Remaking the Economic Institutions of Socialism: China and Eastern Europe

CONTRIBUTORS

Wlodzimierz Brus

Walter D. Connor

János Kornai

Nicholas R. Lardy

Cyril Zhiren Lin

Victor Nee

Susan Shirk

David Stark

Ivan Szelenyi

Martin King Whyte

Remaking the Economic Institutions of Socialism: China and Eastern Europe

Edited by
VICTOR NEE AND DAVID STARK

with Mark Selden

STANFORD UNIVERSITY PRESS
Stanford, California 1989

Stanford University Press
Stanford, California
© 1989 by the Board of Trustees of the
Leland Stanford Junior University
Printed in the United States of America

CIP data appear at the end of the book

Preface

When the idea for this book was first discussed by the editors in 1983, there was little cross-fertilization in the study of state socialism. Scholars of contemporary China and Eastern Europe worked on similar problems without the benefit of the current scholarship on the other state socialist societies. To initiate an exchange of perspectives and research findings, and to encourage the development of comparative analysis of China and Eastern Europe, we convened the "Conference on Economic Reform in China and Eastern Europe," May 8–11, 1986, at the Casa de Maria Conference Retreat in Montecito, California. The Conference was sponsored by the Modernization of China Project of the University of California, Santa Barbara, and the American Sociological Association. Travel funds for the East European scholars were provided by the International Research and Exchange Board. Scholars presenting papers at the Conference were Thomas Bernstein (Columbia University), Wlodzimierz Brus (Oxford University), Ellen Comisso (University of California, San Diego), Walter Connor (Boston University), Dong Fureng (Chinese Academy of Social Science), Zsuzsa Ferge (Hungarian Academy of Science), István Gábor (Karl Marx University of Economics, Budapest), Nicholas Lardy (University of Washington), Cyril Lin (Oxford University), James Millar (University of Illinois), Victor Nee (Cornell University), Mark Selden (State University of New York at Binghamton), Susan Shirk (University of California, San Diego), Dorothy Solinger (University of California, Irvine), David Stark (University of Wisconsin, Madison), and Martin Whyte (University of Michigan).

The papers and discussion at the conference suggested to us that a new perspective was emerging in the field. Not a single paper presented at the conference drew its intellectual inspiration from the totalitarian and modernization perspectives that had organized the field from the 1950s through the 1970s. The new perspective, implicit in the papers, had not yet been formally articulated. The introductory chapter to this volume, "Toward an Institutional Analysis of State Socialism," represents an initial effort to state the new perspective emerging in the field.

We regret that we were unable to use all of the papers presented at the conference; instead we selected papers that in some way exemplified the institutional approaches within economics, political science, and sociology. In addition we included contributions by János Kornai and Ivan Szelenyi, who were invited to the conference but were unable to attend. We wish to express our appreciation for the engaging discussion of the papers given by the conference discussants: Steven Caldwell (Cornell University), Roger Friedland (University of California, Santa Barbara), David Granick (University of Wisconsin, Madison), Samuel Popkin (University of California, San Diego), and Vivienne Shue (Cornell University).

The editing of the book was the result of the equal and joint efforts of the co-editors. We wish to thank Mark Selden for his careful comments on a number of the essays in this book.

Last, we thank our editor at Stanford University Press, Muriel Bell, for her assistance, and our copy editor, Trudi Calvert.

Victor Nee and David Stark

Contents

Contributors

WLODZIMIERZ BRUS received his undergraduate training in economics in the USSR during World War II, and his Ph.D. in Warsaw. He was Professor of Political Economy at the University of Warsaw until 1968, when dismissed for political reasons. Since 1972 he has been Professor of Modern Russian and East European Studies (now Emeritus Professor) at the University of Oxford. His work on institutional change in communist economic systems is reflected in a number of publications, ranging from his book *General Problems of Functioning of a Socialist Economy* (Warsaw, 1961, translated into ten languages; into English as *The Market in a Socialist Economy*, 1972) and in his contribution to the multivolume *Economic History of Eastern Europe, 1919–1975* (1985 and 1986).

WALTER D. CONNOR received his Ph.D. from Princeton University in 1969, and is now Professor of Political Science and Sociology at Boston University, and a Fellow of Harvard University's Russian Research Center. A recipient of Guggenheim and ACLS fellowships, he served in the U.S. Department of State (1976–84) and received the Department's Meritorious Honor Award. His publications include *Deviance in Soviet Society: Crime, Delinquency and Alcoholism* (1972), *Socialism, Politics and Equality: Hierarchy and Change in Eastern Europe and the USSR* (1979), and *Socialism's Dilemmas: State and Society in the Soviet Bloc* (1988). His current interest is in the linkage of Soviet bloc domestic change to foreign policy and East-West relations.

JÁNOS KORNAI is Professor of Economics at the Hungarian Academy of Sciences and at Harvard University. He has specialized in the economic problems of socialism, mathematical planning, and economic theory. His books include *Overcentralization of Economic Administration* (1959), *Mathematical Planning of Structural Decisions* (1967), *Anti-Equilibrium* (1971), *Economics of Shortage* (1980), and *Contradictions and Dilemmas* (1986). At present he is interested primarily in the study of the political economy of socialism.

NICHOLAS R. LARDY received his Ph.D. in economics from the University of Michigan. From 1975 to 1983 he was a member of the faculty of the Department of Economics at Yale University, and since then he has taught at the University of Washington, where he is Professor of International Studies in the Henry M. Jackson School of International Studies. He is the author of *Economic Growth and Distribution in China* (1978), *Agriculture in China's Modern Economic Development* (1983), and *China's Entry into the World Economy* (1987).

CYRIL ZHIREN LIN did his undergraduate work at MIT and his graduate work at Harvard and Oxford universities. He specializes in socialist economics, with special reference to China. He was formerly a Fellow of the Contemporary China Institute at the School of Oriental and African Studies, London, and since 1981 has been a Research Fellow in Chinese Economics at St. Antony's College, Oxford, where he is also Programme Director of the Centre for Modern Chinese Studies. He is the author of articles on planning theory, economic reforms, and development in China. He is engaged in a collaborative research project with the Chinese Academy of Social Sciences on ownership reform and economic efficiency in China.

VICTOR NEE received his Ph.D. in sociology from Harvard University in 1977, and is now Professor of Sociology at Cornell University. From 1978 to 1985 he was on the faculty of the Department of Sociology at the University of California at Santa Barbara. He has written on contemporary Chinese society and politics, and on immigration and ethnicity in the United States. His books include *Longtime Californ': A Study of an American Chinatown*, with Brett de Bary (1973) and *State and Society in Contemporary China*, coedited with David Mozingo (1983). He has done extensive field research in China and is presently working on the analysis of village and peasant household surveys conducted in Fujian Province in 1985.

SUSAN L. SHIRK received her Ph.D. in political science from MIT. She holds a joint appointment in the Department of Political Science and Graduate School of International Relations and Pacific Studies at the University of California, San Diego. She is the author of *Competitive*

Comrades: Career Incentives and Student Strategies in China (1982) and editor of *The Challenge of China and Japan: Politics and Development in East Asia* (1985). She has done research in China several times. In 1984 she spent five months interviewing Chinese economic officials for a book on the political dimensions of the post-1978 economic reforms.

DAVID STARK received his Ph.D. in sociology from Harvard University in 1982, and is now Assistant Professor of Sociology at the University of Wisconsin—Madison. His research in the field of economic sociology on problems of work and organization in capitalist and socialist economies has appeared in *American Sociological Review, Politics and Society*, and *Theory and Society*, with publications abroad in *Actes de la recherche en sciences sociales, Soziale Welt*, and *Stato e mercato*. A book based on field research in Hungary is forthcoming under the title *Politics at Work in a Socialist Mixed Economy*.

IVAN SZELENYI is Professor of Sociology at UCLA. He was Distinguished Professor at the Graduate School of the City University of New York (1986–88), Karl Polanyi Professor at the University of Wisconsin—Madison (1981–86), the Foundation Professor of Sociology at the Flinders University of South Australia (1976–80), and Research Fellow at the Institute of Sociology, Hungarian Academy of Sciences (1963–75). He is coauthor of *The Intellectuals on the Road to Class Power* (1979) and author of *Urban Inequalities Under State Socialism* (1983) and *Socialist Entrepreneurs* (1988).

MARTIN KING WHYTE received his Ph.D. in sociology from Harvard University in 1971. He is now Professor of Sociology and Associate in the Center for Chinese Studies at the University of Michigan. His major works are *Small Groups and Political Rituals in China* (1974), *Village and Family in Contemporary China* (1978), and *Urban Life in Contemporary China* (1984), the latter two coauthored with William L. Parish. He is currently engaged with Chinese sociologists in collaborative research involving a survey on mate choice and marriage relationships administered in Chengdu, Sichuan, in 1987.

Abbreviations

CCP Chinese Communist Party

COMECON (or CMEA) Council for Mutual Economic
    Assistance

CPSU Communist Party of the Soviet Union

FRG Federal Republic of Germany

GDP Gross Domestic Product

GDR German Democratic Republic

NEM New Economic Mechanism

NEP New Economic Policy

NMP Net Material Product

PRC People's Republic of China

SEC State Economic Planning

SEZ Special Economic Zones

SPC State Planning Commission

VGM Enterprise business work partnerships

Remaking the Economic Institutions of Socialism: China and Eastern Europe

ONE

Toward an Institutional Analysis of State Socialism

David Stark and Victor Nee

Thirty years ago, during the first years of de-Stalinization in their countries, young economists in Poland and Hungary began charting a new model of the socialist economy. Although the institutions of a command economy had been in place for less than a decade in Eastern Europe, it was already clear to many that the reality of central planning fell far short of the vision. Today in Eastern Europe and the Soviet Union, many of the same problems of sectoral distortions, chronic shortages, low productivity, slow technological progress, and inefficient allocation of resources are being discussed once again and proposed solutions debated with renewed intensity. In Hungary, where reforms have stopped and started, zigged and zagged since the introduction of the New Economic Mechanism (NEM) in 1968, politicians debate whether lifting the brakes on the emerging private sector will solve the nation's economic crisis or only exacerbate inflationary and balance-of-payments problems. In Poland, where the activities of the world's largest independent trade union were curtailed by a military coup, General Wojciech Jaruzelski and the Polish parliament propose a plebiscite to marketize the relations of purchase and supply between enterprises in the socialist sector. And even in the Soviet Union, where long-dormant efforts at complete de-Stalinization are only recently awakened and Mikhail Gorbachev's reforms are still more rhetorical than real, proposals for restructuring the economy are beginning to be translated into legislation.

Also thirty years ago, China experienced a period of relative liberalization. The debate about the merits of this opening to the intellectuals ("Let a Hundred Flowers Bloom") turned on how various factions of the Chinese leadership interpreted the policies of de-Stalinization in Eastern Europe and especially the events of 1956 in Hungary. The outcome was the anti-Rightist campaign against the intellectuals and the eventual disasters of the Great Leap Forward (1958–59) and the Cultural Revolution (1966–76). Today in China the limits of political liberalization are again being redrawn; and once again, contending factions can use discussions about Eastern Europe as a basis for articulating policy preferences. Current debates, however, occur within a different context than those of the late 1950s as China, too, has stepped onto a road of economic reform. Largely in response to the perceived damages of the Cultural Revolution and mainly in agriculture, Chinese reforms were initially introduced in highly piecemeal fashion in 1978. But in 1984, after the establishment of a special reform commission influenced by the Hungarian experiences, far-reaching reforms were more systematically implemented. Thus in the current situation some segments of the Chinese leadership are looking to Eastern Europe (and to Hungary in particular) not for material as object lessons in morality plays, but for the economic lessons that can be learned about reforming a centrally planned economy. As a result, some of the same economists from Eastern Europe who were writing pioneering dissertations in the 1950s on new approaches to socialist economics are now being invited to China to engage in discussions with their counterparts about the prospects and problems of market reforms in socialist economies.[1]

With the implementation of market reforms in China and momentum building for their introduction in the Soviet Union, reform of the socialist economy is no longer in an experimental stage. If the theoretical tools and alternative practicable models for reforming central planning were generated in socialism's periphery, they are now being introduced (or seriously contemplated) in some of its largest national economies. In world-historical terms, when decentralization and privatization give 10 million Hungarians more economic autonomy, the efforts are path-breaking; but when reprivatization gives more than 800 million Chinese peasants the right to manage their own production, the consequences are epochal. Far from belittling the importance of Hungarian developments, the magnitude of portending changes in China increases the significance of the lessons that can be drawn from Hungary's nearly twenty years of experimentation with reform. With reform on the agenda in the Soviet Union, and with the success or failure of Soviet and Chinese reforms sure to have major effects on international developments into the next century, an understanding of reform takes on added urgency. It is at this moment, then, that the length of reform in a country like Hungary and its breadth across settings as culturally and historically diverse as China and Eastern Europe provide a critical mass of evidence for analyzing the problems endemic to centrally planned economies and the dilemmas faced in efforts to reform them.

This book takes the first steps toward such a comparative analysis by presenting the results of new research on reforms in China and Eastern Europe. Its contributors include Wlodzimierz Brus and János Kornai, economists who have contributed to each stage of the reform debates in Eastern Europe and whose works are now stimulating much discussion in China, as well as representatives of a younger generation of economists, sociologists, and political scientists, many of whom report on field research recently conducted in factories, cities, and villages in China and Eastern Europe. This set of essays is brought together, however, not simply to reach across the boundaries of disciplines and area studies or to publish a compendium of related findings, but because the research and analysis in these papers exemplify an emerging new perspective in the study of state socialism. This new perspective, whose broad contours will be outlined in this introduction, is developing as an alternative to the two major traditions—the theory of totalitarianism and modernization theory—that have dominated the specialized study of socialist societies in the postwar period.

Theoretical Antecedents: From Ideology to Industrialism

Initially developed to analyze the overthrow of the old order (be it through revolution or in the aftermath of war) and the rapid consolidation thereafter of new regimes, the theory of totalitarianism gave explanatory primacy to global ideologies, Leninist parties, and individual leaders.[2] In its classic expression, the totalitarian model portrayed the Leninist party as bent on establishing total control over Soviet society through mass terror and party-dominated hierarchies, destroying the boundaries between state and society and eliminating any autonomous social institutions and processes.

Less thoroughly entrenched in the study of Chinese communism, the theory of totalitarianism had enormous influence in the field of Soviet and East European studies, molding the orthodoxy in Western

scholarship between the late 1940s and early 1960s.* The end of the
Cold War and the changed academic climate during the Vietnam War
in the late 1960s and early 1970s, however, produced the first critical
assessments of the totalitarianism school. Within the totalitarianism
framework, critics charged, the analysis of change in socialist societies
was limited to the transition, however dramatic, from the old order
to the new. The possibility that existing socialisms might evolve or be
transformed was precluded by a theory that portrayed an atomized
citizenry, a frozen society, and an immutable state. Moreover, it was
argued, the analysis of diversity across socialist societies was limited
to national differences in party leaders' interpretations of Marxist-
Leninist doctrine. Similarly, the analysis of differences across social
systems was confined to the contrast between communism's night and
democracy's day, and hence the study of state socialism was unable to
benefit from insights produced by theoretically guided transystemic
comparisons.

The search for an alternative framework began by accepting as
given totalitarianism's account of the Leninist project as directed toward total control by the party-state over society but then went on to
elaborate the unintended consequences of such a project.† The typical

---

*A notable exception to the almost unchallenged prevalence of the totalitarianism
perspective in Soviet studies was Barrington Moore's *Terror and Progress, USSR* (Cambridge, Mass.: Harvard University Press, 1954). Though scholars at the height of the
Cold War between the United States and the People's Republic of China sought to extend the totalitarian model to China during the 1950s, applications of this model to
the complex and protracted processes that gave rise to Chinese Communism, with its
base in the peasantry and the Chinese hinterlands, seemed to raise more questions
than they answered. By the early 1960s mainstream scholarship on China began to
turn away from the totalitarian model, emphasizing instead the social and economic
origins of the Chinese revolution. Influential studies that compared the rise of Chinese Communism with the partisan movement in Yugoslavia (Chalmers Johnson, *Peasant Nationalism and Communist Power: The Emergence of Revolutionary China, 1937–1945*
[Stanford: Stanford University Press, 1962]), analyzed the societal sources of Chinese
Communist organizational dynamism (Franz Schurmann, *Ideology and Organization in
Communist China* [Berkeley: University of California Press, 1965]), and described with
ethnographic detail land reform in a Chinese village (William Hinton, *Fanshen: A Documentary of Revolution in a Chinese Village* [New York: Monthly Review Press, 1965]) both
reflected the weaker grip of the totalitarian model on the China field and accelerated
its rejection.

†The new direction in the study of socialist societies was charted in 1967 and 1968 by
a group of social scientists appointed to the Planning Committee for Comparative Communist Studies under the auspices of the American Council of Learned Societies. The
results of a two-month workshop at the Center for Advanced Study in the Behavioral
Sciences at Stanford sponsored by the committee and attended by twenty scholars were
published in Chalmers Johnson, ed., *Change in Communist Systems* (Stanford: Stanford
University Press, 1970).

steps in such an analysis can be schematized as follows. Having consolidated its position after a revolution, a ruling Communist party, to remain in power in contemporary historical conditions, must be devoted to economic growth. Such growth requires industrialization and the introduction of modern technologies, which in turn require a set of modern values and institutions at odds with the revolutionary enthusiasm, efforts at top-down mobilization, and attempts at totalizing control that initiated the chain of consequences. As Richard Lowenthal argued in a formulative essay, the dilemma facing communist regimes was the irreconcilability of their twin goals of utopia and economic development. According to Lowenthal, "The very success of economic development tends in the long run to strengthen the forces of spontaneous, self-sustaining change, which are typical of modern societies everywhere, while making the cost of further imposed revolutionary change not only higher and more obvious, but less likely to be recovered by a new upsurge of enthusiasm."[3] By extending the logic of modernization observed in Western societies to development in communist societies, Lowenthal predicted that as communist societies approached the level of development of the advanced industrial societies, the institutional structures of the former would inevitably change to reflect functions and values in line with a modern technocratic society. By analyzing how revolution and mass mobilization were giving way to routinization and institutionalization, the early modernization theorists in the field of communist studies viewed bureaucracy as, in a sense, a positive development: in its initial stages, modernization theory saw bureaucratization as the key step on the road to modernity. Later, with bureaucracy taken for granted, the introduction of modern technology and modern values became the defining feature of the process of modernization. Still later, analysts began to question the compatibility of socialist bureaucracy and modern technology. But regardless of the hypothesized link between bureaucracy, technology, and values, it was clear that modernization theory had altered the terms of debate from assertions about the "logic of totalitarianism" to discussions about the "logic of industrialism." Whereas the theory of totalitarianism had identified a totalizing ideology as the propelling force of communist society and focused on the party-state as the sole historical agent in the socialist system, modernization theory shifted the problem to that of the functional prerequisites of industrial economies in socialist states. At the same time, it focused analysis on modern technology and the values that were believed to be its necessary correlates.

The application of modernization theory in the Soviet field in particular tended to view industrialism as a set of technological imperatives. Not entirely unlike Marxism with its notions of "base" and "superstructure" and its technologically determinist tendency to view historical development as the unfolding of the "forces of production," this version of modernization theory defined the economy primarily as a set of technical relations and regarded other institutional spheres such as culture, education, and political participation as derived from the economic base. For many, the "scientific-technological revolution" would gradually but inevitably transform Soviet-type societies as technological imperatives for greater openness and ease of communication would lead to the generalization of scientific values and the creation of more democratic institutions.[4] The key social actors in the modernization paradigm were everywhere the "intellectuals." Intellectuals —variously described or delimited as "the scientific-technical intelligentsia," "professionals," "experts," "engineers and technicians," "technocrats," "university educated," and the like—were seen as the carriers of modernization and the principal agents of change. Within the framework, debate centered on the question of the impact of intellectuals on regime stability. Could the socialist intelligentsia, as some argued, be successfully incorporated at the highest levels and gradually enfranchised in intermediate staff positions to become the counterparts of the technocratic managers of the new industrial state? Or, as others claimed, would the posited antagonism of "reds versus experts" lead to an open battle between the two segments of the "new class" and thereby threaten regime stability?[5] It was by analyzing the problem of the relationship between "intellectuals" and "bureaucrats" that modernization theory addressed the question of whether the eventual transition to full modernity would be disruptive or smooth.

In addition to applying the modernization framework from sociology and economics (associated with such figures as Talcott Parsons, Clark Kerr, and Walt Rostow), the comparative study of communist regimes was reinvigorated in the 1970s by the extension of pluralist theory from political science. "Interest group theory," H. Gordon Skilling maintained, challenged the "concept of a totalitarian system in which a single party, itself free of internal conflict, imposes its will on society" with "an approach that took account of the conflicting groups that exert an influence on the making of policy by the party."[6] The consequence was a body of research on the party administration, the military, enterprise directors, and similar groups deemed influential by the new pluralist theory.

Thus dissatisfaction arising from the limited utility of the totalitarian model in explaining change and diversity in communist societies stimulated interest in applying new conceptual developments in the behavioral sciences to the study of communism. Modernization theory, coupled with interest group pluralism, posited an optimistic framework of evolutionary change that, over the long run, would result in the inevitable death of the utopian goals espoused by revolutionary Marxism. Processes generic to modernization would work out their inexorable logic and remake state socialism after the image of the advanced industrial societies. The analytic tools for the comparative study of modern communism need not be taken from the analysis of Hitler's Germany but could be applied directly from the analysis of other Western democracies because, in fact, the two systems were becoming alike. Whereas totalitarian theory had viewed capitalism and communism as polar opposites on divergent trajectories, modernization theory saw existing socialism on an evolutionary course convergent with that of all modern industrialism.

Throughout the 1980s, researchers involved in the study of socialist societies have become increasingly dissatisfied with the reigning orthodoxies in the field, in part because the shift to attempted reforms dramatized the lack of fit between the analytic problems constructed by the competing theories and those faced in the societies themselves. Contrary to the typical problematic of the totalitarian theory, in the current epoch reforming a socialist economy does not involve overthrowing a prerevolutionary order and consolidating a new one but, rather, transforming a long-established socialist order. Similarly, in contrast to modernization theory, the problem of contemporary socialism is not whether the elites of the Soviet Union, Eastern Europe, and China have modern values but whether their economies can be organizationally restructured.

The dissatisfaction with totalitarian and modernization theories, however, has gone much deeper than a simple charge that the appropriateness of the frameworks is limited to particular periods. The new perspective emerging in the field questions not only the application of the earlier theories to the contemporary period but also many of the fundamental assumptions of those paradigms. Taking the criticisms of the totalitarianism school as its starting point, it goes on to challenge modernization theory on several basic points. First, by projecting features of an idealized image of Western development onto their hypothesized socialist counterparts, modernization theory misuses the comparative method and consequently produces an inade-

quate understanding of the distinctive features of the economic institutions of socialism. Second, by limiting its examination of interest
groups only to elite actors in or around official circles, modernization/
pluralist theory unnecessarily restricts our analytic field of vision and
precludes the possibility that social groups outside the state play a role
in shaping society. Thus whereas the totalitarianism school attributed
primacy to parties and ideologies and modernization theory saw technology and values as the keys to explain modern developments, the
emerging framework focuses on institutions and social groups.

THE ECONOMIC INSTITUTIONS OF SOCIALISM

If modernization theory broke with totalitarianism's portrayal of
communism as capitalism's polar opposite, its comparative methodology continued to analyze socialism in terms of the West. As the
image of socialism's inevitable future, the advanced market industrial
societies represented the "normal" case: the institutions of socialism
could then be understood according to the degree of their conformity
to or departure from this standard. Initial criticism of this aspect of
modernization theory came from a younger generation of scholars,
who, with preoccupations colored by experiences in the antiwar movement of the 1960s, looked for new terms of analysis. The problem
with this revisionist scholarship was that the categories it tended to
accept were often too ready-made, whether Maoist concepts of class,
politics, and ideology to analyze Chinese society, or Marxist categories
of modes of production and propertied classes to study Soviet-type
societies.[7] In part this approach reflected the dependence of the first
wave of revisionist scholarship on communist documentary sources
and the lack of access for field research in China or the Soviet Union.
It also stemmed from the attempt to portray these societies through
categories that were indigenous rather than imposed from outside.
Like totalitarian and modernization theories, revisionist studies also
had an ideological tenor. They tended to project an idealized view of
social and political processes in communist societies. A series of new
developments was required for Western studies of communist societies
to reach maturity: the openings provided for field research in Hong
Kong, China, and Eastern Europe and the intellectual influence of a
new generation of Eastern European scholars on state socialism.

It is perhaps ironic that the light to guide a course out of revisionism's blind alleys came from inside state socialism, in this case from
the East European social sciences. To East European social scientists

both outside and inside state-sponsored academic institutions, it had become increasingly clear that neither Marxism nor modernization theory could yield an undistorted picture of the complex reality of societies whose underlying dynamics were not those of "mature socialism," nor of "state capitalism," nor of some generic "industrialism."[8] Conceptual developments in West European and North American social sciences were to be drawn upon only to borrow tools to analyze the distinctive configuration of institutional arrangements, not mechanically to find one-to-one correspondences (or to pinpoint areas of convergence) between capitalist and socialist institutions.

It was in Hungary, above all, that social scientists attempted to identify the distinctive institutional processes by which state socialism was stably (if inefficiently) reproduced. The mid- and late 1970s saw a wave of creative investigations covering almost every major institutional arena. These studies demonstrated, for example, that state socialist economies have business cycles but that their distinctive features are related to the ways in which enterprise directors "hook onto the plan" rather than to fluctuations in demand.[9] Likewise, the socialist economy shows sectoral segmentation; but unlike capitalism, labor shortage rather than unemployment regulates the distinctive dynamics of the informal sector and the patterns of socialist labor markets.[10] Patterns of workers' shop-floor wage bargaining, regional development, housing inequalities, and social policy in the fields of education and welfare[11] were similarly examined within frameworks that, without apologetics, highlighted how these institutional arrangements differed qualitatively, rather than simply in degree, from their counterparts in Western Europe.

In this intellectual context of a search for concepts to understand patterns of institutional regularity and thus form the basis for genuine cross-systemic comparisons, the work of János Kornai occupies exemplary status. Kornai's doctoral dissertation, alluded to in the opening paragraphs of this introduction, was completed in the summer of 1956 under the title "Overcentralization in Economic Administration" and published in 1957.[12] Based on field research in a number of Hungarian enterprises, the study has been described as the first examination of the socialist economy which "did not explain what the mechanism of the economy under central plan directives *ought to be*, but how *it did operate* in reality, and why it did not ensure the expected development and efficiency of the socialist economy."[13] A model of rigorous empirical research, Kornai's work set the standard for a generation of young economists trained in the late 1960s and 1970s. Kornai's subsequent books, *Anti-Equilibrium, Rush versus Harmonic Growth*, and, most important, *The Economics of Shortage*, provided the theoretical breakthroughs that made possible the analysis of such phenomena as investment cycles, the second economy, and plan bargaining.

The significance of Kornai's theoretical breakthrough is that he showed how the same mechanisms that produced rapid economic growth in planned economies give rise, in the long run, to an economy of chronic shortage, hindering further economic growth. In Kornai's view, the problem of shortage is the central, unavoidable feature of planned economies. It is rooted in the budgetary constraints facing the socialist firm, which are "soft" because the firm's survival and growth are not dependent upon its present or future financial situation. In contrast to firms operating in competitive markets in which sustained losses result in the firm's exit and profits generate the conditions for growth, firms in soft budget conditions can acquire resources and investments without demonstrating credit-worthiness or ultimately covering costs through the proceeds from sales. In other words, the socialist firm is not required to be sensitive to cost and price considerations, except as an accounting procedure.

The paternalism that Kornai sees institutionalized in public ownership guarantees the firm's survival by the state regardless of its performance, and its growth is determined by central planners who allocate resources on the basis of bureaucratic procedures. Because budget constraints are lax, the firm has little pressure to use resources and investments efficiently. In fact, it often has every incentive to use them inefficiently: rewarded for expansion and physical output, the socialist firm's managers seek to hoard and hide reserves and to maximize the resources and investments allocated to it. For this reason, the firm's demand for resources is theoretically limitless. This perpetual hunger for resources, in turn, gives rise to chronic shortages throughout the economy as firms pump the state for more workers, equipment, raw material, and investments irrespective of their financial situation or ability to use those resources efficiently. In terms of the systemic limits of production, on the basis of Kornai's analysis we might say that whereas the firm in a competitive market stops production at the point at which demand has ceased, the socialist firm keeps on producing at whatever the cost; it will stop only when it runs out of mobilizable supplies. The problem for the socialist consumer is that the chronic shortages produced by soft budget constraints lead firms to exhaust available supplies and resources before they exhaust consumer demand. It is in this sense that Kornai labels the planned economy "resource-constrained" at the macro level as opposed to the typically "demand-constrained" market economy.

Kornai's analytic strategy thus works by building up from a set of careful observations of the socialist economy and combining them with pointed contrasts of a comparative nature. Although the concept of soft budget constraint, for example, is clarified by reference to its market counterpart of "hard budget constraint," the complex processes (for example, managerial behavior such as hoarding, forced substitution, and plan bargaining) that can be explained with the ensemble of concepts around the notion of shortage are in no sense deduced or derived from the simple absence of hard budget constraints. The concepts of hard and soft budget constraints are analytically separable from those of market and planning per se. This distinction has important theoretical consequences in the analysis of reforms for, as we shall see, state ownership of large Hungarian firms can reproduce budget constraints that continue to be soft even when the firm is operating in a more decentralized and marketlike environment. Moreover, Kornai's schema makes it possible to reverse the direction of the conceptual borrowing that has for so long characterized the field of comparative economics as the concept of soft budget constraint has obvious applicability to certain sectors and industries in economies with predominantly market-regulating mechanisms.

In sum, Kornai's contribution to comparative economics has been to demonstrate that it is not only market economies that have an "invisible hand": the economies of state socialism, too, have self-reproducing institutional mechanisms.[14] Such concepts as shortage and soft budget constraint give us a comprehensive model to explain their operations. Kornai's contribution to economics and the social sciences more generally has been to demonstrate that a rejection of the modernist assumption of neoclassical economics does not mean that the analyst cannot construct a powerful explanatory model—one, moreover, with a high degree of formalization.

Kornai's careful attention to institutional features of the economy and his rigorous efforts at their formal modeling might once have seemed unlikely concomitants, yet it is precisely in this combination that Kornai's work resonates with new intellectual currents in American social science. Over the past decade, "new institutionalist" paradigms have been developed in every one of the social science disciplines, brought about in political science because internal developments in public choice theory undermined rational choice models lacking institutional constraints;[15] in economics because market fail-

ures could not be explained with the standard analytic tools;[16] and
in sociology because efficiency models failed to explain economic behavior and patterns of organizational survival in the institutionalized
sectors of the economy.[17] These diverse "new institutionalisms" share
a critique of the limitations of neoclassical economics, an emphasis on
the interpenetration of economic organizations and social institutions,
and a commitment to represent complex relationships in formalized
models. These same traits, rather than an allegiance to any one of the
particular neoinstitutionalisms, characterize the recent institutional
analysis in the study of state socialism.[18]

With Kornai's analytic schema as a backdrop, much of this new work
examines the economic institutions of socialism through systematic
comparison. For example, in an innovative comparison of the foreign
economic policies of the Council of Mutual Economic Assistance
(CMEA) economies of Eastern Europe and those of the newly indus-
trializing countries (NICs) of East Asia, Laura Tyson demonstrates
that foreign debt can have entirely different consequences when acquired to confront systemic shortages rather than to take advantage
of favorable conditions in financial and product markets.[19]

Similarly, Ivan Szelenyi adopts a comparative analytic strategy to explore the relationship between markets and inequality. As does much
of the new institutional analysis, Szelenyi's work shows the influence of
the economic anthropology of Karl Polanyi as he adopts the Polanyian
term *redistribution* to characterize the budgetary processes analyzed by
Kornai. Under state socialism, inequalities in areas such as income
and housing are produced and reproduced, Szelenyi maintains, by the
redistributive processes of bureaucratic allocation. Szelenyi's contribution to the comparative study of social policy is the suggestion that
in societies where inequalities are produced by the market, redistribution by the state will reduce inequalities. In societies in which redistribution is the dominant mode, however, inequalities can be reduced
by giving greater scope to market mechanisms.[20]

Victor Nee extends the Polanyian concept of redistributive economy and Szelenyi's hypothesis that markets will reduce inequality in
state socialism to develop a theory of market transition.[21] Nee argues
that the transition from redistribution to markets in state socialism
results in net transfers of power and privilege from the redistributive class to direct producers, that markets provide efficient incentives
for direct producers whereas the redistributive mechanism depresses
individual-level incentives, and that market reform creates new struc-

tures of opportunities centered on the marketplace, eliminating the monopoly of the redistributive sector. Nee tests the market transition theory with Chinese data and opens up the prospect of theoretically driven comparative analysis across state socialist societies.

The idea that research should address institutional configurations rather than comparing particular elements was further developed by David Stark in his model of mirrored opposition to analyze organizational features of the capitalist and the socialist firm. In economies in which the firm operates in a market environment, Stark argues, systemic uncertainties regarding labor are reduced through internal bureaucratic rules. In the socialist economy, by contrast, where systemic uncertainties are produced by a bureaucratic environment, workers and managers respond through internal market transactions.[22] Szelenyi's comparative schema challenges conventional views that markets necessarily increase inequalities; Stark's model suggests that the "internal labor markets" of the capitalist firm are a set of bureaucratic rules whose logic is more classificatory than transactive. Whereas modernization theory posited the West as the standard from which to gaze at the "other," in these and other studies the new comparative institutional analysis provides a vantage point from which to look back at the institutions of capitalism as the specific features of each system are revealed in their mutual contrast.

A FOCUS ON SOCIETY

If familiarity with the work of scholars from state socialist societies has stimulated new concepts to analyze the economic institutions of socialism, so the opportunities provided by détente for fieldwork in the societies themselves have stimulated Western social scientists to analyze the social relations in which these economic institutions are embedded. No longer confined to reading party documents, official newspapers, and the writings of ideological leaders, social scientists could now directly observe behavior in natural settings and interview informants to understand their motivations, perceptions, and interpretations. A new set of methods could be applied to understanding and explaining patterns of social life and the workings of organizations. Village society could be richly documented by field researchers, who could interview informants or live with peasants observing and recording patterns of economic, communal, and political life.[23] From the village up, interviews with party cadres revealed a complex social world in which rural cadres acted within networks of exchange and obligation.[24] Fine-grained accounts of the labor process and factory management emerged from field observation, in-depth interviews, and examination of enterprise records. Seen from the shop floor, the picture of the state socialist factory was not one of despotism but an arena of bargaining and negotiation.[25] Survey research using probabilistic samples opened up the possibility for modeling the causal processes of occupational mobility, income determination, and mate selection in socialist societies.[26] Economists, for their part, gained access to detailed enterprise records which permitted a new microeconomics of the socialist firm. Détente also opened up new sources of macroeconomic data, providing economists and economic historians the opportunity to reconstruct the economic history of communist development.[27] Historians used previously unavailable archival sources and oral histories to write local and regional histories.[28]

In short, the result of new research methods and new theoretical models has been a profound shift in the kinds of problems studied in the most recent work on socialist societies. The new social histories, for example, are more likely to analyze the speech patterns of workers and peasants than the speeches of party leaders.[29] Similarly, though not ignoring the ideological categories of official proclamations, social anthropologists are attentive to how symbolic categories influence the negotiations of everyday life.[30] Whereas the modernization school once attended to the careers of the technocratic elite, researchers today can map the patterns of occupational mobility and income determination among several generations of manual workers and nonmanual employees.[31] And whereas Kremlinologists traced changing cliques and factions from the lineup of party leaders on the May Day reviewing stand, the new sociology of socialist societies examines shop-floor patterns of clientelism and obligation on the assembly line and charts networks of reciprocity and friendship in the markets for houses and spouses.[32]

Far from trivial, this close attention to spontaneous processes in the everyday life of factories, villages, and neighborhoods raises important theoretical questions about the sources of change in communist societies as it reveals significant spheres of social action outside the direction and control of the party-state. Earlier, of course, in arguing that even a "mono-organizational" society would have organizational infighting,[33] interest group theory had challenged the view of a monolithic, undivided ruling class and stimulated research on the bureaucratic politics among competing interests within the elite. Building on this organizational emphasis, the new research in the field, however, studies how the dynamics of organizations are shaped by the actions of subordinate groups as well as by those of leaders and staff.[34] In place of pluralist theory's exclusive focus on interest groups within the bureaucracy, institutional analysis examines the activities of subordinate social groups within society.

If the shift to bringing society into the analysis of state socialism was facilitated by new research methods and new institutional models, the emphasis on subordinate groups such as workers and peasants was stimulated by events in Poland in 1980 and 1981. As millions of industrial workers and white-collar employees organized in Solidarity and their village counterparts joined Rural Solidarity, it was impossible to look solely to intellectuals as agents of change in socialist societies. Whether as a trade union defending the interests of those employed by the state, as a political party articulating policy options to the state, or as a social movement representing "society" against the state, Solidarity was the organized expression of transformative strivings from below.[35] Its defeat and current underground existence, however, do not signal the wisdom of the totalitarianism thesis or the payoffs of focusing on modernizing elites: the failures of the Jaruzelski government in the martial- and post-martial-law periods of the 1980s, no less than the limitations of the Gomulka and Gierek governments toppled in the preceding decades, can be understood only by studying a working class that was not allowed to make policies but was strong enough to veto them.

An analysis of the economic institutions of socialism requires careful examination of the ways state officials are limited by the resistance of subordinate groups. The Polish case is exceptional in the degree to which workers and peasants achieved an organized opposition. Elsewhere, in Hungary, for example, the activity of subordinate groups occurs less through formal organizations of a representational character than through networks of social organization involving reciprocity and exchange. Outside the direct control of the central planners, the "second economy" is a sphere of increased maneuverability for subordinate groups. Its expansion not only limits the scope of action of state officials but also provides shelter to incubate new institutional forms.

Thus if the political sociology of the advanced democracies has been revitalized by attention to the "relative autonomy of the state" and by the analysis of state and party institutions as not shaped directly by class or societal interest groups,[36] the political sociology of state socialism is now moving away from its almost exclusive preoccupation with state and party organizations as its research findings point to the relative autonomy of society and to the institutions in society that place limits on the scope of the state and on the power of state managers.

Remaking the Economic Institutions of Socialism

Our discussion now turns from broad developments in the study of state socialism to outline central problems of reforming socialist societies addressed by the essays in this book. First, we examine the problem of the transition from bureaucratic to market coordination. Specifically, we focus on the dilemma posed by attempting to carry out partial reform in which a mix of bureaucratic and market co-ordination is pursued simultaneously. Next, we examine reforms as redrawing the boundaries between the state and society and shaping new patterns of transaction, mediation, and bargaining across them. In particular, we focus on the shift from a conception of reform as a mix of plan and market within the state sector to a conception of reform as the transition to a mixed economy of public and private property forms with implications for the emergence of new social groups and autonomous social organizations. Finally, we introduce the political dynamics that give rise to cyclical patterns of reform and retrenchment.

HIERARCHIES AND MARKETS

Just as the evolution of hierarchical organizational forms has been explained as a means to economize on transaction costs under con-ditions of market failure in capitalist economies,[37] so the shift from hierarchies to markets should be understood as a response to organi-zational failures in socialist economies. Kornai's soft budget constraint, for example, can be viewed as an organizational failure generic to cen-trally planned economies. Organizational failures in state socialism are rooted in the relationship between the firm and the state, that is, in the allocative processes of central planning. Public ownership, Kornai argues, fosters paternalism on the part of central planners. Ultimately responsible for the well-being of the economy and of the enterprises put under their care, central planners want organizational instruments that can allow them to steer production directly when necessary. The problem is that once the tools for central management are available, they tend to be used.[38] The hyperactive role that comes with public ownership and the resulting multitude of direct microinterventions on the firm have the effect of distorting the regulation of the firm's survival and growth. Moreover, central planners undertaking these interventions are disadvantaged in making rational allocative decisions because prices set by bureaucratic procedures cannot convey detailed information on changing conditions.[39]

These allocative inefficiencies of central planning led early reformers in state socialist societies to advocate incorporating the market mechanism into central planning. The socialist state would control the commanding heights of the economy, regulating the market mechanism by manipulating investment credits, amortization rates, depreciation allowances, interest rates, prices, wage structures, and other macroeconomic controls. With the correct mix of plan and market, the market mechanism would not generate spontaneous economic processes but instead would serve as an instrument to reduce the transaction costs of central planning. In short, early reformers believed that the most efficient governance structure for socialist economies was a combination of market and central planning. In the words of Brus, "The use of profitability as the main efficiency criterion and the basis of incentives is intended to foster rational management in production and exchange efficiency."[40]

The outcome of market reform in Eastern Europe has been largely disappointing, especially in light of the early reformers' extreme confidence in the harmonious, mutually correcting duality of plan and market. Instead, partial reforms both perpetuated problems of the prereform economy and created new distortions and imbalances. As Kornai suggests, the naiveté of the early reformers was to believe that in combining central planning with the market mechanism they could achieve the best of both worlds. They failed to consider fully the possibility that partial reform would result in the worst of both worlds. The command economy was replaced by a hybrid economy, which Kornai argues in Chapter 2 operates in a condition of "dual dependence" in which the economy is coordinated by both vertical bureaucratic and horizontal market relationships. The essence of dual dependence, however, is the continued dominance of hierarchical forms of coordination over the socialist firm and the debilitation of the market mechanism by persistent and pervasive bureaucratic microinterventions. Kornai's analysis points to the dilemma of partial reform, that despite giving a greater role to the market, all of the critical decisions—entry, exit, investments, prices and wages, output, credit—still depend more on processes internal to the planning governance structure than on the market. As a result, the problems of the soft budget constraint, shortage economy, and investment fever of the prereform

socialist firm persist in the postreform economy. Kornai's analysis of
the reforming socialist economy reveals the relative weakness of the
market mechanism when confronted with an intact bureaucracy accustomed to controlling economic action. Whether the actual mechanism
of bureaucratic control is direct or indirect, the effect on the firm is
to weaken its responsiveness to the market and perpetuate the conditions of inefficiency associated with central planning. Kornai concludes from the Hungarian experience of partial reform that without
a decisive shift from plan to a structure of market governance, characterized by hard budget constraints and market competition, there
can be no escape from the dilemma of dual dependence.

The transition from bureaucratic to market coordination in China's
industrial sector, Nicholas Lardy argues, has proceeded far more
slowly than the stated intentions of Chinese reform leaders would suggest. Though there are indications of a renewed attempt to carry out
financial reforms in the urban-industrial sector, the urban reforms
have clearly lagged behind the rural reforms, which have resulted in
sweeping structural transformations. Despite the stated intention of
reducing China's high investment rate of over 30 percent per annum,
during the reform years the rate has remained at essentially the same
level as in the past, indicating a continuation of the prereform reliance on resource mobilization for extensive growth. Intersectoral
allocation continues to follow the essence of the Stalinist model in
which the state procurement system sets the price of agricultural products at lower than market prices and in turn sells industrial products at higher than world prices through the state monopoly over
sales of industrial products to farmers, resulting in a net outflow of
resources from agriculture to help finance urban-industrial growth.
Unlike Hungary, the Chinese did not reform their price structure
in preparation for market reform but instead continued to rely primarily on a central price-determination system. Not only does this
severely undermine the potential for a shift to market coordination,
but the disparity between domestic and foreign prices also gives rise
to distortions in foreign trade. Chinese reformers have been unwilling to shift to market-determined prices, despite the acknowledged
constraint that an irrational price system has on reform, in part because of the political complexity and costs of overhauling the price
structure. Changing price structures can result in major disruptions
to firms accustomed to hidden subsidies passed on through the price
structure. In these crucial areas, argues Lardy, China has yet to go as

far as Hungary and Yugoslavia in changing the governance structure from hierarchical to market modes.

The difficulties of bypassing hierarchies and shifting to market co-ordination point to the extraordinary staying power of established bureaucracies in charge of economic allocation. Kornai's view of the tenacity of the bureaucratic mode of organization echoes Weber's "iron cage" metaphor in which humanity becomes imprisoned by bureaucratic rationalization. Kornai asks: "What caused this tenacity? What is the explanation for the fact that the growth of bureaucracy is an almost irreversible process?"[41] There are distinctive aspects of reforming socialist economies that contribute to the tenacity of hierarchical modes of control. In a shortage economy, when markets cannot accomplish the mutual adjustment of supply and demand, bureaucratic coordination, argues Kornai, becomes indispensable. Bureaucratic allocation encourages firms both to make exaggerated claims for resources to strengthen their bargaining position and to hoard, actions that, when aggregated to the economy as a whole, are reflected in excessive or limitless demand and therefore in permanent shortages. The existence and perception of widespread shortage in turn necessitate continuation of bureaucratic allocation. Moreover, the same bureaucracy entrusted by reformers to implement market reform has strong vested interests in maintaining its power and prestige, which are based in its control over economic transactions.

Contributing to a conservative bias, firms and individuals develop vested interests in maintaining bureaucratic allocation. Lardy points to the hidden subsidies built into the price structure, which redistribute profits among firms, localities, provinces, and ministries so that price adjustments are "fiercely contested." Subsidized industries are net losers when the rigors of the market determine the allocation of resources and investments. Similarly, workers are ambivalent about economic reform in that while they may enjoy the greater range of personal choice and economic opportunities afforded by a mixed economy, they too have a vested interest in secure jobs and benefits, which are threatened if competitive markets impose hard budget constraints on firms, making the prospect of bankruptcy and job layoffs real threats to workers' livelihood.

Are markets and hierarchies incompatible dualities, fundamentally at odds with each other as forms of coordination in socialist economies? The distinction between bureaucracy as a control-allocative mechanism and the qualities of the modern legal-rational bureaucracy is the central theme of Martin Whyte's analysis. Whyte points out that analysts often confuse the two distinct aspects of bureaucracy and bureaucratization. Bureaucratization in one sense refers to the expansion of hierarchical forms of control and allocation over spheres of social and economic life. In its other meaning, it refers to Weber's analysis of the rise of the legal-rational ideal type in the functioning of organizations. The abuses and inefficiencies associated with bureaucracy as a method of allocation and coordination are the foci of criticism by both radicals and market reformers in state socialist societies.

Whyte agrees with Alec Nove's view that there can be only two alternative forms of economic coordination in socialist societies, market and bureaucratic, and differs with those who conceived of the Maoist mobilizational approach as an alternative to central planning and market. Whether or not it is mass mobilizing does not alter the essential form of coordination if hierarchical rather than market forms are the dominant means of economic allocation. Thus despite Mao's avowed intentions of doing away with bureaucracy, the Great Leap Forward and the Cultural Revolution resulted in an enormous expansion in the scope of human activity under the control of state regulation and allocation as private markets and autonomous social action came under relentless attack. During the Great Leap Forward and Cultural Revolution periods bureaucratic coordination was pushed to its extreme pure form through mobilizational politics. The collapse of these Maoist reform efforts bears some resemblance to the aftermath of War Communism in the Soviet Union, suggesting the instability of pure forms of bureaucratic modes of coordination in the absence of the market mechanism.

Both Nee and Whyte concur that the post-Mao market reform has brought about a reversal in the ascendancy of the Maoist mobilizational bureaucracy. The expansion of markets in the post-Mao reforms, Whyte suggests, has been accompanied by the reduction of substantive bureaucratic control over social and economic processes and the emergence of legal-rational modes of organizational functioning. Nee extends Weber's analysis of the relationship between competitive markets and bureaucratic rationalization to develop an institutional theory of changing state-society boundaries in China, showing that the process of establishing the institutional framework of a mixed economy generates pressures for bureaucratic rationalization within state socialism. As the state withdraws from direct control over the economy, and as markets expand in scope and generate new entrepreneurial activity in the private sector, the state must adopt a regulatory role in specifying and enforcing rules and procedures within which economic actors operate and which define the limits of state power. Modern markets seem to require not only rules and procedures within the firm but also a legal-rational institutional environment in which firms and individuals coordinate economic activity within a mutually understood framework of action. Nee contends that the growth of competitive markets generates organizational dynamics that may result in greater reliance on legal-rational procedures and indirect macroeconomic regulation to economize on transaction costs.

In addition to restructuring the relations between firms and ministries in industry, reforms in socialist societies involve remaking economic institutions outside the state sector. Kornai writes that "it has been exactly the nonstate sectors that have brought the most tangible changes into the life of the economy." As with reforms in the bureaucratic sector, the expansion of petty commodity production has gone furthest in Hungary and China. In Hungary, dramatic changes have taken place among private household farms, many of which were originally set aside to help provide for the subsistence needs of cooperative members. Since the reforms of 1968, however, production for the market has grown rapidly, although not continuously, and the entrepreneurial character of petty commodity production can be seen in the sophisticated marketing network through which Hungarian private farmers sell their livestock and produce on foreign as well as domestic markets.

Similar market-oriented policies were introduced in China in the early 1980s, but the Chinese agricultural reform opened up new possibilities for private market production and exchange in the institutional context of a mixed economy. Whereas the private sector in Hungary is still based primarily on the relatively small proportion of land set aside for household and auxiliary plots, in China virtually all the arable land has been assigned to households to farm. Once peasants have met the assigned quota production for sale to the state, they are free to produce for the marketplace. Central to the Chinese strategy has been the state's emphasis on encouraging private investment in starting up small industrial firms in villages and small rural towns throughout China. As private household farms increased agricultural productivity, the surplus agricultural labor pool fed new labor markets opened up by the diversification of the rural economy. The increase in agricultural productivity has already resulted in the diversion of 20 percent of the total rural labor force—about 76 million peasants —from agriculture to village industry, construction, trade, transport,

and other services in the rural market economy. Chinese labor economists anticipate that by the end of the century, another 100 million
peasants will have left farming for other lines of private sector business. By 1986 nonagricultural production accounted for 46.9 percent
of the total output in rural areas. In both China and Hungary changes
in the nonstate sector have been so dramatic that they are leading to a
fundamental transformation in thinking about the process of reform.
Whereas for several decades debate centered on finding a harmonious
mix of plan and market in the state sector, today in China and Hungary one is more likely to find economists arguing about the most
advantageous mix of public and private property forms across sectors
of the economy.

REDRAWING THE BOUNDARIES OF STATE AND SOCIETY

The classificatory and organizational struggle over the changing
boundaries of public and private, state and society, the political and
the personal, is a characteristic feature of every modern society.[42]
Redrawing the boundaries of the state is especially marked in societies with Stalinist or Maoist legacies in which, for longer or shorter
periods, a concerted effort had been made to deny these boundaries
altogether. The penetration of the state into all realms of life did not
extend a public sphere so much as negate it, for without attachment
to the party or one of its subsidiary organizations no particular individual could make claims with any general validity. Yet at the same
time, the omnipresence of ideas about universal interests threatened
to eliminate the particular as individuals lived in fear that the simplest
particularity—a joke between workmates or an innocent remark on
the sidewalk—could be interpreted as intending to convey a general
comment. For the everyday citizen there was little space for politics because everything could be politicized and affairs of heart and hearth
be treated as affairs of state.

In an important sense, reforms in a socialist society, even when they
do not challenge the sacrosanct institutions of the Communist party
or raise the issue of political democracy, always involve a reconceptualization of the relation between particular and general interests. At
a basic level, genuine reforms legitimate the particular—in the sense
that particular interests can have validity without being expressed in
immediately universal terms. To take the problem of enterprise autonomy seriously, for example, means that an enterprise director can
legitimately justify a decision on the grounds that it is good for his

firm. He might go on to make a link to general interests, adding that if it is good for his firm, it is good for the country; but that is quite different from the earlier situation in which the argument from the central planners usually ran the other way around: since it was good for the national economy, it followed that it would be good for the firm. Similarly, legalization (as opposed to mere toleration) of private ventures involves a legitimization of particular interests.

Thus remaking the economic institutions of socialism involves re-defining the conceptions of interests and redrawing the boundaries of state and economy as well as of state and society. Nee, for exam-ple, documents how Chinese state elites at the beginning of the 1980s devoted considerable organizational resources and propaganda in-struments to persuade local-level party cadres to regard the pursuit of private profit by rural entrepreneurs within their jurisdiction as legitimate activity. Entrepreneurship, they argued, could contribute to public goals by promoting economic growth and, in villages or prov-inces with surplus population, by providing new workplaces for the underemployed. This policy called for new measures to alter both the frequency and the type of exchanges that occur between cadre and peasants at the state-economy boundary requiring a modification from the open or porous state-society boundaries of the Maoist mobi-lization era (in which the penetration of society by the state can also be seen as a penetration of the state by society) to a system in which state and society are insulated from each other to a greater degree. In the new arrangement cadres, ideally, are not mobilizing but monitor-ing behavior in the economy. Nee's study of state policy toward rural entrepreneurs thus provides a specific illustration of Martin Whyte's more general argument that reforms that increase bureaucratic pro-cedures in the internal administration of the state can reduce bureau-cratic intrusion in the everyday life of society.

But the state-society boundary is not only redrawn by state policy makers; it is also reshaped by society, that is, by the activities of peas-ants, manual workers, and other employees who are not functionaries in the bureaucracy. Stark's analysis of Hungary's second economy, for example, demonstrates that subordinate groups in socialist economies can create and maintain spheres of activity that are relatively autono-mous from the state. In the late 1960s and throughout the 1970s, the second economy expanded because peasants and workers did not wait for the government to pass new legal measures before venturing into activities in agriculture, construction, and repair. Because so many did so, they opened wider the border zone of the "not illegal," forcing the state to tolerate activities that were once illegal but were not yet legalized. Stark's analysis of the politics of the shop floor similarly points to the strategic actions of workers who attempt to enlarge the zone of limited but significant autonomy which is produced by the systemic uncertainties inherent in the production process of a socialist economy.

Ivan Szelenyi's important contribution to bringing society into the analysis of state socialism is to suggest that it may now be appropriate to speak of an embryonic "civil society" in Eastern Europe. The scope and the depth of such relatively autonomous spheres are not, of course, uniform throughout the region. Moreover, the roads to a civil society and its eventual character can differ fundamentally, as Szelenyi's comparison of the Hungarian and Polish cases demonstrates. If the term *civil society* is not to be used capriciously, it must refer to the self-organization of society, and in Hungary Szelenyi finds such activity in the economy. It is above all in the second economy, whether in the dense network of exchanges outside the state enterprises or in the semiautonomous units spawned by the second economy inside the official enterprises—that Hungarian society is organizing (and not of course without limits) its affairs. The Polish road to civil society, by contrast, bypasses the economy as institutions such as Solidarity or independent publishing houses have sought to create an autonomous public sphere within the polity. Although Szelenyi does not use Albert Hirschman's terms,[43] it is as if Hungarians through their second economy have taken the path of "exit" whereas, through Solidarity, Poles have attempted the avenue of "voice." In such a scheme, East Germany, with its strategy of rationalizing an unreformed economy without an embryonic civil society, represents the path of "loyalty."

In his comparison of East European economies, Szelenyi concludes that the Hungarian trajectory toward a socialist mixed economy is the most likely course for a transition to "intensive" economic development. Such a mixed economy cannot occur through the simple quantitative growth of the second economy. In order to speak of a genuine mixed economy, privately owned productive units must be motivated and able to expand their operations. From their current aims of supplementing income, existing second economy producers would, in a mixed economy, calculate with an aim to accumulating capital. Such a development requires a double ideological shift as state functionaries must eye private producers with less suspicion and private producers must have some confidence that the state will not expropriate their businesses. Nee's analysis of China indicates that these obstacles are enormous but perhaps not insurmountable. Stark's analysis of Hungary suggests that the institutional prerequisites for a mixed economy are a wide range of intermediate property forms. Rather than a strict dividing line between private and public (in which the private always needs to fear expropriation if it should grow too large), such a framework might encourage the private entrepreneur to grow—provided that the private unit grows into an intermediate form. Similarly, private individuals would be able to own stock in public companies and state firms could hold shares in private ventures. The boundary between public and private sectors would thus be crisscrossed by multiple strands of joint ownership forms and related leasing arrangements. The legalization and institutionalization of a private sector in a socialist mixed economy might, in this sense, have the paradoxical effect of reducing the dualistic character of the present-day economic structure of state sector and second economy. Redrawing the boundaries between private and public, between state and society, need not entail making them more distinct and clearly defined but may mean widening the boundary zones and blurring the distinctions.

POLITICS OF REFORM CYCLES

The history of market reform in socialist economies has been marked by cycles of decentralization and centralization, expanding markets and restoration of hierarchies, and alternating periods of reform and counterreform. From the 1960s to the present, reforms in Eastern Europe have taken a zigzag course of initiatives and retrenchment. Stimulated by the post-Stalinist climate of greater flexibility and openness to change as well as by anxiety over the loss of dynamism under central planning (reflected in the downturn in the rate of growth of the Czechoslovak economy in 1963), a wave of reform fever swept through Eastern Europe in the mid-1960s infecting even the most deeply conservative regimes such as the German Democratic Republic (GDR) and the Soviet Union. With the exception of Hungary and Yugoslavia, these reforms proved to be short-lived, and by the 1960s, retreat from reform policies was in full progress, as central planning bureaucracies reasserted their dominant control over the economy. Such was the fate of reforms in the GDR, Czechoslovakia, and Bulgaria. Reforms in Poland, halfhearted at best, were derailed after the 1970 workers' rebellion resulted in the overthrow of Gomulka, though attempts were resumed in 1972–73. By 1975 reform measures were tabled under the pressure of Poland's rapidly deterio-

rating economic conditions. Only Hungary and Yugoslavia retained
the basic features of the reform programs, though the efforts in these
countries also fell short of reformers' expectations.

In China developments in the 1950s and 1960s also reflected dissatisfaction with the Soviet-style central planning model. In contrast
to the East European reforms, however, the Maoist Great Leap Forward and the Cultural Revolution experimented with mobilizational
approaches in the attempt to adapt the Soviet-style command economy to Chinese conditions. Both the Great Leap and the Cultural
Revolution ended in economic as well as political failures for Mao. Significantly, Chinese market reforms emerged in response to perceived
organizational failures of the Maoist mobilizational approach to economic growth. Both sources of opposition to Mao's economic policies,
central planners and market reformers, joined hands in the reform
coalition that sought to restore economic efficiency and normalcy in
the aftermath of the failed Cultural Revolution.[44] Like the Eastern
European reforms, the current Chinese market-oriented reforms appear to be following a cyclical pattern of development. In striking ways
the early years of Deng Xiaoping's reform were similar to Mao's trial
and error approach, which like the start of current reform lacked a
prior blueprint or clearly charted course of action. This open-ended
process of economic reform has allowed the Chinese greater flexibility
and creativity in the implementation of their reform.

As Cyril Lin points out, the Chinese reform follows a logic in which
the politics of reform cycles pushes reformers to assume more radical
positions, while more conservative reformers and hard-line opponents
pressure for retrenchment, establishing a dialectics of reform that
alternates between retrenchment and radicalization. By bringing firms
under market pressure in which some will fail, genuine reforms can
produce a constituency for reversal. As Ellen Comisso has illustrated
with her analysis of the Yugoslav case, hierarchical arrangements give
rise to pressures for decentralization and market alternatives, while
competitive markets stimulate demand for protectionist measures or
hierarchical allocation of resources on behalf of threatened firms and
sectors of the economy.[45] Thus the underlying dynamic of reform in
Yugoslavia is the oscillation between plan and market in which initiatives in one direction set off political pressures to correct for resulting
imbalances by resorting to the alternative coordinating mechanism.

A central contradiction of reform efforts in socialist economies derives from the reform leadership's failure to cut back sharply or dismantle entirely the bureaucracy that managed the command economy.

This is largely because inherent in any reform effort is the fear that the reform may fail to realize desired results. The difficulties and uncertainties of changing a pricing system, or moving away from wage regulations, or imposing hard budget constraints on firms and thus risking plant closures and large-scale layoffs of workers have a conservative influence on reform leaders. To minimize the risk of failure, reformers tend to move gradually in carrying out organizational reforms that are aimed at sharply reducing the size of the economic bureaucracy. Moreover, the political coalitions required to get reform on the agenda may require compromises with more conservative party and ministerial factions. The compromise means that conservative factions remain within the ruling coalition monitoring the reform process, posing a political threat to the reform if turbulence, whether economic or political, appears, which is almost inevitable. The presence of conservatives within the reform coalition and the ready availability of the prereform economic bureaucracy, which only requires reactivating from its dormant or reduced state, suggest that the reform faction is always vulnerable to political opposition from conservatives or hard-liners who were skeptical about reforms in the first place.

In a one-party Leninist state, without competing political parties, there is little scope for open debate to ensure thoughtful consideration of alternative visions, programs, agendas, and public policies. Progress and successes in reform typically have no secure institutional basis or guarantees. "Those groups in society which are interested in the reform do not articulate their interests," argues Erzsébet Szalai on the basis of the Hungarian reform experience, "they are isolated from each other, they have no autonomous institutions, and within existing institutions the positions of those who represent them are vulnerable."[46] The reform opposition, on the other hand, is entrenched at all levels of the party-state; moreover, the decision to recentralize invariably is made at higher levels of the party, where organizational boundaries are closed to societal influences.

Some analysts believe that the concentration of political power in a Leninist party-state without electoral accountability and public scrutiny seriously complicates, if not ultimately jeopardizes, any attempt at market reform. There is no political penalty for failure in the absence of genuine opposition parties capable of mounting political challenges through electoral politics. Thus, for example, despite Deng's admission of more than two decades of economic and political failures under the leadership of the Chinese Communist party before the current reform, the same political party that was responsible for a dismal record of failures still presides, unchallenged, over the reform. Wlodzimierz Brus argues that without the capability for autonomous economic decisions, neither the firm nor the bank is capable of making investment decisions on the basis of market considerations; instead they are subject to the potential or actual microinterventions of the local party organization, thus imposing political priorities on economic transactions. Brus, Whyte, and Lin thus contend that the Leninist state is the main obstacle to remaking the economic institutions of socialism.

In marked contrast, Susan Shirk argues that it is precisely the concentration of power in a few top leaders in setting the reform agenda, shaping the reform ideology, and managing conflicts in subordinate agencies that provides the tools to manage the implementation process. Far from an obstacle, the Leninist state is the instrument of reform. To support this position, Shirk notes that although reform in Hungary and China has not brought about a decisive shift from bureaucratic to market coordination, we should not lose sight of the larger cumulative trend across cycles toward the increased role of the market mechanism in these reforming socialist economies. Shirk points out as well that the "minicycles" of decentralization and centralization in China reflect temporary compromises and adjustments, not the abandonment of reform. The success of reform is to a large extent dependent on the political skills of top reform leaders such as Deng Xiaoping and Zhao Ziyang in proceeding cautiously with the reform agenda, compromising when faced with stubborn bureaucratic opposition, and artfully building consensus to sustain the reform through its various minicycles. In East Asia, as illustrated in the cases of Taiwan, South Korea, Singapore, and to a more limited extent Japan, where the LDP party has ruled uninterrupted since the Allied Occupation, market economies have thrived in states governed by a single dominant political party. If China remains a one-party state, which it is likely to do, and succeeds in creating an economy that relies on a mix of market and state coordination, it will not be the first East Asian country to have done so.

The cycles of reform resulting from the interplay of politics and economics, moreover, are not simply the result of internal factors but are rooted in external forces as well. The limits of market reform in Eastern Europe, Walter Connor states in Chapter 10, are to a large extent defined by its relationship with the Soviet Union. The reversal of domestic reform movements in Czechoslovakia and Poland illustrates how the Soviet Union, through direct intervention or the threat of it, has in the past aborted reforms in these countries.

Connor argues, however, that within these limits Eastern European countries may, nonetheless, move further in remaking the economic institutions of socialism than the Soviet Union even though the technological needs of a great military power exert enormous pressure for economic change. Satellite status attenuates risks associated with reform; superpower status exacerbates the risks. In such a view, what the East European nations lack in sovereignty, they gain in room for experimentation. But what will be the impact on the other socialist economies if the Soviet Union under Gorbachev launches its own market reforms? What are the prospects for reform in the Soviet Union?

The consensus among scholars of the Soviet Union suggests that thus far Gorbachev's reform in the USSR is more rhetorical than substantial and that the Soviet economy is far less changed than Gorbachev's speeches would indicate. To date, the Soviet reform efforts have centered on improving the quality of central planning through streamlining the ministerial system, improving the quality of central directives, and stressing the "human factor" in filling key posts with new personnel.[47] In many respects, Gorbachev's reform echoes the earlier Kosygin reform effort. "Their actions demonstrate the conviction that reorganizing hierarchical structures will solve deep-rooted economic problems," observes Gertrude Schroeder. "Central planning in the view of Gorbachev and his advisors is a sine qua non of socialism that needs to be 'strengthened.' "[48] Ed Hewitt notes that it is "clear, from what Gorbachev has both said and not said, that he does not intend to imitate the Hungarian economic reform model, which virtually abolishes the ministerial system and moves to a system in which enterprises operate without an obligatory plan from the center. Nor has he indicated a willingness to follow the Chinese in their dramatic shift from collectivized agriculture to a decentralized system emphasizing family farming."[49]

Despite the scholarly consensus that the USSR is not likely to pursue a genuine reform strategy—one that seeks to bypass bureaucracies and resort to markets—to rule out the possibility of market reform in the Soviet Union may prove shortsighted. At least one Soviet scholar predicts that by 1993 the USSR under Gorbachev's leadership will have gone further than both Hungary and China in the scope of economic reform. Jerry Hough notes that neither Hungary nor China has made significant progress in shifting to market coordination in the core heavy industrial sectors.[50] Whereas Hungary and China have made their most dramatic breakthroughs in the nonstate agricultural sector and in the second economy, Hough believes that Gorbachev can

be expected to make a move at the periphery of the socialist economy as well and then move to reform the core industrial sectors. Thus
far, conjectures about the future of Soviet reform are just that. But
as Connor argues in this book, whatever the outcome of Gorbachev's
reform, whether he does or does not lead the USSR on the road to
remaking its economic institutions, the Soviet Union will continue to
define the limits of reform in Eastern Europe. If, however, the USSR
also embarks on an ambitious agenda of market reform, the consequence of this departure is likely to encourage more radical reforms
in Eastern Europe and China.

The new institutional analysis of state socialism, defined in opposition to the earlier theories of totalitarianism and modernization, posits
an orienting framework within which theories drawn from the social
sciences can compete. The ground rules of this intellectual competition are based on the assumption that state socialism represents a
distinctive social formation that has its own institutional logic and dynamics of development. This logic is not derived from capitalist development, either as its polar opposite or its convergent future. The institutional perspective insists, first, that theories explaining processes
and outcomes in state socialism must take into account the institutional arrangements specific to state socialism. Second, rather than
an exclusive focus on party and state elites, the new institutional perspective opens up society and economy and their relationship to the
state as arenas of research. Thus subordinate groups, popular culture, social networks, markets, entrepreneurship, organizational innovations, political coalitions, local-level administration, and new forms
of interest representation become objects of study.

Market reform and its social consequences will no doubt stimulate interest in models of convergence between capitalism and state
socialism. Projecting the logic of capitalist development onto reforming socialist economies, journalists and scholars speculate about the
rise of social inequality. Increased imports of Western technology and
science fuel the fascination with modernization theory's predictions
of homogenization of social, economic, and political institutions. Far
from convergence as a likely outcome of market reform in state socialist economies, the societies of China and Eastern Europe are giving
rise to a new diversity in social life that stems from dynamics peculiar
to state socialism. Images that may have appeared incongruous now
blend together, juxtaposing elements of socialist realism with Western commercial culture, traditional cultural forms with contemporary
practices. Boys in Belgrade wear cowboy hats with red stars, and a

billboard in Beijing extols the virtuous one-child family alongside an advertisement for Seiko watches. At a high school graduation dance in Budapest, village women in folk dress sing the chorus of "Honky Tonk Woman" as backup to a rock band and a sixteenth-century prisoners' melody used by Bartók blares from the bass guitar. But it is not only in culture that the incongruous are juxtaposed. Pigeons are raised for sale in the Department of Chemistry of a Chinese university to upgrade faculty benefits. With a photograph of Lenin over his shoulder the president of an agricultural cooperative computes hypothetical profit margins at variable interest rates with a pirated version of Lotus 1-2-3, and the owner of a truck repair shop contemplates joining the newly formed Communist party cell for private tradesmen. The plurality of property forms in reforming socialist societies thus is giving rise to a hybrid version of socialism that accepts practical compromises and mutually contradictory principles as a given condition of social life.

TWO

The Hungarian Reform Process: Visions, Hopes, and Reality

János Kornai

The Hungarian economy has undergone major systemic changes in the last thirty years. The impact of the reform is felt by every Hungarian citizen. The influence of the Hungarian experience, however, does not stop at the borders of this small Eastern European country. At least the temptation to follow a similar road appears in other socialist countries. The leaders of the Chinese economy are studying the Hungarian situation carefully in an effort to learn from its successes and failures. In the Soviet Union and in a few smaller Eastern European countries, where a genuine reform has not yet begun, the advocates of more far-reaching changes refer to Hungary frequently. Perhaps it is not an exaggeration to say that the Hungarian reform has some global relevance.

According to a widespread view, the Hungarian economy has become or is close to becoming a system of "market socialism." Referring to Oscar Lange's famous model of socialism, Paul R. Gregory and Robert C. Stuart write: "In a general way, NEM [the New Economic Mechanism of Hungary] bears a close resemblance to the Lange model."[1] I am convinced that this interpretation of the Hungarian reform is erroneous, and the purpose of this paper is to support my rejection of this view. At the end of the article different "visions" of market socialism will be reviewed and confronted with Hungarian reality. But before this confrontation of vision with reality, a positive description is needed. I try to answer the following question: if it is not "market socialism," what is the true nature of the present Hungarian system? For an answer, we have to review the Hungarian situation in some detail to avoid oversimplification.

There are dozens of books and hundreds of journal articles about the Hungarian reform.[2] Although taking account of alternative explanations, this paper is a *subjective* description and appraisal of the Hungarian reform, its intellectual background, and its real development, in the light of my own views. Although my writings are not without some intellectual influence in my country, I do not claim to be regarded as one of the "architects" of the reform. I was not and am not a government official, a member of any decision-making body, or a formally appointed adviser. In other words, I am accountable neither for the great results of the reform nor for its shortcomings. At the same time, I was and still am a firm supporter and a critical observer of the reform process. It is hoped that this special position gives me a certain closeness to the events, but also some distance needed for a frank and fair appraisal. In some respects this paper reflects a wide consensus shared by a larger group of Hungarians. That does not imply that something like a universally accepted "Hungarian view" exists. Economists in Hungary are not less divided in their opinions than their colleagues in any other country.

The review is not value-free; my own set of desiderata will become clear to the reader as he goes through the paper. Yet the article will remain in the domain of positive analysis and the discussion of a few intellectual currents; there is no attempt to present my own updated blueprint of an "ideal" socialist system.

Because this paper deals with institutional changes, it inevitably touches on problems in the domain of sociology, social psychology, political science, and political history. Nevertheless, this is the work of an economist concentrating on economic issues without aiming at a thorough analysis of their political aspects.

The Hungarian reform was not a one-stroke action, but a long process. Its intellectual history started with papers of György Péter presenting a penetrating criticism of the old system and a draft of the reform. The history of practical reform measures began in 1956–57 with the abolition of compulsory deliveries in agriculture, although the dominant feature of the period 1957–64 was the conservation of the old bureaucratic economic mechanism. An important milestone was reached in 1968, when a whole package of substantial changes was introduced. Further steps came later. But the reform process did not follow a one-way road even after 1968: phases of progress were followed by reversals. After the great reform wave of the late 1960s the years 1972–79 represented again a period in which antireform forces could break through. A new wave of reform measures started in 1979 and has been going on since. Apart from consecutive ups and downs, proreform and counterreform tendencies have been manifest side by side all the time.

Unfortunately, limitations of space do not allow a discussion of the historical evolution of the reform. This paper focuses on phenomena that prevailed throughout the 1968–85 period and characterize the present state of affairs, with only occasional backward glances.

Conceptual Clarification

There are a few general concepts that do not have an unambiguous content in the literature. I wish to clarify their meaning in the context of the present paper.

ECONOMIC SYSTEMS

We use the term *economic system* to mean not only "grand" systems, like capitalism or socialism, which could rather be regarded as system "families," but also the particular members of such a family. Contemporary Czechoslovakia, Hungary, and Yugoslavia, for instance, have different systems, although all three are socialist countries.

Instead of an abstract definition, I give a summary list of the main components of an economic system:

The organizations functioning in the economy: for example, administrative organs, nonprofit institutions, firms, households, associations.

The distribution of the various forms of ownership and property rights.

The distribution of decision-making power.

The information structure: types of information flowing between organizations.

Incentives motivating the decision makers.

The role of political organs and the government in economic affairs.

Laws and government resolutions, that is, the formal legal regulation of the economy's operation.

Informal "rules of the game": routine behavioral patterns enforcing, hindering, or complementing the formal legal regulation.

The list is not exhaustive.* The components are interdependent; they cannot be chosen arbitrarily.

---

*The literature of comparative economics offers various, mostly overlapping interpretations of the notion *economic system*. See, for example, Egon Neuberger and William Duffy, *Comparative Economic Systems: A Decision-making Approach* (Boston: Allyn and Bacon, 1976); and John M. Montias, *The Structure of Economic Systems* (New Haven, Conn.: Yale University Press, 1976).

In the Hungarian literature the terms *economic mechanism* or simply *institutional circumstances* are used more or less as synonyms for *economic system*.

The concept of *policy* contrasts with the concept of *system*. The former is the determination of certain variables by policy makers within the framework of a given system. In this respect I follow the usage of Hungarian discussions, which consistently apply the distinction between issues of economic policy and issues of the economic mechanism.

BUREAUCRATIC AND MARKET COORDINATION

A system coordinates the activities and interactions of its members, that is, individuals and organizations. I distinguish two pure types of coordination.[3]

Form No. 1: Bureaucratic coordination.* There is a *vertical* relationship between the coordinating individual or organization and the coordinated individuals or organizations. Control is exerted by a multi-level hierarchy. Administrative coercion and legal sanctions compel individuals and organizations to accept orders and prohibitions from above. The vertical relationship is lasting and institutionalized; it is mutually acknowledged both "above" and "below." The transactions are not necessarily monetized, but if they are, the subordinated individual or organization is financially dependent on the superior. The bureaucracy is active in the allocation of resources and in the redistribution of income.

Form No. 2: Market coordination. There is a *horizontal* relationship between the buyer and the seller individual or organization; the two participants are equal from the legal point of view. The individuals or organizations are motivated by financial gain. In its pure form market coordination takes place at prices based on agreement between buyer and seller. The transactions are monetized.[†]

Some writers prefer a wider definition; the present paper, however, will apply consistently the narrow definition outlined above. I refer to market coordination only if money, prices, and profit are at work.

The debate over the reform of socialist systems can be translated into the language of the above classification: the participants suggest alternative combinations of the basic forms. Systemic changes in the

---

*The term *bureaucratic* is frequently used pejoratively in the Eastern European literature. The present paper does not follow this usage; according to the Weberian tradition, the term is a value-free denomination of a particular form of coordination.

†Other basic "pure" forms exist also. As important as these might be, for our topics the consideration of Forms No. 1 and No. 2 will suffice.

TABLE 2.1
Share of Social Sectors in Employment and National Income
(percentage distribution)

Sector	Distribution of active income earners				Contribution to national income		
	1966	1975	1980	1984	1975	1980	1984
1. State sector	65.0	70.9	71.1	69.9	73.3	69.8	65.2
2. Nonstate sector							
a Cooperatives	30.7	24.9	25.5	25.9	17.8	19.8	20.6
b Household farming	–	–	–	–	4.0	3.2	2.8
c Auxiliary production of employees	–	–	–	–	3.0	3.7	5.9
d Formal private sector	4.3	4.2	3.4	4.2	1.9	3.5	5.5

SOURCE: Central Statistics Office, Hungary. Data broken down according to our classification are not available for the contribution to national income in 1966.
NOTE: The nonstate sectors are discussed in a later section. "National income" is a net output concept within the framework of the "Material Product System" (MPS), the accounting system used in socialist countries. Except for sectors 2b and 2c, the table does not cover the informal private sector.

real world can be described as new combinations of the two basic forms with shifts of relative weights and new linkages between them.

REFORM

Reform is a notion widely used by many parties and political movements all over the world. The present article will apply a narrow definition designed especially for this discussion. The term *reform* indicates the change in a socialist economic system, provided that it diminishes the role of bureaucratic coordination and increases the role of the market.

The modernization of a highly bureaucratic regulation of the economy with the aid of computers is not reform; nor are efforts aimed at tighter labor discipline. Useful as these policy measures might be, they do not imply the change of the system; they do not lead to diminishing the role of bureaucracy and to increasing the role of the market.

In this sense there are only three countries where a genuine reform process is in progress: in the order of starting, these are Yugoslavia, Hungary, and China. There are signs that perhaps Poland will follow suit.

The State Sector

The economy may be divided into two main *social sectors*: organizations working with capital owned by the state and the rest of the economy, that is, the nonstate sector. (The adjective *social* will be used throughout to refer to the sectors distinguished by ownership.)

The state sector, it must be emphasized, was and still is the dominant sector of the Hungarian economy. As shown in Table 2.1, about two-thirds of officially recorded total national income is produced by state-owned firms.[4]

THE ABOLITION OF MANDATORY PLANS

In the prereform period the state sector was administered by the *command economy*. Usual synonyms are the traditional centrally planned economy or classical socialist economy, economy of the Soviet type, or simply, the "old" economic mechanism contrasted with the reformed "new" one.

The national plan is elaborated by the Central Planning Board and approved by the highest political bodies. After that, the plan is strictly mandatory. The economy is governed by a bureaucracy, organized in a multilevel hierarchy.* The plan indicators at the top are successively disaggregated from higher to lower levels. At the bottom, the state-owned firm gets hundreds or thousands of mandatory plan indicators each year, containing four sets. First, the set of output targets, whenever possible, in physical terms or in aggregate real terms expressed in base-year fixed prices. A multiproduct firm may get as many output targets as it has products or groups of products. Second are input quotas, again in physical or real value terms. This set contains the rations of the centrally allocated materials and semifinished products, indicating not only quantity and quality but also the supplier obliged to deliver. There are also labor quotas and wage funds. Third are mandatory financial indicators concerning production costs, profits, and credit ceilings. Fourth is a list of certain actions to be taken by the firm: introduction of new technologies or products, investment

---

*The role of the party is not discussed separately. The party is not simply a political movement as in a nonsocialist country but also an apparatus in charge of running all affairs. Although from a legalistic point of view the party and the government are separate entities, in practice they are intertwined, and they work jointly in all relevant control processes. The party has the leading role in the joint operation. Hence the term *bureaucracy* or *bureaucratic control* in this paper refers to the role played by the party apparatus.

projects, and so on. Although all plan indicators are compulsory, certain "priority indicators" are enforced more strictly. Typically this is the case with at least one indicator of aggregate output, with some ceilings on wage expenditures, and sometimes also with a few specific export targets.

The flow of information is not unidirectional. The firms submit proposals in the course of plan elaboration, and they report results during and after the plan period. The more important flow, however, is the flow downward: commands given by the higher level to the lower level of hierarchy.

One of the most tormenting properties of the command system is rigidity. Commands once given are hard to change. Any change must go through a multistage process of approval at different sections and different levels of the hierarchy. The system of detailed plan indicators is, of course, interdependent; it is a "general equilibrium" image of future economic processes. It is required that the spillover effects of any significant change be followed in all other segments affected and appropriate adjustment be made. Planners understandably are not fond of such extra work. As a consequence, response to unexpected shifts in supply, demand, or technology is slow and incomplete.

Top planners seek to assure "taut planning."[5] The plan must have a "mobilizing" effect, extracting maximum output from given resources. This is one more reason for rigidities: there are no easily accessible reserves left to be used for quick adjustment. Furthermore, the plan leads to defensive tactics on the part of subordinates. It is in the interest of the firm's manager to hide the genuine capabilities of the firm and to obtain a more lax plan that can be fulfilled comfortably even if supplies do not arrive on schedule. Of course, the staff of the higher authorities knows the firms well. "Plan bargaining" evolves: the superior planner wants more output out of less input, the subordinate wants the opposite. In the course of realizing the plan, the manager's motivation is to achieve fulfillment, perhaps even a modest overfulfillment, but this must not be overdone. Otherwise the overfulfillment of this year will be incorporated into the mandatory target of the next year. As a consequence, a restrictive practice is common.*

*The problem has been discussed in Eastern Europe since the 1950s. There the phenomenon is called "base-year approach." The Western literature introduced the apt name "ratchet principle"; see Joseph S. Berliner, *Factory and Manager in the USSR* (Cambridge, Mass.: Harvard University Press, 1957); Michael Keren, "On the Tautness of Plans," *Review of Economic Studies*, 39 (Oct. 1972): 469–86; and Keren, Jeffrey Miller, and James R. Thornton, "The Ratchet: A Dynamic Managerial Incentive Model of the Soviet Enterprise," *Journal of Comparative Economics*, 7 (Dec. 1983): 347–67).

Input-output combinations are distorted. The direction of distortion depends on the exact nature of the "priority" indicators. If, for example, gross output in aggregate value terms is enforced most rigorously, the manager's interest is to produce goods containing large quantities of expensive material. If the output target is given in tons or, as in textile industry, in meters, the manager is motivated to produce heavy goods or thin textile. Output plans must be fulfilled at any price, neglecting all other nonpriority objectives or those the authorities are less able to check, such as the improvement of quality, the introduction of new products, reduction of costs, and proper maintenance of machinery and buildings.

The abstract model of the command economy operating in the state-owned sector is a strictly vertical bureaucratic control, executed by a disciplined bureaucracy in a consistent way. Real command economies are not as pure as the model; some horizontal coordination exists too. This proceeds partly on a nonpecuniary basis: informal agreements of reciprocal help are made between cooperating producer and user firms, complemented by some incentives in money terms to the suppliers for the sake of more reliable deliveries (that is, a half-tolerated, half-forbidden "market" relationship). In any case, the system in the Hungarian state sector in the early 1950s was fairly close to the model of a pure command system.

Minor changes were introduced in the late 1950s and early 1960s, for example, some limited forms of profit sharing for employees. When the dispute over reform revived in the mid-1960s, there were discussions about how far the country should go in the abolition of commands. Finally, the leadership opted for a radical solution. After careful preparation, the whole short-term command system was abolished in one stroke, beginning on January 1, 1968. The state-owned firms were formally declared to be autonomous with regard to short-term output and input plans.

Orthodox economists in Eastern Europe had been afraid that the socialist system would collapse without mandatory planning. It turned out that they were wrong. This paper will make many critical comments about the Hungarian reform, but this must not overshadow one of the most impressive and undeniable conclusions concerning the Hungarian systemic changes: the radical abolition of short-term mandatory planning is viable even without a fully developed market mechanism.

DUAL DEPENDENCE

What replaced the command system? A state-owned firm of the reformed Hungarian economy operates in a condition of *dual dependence*. It depends vertically on the bureaucracy and horizontally on its suppliers and customers. A brief look at the life of a state-owned firm will illustrate how the system of dual dependence works.

Entry. The creation of a state-owned firm is the result of a lengthy bureaucratic process. It might be initiated by an individual or a group, but the active support of bureaucratic organs is needed for success.

Recently the legal conditions for establishing small state-owned enterprises have been eased. Existing firms can "branch out" and create subsidiary enterprises half subordinate to and half independent of the founder. There is also some possibility of entry by nonstate producers as potential competitors of the state-owned firm, but this is subject to severe restrictions.

Exit. There are state-owned firms that go out of business, but their number is small and the exit (both final liquidation and absorption by another state-owned firm) is decided by bureaucratic procedures. "Death" is not the outcome of a natural selection process on the market. No substantial positive correlation can be found between exit and persistent loss making or insolvency.*

Selection and appointment of top managers. This remained the most important vertical linkage. Until some changes in the mid-1980s the leading executives of a firm were appointed by the superior authority. A successful manager will be promoted either by moving upward within the same firm or by transfer to another firm or to some state agency. Similarly, a successful official in a ministry may be appointed to the directorship of a large firm. There is no genuine job market for managers; their careers depend to a large extent on the opinion of the top bureaucracy. Therefore, it is understandable that one of the main objectives of managers is to please their superiors.

In 1985 new regulations were introduced. The top managers in the majority of state-owned firms are no longer appointed by the higher authority but are elected, directly or indirectly, by the employees of the firm. The administrative and political organizations have formal

*This observation and a few more to which I refer in the paper are based on a large-scale project examining the balance sheets of all Hungarian state-owned firms during 1975–82. This project is directed by the author and Agnes Matits; results are discussed in Kornai and Matits, "Softness of the Budget Constraint—An Analysis Relying on Data of Firms," *Acta Oeconomica*, 32 (1984): 223–49.

or informal veto powers over both the preselection of the candidates and the outcome of the election. It is too early to appraise the results of these arrangements.

Determination of output. The firm's autonomy has increased a great deal in this respect. Short-term annual plans are determined by the firm. The superior authority does not set aggregate output targets and that is an important change. It still puts forward, however, informal "requests" telling the firm what is "expected" from the managers. Typically, certain deliveries are urged for export or for a customer who is a protégé of the intervening official or for the elimination of certain pressing shortages. In any case, the management of the firm is usually willing to comply.

Determination of inputs. The all-encompassing system of formal material rationing and allocation has been dissolved, though a few goods are still centrally allocated. There are, however, informal quotas, licenses, or other restrictions.[6]

Horizontal linkages between state-owned firms in their capacities as sellers and buyers certainly have become stronger than they were before the reform. The linkages are mixtures of genuine market contracts following business negotiations about prices, quality standards, and delivery dates, and of "gentlemen's agreements" based on reciprocal favors. But the horizontal linkages are still not insulated from the decisive influence of vertical regulation. In case of disagreement or contract violation, complaints are addressed to the bureaucracy, which is asked for judgment and intervention.

Choice of technology. Administrative intervention occurs, but it is not widespread. The firm's autonomy has increased substantially in this respect.

Determination of prices. Before the reform, the price of almost all goods produced by state-owned firms was set arbitrarily by administrative organs. The relative prices were grossly distorted. The rules have changed several times in the course of the reform process. Some prices are still determined administratively, although usually under some influence and in many cases under strong pressure from the firms. The majority of prices ceased to be administrative, at least nominally, after 1968. Most of such prices have still not become genuinely free market prices either. Bureaucratic price control has different ways and means to exert strong, in some cases decisive influence on price formation.

First, for many goods strict rules prescribe how to calculate the price. Regulations determine when a "cost-plus" principle must be implemented. For such calculations there are strict instructions as to how costs should be calculated and what profit margins are permitted. In some other cases the application of the so-called competitive pricing principles is mandatory. Profit margins for goods sold on the domestic market must not exceed the profit margins achieved on export markets. Similar correspondence is prescribed between price increase for domestically sold and exported goods. There are many exceptions to the declared calculation principles, again determined by a long sequence of bureaucratic rules.

Second, many of the price changes nominally decided within the firm must be reported in advance by the producer to the price authority, which may or may not intervene, formally or informally.

Third, there are laws against "unfair profit" and "unfair price." These are, of course, vague concepts; much depends on interpretation and arbitrary judgment. Because firms are audited frequently, there is always the concern that their pricing practice may be condemned.

Unfortunately, there is no study available that would give a clear appraisal of how the present Hungarian relative price system compares with a rational one, reflecting relative scarcities more or less correctly. Some authors argue that prices have come much closer to rational proportions than they did before the reform, mainly because the main raw materials, energy, and many tradable goods are closer to relative prices on the world market. Others, the author among them, accept these results but maintain that a large degree of arbitrariness still prevails because of the widespread and bureaucratic interventions mentioned above. In an interdependent price system each bit of arbitrariness spills over and leads to further distortions. As we shall see later, an arbitrarily differentiated system of positive and negative taxation exists, which inevitably leads to price distortions. An indirect piece of evidence supporting the views of the critics is provided by a study of László Halpern and György Molnár, who calculate a "cost-plus" shadow price system based on uniform profit rates with the aid of an input-output table. The calculation shows a strikingly wide dispersion of the shadow-price/actual-price ratios.[7]

The impact of prices on firms' decisions has become somewhat stronger in the wake of the reform, but it is still not decisive. But even if firms eagerly watch prices, they may still give the wrong signals.

Determination of wages and employment. An important change was that absolute ceilings on the total wage bill, which had been one of the most powerful plan figures in the prereform era, were abolished. There are still several bureaucratic instruments of interference in wage formation. The instruments have changed several times since the beginning of the reform process. Among them are progressive taxation of the firm linked to average wages or to wage costs or to the increase of wages and wage policy guidelines associated with strong pressures to follow them.

As a result of the reform, mandatory employment quotas were abolished, but formal and informal restrictions on hiring labor reappeared in the 1970s, as a reaction to growing labor shortages.

Credit. Hungary has a highly centralized monetary system. There is permanent excess demand for credit. The banking sector, except for new institutions to be discussed later, acts as a credit-rationing administrative authority and not as a genuine bank following commercial principles. It is strongly connected with the planners' and the other authorities' supervision of the state-owned firms. Granting or denying credit is almost uncorrelated with the past or present profitability and credit worthiness of the firm. To some extent, the opposite relationship is true. The credit system is used frequently to bail out firms failing on the market. Perhaps a more market-oriented practice will evolve in the near future following recent changes in the financial sector.

Taxes and subsidies. Before the reform firms had to pay all gross profits, except for a minor profit retention, to the central budget. The introduction of taxation, which leaves the post-tax profit with the firm, is an important change. The tax system is, however, extremely complicated. The total number of taxes and subsidies to be paid by or to state-owned firms is between 290 and 300. Few of them are based on rules that affect all firms uniformly. Many tax or subsidy regulations appear to be general, but a closer look shows that they are calibrated to affect only a small targeted group, in many instances only a few dozen out of 1,600–1,700 firms. These are "tailor-made" rules. In addition, ad hoc tax exemptions are granted or payments due are postponed to help firms in financial trouble. Firms suffer from the unpredictability of taxation. Any time that the central authorities feel that firms have "too much money," tax rates may be arbitrarily increased or new taxes introduced or firms might be forced to save (for example, by prescribing mandatory deposits or reserves).

The total of all subsidies for the entire state-owned sector is about equal to the total gross profit before taxation; the total taxes are even larger than total gross profit because the state sector is a net taxpayer. This means that a huge reshuffling of gross profits goes on taxing away and handing out money through hundreds of channels.

Investment. Investment decisions and financing were highly centralized before the reform. As a result of the reform, the firm's discretion
has increased; a substantial fraction of profit can be retained for investment purposes. Nevertheless, central power is still very strong. For
major projects the firm needs additional capital either from the bank
or from the government budget. Only a small part of state sector investments, about one-fifth of the total, is decided at the firm's level
and financed exclusively from the firm's own savings. As for the rest,
the firm must come to an agreement with those who give external
assistance; consequently, the bureaucracy can have a decisive influence
on the allocation of investments. Another form of intervention is to
freeze the firm's savings originally reserved for investment purposes.

The central allocation of investment resources is not guided by profitability criteria. Almost the opposite can be said. Redistribution assists
the losers with money taxed away from firms making large profits.
There is no substantial correlation between pre- or post-tax profitability in a certain year and investment activities in later years (no
effect of past and present profitability). And there is no substantial
correlation in the opposite direction, either, namely, between investment activity in a certain year and pre- or post-tax profitability in
later years. Thus, expected future profitability has no effect, assuming that there is substantial correlation between expected and actual
profitability.

The situation is eased to some extent by recent developments. New
financial intermediaries have been created, and new ways of raising
capital are permitted.

SOFT BUDGET CONSTRAINT AND WEAK PRICE RESPONSIVENESS

In official declarations, profitability is the main criterion in apprais-
ing a firm's performance. The managers' bonus is linked to profitability and there is also profit sharing for employees.* It was hoped
that these measures would transform the firms into genuine profit
maximizers. That has not happened, as is illustrated in Table 2.2.

First let us look at the losers. Loss, even if long lasting, can be compensated for by different means: ad hoc or permanent subsidies, ad
hoc or permanently favorable tax conditions or bail-out credits. Price
authorities can be permissive, allowing increase of the administrative

---

*A manager's bonus is linked to post-tax profitability, giving the manager an extra
stimulus to fight for less tax and more subsidy. Profit sharing is leveled off; in contrast
to the high variance of profitability, the ratio of profit sharing and wage per worker has
a very small variance (Kornai and Matits).

TABLE 2.2
*Transition Probabilities Due to Fiscal
Redistribution in the State Sector of
Manufacturing in 1982*

	To final profitability			
From original profitability	Loss maker	Low profitability	Medium profitability	High profitability
Loss maker	.233	.500	.122	.145
Low profitability	.038	.853	.103	.006
Medium profitability	.000	.734	.206	.060
High profitability	.008	.394	.515	.083

SOURCE: Ágnes Matits, "A redisztribúció szerpe az állami vállalatok jövedelmezöségenek alakulásában: 1981–82" (The role of redistribution in the profitability of state enterprises: 1981–82), ms., Budapest, 1984, p. 48.

NOTE: *Transition* means the proportion of firms in any given original profitability class that became members of a given final profitability class as a result of fiscal redistribution. The transition from "original" to "final" profitability means the transition from the pretax and presubsidy position to the post-tax and postsubsidy position.

price or deviation from certain interventionist price rules. I coined the term *soft budget constraint* to describe this phenomenon.[8] The financial position of the state-owned firm is not without influence. Although there is a budget constraint that forces some financial discipline on the firm, it is not strictly binding, but can be "stretched" at the will of the higher authorities. In principle, the firm should cover expenditures from revenues made on the market. In practice, earnings from the market can be arbitrarily supplemented by external assistance.

The crucial issue is the fate of the chronic loss makers. Their fate will clearly show whether profit is something "dead serious" or only an illusion. The state bureaucracy exhibits a paternalistic attitude toward state-owned firms. This is understandable, for they are creations of the state, and the creator cannot let them down. There are strong social and political pressures to keep ailing firms alive for many reasons, for example, for the sake of job security or of import substitution.[9] But then many observers ask the following question. If the firm is in deep financial trouble and for sociopolitical reasons it cannot be shut down, why at least are the managers not fired? Such harsh treatment would —these observers say—increase the influence of the profit motive. In fact, the managers may either stay or be transferred to another job without significant loss in income and prestige. The reason is simple.

Because of the thousands of bureaucratic interventions, the manager does not have full responsibility for performance. In case of failure he can argue, perhaps with good reason, that he made all crucial decisions only after consulting superiors. Furthermore, many of the problems are consequences of central interventions, arbitrarily set prices, and so on. Under such circumstances, the bureaucracy feels obliged to shelter the loss makers.

On the other end of the spectrum are the firms making large profits. Table 2.2 shows that there is a peculiar egalitarian tendency operating to reduce the larger profits. The budget constraint is not only soft, but also perverse. Because of the ceaseless and unpredictable changes of the financial rules, taxes, and subsidies, firms feel insecure and exposed to the arbitrary improvisations of the bureaucracy.[10]

There are differences in terminology, but in substance a large group of Hungarian economists agree: financial discipline is lax, and there is no strong market coercion to enforce the search for profits. This "soft budget constraint" syndrome has many negative consequences. Only one will be mentioned at this point, namely, weak responsiveness to prices, especially on the input side. If a wrong adjustment to relative prices does not entail an automatic penalty through a well-functioning selective market process, the firm does not have a strong stimulus for quick and complete adjustment. There are some studies, unfortunately not many, that show the firms' weak response to relative prices. For example Judit Szabó and Imre Tarafás, with the aid of multiple regression analysis, demonstrate that changes of the foreign exchange rate have only a weak impact on producers' choice of the output and still less of inputs.[11]

We are facing a vicious circle between the arbitrariness and irrationalities of the relative price system on the one hand and the soft budget constraint syndrome on the other, as argued by Halpern and Molnár and Kornai and Agnes Matits.[12] Because prices are arbitrary and distorted, firms have legitimate reasons to ask for compensation. And when external assistance is granted, it leads to the preservation of the wrong price.

SIZE DISTRIBUTION, MONOPOLIES

The size distribution of firms in Hungarian production is much more skewed in favor of large units than in developed capitalist economies, as illustrated in Table 2.3. In 1975 in Hungarian industry the three largest producers supplied more than two-thirds of production

TABLE 2.3
Size Distribution of Firms in Manufacturing

	Hungary	Sample of capitalist economies
Average number of employees per firm:		
	186	80
Percentage distribution of employees by size categories:		
10–100	14	35
101–500	26	33
501–1,000	19	13
>1,000	41	19

SOURCE: Éva Ehrlich, "A termelöegységek méretstruktúrája 18 ország feldolgozóiparában" (The size structure of manufacturing establishments in 18 countries), *Gazdaság*, 19, no. 3 (1985): 92.

NOTE: The figures refer to averages of various years in the 1970s. The capitalist economies sampled are Austria, Belgium, France, Italy, Japan, and Sweden.

in 508 out of 637 product aggregates.[13] The extremely high concentration weakens or eliminates potential rivalry and creates monopolies or oligopolies in many segments of production.

There are quite a few organizations that have the legal status of a state-owned firm, but are practically playing the role of a state authority. Their number at present is smaller than before the reform but still not negligible. They have the power to determine the rationing of the goods or services they supply to customers. For example, this is the situation with the monopoly company delivering automobiles. There is a monopoly bank with the exclusive right to grant consumer credit and mortgage loans.

In the last few years, there have been serious efforts to break up monopoly positions and to partition large entities into several smaller ones. The size distribution has become somewhat less extreme, shifting a bit toward smaller units. But the process is slow and meets with strong resistance.

There is a peculiar disparity in the treatment of large and small state-owned firms. Large firms are much more successful in lobbying for favors, particularly for investment resources. Some of them are in great financial trouble; nevertheless large credits or subsidies are handed out to them. Smaller units, however, count for less in the eyes of the supervisors. They suffer less from frequent inspections, and it is easier for them to evade certain rigid regulations than it is for large firms.[14]

SUMMARY: FROM DIRECT TO INDIRECT BUREAUCRATIC CONTROL

The reform has improved the performance of the Hungarian state sector. Firms now have more room for maneuver; they have become less rigid and more adaptive. They respond in a more flexible way to changes in demand and pay more attention to improvement of quality and technical progress. These achievements become even more visible if one compares Hungary with the unreformed socialist economies.

This appreciation notwithstanding, the reform went only halfway. Hungarian state-owned firms do not operate within the framework of market socialism. The reformed system is a specific combination of Forms 1 and 2, that is, of bureaucratic and market coordination. The same can be said, of course, about every contemporary economy. There is no capitalist economy in which the market functions in the complete absence of bureaucratic intervention. The real issue is the relative strength of the components in the mixture. Although there are no exact measures, I venture the following proposition. The frequency and intensity of bureaucratic intervention into market processes have certain critical values. Once these critical values are exceeded, the market becomes emasculated and dominated by bureaucratic regulation. That is exactly the case in the Hungarian state-owned sector.* The market is not dead. It does some coordinating work, but its influence is weak. The firm's manager watches the customer and the supplier with one eye and his superiors in the bureaucracy with the other. Practice teaches him that it is more important to keep the second eye wide open: managerial career, the firm's life and death, taxes, subsidies and credit, prices and wages, all financial "regulators" affecting the firm's prosperity, depend more on the higher authorities than on market performance.

In the course of the reform the bureaucracy itself has changed: it has become less tightly centralized. It is a peculiar complex of partial

*Richard Portes, in "The Tactics and Strategy of Economic Decentralization," *Soviet Studies*, 23 (Apr. 1972): 657, made the same general point much earlier, writing that "there is a threshold beyond which decentralization must go to take firm roots." He was, however, confident that Hungarian "strategy and tactics has brought the reform across the border." I differ, believing the Hungarian reform did not cross the critical threshold that separates a genuine market economy (associated with a certain degree of bureaucratic intervention) from an economy basically controlled by the bureaucracy (with certain elements of market coordination).

multilevel bureaucracies that often act in an inconsistent manner; it is more polycentric than before the reform. The head of each branch has his own priorities and performs his own interventions, granting favors to some firms and putting extra burdens on others. The more such lines of separate control evolve, the more they dampen each other's effects.

The "rules of the game" are not generated in a natural, organic way by economic and social processes; rather, they are elaborated artificially by the officers and committees of the administrative authorities. They are, of course, never perfect: they do not produce exactly the results expected and are therefore revised time and time again. Hence they are unable to provide stable guidance for the behavior of the firm. Once the reactions of the firms become manifest, the rules are revised again.

The role of the state is not restricted to determining or influencing a few important macroaggregates or economy-wide parameters like the exchange rate or interest rate. As we have seen, there are millions of microinterventions in all facets of economic life; bureaucratic *microregulation* has continued to prevail.

The firms are not helpless. Every new tactic of the higher organs evokes new countertactics. Bargaining goes on about all issues all the time. This is a bargaining society, and the main direction is vertical, namely bargaining between the levels of the hierarchy, or between bureaucracy and firm, not horizontal, between seller and buyer. All issues mentioned above—entry, exit, appointment, output, input, price, wage, tax, subsidy, credit, and investment—are subject to meticulous negotiations, fights, lobbying, the influence of open or hidden supporters and opponents. The Hungarian literature calls this phenomenon "regulator bargaining"; it has taken the place of "plan bargaining," which prevailed in the command economy. Firms had quite a bit of bargaining power even in the classical command system, and their bargaining position improved substantially in the new system, especially in the case of the large firms.

If bargaining does not succeed, there is one more instrument in the hands of the firm: to evade the regulations, preferably not in an explicitly illegal way but by using tricks, seemingly following the letter of the law but violating its intentions. And then, when the lawmaker recognizes that there are loopholes, he tries to create a new, more perfect decree—and the game starts again.

The system that has developed in the Hungarian state-owned sector may be called *indirect bureaucratic control*, juxtaposing it to the old

command system of direct *bureaucratic control*. The name reflects the
fact that the dominant form of coordination has remained bureaucratic control but that there are significant changes in the set of control
instruments.

The Nonstate Sector

THE REFORM IN AGRICULTURE

Agriculture is perhaps the most successful area of the reform. It
is therefore instructive to discuss agriculture as a whole.[15] Contradictory tendencies developed in the last twenty-five to thirty years.
The share of state-owned farms remained stable. There were two big
waves of "collectivization," that is, forced formation of agricultural cooperatives: the first in the early 1950s and the second in 1959–61.
The latter brought more than two-thirds of arable land from private
ownership into the hands of the cooperatives. Members of the cooperatives were allowed to hold only a small private plot and a few
animals. The present shares of the various types of ownership are
shown in Table 2.4. Still, in spite of dramatic changes in the direction
of collective ownership, Hungarian agriculture is different from the
prototype "collectivized" organization of agricultural production.

Cooperatives. This has remained the largest social sector in agriculture. Many important changes have occurred in their functioning. In
the prereform system the position of a cooperative was not far from
that of a state-owned farm. It was tightly fitted in the framework of a
command economy; it received detailed mandatory plan targets like
state-owned firms. As a result of the reform process, the system of
mandatory plans was abolished in 1966, just as in the state sector two
years later. Frequent informal interventions, however, remained.

Even in the old system leaders of the cooperatives were elected and
not appointed; that was the essential legal difference between a state-
owned and a cooperative enterprise. In practice, however, elections
were manipulated and there was only a formal approval of the pre-
selected managers by the membership. This practice has not been
rooted out, although the participation of the members in the selection
and appointment of managers has become more active; the word of
the membership carries more weight than it did.

In the cooperatives of the early 1950s material incentives were weak.
Compulsory delivery quotas at very low administrative prices absorbed
the largest part of production. In other words, the peasantry carried

TABLE 2.4
*Contribution of Social Sectors to Total
Agricultural Gross Output*
(percentage distribution)

Sector	1966	1975	1980	1984
State-owned farms	16.4	18.0	16.8	15.3
Cooperatives	48.4	50.5	50.4	51.1
Household farming	23.7	19.0	18.5	18.4
Auxiliary production and private farms	11.5	12.5	14.3	15.2

SOURCE: Central Statistical Office, Hungary.

a heavy tax burden. In years of poor harvest even seeds for the next year and foodstuff for the farmers' own consumption were barely left in the village. In the expression coined during those times, the attics of the farmers' houses were swept clean by compulsory deliveries. The sale of surplus on the market was legally permitted, but little or no surplus was left to sell.

There have been substantial changes in this respect. Some (though not all) price distortions, both on the output and on the input side, have been eliminated. Material incentives are strong. As has been mentioned, the compulsory delivery system was abandoned as early as 1956–57. The cooperatives can sell to state trade organizations on a contractual basis, but they are allowed to do their own marketing if they prefer. The cooperative as a whole is motivated to earn more income and more profit. The cooperatives have more autonomy in deciding on the use of their own profit. In many areas a special form of decentralization is applied within the cooperatives: working teams or individuals are in charge of a certain line of production and get their own share of their production line's net income.

Before the reform, agricultural cooperatives were prohibited from engaging in any but agricultural activities. In the reform process nonagricultural activities have developed. The cooperatives have engaged in food processing, in the production of parts for state-owned industry, in light industry, in construction, in trade, and in the restaurant business. The share of nonagricultural production in the total output of agricultural cooperatives was 34 percent in 1984. In this way profits have increased and seasonal troughs of employment can be bridged more easily.[16]

Private household farms of cooperative members. Here one finds the most spectacular changes. Whereas the legal limitations on the size of the household plot have remained unchanged, much more family work is devoted to this special kind of private agriculture. Restrictions on keeping animals and on owning machinery have been lifted. Household farms produce a large fraction of meat, dairy and other animal products, fruits and vegetables. With few exceptions, there is no legal restriction on selling output, and prices are determined by supply and demand on the free market for foodstuffs; hence the peasants have a strong impetus to work hard and produce more. The attitudes of both the cooperative and the agricultural administrative apparatus toward the household farm are now very different from what they were. In the old system the cooperative was hostile; private household farming was regarded as a "bourgeois remnant" that should be replaced by collective forms of production. Now private household farming is declared a permanent component of agriculture under socialism. Cooperatives render assistance in different ways: they provide seeds, help with transport, lend machinery, give expert advice, and assist in marketing. A remarkable division of tasks has evolved in which the cooperatives concentrate more on grain and fodder, which can be produced most efficiently by large-scale operations, and private household farms focus on labor-intensive products for which small-scale operations succeed better.

I do not want to paint an idealized picture: in fact, there are many troubles in this sphere. There have been periodic capricious bureaucratic interventions into the household farming sector, confusing the farmers and weakening their confidence. There are gross distortions in prices offered to private producers by the state trade organizations, who are the main buyers of many agricultural products. In spite of these problems, the household farms are relatively successful.

Auxiliary agricultural production. Hungary is a country with a strong agricultural tradition. People working in nonagricultural professions like to have a garden or a small plot, where they can grow fruit and vegetables or raise poultry or pigs. The liberalization measures in agriculture gave new impetus to these activities. Auxiliary agricultural production turns out to be a nonnegligible fraction of total output, covering not only a substantial portion of the participating households' own consumption, thereby decreasing demand for marketed products, but also contributing to the marketed supply. Some of these producing units developed into specialized, capital-intensive private farms producing commodities almost exclusively for the market.

State-owned farms. The share of state-owned farms in total agricultural output has not changed much, but their situation is now different. Systemic changes appear in the state-owned part of agriculture also. Here we also find dual dependence, but the relative strength of the market is stronger and that of bureaucratic coordination is weaker than in other branches of the state-owned sector. Prices are more reasonable, managers are more "entrepreneurial," and the profit motive is more intense. The main difference is that in agriculture a small number of state-owned enterprises are surrounded by a very large number of more competitive, more market- and profit-oriented cooperatives and private household farms. The minority's behavior adjusts to some extent to the behavior of the dominant parts of the branch.

Hungarian agriculture shows a particular blend of spectacular successes and unresolved problems. The main achievements are the significant improvement of domestic food supply, some good results in exports, and the stronger motivation for work in all subsectors. But all these results were obtained at high cost: with the aid of a very large investment of capital and of the peasants' hard "self-exploitation."

The present size distribution is unsatisfactory; medium-sized units, smaller than the large-scale state-owned and cooperative units and larger than the "mini"-scale units in household farming, are almost nonexistent. In other countries with highly developed agriculture the dominant form is a farm operating with a small number of people, but with high capital intensity. Such an efficient and highly productive form has not yet developed in Hungary either in the cooperative or in the private sector. Development in that direction has been hindered by the privileges of the existing large-scale units and by conservative bureaucratic restrictions.

NONAGRICULTURAL COOPERATIVES

The significance of the nonagricultural cooperatives has increased in the reform process in manufacturing, construction, commerce, and services. They are similar to the agricultural cooperatives in many respects. One important distinction is that there is less favorable treatment of nonagricultural than of agricultural cooperatives as far as credit, tax, subsidy, and import are concerned.

The abolition of mandatory plans and the dual dependence of the enterprise applies to the cooperatives as well. There is, however, a difference in relative weights; in all issues (exit, entry, selection of managers, price, wage, tax, credit) there is somewhat less bureaucratic intervention and somewhat stronger influence of market forces than

in the state sector. The budget constraint is somewhat harder; nonagricultural cooperatives (especially the smaller ones) cannot expect
unconditional survival* and almost automatic bail-out by the bureaucracy. The cooperative is much more responsive to prices; its profit
motivation is stronger.† The cooperatives receive less favorable treatment than state-owned firms in the allocation of investment credits
and subsidies.

The average cooperative is much smaller than the state-owned firm,
especially in recent years, because more possibilities have opened up
for establishing so-called small cooperatives that work under easier
and more flexible legal and financial conditions than do the rest of the
cooperatives.

The situation of cooperatives is important from the viewpoint of
socialist ideology. The idea that cooperatives will be one of the basic
forms of ownership in socialism, or even *the* basic form, has a long-
standing intellectual tradition in the Hungarian Left. The advocates
of the traditional cooperative idea have always stressed the principle of
voluntary participation. Nowadays this principle is more or less consistently applied in the nonagricultural sector. (The same cannot be said
about the formation of cooperatives in the past.) There is a general
shortage of labor in Hungary. The vast majority of present members
therefore, have a genuine choice between entering and remaining in
a cooperative or getting a job in other sectors. Those who stay seem to
prefer this form because it combines the efficiency of a medium-sized
firm with a certain degree of participation in managerial decisions.
The linkage between individual and collective performance and individual earning is more direct than in the state-owned firm. Of course,
a conclusive test can come only if the economic environment of the
cooperative sector becomes more competitive and market oriented,
and the cooperatives have to demonstrate efficiency and profitability
against more vigorous competitors.

THE FORMAL PRIVATE SECTOR

The most spectacular trend of the Hungarian reform process is the
growth of the private sector. From the point of view of ideology, this
is the boldest break with orthodoxy. The term *private sector* has both

---

*Agricultural cooperatives are much more sheltered. Small wonder that this segment
of the economy stubbornly opposes the introduction of bankruptcy laws and other
measures of hardening the budget constraint.

†All these differences are smaller and the similarities greater between *large* cooperatives and state-owned enterprises.

TABLE 2.5
The Size of the Formal Private Sector
(thousands of persons)

Sector	1953	1955	1966	1975	1980	1984
1. Private craftsmen	51.5	97.6	71.3	57.4	63.7	76.1
2. Employees and apprentices of private craftsmen	4.0	16.0	26.7	19.7	20.1	26.9
3. Private merchants	3.0	9.0	8.5	10.8	12.0	22.4
4. Employees of private merchants	—	1.0	1.5	3.4	8.2	28.5
5. People working full time in business work partnerships	—	—	—	—	—	11.0
6. Total number of people working full time in the formal private sector	58.5	123.6	108.0	91.3	104.0	164.9

SOURCES: Rows 1–4, Central Statistical Office, Hungary; Row 5, Ministry of Finance.
NOTE: Since 1968, persons with a regular full-time job in the state-owned or cooperative sector have been able to get a license for a second part-time job in the formal private sector. In 1984, 47.2 thousand persons worked as part-time licensed private craftsmen, and 31.5 thousand as part-time members of business work partnerships.

narrower and wider definitions. The formal private sector is distinguished from the other private ventures in that it is officially licensed by the bureaucracy.

Table 2.5 shows the size of the formal private sector. The majority of personnel are craftsmen, construction contractors, shopkeepers, and restaurant owners. They work alone or are assisted by family members or a few hired employees. The size of this sector has increased rapidly in the last few years when the authorities began to grant licenses more liberally. Also the regulations concerning employment became less restrictive: at present the maximum number of employees, apart from family members, is seven. This is, of course, a very small number for those accustomed to private market economies, but large in comparison with other socialist countries. It means the legalization of "small capitalism." Medium- or large-scale capitalist business is prohibited in Hungary.

A new form has appeared recently: the so-called business work partnership, a small-scale enterprise based on private ownership by the participants. It is a blend of a small cooperative and a small owner-operated capitalistic firm. This form also belongs to the formal private sector.

The formal private sector is still a minor segment of the economy (see Table 2.1). Nevertheless, its rate of growth is remarkable: mere permission to exist and perhaps also some encouragement in official speeches were enough to induce a sudden boom. Apparently thousands of people had a latent desire to enter private business; at the first opportunity, they ran to join the formal private sector. And this happened in the face of many difficulties. Private business is at a disadvantage in getting inputs from the state sector. It rarely gets credit from the state-owned banking sector and therefore must rely on raising money through private and frequently illegal channels. Private credit does not have satisfactory legal backing.

It is widely believed that tax evasion is common; in any case, enforcement of the tax law is lax. Tougher enforcement could easily scare away many people from private business. This leads to a wider issue, namely the problem of confidence.

At present the majority of people working in the formal private sector are probably satisfied with their current income. Perhaps they are not all aware that their relative position in the income distribution is much better than that of small business people in a private market economy. There, craftsmen or small shopkeepers usually have very modest incomes. In Hungary, many of them are in the highest income group. Yet they cannot be sure how long that will last. These individuals or their parents lived through the era of confiscations in the 1940s. In spite of repeated official declarations that their activity is regarded as a permanent feature of Hungarian socialism, deep in their hearts they are not so sure. That is why many of them are myopic profit maximizers, not much interested in building up lasting goodwill by offering good service and quick and reliable delivery or by investing in long-lived fixed assets. Encouragement and discouragement alternate; quiet periods are interrupted by orchestrated media campaigns crying out against "speculation" and "profiteering." A confidence-strengthening experience of many years is still needed to extend the restricted horizon.

THE INFORMAL PRIVATE SECTOR, THE SECOND ECONOMY

We must start with conceptual clarification. Hungarian experts dealing with private activities and income earned outside the state-owned and cooperative sector do not agree on terminology and definitions. The present paper applies the following notions.

To the *informal* private sector belong (a) all private activities pursued outside the formal private sector as defined in the earlier section and (b) all income that does not originate as payment for labor service rendered in government agencies, officially registered nonprofit institutions, state-owned firms, cooperatives, and formal private business. The activity and income components (a) and (b) of the definition are not completely overlapping.

The *first economy* is composed of the government agencies, officially registered nonprofit institutions, state-owned firms, and cooperatives. The *second economy* is the total of the formal and informal private sector.* A caveat: the decisive mark distinguishing "first" and "second" economy in this usage is not legality versus illegality, or payment of taxes versus tax evasion. (That is the common criterion in the Western literature on the "shadow economy.") Many activities in our second economy are legal; a part of second-economy income is taxed. We apply a system-specific classification. The first economy is the sphere that was regarded by the prereform orthodox interpretation as the genuine "socialist" sector, the second economy was classified as "nonsocialist."

Working time. Hungary, with some delay, follows the tendency of industrialized economies by reducing hours of work in the first economy. Simultaneously, activities in the second economy consume more time than ever before. Some people work in the second economy as their main activity. Some members of a family are active full time in the private household farm, while others are employed in the state-owned farm or in the cooperative. Many pensioners have a full- or half-time (illegal or "half-legal") activity. But the majority work in the second economy as an activity supplementary to a first job in one of the formal sectors. They "moonlight" in the evenings, weekends, and during paid vacations. It happens, illegally, that one works while on sick leave, paid by the national health service, or during regular paid working hours at one's first job.

Aggregate data are shown in Table 2.6. The incredibly high (one to two) ratio between total working time spent in the second and first economies demonstrates the high preference of a large part of the Hungarian population for more income and higher consumption over leisure. This is just one of the secrets of the "Hungarian miracle":

*Here I follow more or less the definition of the second economy used by Gábor, the leading Hungarian expert in the field.

TABLE 2.6
The Relative Size of the Second Economy

Economic activity	First economy (state-owned firms and cooperatives) (percent)	Second economy (formal and informal private sector) (percent)
1. Distribution of total active time (excluding time spent on household work and transport), 1984	67	33
2. Contribution to residential construction (measured by number of new dwellings), 1984	44.5	55.5
3. Contribution to repair and maintenance services, 1983	13	87

SOURCES: (1) Central Statistical Office, Hungary; and János Timár, "Idő és munkaidő" (Time and working time), Közgazdasági Szemle, 32, no. 11 (1985): 1299–1313. (2) Central Statistical Office, Hungary. (3) Pál Belyó and Bela Drexler, "Nem szervezett (elsősorban illegális) keretek között végzett szolgáltatások" (Non-organized, mainly illegal, activities in the service sector), ms., Research Institute on Services, 1985, p. 60.

NOTE: The table covers both the officially recorded and unrecorded part of total activities. The figures concerning the latter are based on estimates elaborated by the researchers who compiled the data base of the table. Figures in row 1 are aggregates of all branches of production, including residential construction. The latter is also surveyed separately in row 2. The "first economy" figures include the activities of so-called enterprise business work partnerships. The "second economy" figures include household farming and "auxiliary production of employees." The "second economy" figures in row 3 are the sum of three parts: formal private sector 14 percent, informal private sector excluding "do-it-yourself" activities 19 percent, and "do-it-yourself" activities within the household 54 percent.

people are willing to work more if allowed; they will exert themselves for the sake of higher consumption. In a large fraction of families, members are working to the point of psychological and physical exhaustion.*

Of the 33 percent of active time spent on second-economy activities, a smaller part is spent in the formal private sector, thus contributing to the officially recorded GDP. The larger part of the 33 percent is spent in the informal private sector. Depending on how productivity is measured in the informal private sector, this subsector may add perhaps 20 percent or more to the officially recorded GDP.

Production for own consumption: the role of the household. Before the

---

*As mentioned in the note to Table 2.5, many individuals have a first job in the state or cooperative sector and a second job in the formal private sector. Although this activity is counted as part of the formal private sector, the comments above concerning the extension of working time apply also to this group.

reform there was a strong tendency to reduce the role of the family and the household as a producing and property-owning institution and to shift more and more activity and property into the domain of large and preferably state-owned organizations. The reform reversed this trend to some extent.

The reversal is not consistent and is accompanied by many frictions. A vacuum is present in some areas: the old forms of socialized services are no longer fully responsible for meeting demands on them, yet the household and the family are not yet in a position to take over these responsibilities satisfactorily.[17]

The trend in the prereform system was toward public housing. All apartment houses were nationalized; tenancy was rationed by the bureaucracy. This trend has been reversed. In 1980 71.4 percent of the total housing stock was in private ownership and the rest was owned by the state. The trend continues: 85.7 percent of the dwellings built in 1984 were private. The new shift is associated with severe social and economic tensions.[18]

A further example is transport. Khrushchev advocated the complete abolition of private cars in favor of public transport as a desirable trend in socialism. Present-day Hungary is overcrowded with private cars. The number of privately owned cars increased 13.7 times from 1966 to 1984. But repair service and the building and maintenance of the road network cannot keep up with the increasing number of private cars.

There are many more examples of the reversal from "socialization" toward self-sufficiency within the family and household: child care, sick care, cooking and other household work, and do-it-yourself repair and maintenance. How far the latter trend has gone is demonstrated in Table 2.6.

Contribution to consumer supply. Another indication of the importance of the second economy is the contribution to consumer supply. Table 2.6 presents a few characteristic data demonstrating the extremely large share of the second economy in this respect. And, of course, there are many more areas not shown in the table.

Yields of private property. Participants in the second economy often combine their own labor and equipment, or they may use, illegally, the equipment of their first-economy employer. There is also another category of person: income earners whose source of second-economy income is a return from some private property. The most common example is the subletting of privately owned housing or renting out second homes in recreation areas, either to long-term lessees or to short-term visitors and tourists.*

Legality. There is a wide continuum running from perfectly legal, "white" and perfectly illegal, "black" activities; only in the latter is the law strictly enforced. An informal private sector, or a second economy exists in all socialist countries. Quantitative comparison is not possible, but experts are convinced that the share of this sector in Hungary is much larger than in most socialist economies. This is a direct consequence of the state's attitude. There is a deliberate effort to legalize formerly illegal activities, or to be tolerant of ambiguous cases, provided that these activities are regarded as socially useful or at least not harmful. This tolerance awakened tremendous energy in a large part of the population. It is not a very satisfactory organization of human activity; it is full of conflicts and unfair actions, but still, without the tolerance, this energy would remain dormant. The spirit of tolerance and the trend toward legalization, however, do not work consistently. What has been said about alternations of encouragement and discouragement of the formal private sector applies even more to the informal sector. As a consequence, the situation here is rather unstable.

COMBINED FORMS

A characteristic feature of the Hungarian reform is the experimentation with different mixed forms, combining state ownership with private activity or private ownership.

Firms in mixed ownership. A few dozen firms are owned jointly by the Hungarian state and foreign private business. A sharing of business by the Hungarian ownership state and Hungarian private business does not exist.

Leasing. This form is widely applied in trade and in the restaurant sector. Fixed capital remains in state ownership, but the business is run by a private individual who pays a rent fixed by a contract and also taxes. He keeps the profit or covers the deficit at his own risk. The lessee is selected by auction; the person offering the highest rent gets the contract. In 1984 about 11 percent of the shops and 37 percent of the restaurants were leased this way.

Enterprise business work partnership. In contrast to "business work

*Tenants in a public apartment have in practice a "quasi-ownership" under the conditions of chronic shortage. Tenancy can be inherited, sold for money illegally to a new tenant or legally to the state. Therefore it is not out of place to put the arrangement of subletting in a public apartment in the same category as using the equipment of a first-economy employer.

partnership," which is a form clearly belonging to the formal private sector, those teams are employed by state-owned firms to do extra work under special contract for extra payment, but in some sense within the framework of the employer state-owned firm. In many cases the team is commissioned by its own firm. Or it gets the task from outside, but with the consent of the employer. In many instances the members are allowed to use the equipment of the firm. The "enterprise business work partnership" can be established only with the permission of the managers of the firm; each member needs a permit from his superiors to join the team.[19]

The purpose of creating this new form is clear. It gives a legal framework for certain activities, formerly not legal, and at the same time allows the employing firm to keep some control over these activities. Many managers support this arrangement because it allows them to get around central wage regulation: the partnership undertakes work for extra payment that it would otherwise do (perhaps in regular overtime) within the framework of its regular job. The number of such units is increasing rapidly. It was 2,775 in 1982 and grew to 17,337 by the end of 1984. Many observers are highly critical and question the efficiency of having a first and a second job within the same organization. Perhaps, however, the arrangement may lead to some healthy intrafirm decentralization later on.

STRONG MARKET ORIENTATION AND BUREAUCRATIC CONSTRAINTS

As we have seen, the reform process has created or strengthened a large variety of nonstate ownership forms and activities. It is a great merit of the reformers that they allowed or initiated such experimentation with courage and open minds.

In the midst of the variety of forms, there are a few common features. The economic units in the nonstate sector (perhaps with the exception of large cooperatives) have a hard budget constraint; they cannot rely on the paternalistic assistance of the state for survival and growth. They enter business in the hope of profits and they go out of business if they fail financially. All activities are more market oriented and price responsive than those carried out by the state-owned firms.

The nonstate sector acts as a built-in stabilizer of the economy, which is less sensitive to the "stop-go" fluctuations so strongly felt in the state sector. It is able to grow even when there are troubles with the balance of payments or restrictions on import and investment.

The nonstate sector is, however, not free from bureaucratic con-

trol. There are permanent restrictions and regulations, and also unpredictable, improvised interventions and frequent changes of the
rules. The same phenomenon I have just praised, namely, bold experimentation, can also be confusing. The lack of stability and the many
bureaucratic restrictions do not give full scope to the initiative of the
individuals engaged in the nonstate sector.

Nevertheless, with all its shortcomings, the appearance of a vital
nonstate sector represents something brand new and important in the
history of socialist countries.

Overall Resource Allocation and Distribution

In this section I will discuss issues that cut across the economy, regardless of the breakdown by ownership forms.

PLANNING

In the usage of socialist countries *planning* has a double meaning.
First, it refers to an ex ante exploration of possibilities and comparison
of alternative solutions. A plan sets targets and assigns instruments to
fulfill them. The "product" of the planners' work is the plan itself—a
document accepted by the political and legislative bodies, which serves
as a working program for the government. Second, the term *planning*
is also used to denote what the present paper calls direct bureaucratic
control. The official ideology of the command economy deliberately
wanted to convince people that these two concepts are inseparable.

I suggest a strict separation of the two concepts and reserve the term
planning only for the first. The official documents of the Hungarian reform adopt this interpretation when they repeat that, although mandatory targets and quotas are abolished, planning must be maintained.

Nominally, these resolutions have been implemented. The planning
apparatus is at work, and plans are elaborated in due time. Nevertheless, a closer examination shows that planning has not found its
appropriate new role. One would expect that after being freed from
the nuisances of "dispatcher work" (that is, setting quotas, checking
performance, urging deliveries, and the like) the planner's time and
intellectual energy could finally be spared for his genuine tasks of exploration, calculation, comparison, and ex ante coordination. These
possibilities have not been fully exploited. There are efforts to elaborate long-term plans, but the linkage between these plans and the
actual regulation of economic affairs is rather weak. Planners have

achieved impressive results in coordinating short-term macropolicy and microregulation in a state of emergency (for example, when tensions developed in Hungary's international credit position). Yet the problem has not been solved. The old methodology suitable for imperative planning is no longer applicable, and a consistent new methodology compatible with the systemic changes is not yet available.

FISCAL SYSTEM

The fiscal system has remained extremely large. Total central government expenditure was 52.8 percent of GDP in 1970, grew to 62.7 percent by 1980, and decreased slightly to 61.3 percent by 1983.

In capitalist economies this ratio is strongly correlated with the level of development (GDP/capita). For the sake of comparison we look at European capitalist countries that have reached about the same level of development as Hungary: in 1980 the government expenditure/ GDP ratio was 37.7 percent in Finland, 36.5 percent in Greece, and 29.4 percent in Spain.*

There are several reasons for the high degree of centralization of financial flows through the government budget. Most of them are associated with issues already discussed, the huge burden of subsidies, the deep fiscal involvement in financing investment, and the expenditures of the large bureaucratic apparatus. These properties of the fiscal system provide remarkable evidence that genuine decentralization of economic processes through market coordination has not gone very far.

The next section will discuss the role of banks and the capital market. One remark can be made in advance. The fact that a very large fraction of the economy's net income flows through the central government budget allows less scope for the activity of banks, other financial intermediary institutions, and enterprises and households in the reallocation of funds. This is eminently clear in the case of investment allocation. The larger the fraction of investment financed by the central budget, the less disposable capital is left to the discre-

---

*The Hungarian ratio in 1980 was somewhat higher even than the ratio of Sweden, Denmark, and the Netherlands, although all three countries are at a much higher level of development and spend relatively much more on welfare purposes. The ratio of government expenditure on production (mainly investment and subsidies) in industry, agriculture, transport, commerce, and service as a percentage of GDP was 25 in Hungary and less than 9 in the average of a sample of 14 industrialized capitalist countries. The figures are calculated on the basis of definitions assuring comparability. They refer to the same set of expenditures (including central and local government expenditures). GDP is calculated according to Western definitions for Hungary.

tion of other actors and the less possibility arises for the creation of a well-functioning capital market.

In that respect there is a trend toward decentralization. The share of investment financed by the central government budget was 40 percent in 1968–70 and diminished to 21 percent in 1981–84; the share of investment financed by bank credit and by the producers' own savings increased accordingly.

MONETARY SYSTEM, CAPITAL MARKET

In a fully monetized market economy money is a means of integrating the whole national economy. That is assured by the possibility that money is a universal medium of exchange, which can be used by each money holder for any purpose he chooses. The classical pre-reform system fragmented the economy in this respect. Certain types of money flows between different segments of the system were permitted while others were strictly prohibited. The state sector paid money wages to the households, but, except for minimal tightly restricted consumer credits granted by the monopoly savings bank, it could not give credit to customers. The household paid the price for goods and services marketed by the state sector, but could not invest its savings in real capital formation by the state sector. Even within the state sector money was "earmarked." The firm had at least three kinds of money: "wage money," "money covering current costs other than wages," and "investment money." These categories of money could be used only for the assigned purpose.[20]

The reform has brought some relaxation in this respect; the economy has come closer to a system integrated by money. It is, however, still far from one with free flows of funds.

Banks. Until recently, Hungary has had a "monobank system." In that respect it has remained similar to the classical socialist economy. The Hungarian National Bank has combined two functions: it plays the usual role of a central bank and also acts as a commercial bank, practically as the monopoly commercial bank for most financial operations of the state-owned and cooperative sectors. There have also been a few specialized banks, for example, the foreign-trade bank and the bank for household savings, but these have enjoyed only a seeming autonomy.

There are now resolutions to establish a two-level banking sector in the near future. There will be a central bank at the top with the usual functions and a set of state-owned, but competing commercial banks on the lower level, regulated by the central bank. Even before

TABLE 2.7
The Availability of Bonds, May 1986

Available to:	Total nominal value (billion forints)[a]	Yield (percent)	Relative size (percent)
Private citizens	4.5	7–13	2.0[b]
Firms and institutions	2.0	7–15	9.7[c]

SOURCE: State Development Bank, Hungary.
[a] Covers all bonds issued prior to May 1986.
[b] Total nominal value ÷ stock of household deposits in savings banks.
[c] Total nominal value ÷ stock of outstanding bank investment credit.

this plan is realized, a few small financial intermediaries that can lend for specific purposes (certain kinds of investment, innovation, export promotion) have been established. In any case, we do not know yet how much genuine autonomy the units of the decentralized banking sector will enjoy and to what extent they will be subject to pressure from the central and local bureaucracy.

Firms. Before the reform, the state-owned firm had almost no choice concerning financial decisions. The portion of working capital that had to be deposited in the central bank was strictly regulated; there was a very small part of gross investment financed from retained profit and depreciation funds. Trade credit was prohibited. The bank had a strictly protected monopoly in granting credit to the firm.

Now the situation is different. Let us start with the asset side. A firm can deposit money in the bank and in the near future it will also be able to choose between banks. It can grant trade credit to other firms buying its output.* It can invest in its own plant or it can establish a small subsidiary, holding only a part of equity in the newly created firm. It can contribute to the capital of a newly founded company jointly with other firms or institutions. It can buy bonds issued by other firms or local authorities and traded on the bond market. Table 2.7 provides information about the size of the bond market.

On the liability side the situation is symmetrical; only a few additional remarks are needed. Interest rates have been raised several times since 1976. The average interest rate for medium- and long-

*This is only partly a sign of healthy "commercialization" of trade relationships. A large fraction of trade credit is involuntary; the buyer simply does not pay the bill in the agreed time, in this way forcing the seller to grant credit. Actually this arrangement is becoming a common method of "softening the budget constraint." Involuntary trade credit was, of course, known before the reform.

term credits granted to state-owned firms was 13 percent in 1985, that is, a real interest rate of about 5 percent. There is no conclusive evidence concerning how firms responded to the increase in interest rates. There is permanent excess demand for credit, though the ratio of rejected to accepted credit applications has declined a little. Most observers agree that the sudden decrease of investment activity was achieved mostly through direct bureaucratic intervention into the approval and execution of large projects, and by cutting credit supply— not by the influence of interest policy.

Formerly the only source of credit for the firm was the central bank. Now if the firm wants to raise capital, it can apply to one of the newly created intermediaries just mentioned. Bonds can be bought by households, which opens a new source of fund raising.

The long list of options gives a more favorable impression than does a closer look at the real situation. There are still many formal and informal restrictions both on the asset and the liability side: blocked or temporarily frozen deposits, constraints on self-financed investment. Many of the options are promises for the near future and not yet facts. For example, it is remarkable that firms are not very enthusiastic about buying bonds; the total number of bonds is very small. Most firms prefer to use their savings for reinvestment in their own production even if the expected yield is lower than the return of bonds issued by other firms or local authorities.*

Households. The set of options open to households has also become wider. Before the reform households could deposit money in the savings bank.† They could also buy, under strong legal restrictions, precious metal or real estate. The reform extended the potential portfolio recently by permitting the purchase of bonds. The first steps were taken to establish a kind of institutionalized bond market. This is an important new possibility, but its true significance is hard to judge at this early stage.

As mentioned earlier, individuals can lend to other individuals or invest money in a "silent partnership" of a private business. Without sufficient legal protection, however, this may involve high risks.

Thus the first vague contours of a credit and capital market are emerging, but the Hungarian economy is still far from overall "mone-

---

*This phenomenon indirectly supports the observation that state-owned firms are not highly profit motivated. They are more interested in the expansion of their own capacity.

†The interest rate paid for a one-year deposit to households by the savings banks is 5 percent; the inflation rate in the last few years has been about 6 to 9 percent, according to official statistics.

tization" and from the solidified institutions of a full-grown, well-operating, flexible credit and capital market.

LABOR MARKET

Although steps toward an extended capital market are modest, movement toward a free labor market is substantial. At the peak of direct bureaucratic centralization, labor was rigorously tied to the workplace. There were various restrictions: administrative prohibition on changing jobs except on the explicit instructions of the authorities, prohibition against taking employment in cities without a special permit, and distribution of many goods and services through employers, the state-owned firms, of such items as housing, child care, recreation, food rations or food, and other consumption goods in kind.

In the course of reform the first two of these restrictions on individual choice were abolished. Remnants of the third still exist in housing, recreation, health care, and child care. These are, however, less binding ties than before.

Not only has overall full employment been achieved, but hidden rural unemployment was also absorbed in the early 1970s. This is an important success. The general chronic excess demand for labor, however, is accompanied by labor hoarding and does not exclude minor frictional unemployment in certain professions or regions.[21] Excess demand, together with the elimination of administrative ties, results in high quit rates: 15.7 percent in 1982, as compared, for example, to 7 percent in Czechoslovakia in the same year. Labor is sensitive to benefits and also to differentials between the wage offers of different firms and moves quickly in the direction of better terms. This is true of the labor movement within the state-owned sector. It applies even more to the relationship between the state-owned and the private sectors. Income offered by the formal and informal private sector attracts labor away from state-owned firms, which pay much less. The formal private sector can offer full-time employment. Or employees of the first economy can engage in informal private activities, such as "moonlighting" or even working illegally during regular working time. In any case, the extra activities exhaust the individual and use up much of his energy; hence he will work with less attention and diligence at his first job. Here lies a hidden cost of bureaucratic regulation. State-owned firms are restricted in raising wages, but the formal and even more the informal private sector can get round the restrictions. That is a painful dilemma; simple deregulation of wages would not help if all other circumstances such as excess demand for labor, weak profit motive, and soft budget constraint remain unchanged. It would only lead to more forceful wage-push inflationary pressures.

SUMMARY: COEXISTENCE AND CONFLICT OF THE SOCIAL SECTORS

Hungary has a multisectoral economy; different forms of ownership coexist and compete with each other. But competition is on unequal terms. With some simplification we may speak about a preference ordering of the bureaucracy: (1) large state-owned firms, (2) small state-owned firms, (3) agricultural cooperatives, (4) nonagricultural cooperatives, (5) formal private sector, (6) informal private sector. This ordering is followed in bail-outs (for 1, 2, and 3; with more certainty for 1), and in handing out credits (1, 2, 3, 4). The formal private sector only occasionally receives these favors; the informal private sector gets nothing. It does not mean, however, that the actual relative position of the various sectors follows the same ranking. With some simplification, one may say that the same ordering prevails regarding the following troubles and burdens: frequency and intensity of microinterventions, inspections and auditing, especially interference with price and wage determination, and enforcement of tax laws. In these respects the informal private sector has the advantage of being farther away from the eyes of the bureaucracy. This is an important, although not the only reason why many people prefer, in spite of fewer formal favors, to work in sectors placed lower on the state's preference scale.

Bureaucratic and market coordination are thoroughly intertwined in all sectors. The lower we go on the state's preference scale, the more freedom for market coordination. That is not necessarily because the bureaucracy would deliberately grant this freedom, but at least partly because it is less able to apply the same methods to several thousands of business units or millions of individuals that it can to a few hundred large firms. But even the formal and informal private sectors do not work in a "free" market; the bureaucracy regulates the scope of legality and has many other instruments of restriction and intervention.

There is a feeling of complementarity, but also a feeling of rivalry between the various sectors; and there are collisions between them. The sectors lower on the state's preference scale suffer because in many allocative processes regulated by the bureaucracy, they are "crowded out" by sectors higher on the scale. At the same time, the same lower-preference sectors may be successful in "crowding out" the favorites of the state in the competition on the market. The most important example, namely bidding for labor in short supply, has just been mentioned.

In short, the Hungarian economy is a symbiosis of a state sector under indirect bureaucratic control and a nonstate sector, market oriented but operating under strong bureaucratic restrictions. Coexistence and conflict exist between the social sectors in many ways and all the time.

Tensions and Imbalances

The idea of market socialism is associated with the expectation that the "marketization" of the socialist economy creates equilibrium of supply and demand. It is a crucial litmus test of reform to see whether such equilibrium has been established in Hungary or whether tensions and imbalances characteristic of the former bureaucratic command economy have remained or others appeared.

THE CLASSICAL SHORTAGE ECONOMY

The prereform classical system in Hungary suffered from chronic shortages, and shortages are characteristic of other socialist economies. The first studies were by Kornai, Franklyn D. Holzman, and Herbert S. Levine.[22] The shortage phenomenon and its causal explanation are analyzed in more detail in my *Economics of Shortage*. There is widespread excess demand on many markets, associated with queuing, forced substitution of less desired but available goods for the goods desired, forced postponement of purchases, and forced saving. Shortage phenomena torment both the consumer and the producer, the latter in his capacity as buyer of inputs. There is also excess demand for investment resources, for foreign exchange, and, in the more industrialized socialist economies, shortage of labor as well. There are spillover effects: short supply of inputs creates bottlenecks retarding production and generating shortages elsewhere. The unreliability of deliveries induces hoarding of inputs. Shortage breeds shortage.*

---

*There is an important school of thought (frequently called the "disequilibrium school") dealing with centrally planned economies which denies that shortage is chronic in the classical prereform socialist system or at least on the consumer market of this economy. The intellectual leader of this school is Richard Portes; see Portes and David Winter, "The Supply of Consumption Goods in Centrally Planned Economies," *Journal of Comparative Economics*, (Dec. 1977): 351–65; Portes and Winter, "The Demand for Money and for Consumption Goods in Centrally Planned Economies," *Review of Economic Statistics*, 60 (Feb. 1978): 8–18; Portes and Winter, "Disequilibrium Estimates for Consumption Goods Markets in Centrally Planned Economies," *Review of Economic*

Chronic shortages do not exclude the appearance of underutilized resources, excess capacities, and excess inventories. On the contrary, shortages even contribute to the creation of unnecessary surpluses, because of hoarding and because of frequent bottlenecks that leave complementary factors of production underutilized.

Chronic shortages damage consumer welfare; the buyer feels frustrated because of unsatisfied demand and/or forced adjustment to available supply. It means the dominance of the seller over the buyer: the latter is treated rudely and is frequently humiliated. In production, the disturbances of supply and improvised forced substitutions in input-output combinations cause losses of efficiency. The seller has a safe market and the buyer is willing to accept unconditionally what he gets. This leads to the most detrimental consequence of shortage: the lack of stimulus for quality improvement and product innovation.

Chronic shortage is the joint result of several interactive causal factors.

In spite of restrictive efforts on the side of macropolicy, there are systemic tendencies for demand to run to excess. The strongest force is the so-called *investment hunger*, the insatiable demand for investment resources. The hunger appears at all levels of hierarchical control, starting with the top policy makers and planners who seek high growth rates and ending with firms' and shops' managers, who also have a drive to expand. This is closely linked to the "soft budget constraint" syndrome. Because potential investment failure does not threaten severe consequences, there is little voluntary restraint on the claimant's demand for investment resources, that is, for project permits, subsidies, or credits. If the budget of the decision maker is not strictly constrained, his desire to expand remains unconstrained as well.

The rush to investment is more intensive in periods when central economic policy is pushing more aggressively for accelerated, forced growth. Central policy pulsates in this respect; stop and go peri-

Studies, 47 (Jan. 1980): 137–59; Portes, Richard Quandt, David Winter, and S. Yeo, "Macro-economic Planning and Disequilibrium: Estimates for Poland" (London: Centre for Economic Policy Research Discussion Paper No. 91, 1986). Many remarkable and valuable studies have been produced using the theoretical ideas and econometric methods of this school. An extended bibliography can be found in Portes, "The Theory and Measurement of Macroeconomic Disequilibrium in Centrally Planned Economies," *Econometrica*, 1986. I have an ongoing debate with the disequilibrium school. The controversy concerns questions of aggregation, measurement and interpretation of the notion of aggregate excess demand, the insulation of the consumer market from the rest of the economy, independence versus codetermination of demand and supply, the existence of forced saving, and the relationship between shortage and forced supply.

ods, decelerations, and accelerations alternate causing cyclical fluctuations.[23]

Demand for intermediate goods is amplified by the tendency to hoard. The buyer does not insist on getting just what he needs right now but is willing to purchase everything that may be of some use at a later time.

Demand of producers for imported intermediate goods is very strong. As a counterbalance, central policy wants to push exports. Importers' demand in foreign economies is, of course, constrained. Yet the foreign trade companies in the socialist country are willing to sell at lower prices to increase the total amount of foreign exchange earned by export. If dumping leads to losses domestically, the loss will be covered by the manifold instruments of the soft budget constraint. In other words, the demand of the state-owned foreign trade sector vis-à-vis producers of exportable goods is almost unlimited, adding a further component to runaway total demand.

Households have a hard budget constraint; in the classical system their income is under tight central control. Therefore excess household demand may or may not appear, depending on macrodemand management exercised, in the first place, through wage and consumer price policy. In some countries in certain periods, however, excess household demand is one of the main sources of runaway total demand (for example in Poland in the last five to ten years.)

Relative prices are distorted. Many goods and services have absurdly low prices or are distributed free of charge, generating almost insatiable demand.

The adaptive properties of the system are poor for many reasons. That applies to short-term adjustment: quick modification of input-output combinations requires mobile reserves of all complementary factors at all points of production. If there are shortages of one or two factors, bottlenecks do not allow flexible adjustment. Long-term adaptation is also slow. Uncommitted slack capital should be available for entrepreneurs who want to make use of unforeseen opportunities. But the irresistible investment hunger ties up all investment resources. The great concentration of net income in the central government budget, the bureaucratic procedures of project approval, and the lack of a capital market hinder a fast decentralized adjustment of investible resources.

Adaptation is also dependent on motivation. The producer seller is in a contradictory position. On the one hand, he cannot be indifferent to the urging of the dissatisfied customer, who is supported by his own higher authorities in many cases. On the other hand, he is interested in preserving shortage, which makes his life easier on the output side, because he need not pay much attention to quality, delivery time, and costs.

The relative weight of the different shortage-causing factors is controversial.[24] There is, however, general agreement that all these factors play an important role in explaining chronic shortage.

The issues of direct bureaucratic control, soft budget constraint, and weak price responsiveness and the problems concerning the causes and consequences of chronic shortage are closely interrelated, or more precisely, they are interacting properties of the same system. Chronic shortage is the necessary consequence of a system that is dominated by bureaucratic coordination and that almost totally excludes market coordination. At the same time, shortage is indispensable for the command economy as a legitimation ("rationing, intervention, taut planning are needed because of shortage"), as a stimulant ("produce more because your output is urgently demanded by the buyer"), and as a lubricant of the creaking mechanism of adaptation (in spite of poor quality, unreliable delivery, and poor adjustment to demand, all output is accepted).

PRESERVATION AND ELIMINATION OF SHORTAGES

Hungary has moved away from the classical shortage economy. In important spheres the change is apparent. All observers agree that the supply of food and of many industrial consumer goods is much better in Hungary than it is in other Eastern European economies. In the winter of 1985–86, Hungarian households were provided with electric energy and heating, while in Romania and Bulgaria drastic measures were introduced to force people to cut energy consumption.

Service supplied exclusively by non-business state organizations free of charge or at nominal prices.* The most important example is medical care. Almost insatiable excess demand prevails: long average waiting time for hospital admission (except for emergency), overcrowded hospitals and clinics, hurried examinations, and so on. There is legal private practice, but only for office visits to the physician. Shortage is accompanied by large gratuities to doctors and other medical staff.

Service supplied exclusively by state monopolies at effective prices. The

---

*Each price has a critical value. Under this value the own-price elasticity of demand is zero; that is, the price is nominal. Above the critical value the own-price elasticity of demand is nonzero; that is, the price is effective. Many goods and services have nominal prices in socialist economies.

most important example is the telephone service. Shortage is very severe in this field. The number of telephone lines increased at an annual rate of 4.5 percent and the number of applications for a line at an annual rate of 7.6 percent in the last twenty-five years. The average waiting time is getting longer and longer; at present it is about fifteen years. The network is overused: customers have to wait a long time for a dial tone, lines are almost always busy, and wrong connections are frequent.

Goods and services supplied by a dual system. The most important example is housing. Most urban apartment houses are publicly owned and rented out at very low rates covering only a small fraction of construction and maintenance costs. Although the right to join the queue has been subjected to severe restrictions, the waiting time in the capital is still several years. The other subsector is composed of condominiums in private ownership, owner-occupied family houses, and sublets. In the private sector, prices and rents are very high. The market operates but with many frictions; real estate intermediaries are few.[25]

Another example of duality is the allocation of cars. The supply of new cars is monopolized by a state-owned company. The average waiting time is two to three years. Supply responses tending to preserve shortage can be observed. If the growth of demand is retarded by price increase, authorities and the car sellers' monopoly retard supply as well.[26] About one-tenth of all new cars is sold to privileged customers jumping the queue. The other subsector is the private market for second-hand cars. Here, prices are determined by supply and demand.

Imported consumer goods. The bulk is both imported and distributed by state-owned firms. Supply is capricious. Equilibrium or excess supply occurs in some cases. Sometimes demand is created by introducing a new good imported from the West and then supply is cut, causing shortages. A small supplement is the private import of Hungarian tourists: imported (in many instances smuggled) goods are sold on the informal market.

Goods and services produced and sold simultaneously by various social sectors, including the formal and informal private sectors. The most typical is equilibrium in the aggregate of a larger commodity group. For example, a sufficient quantity of "shoes" or "meat products" in the shops does not necessarily mean that demand is satisfied: frequently the consumer does not find the kind of shoe or meat product he is looking for and must therefore resort to forced substitution. Excessive inventories and empty shelves may exist side by side. In some markets

TABLE 2.8
International Comparison: Composition of
Inventories in Manufacturing Industry

Country (years of observation)	Ratio of input inventories to output inventories	
	Lowest	Highest
Austria (1975–76)	1.04	1.07
Canada (1960–75)	1.06	1.40
United Kingdom (1972–77)	1.20	1.56
Hungary (1974–77)	5.72	6.38
Hungary (1978–84)	4.90	5.25

SOURCES: Central Statistical Office, Hungary; and Attila Chikán, "Market Disequilibrium and the Volume of Stocks," in Chikán, ed., *The Economics and Management of Inventories* (Amsterdam: Elsevier, 1981), p. 84.

NOTE: "Input inventory" covers stocks of purchased materials and semi-finished goods; "output inventory" covers goods ready for sale.

one finds a healthy competition, with attention paid to the demands of the customer. In some other markets, where shortage persists, the private seller exhibits all the well-known traits prevailing on a sellers' market: he can be rude, may try to cheat, and so on.

Intermediate goods. Shortages are frequent. Firms do not suffer from brutal cuts of energy supply as in some other Eastern European countries or as in Hungary in the early 1950s. It is rather the unreliability of deliveries that causes many losses. That is particularly true for imported intermediate goods, for which short supply can cause great troubles in production.[27] There is an enlightening index, the composition of inventories. In a shortage economy firms hoard on the input side and output is easily sold: therefore, the ratio of input inventories to output inventories is relatively high. In an economy in which selling difficulties are predominant, the reverse tends to be true.[28] Table 2.8 shows that the Hungarian state-owned production sector is still closer to the characteristic situation of a sellers' than to that of a buyers' market.

As mentioned earlier, there is excess demand for credit in general and for long-term investment credit in particular. Pressure for credit became stronger because credit supply was cut in the late 1970s. These cuts were parts of the general macroadjustment program to improve Hungary's position on the international financial market. Following tough central intervention, investment activity and demand for investment goods fell off.

Hungary today is less of a shortage economy than it was before

TABLE 2.9
International Comparison of Inflation

Country	Rate of increase in average annual consumer price index (percent)			
	1960–67	1967–73	1973–78	1978–84
Austria	4.8	4.9	6.8	5.2
Finland	4.8	6.6	13.8	9.2
Portugal	3.4	9.3	22.1	22.9
Spain	4.1	6.8	18.8	13.9
Hungary	1.0	1.6	3.9	7.5

SOURCES: United Nations, *Statistical Yearbook 1969, Statistical Yearbook 1978, Monthly Bulletin of Statistics*, Jan. 1983, Oct. 1985.

reform, and some segments have been able to rid themselves of tormenting shortages to some degree. The change has been caused more by changes in the proportionate weight of the various social sectors and less by changes within the dominant state sector. The formal and informal private sectors play a substantial role in filling the gap left by the state sector. But even then, shortages have not been eliminated because many of their causes have not disappeared. A vicious circle exists: recentralization contributes to the generation of shortages and shortages contribute to the trend of recentralization.

INFLATION

Table 2.9 shows that inflation has accelerated in the past decade.* According to a widespread view, the acceleration in Hungary was caused by the reform. This is an oversimplification, although it is not without some truth. Before the reform started, prices and wages had been tightly controlled and fixed for longer periods. Firms were not particularly interested in profits; hence they had no strong reason to raise prices. Some creeping inflation, however, had been going on long before the first reform measures (not sufficiently reflected in the official price indices). True, the reform relaxed price and wage control in many spheres and strengthened somewhat the firms' interest in higher profits. Yet these changes do not constitute a full explanation of the acceleration; there are other explanatory factors at work as well.

*Hungary is compared with a small sample of capitalist countries that are close to the Hungarian level of development (measured by per capita GDP). I do not make comparisons with other socialist countries concerning inflation rates because adequate information about the statistical methodology of constructing price indices in these countries is not available.

First, in the last few years central macropolicy has been deliberately using inflationary measures as instruments of an austerity program. Hungary has serious problems with foreign indebtedness and with the deterioration of the terms of Hungarian trade; policy makers decided to shift the balance of trade from deficit to surplus by every means possible. As a precondition of such a shift, the growth of domestic consumption had to be stopped or cut back. Prices of many basic consumer goods and services were, therefore, raised again and again by government decrees accompanied by decisions to raise nominal wages as a partial compensation. The deliberate central price and wage increases have put in motion the whole price level, including prices and incomes in the formal and informal private sectors. The change in policy and not the change in the system is the main causal factor. A similar policy was also applied in certain periods before the reform, for example, in the early 1950s when the standard of living was deliberately kept down using the instrument of sudden price increases.

Central policy is ambivalent in this respect. Although centrally decided price increases lead the inflationary process, there are official statements attacking managers of firms and the formal and informal private sectors for forcing prices up and for profiteering. Quite a few academic adherents of the reform show a similar ambivalence. They think that inflation, provided it is not too fast, may help the reform because it makes the correction of distorted relative prices and wages easier. The same argument comes up in the official statements justifying some of the price increases. Other economists, myself among them, feel that, with the protracted sequence of partial price increases, Hungary is walking a dangerous path. Each partial price rise has spillover effects in costs of production and/or in the cost of living. The interminable series of partial upward corrections puts in motion the well-known dynamic process of the price-cost-wage-price spiral. That can do much harm to the core of decentralization: to financial discipline and rational calculation based on prices and profits. Inefficiencies can be comfortably covered up by passing over cost increases to the buyer.

Shortage, acceleration of inflation, deficits in the trade balance, the growing burden of indebtedness, liquidity troubles, or any other tension and unhealthy disequilibrium are good excuses for recentralization. They provide legitimation for suppressing market forces and reviving tight control, formal and informal interventions, and rationing of intermediate goods. This is a trap because recentralization solidifies the deeper systemic causes that created most of the troubles. In some cases recentralization is accompanied by solemn promises that the measures are only provisional and will be applied only as long as the troubles prevail. The trouble is that the provisional bureaucratic measures tend to become permanent, because they restore the systemic roots of the difficulties.

EXTERNAL IMBALANCES

Disequilibrium in the balance of trade and current accounts is not a system-specific phenomenon; many nonsocialist economies are suffering from the same problem. What deserves special attention is some characteristic linkages in Hungary between external imbalances on the one hand and systemic changes and macropolicies on the other.

There is an ongoing dispute in and outside Hungary about the causes of the external imbalances. Did they occur mainly because of the deterioration of external conditions (worsening terms of foreign trade, intensified protectionism of Western importers, less access to foreign credit, increase of interest rates), or because of the delayed and inefficient response to the changing conditions? Nobody denies that both classes of factors played a certain role; the controversy is about their relative importance. I join those who put the emphasis on the latter group of explanatory factors, that is, on the deficiencies of Hungarian adjustment to the changes in the external world.

The dividing point in the time series shown in Tables 2.10 and 2.11 is 1973–74, the first worldwide oil shock. Before this event Hungarian growth rates were similar to those achieved by European private market economies. (The small sample contains countries that are close to the level of development of Hungary.) There is, however, a striking difference in the response to the oil shock. The capitalist economies sank into stagflation and recession following the oil shock, but Hungary was progressing on the path of forced growth. The expansion drive continued without interruption; foreign credit was easily available. The accumulation of foreign debt was a consequence of two closely intertwined factors: macropolicy aiming at uninterrupted growth at any cost and the lack of genuine decentralization, that is, the inconsistencies in reforming the economy. It is difficult to separate "policy" and "system" in this respect. The incomplete change of the system produces (or at least intensifies) the expansionary policy at all levels of the hierarchy. Firms were sheltered from the losses due to the contraction of Western markets and the deterioration of the terms of foreign trade by softening the budget constraint and delay-

TABLE 2.10
Indicators of Growth in Hungary, 1956–1984

	Average annual growth rates (percent)			
Indicator	1956–67	1967–73	1973–78	1978–84
	(in real terms)			
1. National income	7.2	6.1	5.2	1.3
2. Investment	10.4	7.0	7.8	−3.0
3. Wage per wage earner	3.9	3.1	3.2	−1.4
4. Consumption per capita	4.4	4.6	3.6	1.4
		1971–73	1973–78	1978–81
	(at current prices)			
5. Gross convertible currency debt				
a On forint base		13.8	20.0	9.1
b On U.S. $ base		23.8	26.8	2.6

SOURCES: (1–4) Central Statistical Office, Hungary. (5) Hungarian National Bank.
NOTE: The concept of national income is explained in the note to Table 2.1.

ing appropriate changes of domestic relative prices.* This is striking evidence that the reform of the state-owned sector remained superficial: the national troubles were not "decentralized" down to the firms, which consequently were not forced to adjust to the new world market situation. Instead of restraint in undertaking new investment and in carefully selecting projects well adapted to the new composition of external demand, an undiscriminating investment hunger continued and was even encouraged by the macropolicy of forced growth.

Finally, after a long delay, macropolicy responded to the dangers emerging in the external position of the country. Suddenly brakes were applied: radical investment cuts were followed by austerity measures and a decline of real wages. Again, this has been and has remained mostly a centralized policy. It is not the market response of decentralized agents to price and quantity signals (external prices and quantity signals converted into decentralized domestic signals). Or more accurately, such decentralized signaling plays only a relatively minor role. It is more a result of recentralization, a revival of admin-

*The effect of the oil shock was also dampened because Hungary could obtain Soviet energy at prices below world market level.

TABLE 2.11
*International Comparison of Growth Rates
in Construction Activity*

Country	Annual growth rates (percent)		
	1968–73	1973–78	1978–81
Austria	5.5	1.0	0.0[a]
Finland	3.9	1.1	1.8
Portugal	8.9	0.9	—
Spain	5.9	−2.1	−1.9
Hungary	6.6	5.7	−0.6

SOURCES: United Nations, *Statistical Yearbook 1969, Statistical Yearbook 1981, Statistical Yearbook 1982.*
NOTE: Construction activity is used as a proxy for investment activity.
[a] Last period for Austria, 1979–80.

istrative interventions in favor of import substitution and of a costly forced export drive that helped in solving the most burning troubles of trade imbalances and international liquidity. Hungary's balance of trade improved: its credit worthiness is exemplary compared to many other socialist and developing countries. But the deeper roots of external imbalances are alive. Bureaucratic control, both direct and indirect, is incapable of "fine tuning." A system cannot have two faces: rigidities, delays in deliveries, slow innovation and technical progress for domestic use and the opposite for the foreign customer. Efficient foreign trade can be assured only by a breakthrough in the reform process.[29]

INDIVIDUAL CHOICE AND DISTRIBUTION

One more problem remains to be raised before turning to the discussion of "visions." How do the systemic changes and the remaining or newly emerging tensions and imbalances affect the individual citizen? As shown in Table 2.10, real consumption was increasing impressively for a while but was then followed by a slowdown. I pointed out in the previous section that the deceleration cannot be charged to the account of the reform. It is explained by an unfortunate coincidence of deteriorated external conditions, policy mistakes, and poor adjustment to the external changes due to the inconsistency of systemic change. Something more should be said, however, not about real consumption recorded in official statistics, but about a different aspect of the quality of life: the individual's rights of choice.

This discussion is limited to economic aspects; choice in political, cultural, and moral dimensions is not the topic of the present paper.

One more qualification: freedom of economic choice is not a simple question of "yes" or "no," but a matter of degree.

In the classical command economy the household could choose between marketed goods and services within its budget constraint. But the situation was very far from consumer sovereignty for many reasons.[30] A large part of total consumption was distributed through nonmarket channels by bureaucratic procedures as fringe benefits. As for the marketed part, chronic shortages created a situation in which the buyer bought not what he wanted but what he could get. Recurrent forced substitution is a violation of economic freedom. Prices did not reflect relative scarcities, and supply did not respond to prices. The consumer's choice had only a weak influence on the composition of supply. On the contrary, arbitrary relative consumer prices shaped demand.

A part of saving was forced by shortage; even after forced substitution some money remained practically unspendable. There was no choice between alternative schemes of sick care or retirement; these were fully institutionalized by bureaucratic arrangements. Savings could not be used for productive investment.

The individual's choice of work was limited. He was free from the great suffering of unemployment, but his choice of profession was, if not dictated, at least "channeled" in the prescribed directions. The working place was assigned in many instances and movement to another job was greatly restricted by administrative prohibitions.

The great achievement of the Hungarian reform is the significant extension of choices. And the great shortcoming of the reform is that it did not go far enough in this extension.

Consumers' choice has become wider. Shortages are less intensive and less frequent, but they still exist. The domain of bureaucratically rationed goods and services has become narrower but has not been eliminated. For some goods and services prices convey the consumers' signals to the producer, who responds with changes in supply. But this linkage is restricted to certain spheres, mainly where the consumer is served by the nonstate sector, and even there the functioning of the market is distorted. In the rest of the economy the composition of supply is controlled by a peculiar combination of influences: in part by legitimate protection furthered by well-considered plans that promote society's general long-term interests against myopic and individualistic decisions, but also by arbitrary paternalistic bureaucratic interference with the consumer's free choice, by the influence of the consumer's decision, and, finally, also by merely random effects.

The choice set concerning saving and investment has become wider as well. The most important change is that individuals can invest in their own private housing instead of passively waiting for bureaucratic allotment. True, the purchase or building of a private house or condominium requires tremendous sacrifices caused by bureaucratic obstacles, shortages, and scarcity of credit. There are new options in holding financial assets, although the number of alternatives is still small. There is still little choice between alternative schemes of medical insurance or retirement.

The individual now has much more choice in deciding on a profession and job. Administrative restrictions of labor movements have been eliminated. The most important new opportunity is the impetus given to the formal and informal private sector. Those who feel they have entrepreneurial abilities have some (rather modest) possibilities of using them. Those who are willing to work more for the sake of higher consumption can enter the second economy. A study showed that in response to the stagnation or decline of real wages, 47 percent of the families opted for working more in the first and second economies because they wanted to maintain their standard of living. Again, the choice set is still rather restricted by frictions and administrative limits.

The problem of individual choice is strongly linked to income distribution. The prereform system associated the narrow limitations of individual choice with a certain egalitarian tendency. Income differentials of employees of the state-owned and cooperative sectors were moderate, although there was never a perfectly egalitarian distribution. Privileges existed for people higher up in the bureaucracy, not so much in the form of higher money wages as in perquisites: a service car, allotment of better housing, special shops with better supply, special hospitals and places of recreation, and so on.

The Hungarian economy achieved full employment and job security. The latter is a controversial issue; several economists point out negative side effects on working morale and on the artificial preservation of inefficient production lines. Income differentials in the first economy exhibit a mild decreasing trend as demonstrated in Table 2.12. There are suggestions that the rapid growth of the second economy counterbalanced this change or perhaps led to some increase of inequality, but there is no reliable evidence supporting these conjectures. Careful studies show that Hungary now exhibits neither the characteristic inequalities prevailing in the prereform classical socialist system, nor the typical inequalities of a capitalist economy, but a peculiar combination of these.[31] We still see differentials based on one's position in the hierarchy, but these appear less in the form of fringe

TABLE 2.12
Income Distribution

	Shares in total recorded money income (percent)			
Decile	1967	1972	1977	1982
1st	4.1	4.0	4.5	4.9
2d	6.0	5.9	6.3	6.4
3rd	7.1	7.0	7.3	7.3
4th	8.0	7.9	8.1	8.1
5th	8.9	8.8	8.9	8.8
6th	9.9	9.8	9.8	9.6
7th	10.9	10.8	10.8	10.7
8th	12.2	12.1	12.0	11.9
9th	14.0	14.0	13.7	13.7
10th	18.9	19.7	18.6	18.6
Measure of inequality	1.92	1.96	1.84	1.82

SOURCE: Central Statistical Office, Hungary.
    NOTE: The interpretation of the first 10 rows is as follows. The population is ranked in increasing order according to recorded per capita money income and divided into 10 classes. The first figure in the first column means the poorest 10 percent of the population received 4.1 percent of the total recorded money income of the population in 1967.
    The term *recorded money income* excludes recorded but nonmoney income (for example, benefits in kind), and also unrecorded income, mostly earned in the second economy.
    The last row shows a synthetic measure of inequality calculated by the Central Statistical Office in Hungary. Income earners are divided into two classes. Group 1: income earners above average; group 2: income earners below average. "Measure of inequality": ratio of average income of group 1 to average income of group 2.

benefits handed out in kind; they are more often reflected in money income differentials. (Although the shift is not complete, privileges in kind still exist.) At the same time, new inequalities have been created by the market, and in particular, by the appearance of the formal and informal private sector. Although incomes at the upper end of the distribution increased, social policy at the lower end did not develop sufficiently. For a long time, reformers had a one-sided technocratic orientation, concerned only with growth, efficient adaptivity, trade balance, and financial regulators and did not pay sufficient attention to the great moral objectives of social justice.

In this respect as well, Hungary is a mixture of the distributional consequences of both bureaucracy and market.

Confrontation of Visions with Reality

Having described the reformed Hungarian economy we turn to alternative visions of market socialism. Some visions took the form of pure theory as in the Lange model; others are blends of normative theory and practical proposals.

OSCAR LANGE'S MARKET SOCIALISM

The literature of the celebrated debate about socialism in the 1930s, including the original writings and the later appraisals, fill up a library.[32] Here I will concentrate on Lange's classical paper (1936–37), which is the central piece in the debate.

The first question is a positive one: is the reformed Hungarian system a "Lange economy" or anything that comes close to a Lange economy? From information provided in earlier sections of this paper, the reader has the answer already: a definite "no."

Caution is needed in formulating a fuller reply. Lange presents in a brief paper a *model*. Model building inevitably abstracts from complications of reality irrelevant to the main line of argument. It is a cheap and unfair criticism of a theoretical model to point out that reality is richer than the model. With certain simplification I will focus on the most substantial assumptions and properties of the theory, both in a comparison with Hungarian reality and in considering the criticism of the theory that follows later.

Because a description of the Hungarian system has been presented already, very brief references will suffice. Lange thought of the possibility that socialism would be a dual economy consisting of a public and a private sector, but he formulated his disputed suggestions for the sector in public ownership. Therefore, it is legitimate to compare the Lange model with the Hungarian state-owned sector.

The Lange economy has a Walrasian information structure. Sufficient information is provided by the price system and by the observation of excess demand. A trial and error method generates Walrasian equilibrium prices or at least prices that converge toward them. Agents respond to prices. In contrast, the prices of the output produced by Hungarian firms even since reform are not Walrasian prices and do not converge to such prices. Official declarations do not reveal even an intention to generate market-clearing prices everywhere in the economy. The prices of products or services originating in the state-owned sector do not reflect relative scarcities. The prices of products and services originating in the nonstate sector may come closer to Walrasian prices but only with severe distortions. The nonmarket-clearing prices of the state sector spill over to the rest of the price system. Apart from the question whether prices give the right signal, the main problem is that price responsiveness of the state-owned firms is weak. They give as much or, in many cases, more attention to other signals.

In the Lange economy the firm is essentially a profit maximizer. In contrast, the Hungarian firm has multiple objectives; the search for more profit is only one of its set of objectives and not necessarily the strongest one. The profit incentive is weakened by the soft budget constraint syndrome. The firm's vertical dependence on the superior bureaucracy dominates its horizontal dependence on the market.

In the Lange economy the central authorities restrict their activities to price determination. In the Hungarian economy the bureaucracy is busy intervening in all dimensions of economic life. Intervention into price formation is only a small part of its hyperactivity.

The question is still open: is the establishment of a Lange economy viable and desirable? The first is the primary question because in case of infeasibility the second question loses relevance. Of course the experience of a single country cannot give a convincing answer, but it can help in the reconsideration of speculative argumentation.

Lange's model is based on erroneous assumptions concerning the nature of the "planners."* The people at his Central Planning Board are reincarnations of Plato's philosophers, embodiments of unity, unselfishness, and wisdom. They are satisfied with doing nothing else but strictly enforcing the "Rule," adjusting prices to excess demand. Such an unworldly bureaucracy never existed in the past and will never exist in the future. Political bureaucracies have inner conflicts reflecting the divisions of society and the diverse pressures of various social groups. They pursue their own individual and group interests, including the interests of the particular specialized agency to which they belong. Power creates an irresistible temptation to make use of it. A bureaucrat must be interventionist because that is his role in society; it is dictated by his situation. What is now happening in Hungary with respect to detailed microregulation is not an accident. It is rather the predictable, self-evident result of the mere existence of a huge and powerful bureaucracy. An inherent tendency to recentralization prevails.[33]

Lange's model is based on an equally erroneous assumption con-

---

*What Lange had in mind concerning the role of the Central Planning Board and the market when he wrote his paper is controversial. In a private letter addressed to Hayek, he stressed the importance of market forces directly determining prices in sectors where genuine competition prevails; see Tadeusz Kowalik, "Review on the Economics of Feasible Socialism Written by Alec Nove 1983," *Contribution to Political Economy*, 3 (Mar. 1984): 91–97. I do not discuss Lange's thinking in the 1930s here but the so-called Lange model as perceived by the profession.

cerning the behavior of the firm. He expects the firm to follow the Rule designed by the system engineer. But society is not a parlor game where the inventor of the game can arbitrarily invent rules. Organizations and leaders who identify themselves with their organizations have deeply ingrained drives: survival, growth, expansion of the organization, internal peace within the organization, power and prestige, the creation of circumstances that make the achievement of all these goals easier. An artificial incentive scheme, supported by rewards and penalties, can be superimposed. A scheme may support some of the unavowed motives just mentioned. But if it gets into conflict with them, vacillation and ambiguity may follow. The organization's leaders will try to influence those who imposed the incentive scheme or will try to evade the rules.

These remarks are well known in the modern sociology, economics, and social psychology of bureaucracy, hierarchy and organizations. The Lange of the 1930s, although a convinced socialist, lived in the sterile world of Walrasian pure theory and did not consider the sociopolitical underpinning of his basic assumptions.

Lange hoped that a market could be *simulated* by a bureaucratic procedure. This hope appears time and again in contemporary writings, for example in Hungary. There is an inner contradiction in the logic of the idea. An army of bureaucrats is needed to adjust and readjust millions of prices almost continuously. The contemporary successor of Lange might say: determine with the aid of computers only price indices of large aggregates and give Rules to the actors prescribing calculation principles for breaking down the aggregates. This is happening, more or less, in Hungary. But as was said above, the firm can get around the calculation principles if these conflict with its interest. As a countermeasure, the authorities will add more detailed instructions, restrictions, and prohibitions. What emerges from this procedure is not a successfully simulated market but the usual conflict between the regulator and the firms regulated by the bureaucracy.

The next objection concerns competition. Don Lavoie rightly points out that in the neoclassical debate about socialism, the emphasis shifted one-sidedly to the issue of computing the correct price signals. What got lost was the crucial Mises-Hayek-Schumpeter idea regarding "rivalry." In a genuine market process actors participate who want to make use, and can make use, of their specific knowledge and opportunities. They are rivals. In that sense the market is always in a state of dynamic disequilibrium. The total potential of all rivals normally exceeds actual demand. Some win and some lose. Victory brings rewards: survival, growth, more profit, more income. Defeat brings penalties: losses, less income, and in the ultimate case, exit. Using the vocabulary of the present paper, the Mises-Hayek-Schumpeter market implies a hard budget constraint and a buyer's market. As long as the system and the policy do not assure the prevalence of these two conditions, there is no genuine market. The great shortcoming of the Lange model is that it does not even contemplate these conditions, and many of Lange's followers committed the same error.

This argument is related to my last remark. Lange had in mind a market using a Walrasian feedback mechanism that equilibrates supply and demand. There are, however, built-in tendencies in a centrally controlled system based on state ownership generating chronic excess demand in various spheres of the economy.

THE NAIVE REFORMERS

"Naive reformers" is a name I give to a group of economists who were the pioneers of the reform process. In Hungary, György Péter must be mentioned first. Others are Sándor Balázsy, Péter Erdős, Tamás Nagy, and István Varga. My first book, *Overcentralization*, in 1955–56 (published in English in 1959), can be put in the same category. Brus in Poland, Evsey G. Liberman in the Soviet Union, and Ota Sik in Czechoslovakia belong to the same group. This is an arbitrary and all too short list, just to illustrate the concept of naive reformer. I refer here to early works of authors who, with the exception of Péter and Varga, are still alive; most have deviated more or less from their early theoretical position.

The group is heterogeneous; the members did not share exactly identical opinions. Their common characteristics seem to be all the more significant because it was exactly this set of common ideas that was so clearly reflected in the official resolutions and documents of the Hungarian reform in 1968. What is more, similar ideas appear in Chinese official writings nowadays. Most Hungarian economists have lost their naiveté through long and sometimes bitter experience. But many of their colleagues in other socialist countries, impatiently advocating the start of a reform, having no firsthand experience as yet, show the same naiveté today and are irritated by the critical attitude of Hungarians.

Before turning to critical remarks, first a word of acknowledgment. The inclusion of my early work in the list above must not restrain me, out of false modesty, from recognizing the intellectual and political courage of the pioneering works. The descriptive part of these studies contains a deep and still valid critical analysis of the prereform system. The prescriptive part points in the direction of the later practical reforms in Hungary and China and to the reform attempts in Czechoslovakia and Poland: firms' autonomy, right price signals, profit incentive, use of market forces, shift toward a buyers' market, and so on. But the pioneers did not foresee many complications which, as it turned out, are the barriers to consistent applications of their proposals.

The naive reformer does not recognize the conflicts between indirect bureaucratic control and the market. He thinks that abandoning the command system and turning from direct to indirect control is a sufficient condition for the vigorous operation of a market. His line of thought can be characterized as follows. Let us have a profit-maximizing, almost autonomous firm. It will respond with appropriate changes of supply and demand to the signals of relative prices, interest rates, taxes, credit rations. If so, there is no contradiction between central regulation and market. Just the contrary, the market is an "instrument" in the hands of the central policy maker. The officers in the central authorities pull all the strings of indirect control and the profit-maximizing agents respond like obedient puppets. As Hungarian experience demonstrates, this fundamental assumption is wrong.

The underlying philosophy is an optimistic belief that perfect harmony can be achieved or at least approached. A market is a good but not perfect automaton. Market imperfections should be corrected by central interventions because the center knows social interests ex officio better than do blind market forces. The naive reformers admit that central planners are not infallible. But then, planners' imperfections can be eliminated with the aid of the market, which makes some corrections automatically. The faith placed in the harmonious, mutually correcting duality of "plan" and "market" (or, in the language of the present paper, bureaucracy and market) is the centerpiece of the pioneers' naiveté.

The coexistence of bureaucratic and market coordination does not guarantee that we get the best of two worlds. It does not lead inevitably to the opposite case either—the worst of two worlds. These are extreme simplifications. Certain mutual corrections are possible. If market forces lead to income distribution that is judged to be unfair by society, or to undesirable externalities damaging to the environment and so on, the bureaucracy can and should apply corrective measures. (Even these corrections, however, are not made sufficiently in Hungary.) If state interventions have undesirable side effects, market disequilibria can give a signal and the planner can make adjustments, provided that he listens to the signal. But such favorable complementarity cannot be relied on too much. As I have pointed out, the greater the bureaucratic intervention, the more one intervention weakens the effect of the other. Each string puller thinks that he can control the firm; the firm, confused by a hundred strings, starts to twitch. It does not respond clearly to bureaucratic regulation, but it does not respond to market signals either. This is what László Antal aptly termed the "illusion of regulation."[34]

The naive reformers searched for a reasonable line of separation between the role of the bureaucracy and the role of the market. Many of them thought that such a separation line could be drawn like this: "simple reproduction" (in Marxian terms) regulated by the market and "extended reproduction" by the planners. In other words, current production controlled by the market and investment by the planner. It turned out that this separation is not viable. On the one hand, the bureaucracy is not ready to restrict its activity to the regulation of investment. On the other hand, the autonomy and profit motive of the firm become illusory, if growth and technical development are separated from the profitability and the financial position of the firm and are made dependent only on the will of higher authorities.

The pioneer reformers wanted to reassure all members of the bureaucracy that there would be ample scope for their activity. Their intention is understandable. The reform is a movement from "above," a voluntary change of behavior on the side of the controllers and not an uprising from "below" on the side of those who are controlled. There is, therefore, a stubborn inner contradiction in the whole reform process: how to get the active participation of the very people who will lose a part of their power if the process is successful. The reassurance worked too well in the Hungarian case; the bureaucracy was not shattered. The number of people employed by the apparatus of economic administration changed hardly at all.[35] Small wonder that, instead of the harmonious coexistence of "plan" and "market" or the establishment of a "regulated market," we got the phenomenon of dual dependence, which actually gives dominant influence to the bureaucracy. And as was explained earlier, once bureaucratic intervention exceeds a certain critical threshold, the market is more or less deprived of energy.

The naive reformers were concerned with the problems of the state-owned sector and did not give much hard thought to a reconsideration of the nonstate sectors' role. It turned out, however, that up to the present time, it has been just the nonstate sectors that have brought the most tangible changes into the life of the economy.

GALBRAITHIAN SOCIALISM

The present Hungarian economic community cannot be easily classified. In a certain sense, every economist and government official is an adherent of reform: reform is the officially declared policy of the political leadership and the government. What really matters is not general notions but the concrete appraisal of the present system and the practical proposals for the future. In these respects the views are heterogeneous; debates go on about dozens of issues. Two economists who agree about Issue No. 1 may disagree about Issue No. 2. Each individual has his own personal collection of criticisms and proposals. Nevertheless, for the orientation of the foreign reader this section and the next will delineate two "schools." A warning is in order: there is some arbitrariness in my characterizations. Those who undeniably belong to one or to the other school may still maintain some individual reservations or dissents. What I present are rather stylized "prototypes" of two somewhat amorphous currents of thought.

I call the first school *Galbraithian socialism*. John Kenneth Galbraith's work is a very characteristic reference in the writings of the school. A dispute, marked sometimes by sharp polemics, goes on between them and the school of *radical reformers* whose thoughts will be reviewed in the next section. The ideas of the first school can be understood best in the framework of the dispute.

The Galbraithians contend that the radicals advocate an anachronistic system. The radicals, they say, want to introduce a mechanism into a socialist economy that would recall early nineteenth-century Manchester capitalism: a market free from any government intervention and the predominance of small economic units. They are socialistic Friedmanites—so the rebuke goes—although the true nature of contemporary capitalism is quite different. And here comes the emphatic reference to John Kenneth Galbraith[36] and to other authors describing modern private market economies. Contemporary capitalism is a dual economy. The first sector is a small group of huge and very powerful corporations, many of them in monopolistic or oligopolistic positions, intertwined with and sheltered by the government. It operates in an environment created by a large and powerful bureaucracy that intervenes in the economy continuously through Keynesian demand management, price and wage regulation, protectionist measures, and so on. The second sector is composed of small producers, small merchants, and the households, whose activities are coordinated by the market. Although both sectors do exist, the first is the really powerful and dominant one and the second is ancillary and subservient. If that is true in case of modern capitalism—so the argument of the Galbraithian school goes—there is no reason to require more decentralization in socialism. On the contrary: a socialist system has the possibility and the obligation to apply central planning and coordination more consistently and to establish more thorough links between the central planners and the large enterprises. The crucial role of central planning must not be disguised bashfully, but should be openly and proudly declared and, of course, much better organized than before. The large monopolies, oligopolies, and the state associated with them must become "entrepreneurial"; "entrepreneurship" should not be a privilege of the small units.

The Galbraithian school is accused in some writings of desiring the restoration of the prereform command economy. In their published writings, they do not suggest a return to an all-embracing command economy. What they do suggest is the legitimation of the status quo. They justify the dualities of the present system: the coexistence of public and private sectors, bureaucracy and market, large and small firms, provided that the first component in all these pairs has the undisputed upper hand. Some of their writings suggest that they do not have much confidence either in the market or in the private sector and would rather see their roles diminished. They would legitimate the actual state of affairs, suggesting minor changes for improvement, but reject any further radical change that would go much beyond the present situation. For that purpose the school proposes to use all theoretical results and practical experience of contemporary capitalism: Kaleckian and Keynesian macroeconomics, the textbooks of Western business schools, the lessons drawn from study tours to ministries, large banks, and corporations in industrialized countries. Every bit of experience that points in the directions outlined above is welcome.

It is, of course, a paradoxical "ideological" support for present Hungarian practice to say: "Look, the system is in many respects not so very different from the practice of modern capitalism." The trouble is that the similarity is exaggerated. True, modern capitalism is a system very different from a perfectly competitive atomistic Walrasian world. Admitting that, there are decisive differences between today's Hungarian economic mechanism and the system of highly developed capitalist economies (the "West" for short in what follows). Without seeking completeness, I will underline only a few attributes relevant in the present context.

There is a state and a nonstate sector in the agriculture, industry, and commerce of both systems, but the proportions are radically different. The state sector is dominant in Hungary, while it is an important but minor sector in the West.

There are powerful large firms in both systems, but the size distribution is very different. The concentration in Hungary is much higher than in the West, as shown in Table 2.3.

The "soft budget constraint" syndrome appears in both systems. In Hungary it is the normal way of life; in the West similar phenomena are more nearly an exception. Related to this is the issue of price responsiveness, which is rather weak in the Hungarian state-owned sector and strong in Western business life, including large corporations.

There are bureaucratic interventions in both systems. In Hungary it is all-encompassing; millions of microinterventions make the state-owned firm highly dependent on the authorities. In the West the influence of the government bureaucracy is not negligible, but the frequency and intensity of intervention are much smaller. By and large it does not exceed the critical threshold at which the vigor of the market would be diminished.

Shortage and surplus coexist in both systems. In Hungary shortages are widespread; strong competition of the sellers for the favor of the buyer is exceptional. In the West, the reverse is true. Shortages appear sporadically, but the typical situation is rivalry between competitors for the buyers' attention. That applies not only to small business but to the large corporations as well. They too feel the threat of actual or potential competition, of newcomers, large or small, of new products brought to the market by firms in the same sector or in other sectors, and also the competition of foreign sellers.

In the dialectics of the debate, however, the proponents of the Galbraithian school deserve full attention, because they put their fingers on some weak points in the argumentation of the other school, the radical reformers.

THE RADICAL REFORMERS

This is not a group with a commonly accepted consistent reform program. We are talking about economists working in different research institutes or in the apparatus of some higher authorities who share more or less similar opinions about the reform. The most characteristic writings are those of Resző Nyers and Márton Tardos, Tamás Bauer, and László Antal,[37] but there is a much larger set of articles written in a similar spirit.

Radical reformers elaborate profound critical analyses of the present situation; this paper has made extensive use of these studies. The focus here is on their normative proposals. Out of the fragments a blueprint of market socialism takes shape. These are more circumspect suggestions than those of the naive reformers of twenty to thirty years ago. The main ideas may be summarized as follows.

A system of market-clearing prices is needed; this and only this price determination principle is acceptable. Price determination must be left to the market. Deviation from these principles can be allowed only exceptionally. Profit incentives should be strengthened to make them sufficiently responsive to prices. Beyond that, new incentive schemes must be introduced; firms should be stimulated to try to increase their net worth as their primary goal.

The distortion of the size distribution should be corrected. It would be good to encourage the appearance of medium- and small-size economic units by a variety of policies to support the free entry of new units and the breakup of monopolies or overconcentrated, excessively large units. Large firms are needed only when they generate economies of scale and are able to operate successfully in worldwide competition.

Barriers to competition must be eliminated. Various forms of competition should be promoted: rivalry between units belonging to different social sectors, between large, medium, and small units, between domestic production and import.

A reform of the system dedicated consistently to these objectives, together with appropriate macropolicy, should greatly extend the scope of the buyers' market.

Barriers to a free labor market must be eliminated. The state sector must not be at a disadvantage relative to the rest of the economy in acquiring labor. More flexibility of wage determination is needed.

Tough financial discipline, the hardening of the budget constraint, must be assured. This effort must be combined with more decentralization in the allocation of funds and with the creation of a flexible capital market. The possibility of bankruptcy must be an ultimate threat. At the same time, prosperous firms must have the opportunity to expand quickly by self-financing, by loans, or by raising capital on the capital market. As a precondition for such changes the share of the government budget in the total flow of income must be diminished.

A commercial banking system must be fully developed and must operate according to business principles.

More competition must be allowed in export and import activities.

Realistic exchange rates must become more influential. Conditions of import liberalization and full convertibility must be created.

Laws are needed that protect private business and clarify unambiguously the legal possibilities and limitations of private activities.

Political conditions of systemic economic changes must be created; the various social and economic groups must get appropriate political representation. At the same time, the state must continue to play an active role in the economy. Its main obligations are the macromanagement of demand, the regulation of monopolies, the development of the infrastructure, the protection of society against harmful externalities, the redistribution of personal income for the sake of social justice.

The changes listed above and perhaps a few more important measures must be introduced in a consistent manner, as a "package." Any one of these changes, implemented separately without the appropriate conditions created by the other necessary changes can be risky or harmful.

I am convinced that the implementation of these proposals is highly desirable. Yet substantial questions are left open. The problem of ownership and property rights is not clearly elaborated in the writings of the radical reformers. This large issue can be divided into two subproblems.

First, what should be the future of nonstate ownership and, in particular, private ownership in the blueprint of a reformed socialist system? Can its share be enlarged? Is a small unit with seven employees the upper limit of a private enterprise acceptable in a socialist country?

Second, is the traditional form of state ownership compatible with the proposed changes listed above, including strong profit motivation, free entry, hard budget constraint, flexible wage determination, workable capital market? Different authors offer various solutions for separating the firms' management from the government bureaucracy. Some economists suggest labor-management because that might assure independence from the bureaucracy.[38] There are counterarguments: the history of Yugoslav labor-management and also the first experiences with the participation of employees in the selection and appointment of managers are not sufficiently reassuring. Others, for example Tardos,[39] suggest the separation of management from a special institution that would be the declared representative of "ownership interests." The latter, like a board of directors in a capitalist joint stock corporation, would appoint and supervise the managers. Critics are skeptical: can ownership interest be simulated by an artificially created body, which is commissioned (by whom? by the bureaucracy?) to represent society as the "owner"?

Many arguments put forward in earlier sections of this paper come to mind. Is genuine autonomy of the public firm under the conditions of the Hungarian political structure feasible? Will the bureaucracy observe a voluntary restraint of its own activity without exceeding the limits assigned by the proposals surveyed above?

Such questions lead to the ultimate problem: can a reform process in a socialist country go much beyond what has been accomplished in Hungary? Or does contemporary Hungary exhibit more or less the ultimate limits of reform? Other minor systemic changes, whatever their desirability, are irrelevant when considering the essence of this question.

I must frankly confess ambivalence. As a Hungarian citizen I sincerely hope that the answers to the series of questions raised above will be positive. As an occasional adviser I may try to help the process go in the direction outlined. As a researcher I reserve the right to doubt.

One lesson that can be safely drawn from study of the socialist economies is the large degree of unpredictability as far as deep systemwide changes are concerned. The questions raised above cannot be answered by speculation, only by historical experience. Up to now, Hungary does not provide a conclusive answer. We must wait and see what may be revealed by Hungarian or Yugoslav or Chinese experience or by the history of any other socialist country that may take the route of reform.

THREE

Open-Ended Economic Reform in China
Cyril Zhiren Lin

"Happy families are all alike, but each unhappy family is unhappy in its own way."
Leo Tolstoy, *Anna Karenina*

The record of economic reform in Eastern Europe has been largely a dismal one. In Hungary, the one country where reforms have had some success, that success is only relative and qualified. Recent Hungarian debates about the necessity of a "reform of the reform" testify to the shortcomings of reform. In other, slightly better-performing East European economies such as the German Democratic Republic, "reforms" have been tactical improvements in the existing Soviet-type system more than an attempt at fundamental reform.

The East European experience with reform strongly suggests an asymmetry in the directionality of systemic changes. The transformation of an economy into a highly centralized command system of the Soviet type has proved far easier than the transition out of it, as if such systems were economic "black holes" from which there is no escape. And it is difficult to invoke time as a counterargument here, for central planning was established from scratch in the Soviet Union within a decade, and in considerably shorter periods in Eastern Europe and China, which had a prototype to follow. Reforms in Eastern Europe, on the other hand, have been unsuccessfully attempted for three decades.

Reform in China has similarly been compelled by evidence of the classic symptoms of dysfunction of Soviet-type economies: declining growth rates, structural imbalances, slow technological progress, and inefficient use of resources. Reforms there are too current for their success—or failure—to be definitively assessed. Nevertheless, without trying to impute a causal relationship, reforms in China can be correlated with markedly improved *output* performance. In the period of the Chinese Sixth Plan (1981–85), national income grew at an annual rate of 9.7 percent in Net Material Product (NMP) terms (or an estimated 10.0 percent in Gross Domestic Product (GDP) terms), with agriculture and industry registering double-digit growth rates (Table 3.1). Between 1978 and 1985, agriculture in particular grew at a higher rate than in any comparable eight-year period, not only since 1949, but quite possibly in this century.

Several other characteristics render Chinese economic performance since 1977 especially impressive. First, positive growth in 1984 meant that for the first time in the history of the People's Republic growth had been sustained over an eight-year period, breaking the historical pattern of seven-year cycles.* Continued positive growth through 1986 represents an unprecedented decade of sustained growth. Second, the record-breaking ten-year average annual growth rate has been achieved without the structural distortions of earlier high-growth periods. To be sure, infrastructural weaknesses in energy, transport, and telecommunications remain serious, but the overall sectoral relationships between consumer goods and producer goods, and between agriculture and industry, have improved rather than deteriorated. It is especially significant that the increases in living standards and real incomes have been greater in the last decade than they were over the entire 1949–77 period.

Once, however, we include the *input* side in evaluating recent Chinese economic performance, the picture becomes more ambiguous. Statistics on factor productivities are too few and too crude to permit any definitive judgment. In agriculture, land and labor productivity appears to have increased. In industry, annual statistical reports show a marginal but fairly persistent increase in labor productivity, but other indicators of profitability and capital productivity have deteriorated (Table 3.2). All these measurements, however, are fraught with conceptual weaknesses and problems, and lend themselves to conflicting interpretations.* But given that the growth rate of national income has increased while the investment rate has remained basically constant (albeit at a high level), overall productivity must have improved.

*Excluding the recovery period of 1949–52, China's national income (Net Material Product) registered positive growth in the periods 1953–59, 1963–66, and 1969–75; the intervening years were periods of negative growth. Thus, Chinese economic growth until the late 1970s had never been sustained for more than seven consecutive years. Positive growth in 1986 represented an unprecedented decade of sustained expansion. The previous seven-year cycles of growth and recession can be attributed to disruptive political disturbances as well as to structural disproportions.

*For a somewhat different interpretation of trends in economic efficiency, see the article by Nicholas Lardy in this volume.

TABLE 3.1

Growth of Economic Aggregates, 1981–1985

(percent average annual increase)

Category	Planned growth: 1981–85	1953–78	Actual growth:						
			1981–85	1985	1984	1983	1982	1981	1979–85
Gross social product	4.0	7.9	11.0	16.2	14.7	10.3	9.5	4.6	10.3
Gross industrial and agricultural output	4.0–5.0	8.2	11.0	16.8	15.2	10.2	8.8	4.6	10.1
National income	4.0	6.0	9.7	12.3	13.5	9.8	8.3	4.9	8.8
Gross agricultural output	4.0	3.2	11.7	14.2	17.6	9.6	11.1	6.6	10.1
Gross industrial output	4.0–5.0	11.3	10.8	18.0	14.0	10.5	7.7	4.1	10.1
—Light Industry	5.0	9.1	12.0	18.1	13.9	8.7	5.7	14.1	12.6
—Heavy Industry	3.0	13.6	9.6	17.9	14.2	12.4	9.8	-4.7	8.1

SOURCE: *Zhongguo Tongji Nianjian, 1986* (Beijing: China Statistics Publishers, 1986), pp. 38, 45, 54.

TABLE 3.2
Financial Indices of State (Independent Accounting)
Industrial Enterprises, 1978–1984
(billion yuan)

Year	(Per 100 yuan of fixed assets at original value)			(Per 100 yuan of gross output value)		(Per 100 yuan of sales revenue)
	Profits	Profits and taxes[a]	Gross output	Profits	Quota circulating funds	Costs
1978	15.9	35.5	103	15.5	32.0	72.5
1979	16.2	36.3	103	15.8	31.0	72.4
1980	15.7	35.9	101	15.5	30.1	73.7
1981	14.4	34.1	96	15.0	30.2	74.6
1982	13.7	33.4	95	14.4	29.7	75.4
1983	13.4	32.7	95	14.1	28.5	75.8
1984	13.7	34.0	96	14.2	27.4	75.7

SOURCE: State Statistical Bureau, *Statistical Yearbook of China, 1985* (Oxford: Oxford University Press, 1985), p. 375.
[a] Computed over 100 yuan net value of fixed assets.

The conflicting evidence may be explained by the offsetting of declining efficiency in resource use at the micro (enterprise) level by improvements in overall allocative efficiency at the macro level. Qualitative evidence suggests that much recent growth derived largely from the taking up of slack in various areas of the economy and from a sectoral reallocation of resources. If so, the improved performance of the Chinese economy may not be attributable entirely or even primarily to reform; it is difficult to disentangle benefits accruing from policy changes and those resulting from systemic changes. But it is also difficult to see how significant policy changes could have been effective without concomitant systemic changes in the spheres of production decision-making, incentives, and distribution. Thus reform has been a necessary if not a sufficient condition of China's improved economic performance.

More recently, however, reforms in China have displayed the rites of passage familiar to students of Eastern Europe: overinvestment, wage (and bonus) explosions, inflationary pressures, budget deficits, import hunger, and the specter of a rising foreign debt. Gains deriving from policy changes and sectoral reallocation of resources appear to be petering out. At the same time, partial reform and a higher level of economic activity have combined to amplify the problems deriving from what Kornai describes as "soft-budget constraints."[1] The consequent slowdown in the pace of reform in 1986 fueled speculation that China's reforms, like those in Eastern Europe, have encountered insurmountable political and technical obstacles.

In evaluating the Chinese reforms and their long-term prospects from the perspective of East European precedents, however, one would do well to remember Tolstoy's observation about the peculiarities and distinctions of unhappy families, if I may be permitted an analogy between an unhappy family and an economy in difficulty. Generic similarities in Chinese and East European points of departure, (the Soviet-type system), symptoms of systemic defects, and proposed remedies can easily obscure fundamental and decisive differences.

One such difference is the lower level of industralization in China. If extensive sources of growth (e.g., an abundant labor supply) still exist in China, then reforms there may be less constrained by rigid technical input-output relationships. A lower degree of interindustrial interdependence in the less industralized Chinese economy might render reforms somewhat simpler. The extent to which the Chinese actually had instituted a system of the Soviet type may also affect how difficult it proves to be to dismantle centralized command structures. These and other differences deriving from China's low level of development and primitive planning institutions might offer the "advantages of backwardness" to reformers.

The political differences are equally important. China and the Soviet Union share similar geopolitical ambitions: to gain economic, technological, and political parity with the most advanced Western nations. In the Soviet case, parity has basically been achieved, through the traditional centralized economic system, although at high and increasingly unacceptable costs. The Soviet Union's military parity with the United States, in particular, has been realized through the enormous mobilization and diversion of resources to the crucial defense sectors, a task facilitated by centralized, command planning. In China, defense is much less paramount. Parity with the West has not been achieved (and is perceived as unattainable by a Soviet-type system); and the economy remains relatively backward. Thus, in China there is more to gain and less to lose from reform: potential benefits far outweigh potential losses.

Another important difference between China and the East European countries lies in the conceptualization of a reform model and the reform process. The peculiarities of the Chinese political economy have compelled highly generalized Chinese reform principles, which incorporate selective elements of the Hungarian system, of the existing Soviet-type system, and of a system of China's own making. The incipient Chinese economic model appears to be a hybrid that falls far short of the Hungarian model in some respects, as in the retention of obligatory targets, while going far beyond it in others, as in the creation of a nationwide bond and equity market. Indeed, the most distinctive aspect of the Chinese reforms is that they have proceeded without a detailed reform blueprint or coherent theoretical formulation. The result has been a process of open-ended reform unique among the centrally planned economies.*

What follows is an evaluation of the process of open-ended economic reform in China, with special reference to industrial reform. This process will be shown to have a logic of its own, in which tactical adjustments and periodic retrenchments to counter the inevitable distortions in the early stages of (partial) reform implementation have in turn provoked even more radical solutions, propelling reforms, and sectors of the economy targeted for reform, in increasingly radical directions.

Revisions in the Premises of Reform

The leadership that succeeded Hua Guofeng assumed power already convinced that reform was a precondition for reaching China's modernization goals.† But the premises of reform in the late 1970s were highly generalized. First, reforms at that stage appear to have potentially conflicting short-term as well as longer-term objectives. Reforms were intended as immediate tactical measures to reverse the perceived economic crisis of 1975–76, but there was at the same time a recognition of the need for systemic reform of a longer-term, stra-

---

*Open-ended reform is not a post-Mao innovation. It derives from a peculiar post-1949 revolutionary Chinese predilection for experimentation with new policies and institutions without a clear preexisting blueprint. Previous examples are the Great Leap Forward, the rural people's communes, and the Cultural Revolution.

†Deng Xiaoping in his second political reincarnation in 1975 was responsible for the then notorious "Twenty Articles on Accelerating Industrial Development" (later revised to become the "Thirty Articles"), which proposed major changes in industrial planning, management, reorganization and sectoral priorities. The "Twenty (Thirty) Articles" bore close similarities to the "Seventy Articles" drafted in 1961 to rectify policy and institutional mistakes made during the Great Leap Forward and later condemned as evidence of a "capitalist road" during the Cultural Revolution. Excerpts from the "Twenty (Thirty) Articles" are available in *Issues and Studies* (Taipei), Dec. 1978 and Jan. 1979 issues. For a tendentious critique of the "Twenty (Thirty) Articles," see State Planning Commission, "An Ugly Counter-revolutionary Drama of Usurping the Power of the Party," in *Renmin Ribao*, July 16, 1977, pp. 1–3. See also the "Seventy Articles on Industry," translated in Union Research Institute, *Documents of the CCP Central Committee*, (Sept. 1956–Apr. 1969) (Hong Kong: Union Research Institute; 1971), pp. 689–93).

tegic nature. Second, the official or orthodox conceptualization of reform was then mainly limited to improvements in planning and management within the basic Stalinist framework rather than departures from it.*

The approach appeared to assume that Chinese economic policies and institutions had embarked on an erroneous ultra-leftist course in 1958. Thus, long-term reform measures were intended to undo the mistakes of the preceding two decades and to restore the *status quo ante*. Subsequent measures in both agriculture and industry betray a desire to return to the "golden age" of the 1950s.† Finally, the notion of restoring the system of the 1950s entailed the legitimization of a degree of market relations, which in turn meant a repudiation of ideological objections to the market mechanism. Once this was achieved, however, proposals for marketization went beyond the system of the 1950s and cleaved the initial unanimity of the central leadership on the need for limited market relations. At the same time, weaknesses in the economics research infrastructure, a legacy of two decades of anti-intellectualism, as well as the "anti-economism" of the Cultural Revolution, made it difficult to formulate a coherent blueprint for market reforms. Thus political and technical constraints on the drafting of a detailed reform blueprint have made Chinese reforms, initially by force of circumstance and later by choice, an experimental and open-ended process.

Changes in the premises of reform were, however, later compelled by a revised appreciation of past economic performance, which not only made reforms more urgent but also encouraged reforms of a more fundamental nature. Newly reconstructed time-series data for the post–Great Leap Forward period provided information on the input side which showed that growth had been accompanied by gross economic inefficiencies. Various Chinese economists have since argued that growth had been overwhelmingly of an extensive nature, made possible only through extremely high rates of accumulation and drastic suppression of consumption (i.e., a "surplus maximization" growth strategy), which led to a fall in real incomes between 1957 and 1977. Moreover, declining factor productivities and investment efficiency

---

*In industry, for example, immediate short-term measures involved a rehabilitation of the planning and statistical apparatus as well as elements of the "Twenty (Thirty) Articles" and "Seventy Articles"; in agriculture, they similarly reinstated policies contained in the "Sixty Articles on Agriculture" from 1962.

†The present Chinese leadership has argued that policies were basically correct in the 1950s but took an erroneous turn from 1957 on. Cf. *Resolution on CPC History, (1949–81)* (Beijing: Foreign Language Press, 1981).

resulted in a declining trend in long-term growth rates.* The excessive priority given producer goods created profound structural imbalances, which in turn produced sharp fluctuations in growth rates and a structural and institutionalized propensity for recession.

The indictment of previous development strategies and performance was accompanied by an equally critical rejection of previous solutions to the problems of overcentralization. Attempts at decentralization in 1957–58 and again in 1970, which enhanced provincial and municipal planning powers, consistently led to a weakening of national plan coordination and integration and were commonly characterized by spurts of overinvestment followed by recession.[2] Once the intended cure proved worse than the disease; recentralization inevitably followed. This record of cycles in decentralization and recentralization has since been summarized in verse by Chinese economists: "Once centralized, then complaints (by local governments over insufficient powers); once complaints, then decentralization; once decentralized, then chaos; once chaos, then recentralization; once centralized, then complaints."

Previous decentralization attempts were conditioned by a peculiar conceptualization of the problematic of overcentralization. It was one that conceived of overcentralization exclusively in terms of central-local relations. Consequently, redress was sought solely by changing the *locus* of economic control or decision making while preserving intact the *methods* of economic control; thus the system of "dual-track" planning, which placed the majority of state enterprises under local control.[3] But such a conceptualization was not so much wrong as superficial—a half truth concealing the other, more important half. While stressing the problem of plan consistency in terms of reconciling vertical/sectoral and horizontal/territorial plan equilibrium, it ignored the questions of rational economic calculations and allocative efficiency in resource use. To be sure, the planners were concerned with economic efficiency, but again this problem was conceived as efficiency in the *use* of resources at the micro or enterprise level once such resources had been centrally and administratively allocated.

"Official" acceptance by the Deng leadership of the deficiency in these earlier conceptualizations, and the new priority given economic

---

*Declining trends in investment efficiency and long-term growth rates have been the subject of numerous Chinese studies; see, for example, Liu Guoguang and Wang Xiangming, "A Study of the Speed and Balance of China's Economic Development," in *Social Sciences in China*, no. 4 (Beijing: Social Sciences Publishing House, 1980), pp. 15–43.

efficiency (as opposed to plan consistency) led to a reformulation of the planning problematic in terms of state-vs.-enterprise and state-vs.-producer (worker) relations, alongside the traditional central-local dichotomy. Ideologically legitimizing this new conceptualization required reinterpretation of the meaning, existence, and function of Marxian economic categories (commodity, value, price, etc.) and laws (the Law of Value and the "law" of distribution according to labor) under conditions of Chinese socialism.[4]

With some important exceptions noted below, Chinese reform debates in 1978–82 focused largely on enterprise autonomy as the pivot upon which related aspects of reform would or should turn. Yet the voluminous literature on enterprise autonomy that emerged during this period failed to cover one essential point: the overall systemic framework within which enterprise autonomy would operate. The generality of the principle of enterprise autonomy was proportional to the paucity of particulars. For example, enterprise autonomy was consistent with several radically different economic models: it was applicable to, among others, the Leninist New Economic Policy model, an improved Stalinist model (of, say, the GDR genre), as well as to different variants of market socialism. Ambiguities on this point, combined with still extant, though considerably relaxed, ideological constraints, precluded consensus on a reform model or a coherent operational blueprint. The absence of a blueprint in turn precluded a proper understanding and specification of the interdependencies among the different components of reform. It also precluded the formation of a strategy for reform implementation: whether reform (in its component parts) should be introduced all in "one shot," in "blocs" over stages, or individually in piecemeal fashion. Without a clear reform model, it proved difficult to determine the necessary preconditions for reform and the means of achieving them.

The attempt to articulate responses to these problems generated its own ideological problems. While the Law of Value and commodity production were now regarded as legitimate during Chinese conditions of "underdeveloped socialism," other sensitive ideological issues were avoided through a convenient artifice: reforms were defined, and seen to be defined, exclusively as changes in the system of economic management, without any linkages to the existing system of public ownership. In agriculture such a formulation was plausible enough: land was collectively owned to begin with. In industry and commerce, however, state ownership of the means of production was the basis for direct planning and control, and it was debatable whether reforms

could succeed without concomitant changes in the system of ownership. The first to confront this question bluntly was the economist
Dong Fureng, in a 1979 article.[5] Dong implied that such a formulation
was contrary to the logic of Marxism and would prove inconsistent
in practice. In this and subsequent articles, he called for a reexami-
nation of the concept of public ownership, and in particular ques-
tioned whether state ownership (as dominant in China) was the sole
or optimal *form* of public ownership. This was a challenge to received
doctrine and was condemned by the CCP. It was not until 1985, after
nearly seven years of experiments with reform, that Dong's view was
accepted by the majority of Chinese economists and by some members
of the leadership. Its acceptance represented a decisive, albeit highly
controversial, revision in the premises of reform.

Issues of Market-Oriented Reforms in China

The abandonment of earlier conceptualizations of the problems of
central planning and loosening of the ideological straitjacket in China
made it possible to consider marketization as one potential solution to
the country's economic dilemma. But the extent to which marketization is a feasible remedy has become a subject of intense controversy
among Chinese policy makers and academic economists.

A key issue in this controversy is the differing nature of reforms in
agriculture and in the other sectors. Reforms in the nonagricultural
sectors are politically more sensitive (because of the ownership
question) as well as technically more complex. Although agricultural
reforms entail fundamental changes in income rights introduced
through the devolution of decision-making powers to the household
and through a concomitant extension of market relations, property
rights remain formally unaffected. But it is hard to see how the budget constraints on industrial enterprises could be tightened through
systems of production responsibility and market discipline without
changes in state-enterprise relations, including changes in the form
of ownership. Even if this ideological issue were resolved, there is
the further pragmatic question of whether decentralization through
marketization might lead to the effective loss of state control over the
"commanding heights" of the economy and ultimately over its direction. This is a political and economic question with profound implications for the nature of the Chinese state even if public ownership
remains unaltered.

Industrial reforms are technically more complex because of the sector's greater complexity of interindustrial forward and backward linkages, the diversity of technological and production processes, etc. Thus reforms in industry or commerce will have much wider repercussions throughout the system, with a change in one variable generating disequilibrating impacts that cannot be easily anticipated or contained. The more developed the economy, the more serious these problems become; the more serious these problems become, the greater the need to introduce the various components of reform simultaneously, "in one shot," as in Hungary, or at least to compress the period in which reforms are phased in, during which half a reform might prove worse than none.

The greater degree of monetization in the industrial and commercial sectors also renders price reform particularly difficult. In the rural sector, price effects are primarily on the output side (the incentive effects and effects on production costs) given the predominance of remuneration in kind and the relatively low marketed ratios of total output. A larger proportion of the rural household's basic consumption bundle (e.g., housing, food, and clothing) is internally produced and is thus less sensitive to price changes. Extensive monetization in the urban economy, by contrast, amplifies the impact on household income and the social consequences of any price reform, quite apart from effects on production costs, volume, and structure. In the non-agricultural sectors, almost all labor remuneration is in the form of wages; even partial remuneration in kind (e.g., in educational, health, and welfare services and "fringe benefits") would be seriously affected because they vary with the profitability and bonuses of the enterprise. The sociological characteristics of the urban family, in contrast to those of its rural counterpart, are also relevant: e.g., the lower dependency ratio, smaller household size, and other characteristics that have implications for social security. The possible adverse "demonstration effects" of growing disparities in living standards contingent upon reforms might be a greater political problem in the cities. In agriculture, there is a shared sense of belonging to the same sector of society. In the cities, the sense of identification is with a particular *danwei* (work unit) or sector; where reforms alter the balance of interests among enterprises and industries, social (and hence political) discontent is easily fermented. The number of vested interest groups is that much greater in the industrial society.

Industrial reforms are also technically more complex for reasons that are strictly speaking independent of the more integrated nature of industrial activities and relationships. Industry is *the* sector in China where Soviet-style planning has been the most assiduously implemented. And if our observation about the asymmetry of systemic changes has any validity, then it is in the domain of industrial (and related commercial and financial) reforms where such an asymmetry would be most evident. In other words, industrial reforms are more complex because in industry, as opposed to agriculture, the point of departure is the Soviet-type system.*

If we look at the two periods in which industrial reforms have been most widely implemented, 1979–80 and 1984–85, we see that reform implementation has in each case made the Chinese economy appear increasingly like a heart patient suffering from overexertion. Thus one observes evidence of pressures (inflationary and investment), tensions (in material, energy, transport bottlenecks), and breathlessness ("overheating" of the national economy). These are symptoms of what Kornai has described as conditions of shortage, investment hunger, and "soft-budget constraints" intrinsic to systems of the Soviet type. They indicate important generic similarities in Chinese and East European points of departure for market-oriented reforms. But there may well be equally important differences.

The key question here is: to what extent does the Soviet system actually exist or operate in China? My brief answer would be that it operates extensively in China, though in a distorted fashion. It operates primarily at the provincial and municipal government levels rather than at the central or national level as a result of previous decentralization attempts that favored territorial plan equilibrium over sectoral plan equilibrium. The Chinese economic system has a relatively low degree of intersectoral and interregional transactions and linkages owing to a policy encouraging basically autarkic, self-sufficient, and vertically integrated economic units and subsystems. This has created a "cellular" economic structure, described by the Chinese as one in which each and every production or administrative unit, regardless of size, is a self-contained entity. The consequent low level of functional specialization and the paucity of institutions for intersectoral and interregional transactions have positive as well as negative implications for market-oriented reforms. On the one hand, there is

---

*Although direct planning in terms of obligatory production and purchasing targets was dominant in Chinese agriculture from 1956 to 1978, the extent and detail of controls were substantively different from those in the nonagricultural sectors. Moreover, the Chinese rural peoples' commune differed from both state farms and collectives in Soviet agriculture, with consequent differences for methods of agricultural planning.

wide scope for productivity gains through greater specialization. The low level of interindustrial interdependency also means that the unpredictable disruptive side effects of reform implementation can be more easily isolated and contained. On the other hand, the weakness of the infrastructure for interenterprise, intersectoral, and interregional trade, along with the lack of experience in this realm among planners and enterprise managers, means that such an infrastructure must be laboriously constructed, and the necessary managerial skills developed, before market-oriented reforms could function properly. The highly compartmentalized economy also means that market segmentation and discontinuities are likely to persist. These dangers arise not only out of a structure in which economic relations have followed administrative boundaries, but also out of a long-entrenched tradition of "departmentalism" and "regionalism" in which "beggar thy neighbor" and protectionist policies have consistently been pursued by powerful local governments. Efforts to establish appropriate conditions for competition will be hampered by these characteristics; indeed, monopolistic and protectionist tendencies are already evident.

Previous decentralization measures in China were compelled by peculiarities of the Chinese political economy that required an adaptation of the Soviet planning prototype. The problem in the 1950s and 1960s arose from applying Soviet-type planning to a large, underdeveloped, labor-surplus and capital-scarce economy. The same problems exist today in market-oriented reforms. Consider, for example, the traditional problem of central-local relations arising from the sheer size of the country. Can effective state control, however indirectly enforced through a regulated market, be achieved without some kind of regional or provincial economic intermediary? If the answer is no, then what are the appropriate economic relationships between these intermediaries and the primary economic units on the one hand and the central government on the other? The answer must take account of the peculiarities of Chinese political history—namely, the traditional dangers of centrifugal tendencies threatening the political unity and integrity of the nation. Does marketization, or the abolition of tight administrative methods of economic control, abet or contain these tendencies?

A second obstacle to reform arises from the very low level of incomes and living standards. A need to contain politically unacceptable disparities in income and to ensure minimum living standards requires considerable redistribution of incomes and resources. Nowhere has the problem of regional disparities been resolved through reliance on the market mechanism alone. Moreover, the previous policy of encouraging self-sufficient economic units means that Chinese state enterprises are more than just production units: they are mini-societies or, more precisely, mini–welfare states, responsible for a whole range of "cradle to grave" services and activities upon which workers and their families depend. This fact poses almost insurmountable difficulties for attempts to introduce independent profit-and-loss accounting for individual enterprises, as market reforms would seem to require. If enterprises are to be given real power to hire and fire workers, then the state will have to assume the burden of welfare and other services by creating a national social security and pension system; significant changes will also be required to provide the housing, health, and educational services hitherto provided mainly by state enterprises.

This second problem brings us to a third: where labor markets are concerned, the point of departure for reform in China is on an even lower level than in Eastern Europe or the Soviet Union. The low level of development and the huge population have conspired to create peculiar problems in manpower planning. The abundance of labor has forced the Chinese system to retain elements of War Communism in a labor allocation system that is more centralized than that of most other centrally planned economies (the possible exceptions are North Korea, Albania, and Vietnam). A labor market does not exist outside the agricultural sector in China; attempts to create one would be constrained by the specter of massive unemployment, a specter made more ominous by the baby boom of the early 1960s. Yet tackling the problem of unemployment by greatly expanding collectively and individually owned enterprises, with a corollary expansion of factor and commodity markets, might well overwhelm the state sector given the rigidities inherent in the latter, and lead to a brain drain from the state sector.

Fourth, marketization under the conditions of a shortage economy, conditions that are likely to persist for quite some time, might result in perverse enterprise behavior. Chinese enterprises would react to growing market forces and autonomy not by maximizing profits, but by maximizing total revenues or scale of production. Under the existing Chinese promotion system, economic success and political power are determined by the size of operations under one's management rather than profitability. There might also be the tendency, as in Yugoslavia, to maximize average earnings per worker rather than profits, militating against state production and employment objectives. Monopolies and barriers to entry are also real possibilities. Chinese industrial enterprises evince wide disparities in costs, technology, and management skills. Smaller-scale producers employing less advanced technology, and lacking the preferential access to capital and key material inputs that large-scale enterprises enjoy, would simply be unable to compete. Indeed, many of the market imperfections so evident throughout the nonsocialist less developed economies may be replicated in China.

In summary, then, whereas the initial conditions in China may in some respects be more conducive to market-oriented reforms than in Eastern Europe, in other respects they impose stricter boundary conditions for the scope and pace of reform. The distinctive aspect of reform in China is that it is being attempted in a large, low-income, developing economy. As such, in China (as perhaps in the Soviet Union for different reasons) the necessity for retaining some form of direct administrative economic controls is finely balanced against the need to improve economic efficiency through marketization. There is also the larger question of whether the market mechanism could function properly in China (and in other centrally planned economies) without fundamental changes in the political, legal, and social systems that would extend beyond the leadership's definition of socialism. From this perspective, market reforms are inherently open-ended.

The Consequences of Initial Reforms

The absence of a coherent reform blueprint did not prevent an impatient leadership from proceeding with reform experiments based on general principles derived from the lessons of previous decentralization attempts. The two most basic principles concern the decentralization of economic decision-making powers to local governments as well as to primary economic units, and the enhancement of workers' incentives by a more direct relationship between individual work effort and remuneration. The operative framework behind these experiments appears to be the economic system of the early 1950s.

In agriculture, policy and systemic or institutional changes proceeded in tandem. State procurement prices for key agricultural products were raised to reverse the widening of the industrial-agricultural price differential that had occurred since the early 1960s. The "grain first" policy was relaxed, with sideline activities, functional specialization, and more diversified output encouraged in line with the principle of comparative advantage. These policy changes were reinforced by systemic reforms involving the decentralization of decision making to lower levels and the reinstitution of urban and rural free markets.

In industry the trial reforms centered on granting greater *relative* autonomy to selected state enterprises endowed with superior management and economic-technical conditions. The key word here is "relative," for enterprises participating in the reform experiments remained highly circumscribed in both nominal and effective terms.

As exemplified by the pioneering Sichuan prototype introduced in mid-1978, greater relative enterprise autonomy meant autonomy only at the margin.[6] It comprised essentially three basic, interrelated components. The first was autonomy in above-plan production: once obligatory state output (and a whole complex of other) targets were fulfilled, enterprises were free to decide on the input and output of surplus capacity. They could secure inputs and market output for above-plan production on their own, and engage in direct bilateral interenterprise relations. Second, an enhanced material incentive system: a scheme of bonuses geared to overfulfillment of plan targets was introduced. And third, a profit-retention scheme: enterprises were allowed to retain a percentage of profits once profit and various output and economic-technical norms were fulfilled, with the percentage rising along a sliding scale in proportion to plan overfulfillment. Retained profits were to be used in specified proportions for bonuses, workers, welfare, reserves, and the creation of a development fund, to provide working capital for above-plan production, technological renovation and below-norm capital construction. In addition, the enterprise fund was closely allied to new regulations allowing enterprises to retain a larger share of their depreciation funds and to decide on depreciation rates on fixed capital.

It is worth emphasizing that the Sichuan reform experiment, which was applied on a national scale beginning in 1979, was derived entirely from the 1962 "Seventy Articles on Industry." The substance and details of the experiment correspond *exactly* with a normative description of the workings of state enterprises given by Ma Wenguei in 1964.[7] The modesty of this initial industrial reform will be obvious to students of East European economics. It certainly did not go beyond the bounds of Soviet-type planning in any fundamental way. Although financial or value targets were now given greater importance, command planning in physical terms remained dominant. It may be argued that these measures constituted more of a tactical improvement in Soviet-type planning than reform as such. For example, autonomy in the sphere of above-plan production did not necessarily imply a diminution in central controls if it were contingent on fulfilling obligatory targets first or if it derived from existing hidden (hoarded) capacity. The degree of autonomy could easily be varied by adjusting the tautness of state plans and hence the scope of surplus capacity. More important, continued direct state controls over wage rates, the total enterprise wage bill, size of staff and workforce, allocations of key material inputs, working capital, and investment finance —all these significantly restricted the scope of autonomy. Nevertheless, the importance attached to value categories such as profits and prices in both agricultural and industrial reform experiments should not be underestimated.

Modest as the enterprise autonomy experiments were on paper, in practice they proved even more limited owing to competing and often contradictory policy objectives. The industrial reform experiments were introduced in 1979, when unemployment was acknowledged for the first time since the late 1950s as a serious problem. The rehabilitation of individually owned enterprises was one measure to generate employment, but administrative means were relied upon extensively to resolve the problem.[8] State enterprises were instructed to take on additional manpower whether they needed it or not. This effectively meant that the state was taking away autonomy with one hand while giving it with the other. This policy undermined the newly decreed powers of enterprises over input mix and factor proportion decisions, and it made it very difficult for an enterprise to reduce costs sufficiently to benefit from the profit-retention scheme. At the same time, the introduction of bonuses was intended not only as a systemic change to enhance labor productivity, but also as a major change in incomes policy to compensate for the decline in real incomes since 1958 and gain political support for the leadership. Combined with significant pressures from party cadres to award bonuses uniformly and "indiscriminately" irrespective of actual individual performance, this resulted in both the deterioration of cost norms and inflationary pressures. In 1978–79, for example, the total number of staff and workers increased by 4.9 percent (from 94.99 to 99.67 million), but the total wage bill increased by 13.6 percent (from 56.88 to 64.66 billion yuan). However, bonus payments (including piece-rate wage payments and above-quota payments) grew by 332 percent![9] Thus, increases in bonus payments accounted for 37.5 percent of the increase in the total wage bill. Over the same year, national income and industrial output grew by only 7 and 8.6 percent, respectively. This was an instance where a lack of congruence between policy and systemic changes undermined the latter.

A second factor limiting the scope of reform was the power of vested interests. Contrary to the original intentions, the newly decreed powers of enterprises over above-plan output and the disposition of retained profits and depreciation funds were often concentrated not in the hands of the enterprises themselves, but in those of controlling authorities at the municipal, provincial, and ministerial levels. In interviews conducted by the author in 1982 at various state enterprises in Liaoning, Chengdu, Changzhou, and Shanghai, it was learned that many enterprises participating in the reform experiments were required to seek the approval of superior authorities for above-plan output. In most cases they were simply implementing orders issued by their superiors. In many cases, too, depreciation reserves and enterprise funds were held not by the enterprise but by the controlling authority. Local party committees still exerted powerful informal controls over enterprises in their domain. The enterprises' subservience was also due to the partial nature of reforms, notably the absence of factor markets (in any meaningful sense) through which an enterprise could independently and directly secure inputs needed for above-plan production. Enterprises were therefore dependent, through superior authorities, on the still tightly controlled material-allocation system. Similar constraints operated on the output side, with enterprises dependent, in the absence of a sufficiently decontrolled or developed commodity market, on state distribution channels.

The continued dependence of an enterprise on its superior authority for access to inputs had far worse implications than simply undermining an enterprise's autonomy in above-plan output. To the extent that it remained so dependent on superior authorities, these superior authorities in turn remained responsible for any potential losses, which negated any effectiveness that independent profit-and-loss accounting might have had in "hardening" the soft budget constraints on an enterprise.

Where the reform experiments permitted greater relative enterprise autonomy, they were not always welcomed. The gist of readjustment was sectoral reallocation of resources. Consequently, the input-intensive producer-goods industries faced substantial cutbacks in allocated resources. Greater autonomy was therefore anathema to state enterprises in the producer-goods sector. Many such enterprises in the Northeast had their obligatory output targets scaled down and were simply told to use their newly decreed autonomy to make the best of the sudden huge increase in above-plan capacity. With the reduction in planned output came a concomitant reduction in the inputs allocated by the state. For enterprises starved for inputs and faced with high fixed costs and lower orders, independent profit-and-loss accounting associated with enterprise autonomy was, in the words of a manager of a machine-building enterprise in Liaoning, "not appropriate at this time." The overall pattern of responses to the reform experiments of 1979–82 was as follows. Where an enterprise was a "profit center" generating significant revenues for its controlling authority, the authority regarded it as a *feiruo* (tasty morsel) and was reluctant to grant it greater autonomy. Where an enterprise was a "loss center," the authority was eager indeed to devolve control. This was yet another important dimension of the industrial reforms: the differing political attitudes toward reform from region to region in accord with the geographic readjustment of economic costs and benefits.

It is difficult to accept the official Chinese assessment of the early 1980s that the industrial reform experiment was by and large successful. It was at best inconclusive. Statistics cited by various Chinese publications showing higher rates of output and profits among the experimental enterprises are misleading.[10] The majority of these enterprises enjoyed superior managerial and economic-technical conditions to begin with. As indicated above, the real extent to which autonomy was enlarged is questionable. The sample of enterprises upon which the statistics were based was in any case extremely small and highly selective. Moreover, because the majority of experimental enterprises were in industries enjoying preferential access to funds and inputs under the readjustment policy, it is difficult to attribute their improved performance to increased autonomy rather than to readjustment measures per se.

An overall assessment of the industrial reform experiments during 1979–82 is all the more difficult because they were associated with, and seen by many as responsible for, a number of negative macroeconomic developments: growing budgetary deficits, inflationary pressures, foreign trade deficits, excessive capital construction, nonproductive investments, etc. But the imputation of a causal relationship may not be entirely warranted. Inflationary pressures must have been endemic in the Chinese economic system even before the reforms, owing to the structural conditions of a "shortage economy." If this is correct, then the industrial reforms may not have generated inflationary pressures per se but have allowed an existing "repressed inflation"

TABLE 3.3
State Investments, 1978–1985

Year	Investment in fixed assets (billion yuan)		Percent of capital construction	
	Total investment	Capital construction	Budget	Extra-budgetary
1978	66.9	50.1	83.8	16.7
1979	69.9	52.3	80.0	20.0
1980	74.6	55.9	62.5	37.5
1981	66.8	44.3	56.8	43.2
1982	84.5	55.6	49.8	50.2
1983	95.2	59.4	58.2	41.8
1984	118.5	74.3	54.4	45.6
1985	168.1	107.4	39.2	60.8

SOURCE: *Zhongguo Tongji Nianjian, 1986*, p. 446.

to be transformed into an open one.* Moreover, inflationary pressures may have been generated by changes in the government's *incomes policy* (notably the bonus scheme) rather than by the systemic changes per se. Similarly, it may be argued that the decentralization of the foreign trade management system did not generate "import hunger" but simply allowed its translation into actual imports, resulting in growing trade deficits.

"Investment hunger" is also a structural characteristic of Soviet-type economies, where an enterprise's soft budget constraints and uncertainties in supply planning lead to excessive investments in the absence of penalties for wrong investment decisions on the one hand, and the tendency for enterprises to expand capacity and stocks as a hedge against taut plans on the other. The industrial reform experiments have clearly exacerbated this problem (see Table 3.3). What is notable is the growing share of investments undertaken outside the state budget. During the Third Plan (1966–70) and the Fourth Plan (1971–75), extrabudgetary investments accounted for only 10.7 and 17.5 percent, respectively, of total capital construction investments.[11] They were only 16.7 percent in 1978 and grew marginally to 20 percent in 1979. Since 1980, however, they have increased from 37.5 percent to a peak of 50.2 percent in 1982. Inasmuch as extrabudgetary investments are

---

*Some Western economists have disputed the phenomenon of repressed inflation in centrally planned economies, arguing instead that "microeconomic inflation" (disparities in the supply-and-demand structures of consumer goods) exists. For a critique of the concept of repressed inflation, see Richard Portes, "The Control of Inflation: Lessons from East European Experience," in *Economica*, May 1977.

TABLE 3.4
Budgetary Revenue and Expenditures, 1978–1985
(billion yuan)

| Year | National budget | | | Enterprise income | | Industrial and commercial taxes |
	Revenue	Expenditure	Balance	Total	Industrial enterprises	
1978	112.11	111.10	1.01	57.20	44.04	45.13
1979	110.33	127.39	−17.06	49.29	45.12	47.27
1980	108.52	121.27	−12.75	43.52	44.2	50.14
1981	108.85	111.50	−2.55	35.37	41.9	53.84
1982	112.40	115.33	−2.93	29.65	39.1	60.00
1983	124.90	129.25	−4.35	24.05	39.86	64.38
1984	150.19	154.64	−4.45	27.68	38.53	75.75
1985	186.64	184.48	2.16	n.a.	n.a	110.10

SOURCE: *Zhongguo Tongji Nianjian, 1986*, pp. 595, 597.

financed largely from retained profits and other funds (e.g., reserves, depreciation funds, illicitly diverted funds) retained by enterprises and their controlling authorities at the local level, their growth reflects the weakening of *central* controls over investments. In particular, it is the direction of local investments that has proved difficult to control and has resulted in overheating.

The industrial reform experiments have also been blamed for growing budgetary deficits. A budgetary surplus of 1.01 billion yuan in 1978 was transformed into a massive deficit of 17.1 billion yuan in 1979 (see Table 3.4). Budgetary deficits persisted until 1985, when a surplus of 2.8 billion yuan was realized. The deficits of the late 1970s and early 1980s derived from a situation of declining revenues and rising expenditures. In 1979 the decline in revenues was only 1.78 billion yuan; the deficit that year was caused mainly by an increase in expenditures of 16.29 billion yuan. Although there were across-the-board increases in all expenditure categories (except for working-capital allocations to enterprises), the single largest increase was in defense expenditures, an increase occasioned by armed conflict with Vietnam. Defense expenditures accounted for 5.49 billion yuan, or about a third of the total increase. At the same time, a significant drop in *total* enterprise income remitted to the state contributed to the deficit. But remitted income of state *industrial* enterprises actually increased in 1979; since then, there has been a gradual decline owing to the substitution of taxes for profit remittances by enterprises. Thus in 1978, enterprise income accounted for 51 percent of total budgetary revenues, with industrial and commercial taxes accounting for only

40.3 percent. By 1983 their relative importance had been reversed: the former accounted for only 19.3 percent, the latter for 51.5 percent (see Table 3.4). Moreover, between 1979 and 1983 the annual decline in industrial enterprise income was more than offset by the annual increases in industrial and commercial tax revenues; over this period, industrial enterprise income declined by 4.18 billion yuan while industrial and commercial taxes increased by 19.08 billion yuan. Thus, there is no evidence that the experiments in industrial enterprise autonomy resulted in a fall in budgetary revenues contributed by the industrial sector *on balance*; statistics prove the contrary.

Thus, the decline in budgetary revenues must be attributed to other factors. One is the policy decision to increase agricultural procurement prices, which required considerable state subsidies to urban consumers (again, an incomes policy). Another factor is the Open Door policy to expand trade relations with the West. These two factors account for very large losses incurred by state commercial and foreign trade units, which explains why *total* enterprise income since 1983 has been less than *industrial* enterprise income alone. The overall net effects of the industrial reform experiments on budgetary and investment trends require further detailed study. It seems reasonable, in the light of the preceding discussion, to hypothesize that the abovementioned negative macroeconomic phenomena may be attributable more to policy than to systemic changes, or at least to a lack of coordination between policy and reforms than to reforms per se.

The Dual System vs. The Regulated-Market Model

By late 1981, the perceived incompatibility between the industrial reform experiments and the readjustment policy compelled the Chinese leadership to subordinate the former to the latter. A decision, announced earlier in the year, to broaden the experiment in enterprise autonomy to all state enterprises was countermanded. A hiatus in some components of the industrial reform experiments was imposed throughout much of 1981–84, with recentralization effected in spheres such as finance, investment, and foreign trade. This marked the end of the first cycle of Chinese reforms. During this slowdown in industrial reforms the leadership sought to plan the future direction of reforms on the basis of the trial reforms. But the ambiguous results of the experiments lent themselves to conflicting interpretations even within China. What emerged during this period was a growing polarization in thinking and proposals for further reform.

Since 1978 China's leaders have shared a broad consensus on the need for market-oriented reforms. Underlying this consensus, however, was a continued belief in the planned economy as inherently or potentially superior, in terms of both economic efficiency and social justice, to the chaos and inequities of a full-fledged capitalist market system. In particular, conservatives insisted that, given Chinese political and economic realities, extensive state direction of economic activities was essential to the realization of the nation's modernization objectives, whatever economic theory or political ideology might deem optimal. But the Chinese experience with central planning had confirmed that "When you try to plan everything, you plan nothing." Increased market relations were regarded as an antidote to the rigidities and excesses of Soviet-type planning. Within this pragmatic coalition, there emerged two divergent views of what constitutes a planned economy and which elements in it were essential; the differences hinged upon the relationship between plan and market.[12]

The view now associated with Chen Yun and other conservative reformers (including Deng Liqun, Hu Qiaomu, Wang Zhen, and Peng Zhen) is best captured in their slogan "Central planning is primary, market regulation is supplementary." Their views harked back to the "reform" ideas first proposed at the Eighth Party Congress in 1956.[13] Implicit in this view was the continuing validity of the basic premises of the centralistic model. The advantages of a Soviet-type system for resource mobilization and rapid structural transformation were seen as crucial to modernization. But it was also accepted that the virtues of command planning when pushed to the extreme become vices, and this was perceived to be the planning problematic. Consequently, the corrective they advocated was not the abandonment of command planning, but confining its scope to manageable proportions. Direct command planning was to remain dominant in the strategic sectors of the national economy, supplemented by market relations in the nonstrategic sectors, where referential rather than obligatory targets prevailed. Thus it was to be a market dominated by the state, with the state enforcing its overall objectives through its monopolist-monopsonist position. Thus for conservatives, market reform meant in essence a return to the NEP-like mixed-economy model that had existed in China until the wholesale nationalization of industry and commerce in 1956. This was a two-track model, one centrally and directly planned, the other employing the market mechanism, with a clear distinction between the two. Underpinning this model was a perceived antithesis between plan and market; central planning was assumed to be good for some things, the market for other things. They might cohabit but should not be allowed to mate.

Chinese advocates of this dual-system model rejected its identification with the traditional Soviet-type command planning model. Indeed, their entire line of reasoning was founded on the rejection of three economic models they felt that experience and ideology had shown to be unworkable for China: the classic Stalinist model, the Chinese system of the Cultural Revolution period, and the capitalist market system. To the extent that the dual system model explicitly incorporated a market subsystem, this distinction between the dual system and the Stalinist system is justified. But the distinction seems to me a superficial one. The Soviet system (and even the War Communism model) never dispensed altogether with market relations.[14] In both the dual system and the Soviet system, the central leadership relies on direct command planning as the *principal* means of implementing state objectives, with market relations playing a *residual* role. The difference in the role of the subordinate market sector in the two models is essentially one of degree. The dual system can be considered a tactical improvement on the Stalinist system, but not a fundamental departure from it.

Fundamentally different views were held by more radical proponents of market reforms. The diversity of opinion within this group makes it difficult to identify a single model or to attribute such a model to one integral school of thought.[15] Nevertheless, with these caveats in mind, we may distill a representative conception. "Radical" reformers consider the Stalinist command planning system—with its reliance on highly detailed obligatory target, direct controls, and economic calculations in physical terms—to be intrinsically incompatible with the objectives of allocative efficiency, technological dynamism, and equilibrium growth. They advocate the replacement of command planning with an economic model that integrates plan and market within an organic whole.

These ideas in the initial stages were heavily influenced by the writings of Sun Yefang, and later but more importantly by the "regulated-market" model proposed by Wlodzimierz Brus. Sun never produced a clear operational conception of reform as such, but in his discussion of the general theoretical principles of reform he proposed that the degree and methods of economic control should distinguish between economic decisions pertaining to simple reproduction (current or steady-state production) and those relating to expanded reproduction (net investment and growth).[16] This distinction, he wrote, should form the basis for enterprise autonomy: decision-making powers over simple reproduction should be devolved to profit-maximizing enterprises, with the state retaining direct control over expanded reproduction and the setting of prices to ensure that state production objectives are fulfilled. Until the last years of his life, however, Sun consistently rejected the use of a market mechanism, although toward the last years of his life he began to accept increasingly the market principle.

A broadly similar but more sophisticated conception, and one that explicitly advocated the market mechanism, was Brus's model of a regulated market with finer distinctions of different types of economic decisions.[17] His scheme similarly called for direct state control over "fundamental" economic decisions concerning investments, structural change, and growth rates of economic aggregates pertaining to the macroeconomy, while decisions over microeconomic activities would be left to primary economic units. But Brus went further, advocating abandonment of the system of obligatory targets altogether in favor of autonomous enterprises making decisions in accordance with actual market conditions. The market would be a regulated one, with the state manipulating economic levers or value parameters such as prices, taxes, interest rates, etc., to ensure microeconomic compliance with macroeconomic objectives.

The regulated-market model differed from the dual-system model of Chen Yun in several important respects. First, in the former, the market mechanism is posited as an integral element of planning, as a means of plan implementation. It thus denies the antithesis of plan vs. market. The dual-system model insists on the inherent incompatibility of direct planning and markets, on the inability to control important economic aggregates indirectly through the market, and on the need to ensure the dominance of command planning. The model embodies an inherently negative view of the market mechanism; it is merely an expedient made necessary by the limitations of central planning and hence to be tolerated rather than pursued for its own sake.

Second, in the regulated-market model the division of the economy according to the different (direct vs. indirect, administrative vs. economic) methods of control is not drawn along sectoral lines, but along classifications of the short- vs. long-term or micro- vs. macroeconomic nature of economic decisions. The dual-system model, in contrast, advocates command planning in the strategic (mainly producer) goods sector while allowing a state-dominated market to operate in the nonstrategic (mainly nonessential consumer) goods sector.

Third, in the dual-system model, market operations are subordinate or supplementary to the dominant, directly planned sector, and as such are a "residual" predetermined by the requirements of the planned sector and by planners' preferences. Allocation of finance, labor and materials, prices, and other value parameters remain largely in the control of the state. In the regulated-market model, resource allocations occur through the market—albeit with the state manipulating the parameters influencing allocation decisions.

Fourth, all primary economic units in the regulated-market model are in the main autonomous financial entities in the sense of Western firms: they are responsible for their own profits and losses, and they operate within a competitive environment. In the dual-system model, enterprises belonging to the directly planned sector would still enjoy "soft-budget constraints."

Fifth, in the dual-system model, the dominance of the directly planned sector would imply maintenance of planners' preferences in formulating economic objectives, whereas the regulated-market model permits consumer sovereignty, as expressed in market signals, to determine short-term production and long-term investment decisions. Sixth, the dual-system model is essentially a supply-determined system, whereas the regulated-market model is demand-determined.

Seventh and last, the continued dominance of command planning in the dual-system model is dependent on a system of tight political control. The enlarged scope of market forces in the regulated-market model, by contrast, presupposes greater economic freedom among individual economic agents. Economic freedom may be indivisible from political freedom, and the efficient functioning of the market mechanism in the regulated-market model may therefore compel more democratic or pluralistic political structures.

In spite or perhaps because of the absence of a coherent blueprint for longer-term strategic reform, the industrial reform experiments in China during 1979–81 relied extensively upon the transitional system previously tried in the mid-1950s. The reform experiments were intended to adhere to the dual-system model. When a number of negative macroeconomic developments occurred, conservative reformers attributed them to an excessive pace and the premature extension of market relations beyond the scope prescribed by the dual-system model. They argued that before potentially disruptive market relations could be introduced on a wider scale (even if limited to secondary sectors of the economy), the apparatus of direct planning had to be considerably strengthened and improved.

Advocates of the regulated-market model, in contrast, insisted that the problem was not one of too much reform too fast, but rather one of reforms that were incomplete, incoherent, and insufficient. They criticized the larger external macroeconomic environment within which relative enterprise autonomy had to operate, along with the inherently restrictive measures governing the internal operations of an enterprise. On the former point, the two most serious defects were the unreformed and irrational price system and the failure adequately to loosen controls over material allocation. Existing prices were highly imperfect parameters for guiding above-plan (and even planned) production and generated considerable distortions and disparities in the profit-retention and bonus systems. The lack of sufficiently developed factor and commodity markets undermined the exercise of autonomous decisions if enterprises still had to rely on tightly controlled state channels for input provision and disposal of output.

On the issue of an enterprise's internal structure, radical reformers argued that "relative" autonomy in the sphere of above-plan production (and even more limited autonomy for labor and wages) was logically and operationally inconsistent with the plethora of remaining direct state controls over other aspects of enterprise activity. Of particular importance were the rigid state controls over investments. The idea that decision-making powers over simple reproduction could be separated from those in the sphere of expanded reproduction, however neat in principle, was proving increasingly unfeasible in practice. The Chinese industrial reform experiments suggested that the two sets of decisions are continuous rather than discrete, and that it might be impossible to impose such an artificial separation in practice. Finally, an even more fundamental constraint on enterprise autonomy was the dominant role of the party in management.

Tactical Countermeasures and the Acceleration of Reforms

The emerging conflict between the two basic schools of reform thinking coincided with a period of increasing political orthodoxy. This was manifested in the Spiritual Pollution campaign directed against "decadent Western bourgeois influence" allegedly arising from the Open Door policy. In internal party circulars, the regulated-market model together with a host of other policy prescriptions were criticized as an insidious attempt to treat Chinese ills with "Western medicine." By September 1982, academic articles advocating the regulated-market model were openly criticized in national newspapers and journals. The slogan "Central planning is primary, market regulation is supplementary," associated with the dual-system model, became the orthodox principle of reform.

China did not, however, totally abandon potentially important changes in the planning and management system in general and the extension of marketization in particular. Where such reforms were not perceived to challenge the fundamental basis of central planning, they continued to be implemented, though on a cautious and gradual basis. In agriculture, this period saw an acceleration of reform with the introduction of the household production-responsibility systems on a nationwide scale. This was accompanied by the parallel expansion of urban and rural free markets, a diminution of state monopoly purchases, and relaxation in the rationing of staples. In early 1984, regulations were introduced to extend the period of land tenure allowed under the production-responsibility system, thus institutionalizing further the system of private farming.[18]

Systemic changes in the nonagricultural sectors were much more circumscribed and were intended to serve the priority objective of readjustment. Most of the measures introduced during 1981–83 involved efforts to improve the *quality* of enterprise management. This was in part due to a recognition that for many enterprises, mediocre management militated against the proper exercise of their enlarged autonomy, to say nothing of paving the way for further reforms to come. But the measures were primarily designed to reduce the huge financial losses enterprises were incurring and the state's budget deficit to which they contributed. In 1981, the production-responsibility system was introduced in industry, modeled after its agricultural counterpart. Its objective was to enhance microeconomic efficiency in the use of resources and to reduce financial losses through independent profit-and-loss accounting. The next year, 1983, saw the issuance by the State Economic Commission of the "Six Criteria" for consolidating and improving enterprise management.[19]

These measures led to two important developments in industrial reforms from 1981 to 1983. One was the first stage of a comprehensive tax reform. In essence, the profit-remittance system, through which the overwhelming share of an enterprise's net revenues was transferred to the state, was replaced by taxation. The previous industrial-commercial tax was effectively abolished, and in its stead an array of taxes on enterprise income, profits, consumption of energy and scarce materials, bonuses, sales, etc., was instituted. The new tax system was devised partly to facilitate independent profit-and-loss accounting by state enterprises and the production-responsibility system, but mainly to resolve the state's budget deficits. This system regularized the state's revenues and made them more predictable, insofar as revenues are geared to the *volume* of economic activity and not to (uncertain) profits.

The other major reform innovation in the early 1980s was the policy of creating "experimental centers of integrated reforms." Its point of departure was a national program of industrial reorganization introduced in 1982. Its purpose was to rationalize the scale and structure of production by encouraging functional specialization and interregional and intersectoral cooperation. The principal organizational models promoted were the agro-industrial and urban-rural industrial combines through which interindustrial linkages could be strengthened. With these measures in hand a number of key cities (e.g., Chongqing, Changzhou, Shenyang, and Tianjin) were selected for an experiment in integrated reform, combining reforms in production, distribution, marketing, and industrial organization on a city-wide basis. This was later extended to experiments with regional development zones, such as the Pearl River and Shanghai-Jiangsu-Zhejiang development zones.

Another, less successful, reform was what the Chinese termed political reform, involving an attempt to separate political tasks from purely technical and managerial functions. The political leadership role of party cadres in state enterprises was to be strictly defined, enabling enterprise managers to assume full power and responsibility over economic matters. In practice, this proved particularly difficult to implement: some members of the top leadership, including the powerful and highly conservative military faction, objected to what they perceived as a diminution of the role of the Communist party. Their view was strongly endorsed by the vast army of middle- and lower-level cadres seeking to protect their vested interests.

By 1984, however, important changes in the Chinese political and economic environment occurred once again, this time leading to an acceleration and radicalization of reforms. The most important change was the abrupt termination of the Spiritual Pollution campaign in February 1984. With the termination of this campaign, the ideological restrictions on reform were relaxed.

At the same time, macroeconomic equilibrium conditions had improved considerably. Stringent controls on imports had reversed the country's merchandise trade deficits of 1978–80, resulting in sizable surpluses in 1981–83; the state budget deficit had also been considerably reduced. National income and sectoral output had improved, as had structural proportions (although some structural weaknesses remained). The preconditions of macroeconomic equilibrium for further reform were therefore increasingly favorable. The increased availability of supplies and consumer goods provided a vital cushion against potential inflationary tendencies during price and other reforms. These improved conditions provided a window of opportunity, rarely seen in Eastern Europe, that had to be seized.

The improved performance of agriculture was a particularly important factor in the relaunching of the industrial reform. The success of the agricultural reforms gave credence to a somewhat mechanistic argument for extending reforms to the industrial sector. There were, however, two negative but more substantive arguments compelling further industrial reform as a result of agricultural successes. The first was the problem of maintaining peasants' incentives, which had been a critical factor in raising productivity. The incentives deriving from significant growth in rural incomes would be blunted without a concomitant increase in the availability of consumer and other manufactured goods on which those increased incomes could be spent. Ensuring an increased flow of better-quality, more diversified manufactures to the rural sector required fundamental changes in the commercial and industrial systems. Second, without detracting from their effectiveness, the success of the agricultural reforms must be placed in perspective because of its implications for industrial and financial reform. The growth of crop output since 1978 has derived largely from the slack created by a curious mixture of positive and negative historical factors. A positive factor was the extensive capital construction in the countryside during the preceding two decades, which significantly increased the agricultural sector's latent potential. A negative factor was the past failure to exploit this potential fully because of policy errors that discouraged incentives and a rational cropping pattern.[20] The growth in noncrop sectors of the rural economy such as sidelines and rural industries, which has largely accounted for the double-digit growth rates of agricultural output in recent years, was similarly built upon foundations laid down earlier, namely the "five basic industries" policy introduced in rural areas in the mid-1960s. It may thus be argued that agricultural reforms enabled output to move from a point within the sector's production possibility frontier to a point on the frontier, but there is no conclusive evidence that the frontier itself has been shifted outward. Recent agricultural growth has occurred within the context of traditional technologies. Future agricultural growth, as slack in the sector is exhausted, will require fundamental technological change as well as the maintenance of incentives. These in turn depend on fundamental industrial, commercial, and financial reforms.

Such technical considerations, conjoined with the improved political and economic environment, led to the reintroduction of industrial market-oriented reforms with a vengeance in 1984–85. In early 1984, senior leaders such as Deng Xiaoping made highly publicized visits to the various Special Economic Zones (SEZs) and announced that they would be further expanded and liberalized, and fourteen coastal cities were designated as preferential foreign trade and investment areas. At the same time, measures were introduced to convert the People's Bank into a central bank, while a number of new, specialized banks were created or rehabilitated to handle loans for agriculture, working capital, and investments. In May, a "Ten Point Program" for the further expansion of enterprise autonomy and other related industrial reforms was announced.[21] In September, the government announced a wide-ranging decontrol of material allocation. The number of industrial commodities subject to central unified allocation and fixed state prices was reduced from 120 to 60, and of agricultural commodities from 29 to ten. The last measure was immediately followed by the Third Plenum of the Twelfth Central Committee (October 1984), whose communiqué announced that a five-year program of fundamental reform of the urban economy would be the main task for the party and state in the coming year. The next two months saw new regulations promulgated that changed the methods of calculating and allocating quotas for bonuses, wages, working capital, and investments in state enterprises.

In January 1985, changes were introduced in the system of state purchases of agricultural products.[22] In February and April, the government effectively abolished the dual-exchange-rate system in foreign currency transactions by reducing the overvalued official rate of the yuan to the more realistic internal settlement rate.* In May, a major price reform meant perhaps the largest increases in food prices ever attempted in a single stroke by a socialist country.† In July, in-

---

*Until then, the Chinese had copied the Soviet practice of divorcing international prices from domestic transfer prices through a dual-exchange-rate system, with official rates usually overvaluing the Renminbi. Following the Open Door policy, the unrealistically high official rate discouraged foreign equity investments as it undervalued the foreign partner's investment. The convergence of the official and internal settlement rates was intended partly to resolve this problem.

†For example, official urban prices of fish were increased by 240 percent, mutton 80 percent, pork 36 percent, and chicken 47 percent with a resulting average increase of slightly over 50 percent in urban food prices. To limit the decrease in real incomes, a subsidy of 7.50 yuan per worker was introduced.

terest rates on investment loans and personal savings deposits were announced, to take effect August 1, reflecting an increased reliance on value parameters. Throughout the rest of 1985, further measures and laws to liberalize foreign trade, banking, and investments were introduced. During this period, too, the government embarked on a program of "denationalization." Medium- and small-sized state enterprises running at a loss were converted into collective or individually owned enterprises, with the fixed assets of these enterprises given gratis or sold to workers and staff. To avoid ideological objections, this policy was described as introducing "collective" methods of management instead of what it really was—i.e., privatization.

The accelerated pace of reform in 1984–85 represented the most fundamental attempt to reform the Soviet system to date in China. But once again it was undertaken without benefit of a coherent, detailed reform blueprint. Although the Communique of the Third Plenum of the Twelfth Central Committee has sometimes been referred to as a "reform blueprint," it was in reality a political document reaffirming the leadership's commitment to comprehensive reform. Specifics on reform—aside from a statement of the highly generalized principle of "building socialism with Chinese characteristics" and an identification of specific elements of reform—were conspicuously absent. The document's most significant aspect was its deliberate omission of the phrase "Central planning is primary, market regulation is supplementary." In the tradition of subtle Chinese Communist political processes, the omission of this slogan signaled that the party no longer endorsed the dual-system model as the only acceptable one.* The omission in effect supported the more radical view that the economic system of the 1950s from which the dual-system concept was derived was outmoded, and that reforms should develop an economic mechanism that integrated plan and market. Students of Marxian economics will appreciate the finer points of Chinese economic debates since the Third Plenum; the Chinese economy is now described as a "socialist commodity economy," a reworking of the earlier formulation, "Commodities still exist (in the nonstate sector only) under socialism."

Although a reform blueprint remains to be drafted, the outline of the incipient Chinese reform model is emerging. Under the principle of combining mandatory planning with guidance planning, microeconomic decisions are to be devolved to the primary economic units, while the state retains direct control over strategic macroeconomic

*The communiqué went through seven drafts, with the slogan being dropped only after contentious debate over the fourth draft.

variables determining growth rates, structural change, and investment. In such a scheme, the national economy would comprise three basic categories of enterprises. In the first are state enterprises in such strategic areas as energy, transport, telecommunications, and key producer goods. These enterprises would remain under a system of obligatory output targets and unified materials allocation. A second sector comprises the majority of state enterprises, mostly large and medium-sized, where only a small proportion of their capacity would be subject to mandatory planning. The use of remaining capacity is left to enterprises themselves to decide on the basis of market conditions, with concomitant power over wages, the hiring and dismissal of labor, securing of inputs, and marketing of output. The above-plan production and activities would be subject to "guidance" through the regulated market. Finally, in the third sector, smaller state enterprises and all collectively and individually owned enterprises would be freed altogether from obligatory targets, producing wholly in accord with market conditions.

Such a conception of the reform model is clearly not tantamount to either complete acceptance of the regulated-market model or total rejection of the dual-system model. It is a compromise between the two, and as such typical of Chinese policy formation. The virtue of such a compromise formula is the flexibility built into the model: the state can easily vary the degree of mandatory planning and marketization in two ways: by altering the number of enterprises belonging to each sector, and by changing the proportion of capacity subject to obligatory targets in a given enterprise. Such flexibility allows the government to fine-tune or contain the potentially disruptive effects of marketization, obviating the need to resort to a full retreat from reforms in the face of difficulties, as has usually happened in Eastern Europe. This is *the* distinctive feature of the Chinese economic reforms, it is intimately tied to their open-endedness, and it may well determine their success or failure.

The acceleration of reform in 1984–85, however, not only exacerbated existing distortions but generated numerous new distortions as well. In enhancing the importance of financial indicators, the first stage of tax reform only exaggerated existing price irrationalities. It therefore became necessary for the state to introduce widely varying rates of taxation and profit retention to compensate for these distortions, with the rates arbitrarily negotiated with each enterprise and industrial branch. The political influence enjoyed by a given enterprise or its controlling authorities play an important role in rate-setting;

thus a tax reform designed to introduce a greater element of economic rationality has created its own administrative arbitrariness.

Existing irrationalities were compounded by the enlargement of enterprise autonomy in the May 1984 Ten Points circular. The two most important components of the Ten Points were new floating price and wage systems. Under the floating-price system, prices of above-plan output were allowed to vary by 20 percent above and below official state prices. This effectively created a three-tier price structure: official and fixed state prices, floating prices negotiated between producers and users ("negotiated prices"), and free market prices. Given excess demand, prices in the last two tiers moved significantly above officially fixed prices. This meant that enterprises with taut state plans or with little surplus capacity to engage in above-plan production were penalized by not being able to sell their products at decontrolled prices.

The floating-wage system was more varied in its application. The basic idea was to introduce a degree of flexibility into the unified industrial wage schedule without generating inflationary pressures. The general formula was that the wage bill for an enterprise could increase in proportion to its increase in profits and tax payments; the coefficient determining the proportionate increase in the wage bill (or the amount of float) being less than unity but individually set for each enterprise. The ways in which the increment in the total wage bill was to be dispensed varied considerably.[23] In some cases, the increment was used to move exemplary workers up one wage grade for the next planning period, on the condition that no more than 3 percent of the work force could be moved up in any one-year period. If an upgraded worker maintains exemplary performance for two consecutive years, he is then permanently promoted to the higher grade. In other cases, all staff and workers in an enterprise would have only 70 percent of their normal wages paid as the basic wage, and any increment in the floating total wage bill is used (if their performance warrants it) to increase their total wage up to their previous total basic wage including bonuses or even beyond.

The floating-wage system appears to have a number of serious defects. First, distortions in interenterprise profitability deriving from the irrational price structure translate into inequities, though variable coefficients are used to mitigate them somewhat. Second, the floating-wage system weakens state control over the national total wage bill and introduces an element of uncertainty to wage planning, leaving the state with a less effective incomes policy. Third, in practice wages tend to be downward rigid and thus only float upward, creating an upward wage spiral with each measure of decontrol and generating inflationary pressures. Fourth, if the system is designed to enhance productivity, it is misconceived. There is no evidence whatever from other countries that greater wage differentials enhance productivity; higher wages and a closer relationship between effort and remuneration enhance productivity but not greater differentials. Fifth, wide wage disparities resulting from this system have created considerable resentment among workers within an enterprise, for under this system not all workers benefit from improved enterprise performance: one worker's gain is another's loss. Finally, perhaps the most serious defect is that inflationary pressures are not contained as intended inasmuch as the increase in an enterprise's taxes and profits to which the float is geared does not necessarily reflect increased productivity, but may result from "supernormal" profits engendered by irrational prices. These defects have made the floating-wage system controversial; by mid-1986, this system was being reexamined with a view to abolishing it.

The Ten Point Program, together with other reform decrees issued throughout the second half of 1985, also gave enterprises greater powers over labor, capital, and investment. Enterprises were allowed to dispose of idle fixed assets and to determine depreciation rates to account for "invisible" depreciation (moral or technological obsolescence). To curb excessive investment, bank loans and provisions for above-norm working capital replaced budget allocations. In line with wage and capital-management reforms announced in the third quarter of 1984 but scheduled to take effect in January 1985, the government announced that an enterprise's allocation of working capital and investment funds, as well as its total wage and bonus payments, would be subject to a fixed, proportionate increase over actual outlays in 1984. These regulations led enterprises to embark on a wild spending and investment spree in late 1984 to inflate their base norms. As a result, bank loans in 1984 increased by 28.9 percent over 1983 figures, with the increase in December alone accounting for 48.4 percent of the increase for the entire year. The total wage fund for workers and employees increased by a phenomenal 19 percent in 1984, with the fourth-quarter growth accounting for 38 percent of the year's increase. Money supply grew by about 8 billion yuan above plan.[24]

Continuation of these trends in the first quarter of 1985 led to inflation and an overheated economy, the largest foreign trade deficit in post-1949 history, and a drastic drop in grain output. The vigorous expansion of rural industries, particularly on the part of smaller-scale producers who were less technologically efficient and hence more input-intensive, exacerbated both investment hunger and bottlenecks in energy, materials, and transport. At the same time, the major increase in urban food prices in May 1985 (discussed above) added to inflationary pressures, as did widespread illegal and extralegal price increases. Beginning in late April 1985, the government introduced stringent controls over foreign trade, finance, and material allocations. These remedial measures amounted to a return to administrative control. All government departments and economic units were forbidden to issue unauthorized wage increases or bonuses, and were required to deposit their payroll funds into special bank accounts with their disbursement closely monitored by higher authorities. Heavy taxes were also introduced to penalize above-plan investments.

The result was a greater slowdown in economic activity than originally intended—an across-the-board recession in the first half of 1986. Throughout 1986 there were numerous reports in the Chinese press about "cash-flow crises" in state enterprises because of the severe restrictions on working capital allocations, with interbank settlements coming to a near-standstill in certain provinces. Moreover, the overheating of the economy from the third quarter of 1984 to the third quarter of 1985 had involved a very significant drawing down of material reserves; the depletion of stocks by late 1985 and early 1986 exaggerated the braking effects of the stringent administrative countermeasures. Shortages of materials in turn exerted tremendous upward pressure on prices of inputs, generating cost-push inflationary pressures. The second round of accelerated reform in 1984–85 therefore came to be closely associated, like the first round in 1979–81, with serious negative macroeconomic trends.

The Prospects for Open-Ended Reform

With the overheating of the economy in 1985, further reforms in wages, labor, prices, material allocations, and finance and banking, scheduled for implementation in 1986, were shelved. It was announced that 1986 would be a year of "digesting" the impact of earlier reform. Since then, the pace of economic reform in China has reached a near-standstill.

The latest slowdown in reforms has also been accompanied by a reintensification of political conflicts over the appropriate model and pace of reform. Opponents of the regulated-market model were quick to make political capital of the overheating of the economy. But the negative macroeconomic trends, while serious, must again be placed in perspective. Just how adverse the economic consequences of the decline in grain output or of the growing trade deficit really were is unclear. Even without the cushion afforded by ample grain reserves accumulated in previous years, 1985 grain output was apparently more than sufficient to meet domestic needs because China in that year became a net exporter of grain. Similarly, the issue of trade deficits may have greater political than economic significance. To be sure, an uncontrolled and irrational structure of imports was in the long run potentially serious. But the present relatively low (by international standards though not by historical Chinese standards) Chinese debt-service ratio and foreign debt level suggests that recent trade deficits and declining foreign exchange reserves may also have more political than economic implications. Both the fall in grain output and the rising trade deficit, however, run against the deep-rooted historical conviction of the need to be basically self-sufficient in food and the equally deep-rooted aversion to being in debt to foreigners. And any hint of inflation raises the specter of the hyperinflation of the 1940s that helped bring down the Guomindang government.

The renewed reform debates resulted in a restatement of previous positions. The tenor of conservative opinion, as expressed in the Chinese press throughout late 1985 and 1986, was that reforms in general and marketization in particular had once again gone too far too fast. One instance cited was the extended market relations concomitant with the growth of village industry; with industrial and commercial undertakings more profitable than agricultural ones, many rural households and village authorities diverted land and labor away from grain toward more lucrative activities. This was seen as a clear lesson in the pitfalls of relying on prices to regulate output. If relative prices were readjusted to encourage the desired crop output mix, the proportionate increase in state subsidies would exacerbate budget deficits as well as inflationary pressures. The critics' prescription was to strengthen central planning, reinforced by a revitalization of moral incentives and political education led by party cadres.

The general view among radical reformers, though less uniform, was that the negative macroeconomic trends of late 1984 and 1985 were an inevitable consequence of a structural excess aggregate demand in the national economy. In other words, the real cause of overheating was not so much reform per se, but rather conditions of a shortage economy, conditions created and perpetuated precisely by Soviet-type central planning. Thus, the reimposition of administrative controls could at best be only a temporary solution, since it addressed superficial symptoms rather than root causes.

Supporters of reform attributed the government's inability to contain industrial overheating to a discrepancy between macro- and microeconomic reforms.[25] It was admitted that the expansion of enterprise autonomy had proceeded beyond the state's capacity for *indirect* regulation (through economic as opposed to administrative methods). The solution therefore lay in *further reforms*: parallel changes in the institutions and methods of indirect macroeconomic regulation —i.e., further reforms in prices, banking, and finance. An instance often cited by radical reformers concerned overinvestment and excess liquidity in the economy in the context of supply rigidities. Since 1978, there have been significant increases in real household incomes and hence in purchasing power; at the same time, the profit-retention scheme has resulted in a sizable pool of funds at the disposal of enterprises or their controlling authorities. Interest rates are too low for the existing banking system to soak up excess liquidity in the economy, leading households to spend their savings on scarce consumer durables and thereby generating inflationary pressures. Enterprises, in the absence of profitable alternatives, either spend their funds to increase productive capacity beyond optimal levels or waste funds in unproductive undertakings, both of which generate inflationary pressures and overinvestment and exacerbate existing energy, transport, and material bottlenecks. At the same time, the state has faced budget deficits and a shortfall in funds for planned investments. Even if interest rates could be raised high enough (and this is doubtful) to mop up excess liquidity, administrative decision making in the existing financial and banking systems is unlikely to ensure an efficient use of the savings thus mobilized. The absence of penalties under a soft-budget-constraint regime and conditions of a seller's market would in any case negate the higher cost of borrowing. In the reformers' view, the real long-term solution lies in the creation of a national capital market as a means to divert funds from consumption to a rational investment structure and thereby contain inflationary pressures, as well as the growing problems of secondary or gray markets symptomatic of repressed inflation.

These arguments for further reforms along the regulated-market principle regard the soft budget constraint of state enterprises as the root cause of excess demand and shortages. The solution to this problem, it is argued, can only be full, not "relative," enterprise autonomy, which would force enterprises to be autonomous financial and economic units, wholly responsible for profits and losses. Such a solution would imply a large number of corollary reforms: strict noninvolvement by the party in enterprise management; devolution of greater investment powers to the enterprises given the indivisibility of some production and investment decisions; the creation of labor and capital markets; the acceptance of bankruptcy as a means of enforcing financial discipline; and many other reforms.

These proposals are evidence of an increasing radicalization of reformist thought in China since 1985. Of particular importance here is the increasing acceptance by a growing number of Chinese economists of the view, first raised by Dong Fureng and more recently by Su Shaozhi among others, that real enterprise autonomy is impossible without corresponding change in the system of ownership. The "entrepreneurial socialism" concept of the Hungarian economist Tibor Liska has aroused considerable interest among Chinese economists, though none of them appear to find such a concept either desirable or workable. What has been increasingly advocated, rather, is the notion of a "socialist share economy," in which, as in a joint-stock company, shares in an enterprise can be owned jointly by the state, the enterprise's workers and staff, other enterprises, and private individuals. With such an enterprise directly accountable to a board of directors comprising shareholders' representatives, real financial autonomy or hardening of the budget constraints could finally be enforced. This is one attraction of the concept; the other is that the degree of state ownership, and hence state control, can vary with the importance of the enterprise through greater or lesser equity holdings by the state.

The articulation of these increasingly radical reform notions, as well as recent experimentation with bankruptcy, bond sales, and stockmarkets, provoked the most serious and acrimonious political controversies since 1978. The conflict between conservative and radical reformers worsened with the second Hundred Flowers campaign, launched in April 1986 to encourage greater involvement by intellectuals in the country's modernization efforts by giving them greater academic and artistic freedom. The campaign precipitated an unprecedented debate on the need for political reform as a precondition for effective economic reforms, with some writers advocating a more democratic political structure as check and balance on the party's monopoly of decision making. Following widespread student demonstrations for greater democracy in December 1986, which conservatives attributed to the political reform debates, party Secretary General Hu Yaobang was dismissed for failing to observe party discipline and sanctioning the "bourgeois liberalization" that the debates and demonstrations allegedly advocated.

Under these political conditions, the plan to finalize a detailed draft reform blueprint for presentation at the decisive Thirteenth Party Congress in October 1987 was postponed. Certainly the pace of economic reforms in 1987 ground to a virtual halt despite official reassurances to the contrary. Given the political and ideological obstacles to the formulation of a detailed reform blueprint, economic reforms in China, if and when they are restarted, can therefore continue only on an open-ended basis.

Any further reforms will have to confront two particularly difficult problems. The first is a direct result of open-ended reform, of reforming without a proper appreciation of the necessary sequencing of reform components. This concerns the relationship between price reform and reform of the material-allocation system. Since mid-1984, reform of the material-allocation system has resulted in a considerable proportion of producer goods being distributed through the market. This decontrol of the supply system was in effect a concealed price reform, with both the negotiated and the free-market prices of decontrolled manufactured producer goods shooting up rapidly. By mid-1986 only eight categories of producer goods prices, mainly raw materials, remained under strict state control.* The ensuing huge discrepancy between the state-controlled negotiated prices and free-market prices of the eight key categories of raw materials renders a price reform of the raw material price system critical. But since raw material price reform entails a major upward revision in the price level, controls on prices of manufactured goods must be reinstituted to prevent cost-push inflationary pressures from getting out of hand. It is evident, therefore, that manufactured goods prices should never have been decontrolled ahead of raw material prices. By the same reasoning, the increases in basic food prices of the spring of 1985 should never have been introduced prior to comprehensive wage reforms, which remain to be implemented.

The second major problem concerns the system of incentives, more specifically the wage, profit-retention, and bonus systems. If *any* pro-

---

*In late 1985, the eight remaining categories of product or service prices under direct state control were coal, petroleum (including natural gas), electricity, cement, timber, nonferrous metals, transport and telecommunications, and special heavy industrial machinery. Interviews in Dec. 1985 and unpublished Chinese internal reports.

portion of an enterprise's production or investment is undertaken on the orders of higher state authorities, then surely the enterprise cannot be held accountable for the financial results of those decisions, however rational the price system might be. How, then, can an enterprise be fully responsible for its own profits and losses? Under these conditions, any profit (or loss) earned (suffered) by the enterprises or the consequent increase (or decrease) in bonuses resulting from those externally determined decisions is not and should not properly be earned (or borne) by the enterprise and its workers.

Both technical and political difficulties are evidently becoming more complex and contentious as reforms proceed. Yet as these obstacles to reform grow stronger, so do the imperatives for reform, for example, the urgent need for the technological transformation of agriculture if output growth rates are to be maintained. Investment in agriculture during the Sixth Plan (1981–85) was lower than in any comparable periods in post-1949 history. If and when the state begins to accelerate agricultural investment, it will have to develop new methods and institutions for financing investment under conditions of private household farming. And as productivity increases in agriculture, labor markets will have to be developed to accommodate the growing army of surplus agricultural workers.

Another factor compelling further reforms is the shift in development strategy contained in the Five-Year Plan for 1986–90. This strategy adopts a more Western approach, stressing the growth of the service and foreign trade sectors, income maximization rather than output maximization, as well as a more consumer-oriented production structure. This implies a gradual transformation of the Chinese economic system from a supply-determined to a demand-determined growth regime. Critical shortages in energy will require considerable increases in energy efficiency and hence major technological renovations. All these considerations compel further fundamental systemic reforms.

The Chinese experience strongly suggests that reform is a process that has its own logic, one that may not be discernible a priori, but that must be allowed to pursue its own course if it is to reach the velocity needed to escape the gravitational pull of the Soviet-type system. Logic here refers to an incremental, natural, and evolutionary process of transition from one economic morphology to another, more efficient morphology for which neither the constituent elements nor the process of transition can be predetermined. The analogy in the natural sciences is Darwinian evolution, in which an organism adapts and improves incrementally through "cumulative" selection and mutation. Open-ended reform is such a process: a process of selective experimentation. Reform in China has so far been such a process, compelled by technical and political constraints. Open-ended reform also has the advantage of providing an invisible or mobile target, upon which ideological opponents find it difficult to fix their fire. But if it is true that economic reform is indivisible from political reform, and if our proposition that a process of open-ended reform leads to increasingly radical solutions has any validity, then over time as the economic morphology takes shape, the political and ideological obstacles will become increasingly formidable.

FOUR

Coexisting Organizational Forms in Hungary's Emerging Mixed Economy

David Stark

Hungary does not yet have a socialist mixed economy. Its state sector is still too large and its private sector too fragile to merit such an attribution. Nevertheless, in their daily lives millions of Hungarians are mixing experiences in a variety of economic forms. We have only to think, for example, of the engineer who works for a socialist firm during the day and drives a private taxi at night, the worker who assembles motorcycles during the week and moonlights plastering walls on weekends, or the kolkhoz peasant who, in his spare time, intensively cultivates strawberries for the West European market in his plastic-covered hothouse. In fact, according to recent official estimates, three-quarters of all households earn some additional income from the "second economy."* Moreover, when they are not mixing

*Competing definitions of the informal or second economy abound. By the term *second economy* I refer to income-producing activities, legal, tolerated, or illegal, of households that occur outside employment in the organizations of the socialist sector. The definition embraces activities such as those of officially registered private entrepreneurs, cultivators of household plots, and unregistered providers of services and repairs. Legality as such is not a dimension: my definition includes more than simply activities deemed illegal by the authorities and excludes some illegal activities, such as robbery, that are deemed criminal by the population. The most rigorous and theoretically cogent definition of the second economy is that of István R. Gábor, presented in full in "Második gazdaság: A magyar tapasztalatok általánosíthatónak tünő tanulságai" (Second economy: General lessons of the Hungarian experience) *Valóság*, 1985, no. 2, pp. 19–37.

The term *second economy* was used by some economists and sociologists in unpublished papers in the 1970s. For a brief history of the concept in this literature see István R. Gábor, *A második gazdaság és 'környéke' Magyarországon—az 1960-as évek második felétől napjainkig* (The second economy and its 'fringes' in Hungary—from the late 1960s to the present), *Társadalmi Struktúra Bulletin*, 1983, no. 6, esp. pp. 69–75. The term first appeared in print in a pathbreaking essay by István R. Gábor published in *Valóság*, 1979, no. 1, pp. 22–37 (reprinted in English as "The Second (Secondary) Economy" in economies as income earners, Hungarians, as consumers, can turn to the second economy for everything from bread for their kitchen tables to software for their computers. As breadwinners and as bread buyers, Hungarians live in a dual economy.

This paper contributes to the analysis of Hungary's emerging mixed economy by examining a recent innovation that involves a mixture of elements from the socialist economy and the second economy. This organizational form, known as the "work partnership," combines public ownership and private initiative. In work partnerships, groups of workers in Hungarian enterprises organize semiautonomous subcontracting units to produce goods or services during their off hours using factory equipment. A worker who belongs to a partnership thus participates in two organizational forms, first as an employee of the firm, working during the regular hours for wages and other benefits, and second in the off hours, as a member of a partnership in which the organization of work, the election of representatives to negotiate contracts, and the internal distribution of earnings are decided by the membership.

Like his counterparts who move back and forth between the state sector and the second economy, the work partner lives in two social worlds. Unlike them, his experiences with two organizational forms, though separated in time ("from six to two we work for them, but from two to six we work for ourselves"), are not separated spatially; they occur within the socialist enterprise and often involve working on the same machines and making the same products. In part because of this proximity in time and space, the partnerships exist as a simultaneously conservatizing and disequilibrating force in the politics of the workplace. On the one hand, the partnership is part of the firm and its very success can reproduce existing patterns of social relations and even give new life to old methods of bureaucratic management. On the other hand, the interdependent ties that link firm and partnership produce pressures to change the status quo. Unlike the informal second economy, which stands outside the gates of the socialist firm, the partnership is located within the firm's boundaries, and, to the extent

Acta Oeconomica, 22 [1979]: 291–311). It quickly entered the social scientific vocabulary. Following the publication of Gábor's article, the concept appeared in periodicals and in daily newspapers first as the "secondary economy" (*a másodlagos gazdaság*, and later, inside quotation marks, as "the 'second' economy" (*a "második" gazdaság*). Reflecting its adoption in political vocabulary, by the mid-1980s the term appeared almost every day in newspapers (including those of the party and the trade unions) without the quotation marks and is now entering everyday language.

that it is perceived to embody new principles of organization, it can lead to new perceptions of the socialist enterprise.

In studying the work partnership form, my purpose is not to examine these arrangements as a Hungarian version of "worker participation" or "job enrichment" schemes that we are familiar with in the West. As we shall see, the partnerships were not devised by "job redesign" experts; nor are they introduced by outside consultants in cooperation with trade unions, as is often the case in advanced democracies. Their establishment is at once both more haphazard and more systemic, springing from a combination of initiatives at the level of the shop floor and at the highest levels of political authority in Hungary. The partnerships are one more illustration of pragmatic improvisation as a characteristic feature (whether a strength or weakness) of reform efforts in Hungary, and their brief history has already been marked by a series of unintended consequences for enterprises and for national politics. Thus empirical focus on the new subcontracting partnerships provides a case to explore the relationship between the dynamics of organizational innovation and the politics of reform in a socialist economy.

My analysis of this new subcontracting innovation is based primarily on field research in eight Hungarian firms across a range of industries in the summer of 1984 with intensive follow-up studies in three of these firms in the winter and spring of 1985.* Eighteen subcontracting units of varying skill composition were included in the study. The research involved observation, participation in meetings, examination of company documents, and above all many hours of open-ended interviews with thirteen managers and fifty-one workers in their factories and homes. These studies at the level of the firm were supplemented by aggregate statistics on the composition of the partnerships, newspaper articles, transcriptions of radio and television broadcasts, and personal interviews conducted with trade union officials at the national level and with key figures in the decision to establish the new subcontracting form, including the former deputy prime minister of the Hungarian government and a current member of the Central Committee.†

---

*This field research was conducted in collaboration with János Lukács in affiliation with the Institute of Sociology of the Hungarian Academy of Sciences. I am grateful to him and to László Bruszt for facilitating access to the firms, for help in translating the interviews, and for fruitful discussions while the research was in progress.

†Teréz Laky, of the Institute of Labor Studies, kindly provided access to statistical data from her major project on small enterprise forms.

The first section of this paper examines the process by which aspects of the second economy were incorporated into the heart of the socialist enterprise. In brief, the timing of the introduction of the partnerships involved a conjuncture of economic crisis, the expansion of the second economy, and the emergence of Solidarity in Poland. The second section analyzes the operation of the partnerships inside the enterprise. Originally regarded by state officials as a mechanism to cope with shortages resulting from restrictive measures intended to bring Hungary's balance-of-payments problem under control, the partnerships came to be used by management to solve the organizational problems of the firm. The third section examines the lessons of the partnership form as voiced by the participants themselves. As they move from being stopgap measures to becoming an institutionalized feature of the socialist firm, the partnerships create an experimental situation, and the experiences of the work partners in a semiautonomous social space lead to the expression of new principles for organizing work, allocating rewards, and representing interests. The conclusion explores the meaning of the subcontracting form for the future course of the reforms. For workers, politicians, and ordinary citizens, the partnerships are a highly visible symbol of the current state of the Hungarian reforms. As a mixed property form they point to the possibilities of a socialist mixed economy with a plurality of organizing principles.

A Second Economy for the Core Industrial Labor Force

Hungarian workers received the right to establish work partnerships through legislation enacted in January 1982. But we must examine events of the previous decade to understand the political and economic framework in which the partnerships were introduced. Although the Hungarian reforms are sometimes seen from afar as an unbroken series of ever bolder departures from the orthodoxies of the centrally planned economy, in fact, in 1972–73, Hungarian authorities altered the course of the economy away from the reform process that had been inaugurated in 1968.[1] In place of the market decentralizing model of the New Economic Mechanism, the Hungarian economy entered a new stage from 1973 to 1978 characterized by the resurgence of many forms of central intervention in pricing, investments, and wage regulations.[2] This period also witnessed a strong trend toward increasing industrial concentration: the number of firms declined dramatically and the proportion of workers in firms employing more than a thousand workers increased significantly as trusts and large enterprises swallowed up smaller firms.[3] Despite external shocks to the economy from the sharp increase in energy prices and the downturn in the international economy, the Hungarian economic leadership remained convinced that rapid rates of growth could be achieved by an only *partially* reformed economy, and the years from 1973 to 1978 saw extraordinarily high rates of investment financed by Western credits and a growing trade deficit.[4]

These illusions came to an end in 1978, when the balance of trade reached crisis proportions and convertible currency indebtedness totaled \$7.6 billion with a highly unfavorable proportion of short-term to medium- and long-term debt.[5] In response to this crisis, Hungarian leaders adopted a tight "restriction" policy: both consumption and investment were curtailed in an attempt to bring the balance of payments to manageable proportions.[6] At the same time, some efforts were made to increase industrial efficiency by breaking up horizontal trusts and some large enterprises. But these steps, combined with greater enterprise autonomy, were hardly enough. Specialization to improve competitiveness required a revitalized "background" industry of small and medium-sized firms—a network of subcontractors to give the large firms and the entire economy greater flexibility. Thus in 1980 a series of discussions began at the highest levels of the state and party in search of ways to improve this background industry as well as to mitigate the shortages in consumer markets and disruptions in consumer services that were accompanying the restriction policy. Very early on in these debates, discussion came to center on the prospects and possibilities of integrating the second economy with the state sector.

During the 1970s, despite the push toward greater centralization within the state sector, Hungarian authorities had tolerated the expansion of the second economy. Or, perhaps more accurately, rather than reforming the first economy, the political and economic leadership had reluctantly allowed the expansion of the second. By the end of the decade, participation in the informal sector was sizable,[7] and debate among political authorities no longer centered on measures to eliminate the second economy but sought to foster closer ties between the informal and the socialist sectors.

The result of the high-level, closed debates begun in 1980 was the announcement, in late 1981, of a series of statutes that established a broad range of intermediate property forms in the Hungarian economy. These new regulations simplified the procedures for establishing subsidiaries; they lifted restrictions on industrial production in the small but very profitable units of the agricultural cooperatives; provided for the establishment of a variety of small semiprivate entrepreneurial forms; and in a highly visible move in the service sector, allowed individuals to place bids to lease state-owned restaurants, grocery stores, and commercial shops on a contractual basis (a kind of franchise arrangement). Included among the allowable small entrepreneurial forms were the "enterprise business work partnerships" (*vállalati gazdasági munkaközösségek*, or VGMs).

Officials initially envisioned the VGMs as serving two functions. First, economic leaders hoped that the partnerships would provide a way to mobilize the substantial financial reserves of the population. The initial presumption was that VGM members would invest part of their savings to purchase new equipment, machine attachments, and material inputs for this auxiliary production. Second, economic leaders stated that the VGMs would be especially useful for mitigating specific shortages by producing goods and services directly for the consumer market. In short, officials explicitly viewed the partnerships as stopgap measures in response to immediate economic difficulties in the restriction period.

But behind the explicit and very specific economic goals stands another political-economic consideration that is especially important for understanding the establishment of the VGMs. The political leaders saw the work partnerships as, above all, a means of maintaining the standard of living of the politically and economically strategic core group of workers inside the large enterprises during a period in which the real wages for the entire working class were growing little, if at all. It was hoped that the VGMs, by providing an additional source of income, would prevent the emergence of tensions among workers whose key position in the labor process (and whose political skills and ability to use their dense social connections) provide a strong basis for informal bargaining inside the large enterprises. The Hungarian leadership was especially attuned to such possible tensions given the emergence of Solidarity in Poland at precisely the time when the establishment of the VGM form was being debated. In a period of stagnating real wages in Hungary and worker insurgency in Poland, Hungary's leaders hoped that the new form would preempt political tensions among key groups of workers and tie their interests to the new wave of economic reforms.

Moreover, the reversals in the reform process in 1972 had been led by national trade union leaders, who claimed to represent the grievances of these same urban industrial workers,[8] and the trade union presence had to be included in the political calculations of those politicians who wished to see the economy taken further along the road to new reforms. The work partnerships were one way for these workers to become partners, and not obstacles, to reform. The VGM form was a specific mechanism to supplement incomes for these key workers, many of whom could not use their skills in the second economy. For although the informal sector had grown rapidly during the 1970s, it did not augment the incomes of all workers. If the washing machine repairman in a state firm could gain clients and spare parts from his regular job for his off-hours "private practice" and if the peasant could intensively cultivate his own hectare of land, how was the furnaceman in a steel mill or a machinist making sophisticated machine tools to use his special skills within the second economy? The VGM provides such an opportunity to gain additional incomes in the off hours. As one young machine designer explained:

The VGM is a more civilized form than the second economy. I can earn extra money according to my skill and not on a lower level. If you do the work at your same level, you regard the extra money as less humiliating. Let's say, if I need the money, I don't have to wash little Aunt Mary's windows or unload wagons but I can do the work that I like and know well. There aren't too many possibilities to do design work in the black for enterprises. To design and make a tool can't be done in "schwartz." But in the VGM I continue my regular work and so it can bring about some professional development too.

Similarly, an older machinist stated: "I can't grow vegetables in a bathtub. Those who live in the countryside have household plots and can earn some money from these, but we in the city don't have these. In the VGM, though, I can stay in the same place, use my same skills, and work with my same friends." Or, as a Central Committee member explained to me in an interview, "The VGMs are the household plots of industry."

Markets Inside the Socialist Firm

By the end of 1986, with 267,000 members in 21,490 partnerships, roughly one out of every ten manual workers in Hungarian industry was participating in a work partnership. The VGMs have indirectly fulfilled the macropolitical goal of reducing tensions among the key group of urban industrial workers, but they have not been used to achieve the specific economic goals stated at the time of their establishment. Rather than mobilizing financial reserves or meeting the immediate shortages in products and services for the consumer, the partnerships have served to fill the shortages and reduce the internal uncertainties of large enterprises.

The director of an enterprise who approves the establishment of partnerships in his or her firm creates a valuable resource to reduce bottlenecks in supplies, to improve auxiliary services, and to mitigate the need for rush work in those parts of the production process that suffer the most acute labor shortages. Partnerships are often set up to perform tasks that formerly were awarded to outside contractors, for example, support functions such as installing equipment, nonroutine maintenance, or special design work. In such cases, the partnerships are a means to reduce dependence on outside firms. Because the background industry was so underdeveloped in Hungary, many of these outside contractors (often small urban cooperatives or the industrial units of the agricultural cooperatives) enjoyed a monopolistic position in the market for their particular product or service, or at least a favorable position in bargaining with the large enterprises. The partnerships regularly underbid these outside units, and their ready availability also gives the enterprise increased flexibility in meeting production deadlines by saving time in contract preparation or the provision of additional information as the project unfolds.

Moreover, because the division of labor within the partnerships is often highly fluid (sometimes dissolving the distinction between mental and manual labor), the VGMs are a source of technical innovation. In some firms, partnerships are established in highly profitable, small-batch specialty production. In one very large firm included in this study, a partnership developed specialized rubber mixtures on a subcontractual basis with the firm. The impetus for this innovation came from the composition of the VGM, which included chemists, engineers, and production technicians, who, in their regular hours, worked in different units of the enterprise. Within this same firm, another group of workers, also from diverse fields, set up a partnership to find a use for scrap rubber. This VGM now produces a wide range of products, the marketing arrangements for which they established themselves. In this case, the firm benefits on at least two counts: it takes a cut of the partnership's "profits," and the salable products are made from unprofitable scrap for which the firm formerly paid a high cost to burn, bury, or otherwise destroy. In yet another factory within this same enterprise, the research, set-up, initial production, and testing of a new unit to produce a specialized pipe for offshore drilling (obviously for export) was carried out by several partnerships working in teams, which combined design engineers, technicians, and maintenance and skilled workers who decided among themselves how to allocate and reward tasks. Management estimates that the turn-around time for this project was cut almost in half by subcontracting the venture to the off-hours partnerships rather than performing it in the regular hours.

Most important, the partnership form provides a means to reward strategic workers differentially, tie their interests to those of the firm, reduce turnover, and improve the likelihood of their cooperation within the production process.[9] Every firm in any advanced industrial economy faces some uncertainties with regard to labor. In the capitalist economy, managers face the uncertainty that workers will take their skills (often acquired on the job) out onto the external labor market. In the socialist firm, this problem is even more acute because the disruptions within the production process (caused, for example, by supply bottlenecks), the need to keep obsolete machinery running during storming periods, and the necessity of a flexible allocation of labor (shifting workers from machine to machine or even across shops within a single day) make shop management even more dependent on those workers who have firm-specific skills or who must perform nonroutinized tasks.[10]

Within the capitalist firm, one organizational solution to reduce turnover among workers with firm-specific skills and to promote co-operation within the production process is to institutionalize internal labor markets by creating a set of bureaucratic rules governing hiring, promotion, and layoffs.[11] In the United States, for example, these rules often take the form of incremental wage and salary increases organized along bureaucratized job ladders.

Within the socialist firm, we find a set of institutions performing comparable functions, yet the socialist internal labor market takes a form quite different from routinized promotions. Like the manager in the capitalist firm, the socialist manager hopes to reduce turnover and ensure cooperation from the workers upon whom he is dependent to meet the plan targets. But in the socialist firm, bureaucratic job classifications and wage regulations imposed by the central authorities are obstacles to be circumvented rather than instruments for the construction of internal labor markets within the firm.*

The result is not collective bargaining but *selective bargaining* within the socialist firm.[12] The bargaining units within these negotiations are informal groups on the shop floor composed of workers who possess the combination of technical skills (human capital), political skills (political capital), and contacts and connections (social capital) necessary to convert opportunities into advantageous bargaining. These resources, of course, are not equally distributed. Those workers who are structurally excluded from the selective bargaining (women and younger and unskilled workers) must resort to individual strategies of quitting jobs in search of higher wages or of engaging in supplementary activities in the second economy. Those workers who can participate in selective bargaining enjoy higher earnings, less fluctuation in earnings, and somewhat greater predictability that increased skills, effort, or both will yield comparable rewards.[13]

Rather than through routinized promotions along narrow job classifications, it is through the transactive exchanges of this selective bargaining that an internal labor market is constructed within the socialist firm. In short, whereas uncertainties in the capitalist firm are mitigated through internal bureaucratic rules, in the socialist firm uncertainties are reduced through internal market transactions. And whereas workers in capitalist economies differ in the extent to which they are protected from the market, workers in the socialist economy differ according to the extent to which they can participate in the market.

By institutionalizing the selective bargaining process, the Hungarian work partnerships make transparent the use of transactive relations to construct an internal labor market inside the socialist firm. The relationship between the enterprise and the partnership is explicitly transactive: through its elected representative the partnership negotiates the price of a particular task, product, service, or aspect of the production process, either in spot transactions or in more long-term

---

*Moreover, the repeated crises within production pose almost insurmountable obstacles to the application of Taylorist principles of routinization. An entirely unintended consequence of central planning is that the labor process in state socialist economies requires a more flexible allocation of labor on the shop floor. One irony of the attempt to bring an entire economy under rationalized control through the redistributive (budgetary) instruments of central planning, it seems, is to obstruct routinization and job fragmentation inside the firm. Despite Lenin's fascination with Frederick Taylor, scientific management in the macro sphere precludes scientific management in the micro sphere.

agreements. In some firms, enterprise management encourages the formation of several partnerships in the same field of activity. The firm then posts jobs and invites the partnerships to bid, with the subcontract going to the partnership that offers the lowest bid. More typically, the partnership and its parent enterprise reach agreement over the price of a task through direct negotiations. These negotiations involve a complex calculus including the timing of the negotiations in the firm's planning cycle or month of the year, the going rate in the private sector for the skills of the partners, the urgency of the task, the costs of subcontracting the task to an outside firm, the costs of undertaking the task on overtime or by employing Polish "guest workers," the hard currency earnings (if any) that might accrue to the firm, and above all the relative strength of the group on the regular hours (itself a complex function of technical skills, possibilities of exit, strategic location, the group's cohesiveness, and the extensiveness of its contacts and connections). In these negotiations the partnerships use all their formal and informal knowledge of the economic difficulties of the firm to bargain for better subcontractual rates.

Not all workers participate in subcontractual partnership arrangements. In most firms in which the partnerships operate, fewer than 10 percent of manual workers are involved. Workers who do participate are able to capitalize on their technical skills and their contacts and connections. Hourly earnings in the partnerships are usually two to two and a half times higher than earnings during the regular hours. In the VGMs studied, it was not uncommon to find partnership members whose hourly earnings from their VGMs were four times the average hourly wage in industry. For most of the work partners, the income from their VGM participation represents one-third to one-half of the total yearly income from their regular job; for some members, however, VGM income equals, and even exceeds, their regular earnings. Managers are willing to pay higher rates to the partnerships not only because the partnerships reduce turnover, increase productivity, and promote flexibility but also because the entrepreneurial fee paid to the partnerships is not charged against the wage fund of the enterprise but considered a cost like a fee or purchase from any other unit in the economy. The autonomy of the partnership (its status as a legally separate economic unit) thus allows enterprise management to augment the earnings of a selected group of workers through an avenue that circumvents the central wage regulations. The limited nature of this autonomy (wherein the partnership is legally recognized only insofar as it has been approved by the director of the enterprise) allows management partially to co-opt its form, to restrict the number of partnerships established within the firm, to prohibit partnerships from making subcontracts with other firms, and thus to reduce the opportunities for the partnership to compete favorably with the regular divisions of the enterprise both internally and on the external market.

Thus the hopes among some reformers that the VGMs would undermine the traditional enterprise hierarchy from within have not been realized in the short run.[14] Some Hungarian analysts such as Teréz Laky have argued that the partnerships have actually given the traditional hierarchical relations a new lease on life. Not unlike some authors such as István Kemény, who regard the second economy as a safety valve venting pressures to reform the socialist economy, this perspective sees the partnerships as reducing rather than increasing pressures to reform the socialist enterprise.[15] But as we shall see in the following section, the partnership is not entirely a stabilizing force in the politics of the Hungarian firm.

Competing Interpretations of a Social Experiment

To this point we have examined the continuities between the partnership form and the preexisting social arrangements between workers and managers in the Hungarian firm. We have seen, for example, that the partnerships represent a formalization of the selective bargaining that takes place on the shop floor during regular work hours. In the following sections we turn our attention to the discontinuities in this field of competing and coexisting social groups. Formalization, for example, can be seen as merely the legalization of the shadow bargaining of the regular hours. Alternatively, the establishment of groups of workers as formally recognized bargaining units, separate from and outside the jurisdiction of the trade unions, can be seen to introduce a new element into the field. By creating an institutionalized system of subcontracting, the partnership form creates a social space in which workers, although without autonomy to choose their bargaining partners, do have considerable autonomy to select their own workmates, choose their representatives, organize their work, and devise systems of internal governance and payment. Moreover, because this social space is not simply ad hoc but institutionalized, it becomes a visible object as a named place in the Hungarian social structure.[16] This visibility promotes reflection by the partnership members themselves.

But it also invites scrutiny by nonmembers: because each partnership has a recognized identity, with clear boundaries, the formerly obscure nature of the socialist internal labor market becomes visible. This visibility, furthermore, extends from the socialist firm to the broader polity as scarcely a week goes by in which the meaning of the partnership "experiment" is not debated in the newspapers and in television and radio broadcasts.

SUBJECTS OF THE EXPERIMENT

The theme of experimentation pervades public discussion about the work partnerships at every level of Hungarian society. In his closing speech at the Thirteenth Party Congress in March 1985, János Kádár called the VGMs an "important experiment" that the party should support.[17] Within the context of the debate about the future of the VGMs, Kádár's remarks had a double meaning. On the one hand, the VGMs are an experiment in the sense that they are a form for testing new ideas that might prove useful for the economy. On the other hand, by labeling the VGMs an experiment, Kádár also signaled that the scope of their activities should remain within well-bounded limits.

The members of the work partnerships experience the experimental nature of the VGMs along multiple dimensions. Sensitive to possible changes in the political climate, members know that an experiment can be terminated, and this uncertainty colors their perceptions. Cognizant of the competing interpretations of the VGMs by other social actors, they also know that an experiment can be extended, and this possibility encourages further investments of time and energy to make their group a surviving beneficiary. Conscious of their own experiences, the work partners draw some lessons of their own, and, as we shall see, they are often highly articulate in stating them. Above all, the work partners are acutely aware of the dual sense in which they are the subjects of an experiment. On the one hand, they are experimental subjects, being observed by others. The members repeatedly use metaphors such as "The VGM is a satellite sent out on a reconaissance mission," or "The VGM? It's a surveying instrument in unexplored territory. They want to see what's possible." On the other hand, the work partners are active subjects, themselves experimenting inside the VGMs as they make innovations in the production process, organize their work differently, and devise and modify internal payment systems in search of better methods for allocating the earnings of the group.

MANAGERS ON INCENTIVES AND INDIVIDUAL
INTRAPRENEURSHIP

Before elaborating the lessons that workers draw from the subcontracting experiment, it is necessary to explore the interpretations
offered by ministry officials and enterprise directors. For officials in
the Planning Office and the Finance Ministry, the principal lesson of
the VGM experiment is to reveal the hidden labor reserves of the large
firms. Enterprise directors, for their part, point to a different conclusion, arguing that the VGM experiment proves that Hungarian enterprises need a more differentiated incentive structure. At the same time
that the VGMs provide an avenue for enterprises to maneuver around
central wage regulations, directors point to the VGMs as demonstrating the achievements that would be possible if central wage regulations were abandoned entirely. For many managers, the principal lesson of the VGMs is the need for changes in the incentive system, not
in the supervisory hierarchy. Other enterprise directors point to the
partnerships as indicating a new direction to expand subcontracting
inside the firm. But their interpretation of the partnerships focuses
on the subcontracting link in itself rather than on the altered pattern
of relations inside the units: many of the preliminary schemes now
under consideration in the firms I studied are built around a model in
which one person (significantly, a manager) will operate as an entrepreneurial subcontractor with almost complete discretion to manage
a particular subunit, sharing profits between the enterprise and the
unit. Presented with these proposals, the work partners argue that this
model is more an application of the leasing arrangement now found in
the service sector than an application of the lessons of the partnerships
as collective entrepreneurs. They interpret the lessons of the partnerships quite differently—as evidence of the ability of worker groups to
self-manage their own activities.

WORKERS ON THE ORGANIZATION OF
WORK INSIDE THE PARTNERSHIPS

The partnership members, of course, are not blind to the ways in
which the structure of incentives differs in the regular hours and in
the off-hours subcontracting units. As a machinist explained:

The goals are different in the regular hours and in the VGM. In the VGM
there is not a goal to be good for the boss, sneaking around for him, to be
made an "excellent worker" [*kiváló dolgozó*]. Here there is only one goal: to do

good work and earn money. For money, nothing else. Because the work task is in front of him, and he knows that, if he does solve the problem quicker and better, he will earn more. The other, the essence of the regular hours is that there is no incentive system there. So, if I actually work two hours or eight hours out of the eight, I earn the same.

A semiskilled worker commented:

In the official hours, the intensity of work doesn't get you anything. If you work harder, they will say, 'you are a very good worker,' but that's it. In the VGM, if you work harder, you will get more.

A skilled machinist stressed that it is not the pace or intensity but the organization of work that differs in the partnerships:

Q. Is work in the VGM basically the same as in the regular hours?
A. There is a difference, but let me say in advance that we don't work at a faster pace—only better held together, more organized, and with better ideas. The intensity isn't greater. [He repeats with emphasis] The intensity isn't greater.
Q. For example?
A. Take our last task. The shop would have got it in regular hours. The foreman would have arranged it among other tasks, fit it among the other work. He would have a fixture made—from *his* point of view. So, the principle of "more eyes see more" is missing. For example, there is a position driller [highly skilled machinist] who puts the piece on his machine and starts the task. In the VGM I can tell him that there is a need for cutting another piece that can also be done on the same machine. That will save a lot of set-up time. And so I tell him to do it. In the regular hours the second piece would be brought to me on another machine. They would bring it to me and I would have to say "if we do it on my machine, we need a special fixture to do that cut, so I can't do it yet." I have to wait till the tool is made—and the time goes. Because of such things the enterprise spends more time. We [the VGM], for example, we take out the blueprints and we make a so-called home technology. What are the successive operations, what tools and instruments are needed? We bring them out, sharpen them, put them in order, and the work goes continuously and smoothly. We always win a certain time against the enterprise.
Q. How does that happen?
A. In the regular hours they [the managers] bring only the *detailed* blueprints that this and this is needed. But from the *master* blueprint I can see quite different things. And I immediately see where are the obstacles, the danger spots. But in the shop we get only the detailed blueprints and the tool is made in pieces and they wait till a problem occurs which is maybe correctable—and maybe not. That's the problem. In the regular hours the tasks are defined almost down to the tiniest detail. It seems a contradiction but it is not. I said at the beginning that here are such craftsmen who can do their task autonomously and they don't need this guidance. But because of the bad, unorganized supervision, others dip their hands in the process and screw it

up. . . . In the VGM we work from the master blueprint. Everyone who is part of the project will look at it at the beginning. *We* plan it in advance. There's no one looking over your shoulder to mess it up. We keep in touch with each other and figure out new solutions while the job is going along, too.

Partnership members often speak about the difference between hierarchical supervision in the regular hours and horizontal coordination in the VGM. One repeated theme in early conversations was that the "boss" is missing in the partnerships. The question was raised in a number of subsequent interviews, as here with a machine operator:

Q. Is the representative [*közös képviselő*] a boss [*főnök*]?
A. The two are not the same. In regular hours I have a boss who has a certificate and the position for supervising me. And he says what's to be done and how it has to be done. But afterwards, in the afternoon [off-hours partnership], I can do it as *I* want. So, they have a supervising system, but this system can only do just so much.*

A semiskilled electronics worker was asked:

Q. How do things work in the VGM?
A. In the official hours the worker waits until work is organized. In the VGM everybody takes part, nobody waits. No one is a supervisor or controller; everybody is an organizer.
Q. Is there a boss in the VGM?
A. A leader but not a boss. In the end the voice of the boss is not allowed. We decide together.

And, most succinctly, a skilled worker stated: "A boss doesn't work. And so there isn't one in the VGM." Referring to the VGM's failure to recognize official classifications of rank and skill, one maintenance worker who was a partnership member explained:

---

*The "they" in this quotation is significant and occurs repeatedly in conversations with partnership members. Some members seldom use the term *regular hours* but simply say, for example, "the way they do it." "They" refers in these cases to managers or to the enterprise in contrast to the partnership. In one group of semiskilled operators, the semantic usage is even more interesting. This shop contains four machines for making latex gloves. Three are used by the enterprise. The fourth is used exclusively by the work partners. In conversations with each other, the work partners refer to the three machines as "the state machines" (*az állami gépek*) and to the partnership machine as "the group's machine" (*a közösségi gép*) or simply as "our machine" (*a mi gépünk*). When meeting at the beginning of a shift, workers in the shop inquire whether one is working on the "state shift" or on the "private shift" (*az állami vagy a maszek műszak*)? *Maszek* is a common term for private sector, coined from *magánszektor*. In the 1950s and 1960s, the term carried pejorative connotations, and it still does among some segments of officialdom. The partnership members, in this case, used the term somewhat jokingly, but without derogatory implications.

You can't compare the VGM work with the official work. During the morning hours, two different types of workers work together. One is skilled and the other is unskilled. At least that's how it's seen officially. So what does the unskilled person do? He has to say to himself, "I'm earning less, so I won't work as much." That makes a lot of sense. But on the VGM, each task has a professional leader. It's not divided up like "skilled" and "unskilled." The professional leader divides up the work; he makes some very general assignments. And then everybody works just as hard. The motivation is very different than during the official hours.

Elite workers putting in long hours of extra effort, exceeding the production norms of the typical working day, hailed by some as exemplars of the new working class that makes technological innovations without the supervision of technical specialists—these observations about the Hungarian partnerships recall the Stakhanovite movement of decades earlier.[18] But we should be cautious before drawing this analogy too emphatically. In the first place, the Stakhanovites were hailed as individuals. More important, behind the bemedaled "heroes of socialist labor" stood the unrecognized unskilled workers whose labor made it possible to achieve the unprecedented production records.* The Stakhanovite organized work in a hierarchical manner and, like the subcontractor in the internal subcontracting system at the turn of the century in the United States, he was unquestionably "the boss." The statements by VGM members quoted above provide a useful counterpoint. These elite workers are a collectivity, and their higher productivity is achieved through internal social relations that are less rather than more hierarchical.

WORKERS ON SELECTION AND PAYMENT

In my conversations with VGM members about the criteria for selecting members, the consistent theme that emerged was that the group should attempt, within the limits of cohesiveness ("there must be good relations between each other"), to maximize the total volume of its capital. Although the subcontracting units rarely involve commitments of personal financial savings, the process of group formation is, nonetheless, conceptualized by VGM members as an investment. Many see the partnership form as an opportunity to pool their technical, social, and political capital.[19] One group of workers, for example,

---

*The reader unfamiliar with the details of the Stakhanovite movement might, nonetheless, recall scenes from Andrej Wajda's *Man of Marble* and the laborers who helped Birkut attain the carefully choreographed bricklaying feat.

formed a partnership to do maintenance work. The composition of the group was heterogeneous with mechanics, pipe fitters, electricians, workers who do gluing and fitting, draftsmen, and so on.

Q. Why so many different skills and occupations?
A. Because when even only one member has a piece of paper [a technical diploma] that makes him qualified, the partnership can make contracts to do that task. If we have someone trained in mechanics, we can do mechanical repairs; if we have someone who is certified as an electrician, we can make contracts to do electrical maintenance. The same with plumbing and pipe fitting. We could bake if we had a certified baker.
Q. So you learned new skills in the partnership?
A. That happens a little bit. It sometimes happens that you can learn a few things from somebody. But for the most part, it's not that we didn't already know how to do it but just that we didn't have a piece of paper.

The key idea here is that the partnership has socialized the educational capital of its membership. What had been the property of an individual (in all the meanings of the term "property") now has become the property of the collectivity. In so doing, the partnership does not simply aggregate the credential capital of its respective members. Rather, by bringing this credential capital into a new form of organization (one in which each member can perform almost any function for which the *unit* is "certified") it greatly amplifies the exchange value of the certificate.

Other groups attempt to improve the information available to their partnerships by choosing members (or self-selecting each other) not simply on the basis of technical credentials but also on social capital (contacts and connections) and political capital (party membership). The net effect of these choices (as well as those of shop supervisors, who, on occasion, are instrumental in shaping VGM membership) is that the work partners are those workers who were already advantaged in the selective bargaining of the shop floor. Tables 4.1 and 4.2 present the distribution of employees and VGM members by skill and sex at a firm I shall call "Minotaur," one of the largest enterprises in Hungary. As Table 4.1 indicates, university graduates, technicians, and skilled workers are disproportionately represented in the partnerships, and semiskilled, unskilled, and administrative staff are considerably underrepresented. Table 4.2 shows that women make up 42.2 percent of the employees in the firm but only 17.6 percent of the VGM members.[20]

When asked to explain why some workers are included in the VGMs while others are not, some partnership members are quick to respond

TABLE 4.1
Skill Distribution at Minotaur and Its VGMs, 1984
(percentages)

Skill level	Minotaur employees	VGM members
University graduates	6.1	10.0
Technicians and skilled workers	33.9	67.8
Semiskilled workers	42.1	18.0
Unskilled workers	6.2	1.2
Administrative staff	11.7	3.0
TOTAL	100.0	100.0

SOURCE: Internal company document at Minotaur.

NOTE: The category "technicians and skilled workers" is composed mostly of skilled workers. "Technicians" are highly skilled workers with special diplomas. The definition is somewhat ambiguous and seemed to vary from factory to factory within this large enterprise. I have merged the categories here.

TABLE 4.2
Gender Distribution at Minotaur and Its VGMs, 1984
(percentages)

Gender	Minotaur employees	VGM members
Men	57.8	82.4
Women	42.2	17.6
TOTAL	100.0	100.0

SOURCE: Internal company document, Minotaur.

that "everyone could be in one if they wanted." Moments later, these same workers would point out the difficulties faced by their partnership in gaining recognition and would note that not all workers have the political skills, knowledge, or information necessary to maneuver through that process. As a supervisor and VGM member observed,

Among about one-third of the workers here there is strong opposition to the VGMs, especially among those who aren't in, but it isn't important why. But these voices are subsiding now because in principle everybody has the possibility to join. . . . The only problem is that for people at the machines to go through that circus [the problem of getting the papers and administrative approval] there is not enough preparedness, not enough time, not enough knowledge. Workers need some experience in managing. Management has to help in the administrative work to get through the official establishment process.

Similarly, another worker in the machinist VGM at Minotaur repeated the standard "in principle anyone can join" and then added,

Many people would like to join the VGM but we don't need more people in our group. The best 17 to 18 skilled workers in the shop [of about 120 workers] are already in the VGM. Those people who could be leading representatives [for other VGMs] are already in this group. No one is left to really lead any other group.

Partnership members are acutely aware of the envy (as they put it) of the workers in their shops who are not members of a VGM and the themes of envy and tensions occur often in their conversations. In some firms, management uses nonmembers to police the rule that VGM work not be undertaken during the regular hours. The relationship between members and nonmembers is most problematic when nonmembers (e.g., crane operators, tool or supply room workers, truck drivers, and the like) must perform support work for partnerships as part of their regular jobs. Some partnerships attempt to resolve the problem by creating a common fund administered by the representative to make illegal but widely tolerated "pocket-to-pocket" payments to these support workers in what one worker described as a "third economy" inside the firm.*

OUTCOMES ON EARNINGS INEQUALITIES

The net effect of the pattern of selection and the system of subcontracting, then, is to widen earnings differentials within the working class in the socialist sector. But the contribution of the partnership form to income differentiation in the Hungarian economy is far more complex than to be simply captured under the label that "market mechanisms produce inequality." First, although estimates vary, a considerable percentage of non-VGM members augment their incomes through participation in the second economy outside the boundaries of the enterprise. VGM earnings, no doubt, widen income differentials within the socialist sector (and perhaps even when second economy earnings are included); but the effect of the VGMs on total income

---

*Here, too, a comparison and contrast with Stakhanovism is instructive. If we were to consider the partnership as a collective Stakhanovite, then the support workers who stand outside the partnerships would be the counterparts of the Man of Marble's unrecognized unskilled helpers. The important difference is that whereas the Stakhanovite's assistants were bureaucratically constrained to participate, the "pocket-to-pocket" payments by the partnerships result from resolute bargaining between the nonmembers and the VGM representative.

differentials would be overstated if we failed to include the second economy incomes of nonmembers.

Second, although the partnerships widen earnings differentials within the working class, they act to narrow income differentials between the working class and managers. In fact, mid-level managers, who are prohibited from forming partnerships, voice strong opposition to the partnerships (often prefacing their remarks with statements that it is the organization's interests and not their own self-interest that motivates their opposition) primarily because their blue-collar subordinates who are VGM members have higher incomes than they.

Third, if the partnerships widen income differentials across the working class, the payment systems within the partnerships are narrower than the pay scales for the comparable range of occupations (or job descriptions) in the official organization. On the whole, blue-collar partnerships seem committed to income equality within their groups.* This equality would seem to be obvious and unexceptional in the cases of partnerships with homogeneous skill composition, but the principle of broad equality is also adopted in groups with heterogenous skills and sometimes even when engineers, professionals, or supervisory personnel participate in VGMs alongside manual workers. Not all partnerships enforce strict equality, but most use payment systems that narrow differentials. Some groups use an internal payment scheme based strictly on the number of hours worked in the partnership, with no difference in rates even when skills differ. Others make great efforts to equalize earnings, using an internal piece-rate system but then rotating the members across jobs with "easy" and "tough" rates. Others pay basic hourly rates but with a rule that at the end of each six months incomes among the members cannot vary by more than plus or minus 5 percent. It becomes the task of the representative to make assignments within a system that allows workers flexibility in scheduling, working more in some months as their family needs require. Still others pay flat rates during the year but create a special bonus fund that is redistributed at the end of the year (voted by the membership) to members who made "special contributions" (for example, developed new products, gained contracts, made some

---

*My impression is that within VGMs composed predominantly of professional or nonmanual employees the internal payment systems increase differentials within the group. This is in marked contrast to the VGMs composed primarily of manual workers. The small number of cases, however, cautions against generalizations here.

technical innovation, or played a crucial role in maintaining the cohesiveness of the group).

NEW PERCEPTIONS OF THE VALUE OF WORK

Whether the internal payment systems of a partnership yield wider or narrower differentials than in the regular hours, the characteristic common to almost all partnerships is that the internal payment system differs from that of the regular hours. And this difference (along whatever dimension) is acutely perceived by the members themselves. For example, a woman in a VGM composed predominantly of semiskilled workers observed: "In the regular hours they pay you for a piece of paper [the diploma or credential]. In the partnership we pay for what you know how to do." With this succinct comment, this worker summarized her view that her partnership recognizes tacit skills, that is, those the worker possesses but are not officially acknowledged and rewarded in the regular hours. Along a related but somewhat different dimension a worker in the same firm noted: "In the regular hours we are selling our time; in the VGM we are selling our skills." This brief observation reflects an important change precipitated by the partnership subcontracting form, a shift in the way workers think about themselves and the value of their work. Not only does the internal payment system reward uncredentialed or tacit skills, but in addition the subcontracting arrangement alters workers' calculations about the employment relationship. As in the case quoted above, calculation shifts from "how much is my time worth?" (with the corollary calculations involving minimizing effort and maximizing rewards) to "how are skills valued?" It is significant, moreover, that in so doing this worker does not use the singular "I" and "my skills" but the plural "we" and "our skills." For this worker belongs to the maintenance VGM noted above, which "socialized" its credential capital. Like many partnerships, the internal payment system in his group is structured around a principle that individual remuneration must promote the maximization of the collective's income. Thus, although the unit of payment is ultimately the individual, in a sense the individual members think about the group as the unit of payment, and they do so in a mode of calculation that is not adequately captured in the term *collective incentive scheme.*

For a sizable minority of VGM members, the reconceptualization is more dramatic. "The partnership made me think about what my work is worth," is a repeated theme in the interviews. Whereas formerly they thought about the value of their labor as "selling time," and later as "selling skills," now they begin to calculate the value embodied in the products produced by the partnership. This new mode of calculation should not be surprising when we consider that, in their negotiations with the enterprise, the partnership members (for the "first time in their lives," as they explain) seek out information on the market value and sometimes even on international markets for the products or services they are subcontracting to the enterprise. The internal subcontracting system thus offers workers concrete experiences that enable them to begin to calculate the value of their work in a mode quite different from the wage-labor, commodity form.

ORGANIZATIONAL REFLEXIVITY AND
REPRESENTATIONS OF SOCIAL GROUPS

Like the informal worker groups involved in selective bargaining during the regular hours, the work partnerships are small work teams; but the contractual nature of their connection to the enterprise yields properties that are distinct from those of the informal group on the shop floor. For however durable, cohesive, and capable of interacting with its organizational environment, the informal group is not an officially recognized unit. The VGM has an official, that is, explicit and institutionalized, identity. Unlike the informal group, it has a name and a list of members. It embraces each of these members, and although it can operate only through their continued interaction, in an important sense it stands outside them.

Because the VGM is involved in more formalized, contractually binding interactions with the enterprise, the work partners must construct a set of social arrangements within the VGMs that have a higher degree of objectification than those within the informal networks and culture of the shop floor. These rules and procedures are often fluid and far from bureaucratic. What makes these regulating mechanisms distinct from the codes of the shop floor is their heightened visibility for the work partners themselves. In deciding how to allocate earnings, for example, an internal payment system may be adopted and later rejected or modified after a lengthy process of debate and discussion. For the members, the VGM with its internal rules and regulating mechanisms can exist as an object to be examined because, in a peculiar sense, they stand both inside and outside it. It becomes all the more obvious that a choice was made, that things were done this way rather than that, when, with the same technology and perhaps even the same personnel, they are done differently during the regular hours in another organizational context.

Most important, of course, for the politics of the enterprise, the VGMs provide a distinct vantage point from which the members can view the enterprise. The experiences of the work partners with different forms of representation, methods of work, systems of payment, and classification of skills always exist alongside their experiences in the regular eight-hour shift. Because the partners' organizational solutions occur within a unit with a distinctive identity, which is itself subject to the gaze of others, these arrangements appear in sharper relief, in heightened contrast to the regular hours. In short, the VGMs promote an organizational reflexivity among their members.*

The phenomenology of the relationship between the informal group and the firm is quite different from that between the VGM and the firm. Because the values and codes of the workers' regular shop-floor culture are reproduced through the activity of work in the firm, they are not a separate sphere but rather an integral part of the organizational life of the firm. The individual's experience of the informal group takes place in the same moment as the experience of work in the dominant form of organization. But, although the VGM must be seen as a functioning part of the overall organization, the organizational features of the work partnership can be experienced in a sphere which is temporally and perceptually distinct from work in the regular hours.

The VGM, then, is formally part of the enterprise, but its forms are analytically and experientially separable from the rest of the organization. This peculiar identity/duality at the organizational level is also manifested at the individual level for the VGM members must construct identities in a situation in which they are connected twice over to the firm: once as employees, once again as members of an affiliated VGM whose internal logic is both inside and outside, different and conjoined, competing and coexisting with the dominant form of organization of the socialist firm. The work partners' participation in two spheres, that of the VGM and that of the regular-hours' orga-

---

*This situation represents a curious paradox. To the extent that the VGM members construct and reproduce institutionalized arrangements they create forms of a more objectified nature. This process is sometimes referred to as reification, the moment when a social relation or set of social relations is experienced as a thinglike property. But in this particular instance, this same moment provides the opportunity to reflect back on the organization of work in the regular hours. The powerful conservatizing element in any organization or system of social action, the preconscious belief that a system of social relations is of the natural order of things, cannot be sustained.

nization, raises the stakes in the game. Because the VGM members are only part-time partners but full-time employees, they maintain a direct and immediate interest in the organization of work and systems of payment in the regular hours.* With a vital stake in the socialist enterprise, the work partners repeatedly point to the organizational forms of the VGMs as positive models for change in the dominant form of organization in the firm. The institutional separation of the two forms permits reflexivity, the proximity invites comparison, concrete experiences yield alternative models, and a stake in the outcome prompts desire for change.

If the partnerships produce new perceptions of the socialist enterprise on the part of the members, they also lead to new perceptions by nonmembers. One consequence of the work partnerships' more objectified institutional existence than that of the informal group (that is, that they have officially recognized identities and clearly demarcated boundaries) is to heighten the visibility of the internal labor market. The presence of the partnerships brings selective bargaining out of obscurity and into the bright light of debate and discussion at the level of the shop floor, the enterprise, and the nation. Especially for nonmembers, it is now much more obvious that some workers are in, while others are excluded from, the socialist internal labor market. Thus, whereas institutionalization provides new resources for the partnership members it also poses new liabilities. Polemically stated, because the partnerships can be named, they can also be blamed.

The existence of the partnerships also poses a challenge to the officials of the trade unions. Because the partnerships contract for entrepreneurial fees, they come under the jurisdiction of the Civil Code and not the Labor Code. As such, their activities are not regulated by the trade unions. Although the Hungarian unions are somewhat more responsive than their counterparts in other East European economies, the trade union leadership is not noted for militant advocacy of working-class interests. The opposition of trade union officialdom to the partnerships stems from perceptions that the partnerships are

---

*In this sense work in the VGM is both similar to and different from work outside the firm in the second economy. Work in the second economy, like that in the VGM, does not sever the principal ties of interest to the firm. Moreover, experiences in the second economy are not irrelevant to workers' evaluations of their jobs in the socialist sector or in the formulation of alternative conceptions of economic organization. But (unlike the VGM) either because the nature of the work is so different or because the institutional context is so radically different, experiences in the second economy do not offer the same opportunities for a direct and immediate comparison with the regular hours.

an intrusion into a sphere long guarded as its own institutional turf. Moreover, the partnerships provide an alternative model for the representation of some working-class interests. To the extent that the unions at the local level could be seen to have a constituency, it had been formed by the core, skilled workers—precisely those most likely to join the partnerships and devote their energies and attentions to an alternative channel of interest representation.

Trade union officials did not initially oppose the work partnerships. Like other organizations, they endorsed the party resolutions favoring the new form. But by the end of 1982, when it became obvious that the partnerships were growing rapidly and would become (unexpectedly) the predominant organizational innovation among the new intermediate property forms, the trade union leaders reversed their position.* The justification of this opposition has taken two formulations of dubious consistency. In 1983, the signals sent from the national trade union council (through its newspapers and the speeches of its leadership) deplored that the partnership members were being overworked in a sphere "unprotected" by the unions. Later in that year and throughout 1984, the posture shifted to one that deplored that not all workers were able to participate in the subcontracting form and criticized the "unjustified" inequalities in earnings that resulted. With this move, the trade union leadership began to exploit the now more visible duality among different segments of the working class. Some politicians have also elaborated these criticisms, charging that the partnerships are a primary cause of the high rate of inflation in the economy. With the increasing attention devoted to the partnerships in highly publicized discussions, the partnerships become an objectified social category, a sign that enters into the political vocabulary at the level of the shop, the firm, and the nation.

The question of who represents the working class is thus bound up with the question of the representational images of "the working class." Is it a unified and homogeneous social category or does it have discrete layers and segments, perhaps with conflicting interests? The existence of the partnerships, involving roughly every tenth manual worker, increases the salience of this question. Thus, together with the question of who represents the partnership is the question of what the partnerships represent. Are VGMs composed of overworked and exploited employees or of opportunists taking advantage of a temporary

---

*The perspectives of trade union officialdom and those of local-level shop stewards are far from identical. Many shop stewards participate in the partnerships and have been noticeably hesitant to articulate the stance of the leadership.

economic crisis? Are the work partners the Hungarian Stakhanovites of the 1980s? Is their initiative and their self-organizing capacity an indicator of the creative potential of the entire working class, or is the predominance of skilled workers in the partnerships an indicator that these organizing skills are specific to a certain segment of workers? In this latter formulation, the partnerships are a vanguard of a "new working class" of lower-level engineers, technicians, and skilled workers. Does the category of working class adequately capture the orientation of the work partners, or does their higher standard of living and their participation in an intermediate property form bring them closer to the class outlook of the ambitious entrepreneurs in the growing private sector? That each of the statements implicit in these questions contains a certain partial truth reflects the complex and contradictory character of this new element in the Hungarian reforms.

The Partnership Form and the Future Course of Reforms

Returning in this concluding section to the relationship between the partnership form and the broader politics of reform in contemporary Hungary, we recall that the leadership of the Hungarian party sought a mechanism to augment the incomes of the elite of the urban industrial working class and thereby preempt political tensions among this strategic social group. The VGMs have accomplished this goal in the short run. But they are now becoming a source of tensions among this same group. VGM members now rely on the higher earnings made possible by off-hours subcontracting. Still, they strongly resent that they must undertake exhausting work in addition to the regular hours in order to improve their incomes. This hostility mounts over time. The following passages, from a highly skilled worker and a skilled machinist, are typical of many similar comments from VGM members:

There is a principle that we should work only eight hours, and several years ago we were fighting for an eight-hour work day. But now we work Saturday and Sunday fourteen to sixteen hours. For health reasons this isn't possible. We come in and take medicine. My colleague and also I went to physicians, we felt dizzy. I felt really bad. And the doctor says, "It's the VGM disease." So, the people are working themselves to death and this can't be continued in the long term. The people are such, and I have experience with it now for the first time, that despite what a lot of people say that we are lazy, careless, that's not true because we can croak in this work. There are unbelievable production results. But it's pure hell what we put ourselves through. We will kill ourselves, we know, and we want to get out of it.

I regard it as exploitation. It requires a lot of energy and at the root of it all is money. But we have to regard that people get tired. And as I mentioned, these men are the kind who try to do their job properly also in the regular hours. They are the best paid workers in the shop. So they must satisfy the regular hours need, because they do most of the tasks. And then after regular hours to stay longer. One can't do it over the long term without complete physical exhaustion. Because of this the VGM has no future.

The experiences within the partnerships with alternative forms of organizing work lead not simply to the articulation of grievances but also to demands that the VGMs should be moved from the off hours into the regular hours. The following statements were made in private conversations, but similar opinions were also voiced in enterprise-level meetings that I attended:

The question is, why don't our managers solve our problems in the regular hours?

From the beginning I've been of the opinion that in the regular hours there should be a VGM-like organization of work. And to pay as in the VGM. I wondered as I heard about these conversations [my interviews] whether or not our firm's economic experts are interested in these topics because they should have solved very flexibly these problems of the differences between regular and VGM work. The experts of the enterprise should be coming here to do these interviews to find out a way to do the work that's done so flexibly in the VGMs also in the main hours.

I'm pessimistic. I don't see a long future. But we have hope that our enterprise will get on such a level that the experiences coming from the VGM can be used for the whole shop, and in the eight hours we will get a wage like that made in the VGMs. That's what we want to achieve.

But as we saw in the previous section, workers, managers, and ministry officials draw different lessons from the VGMs. Thus the future of their incorporation into the official hours (if at all) is not easily predicted.

The present situation of the partnerships represents in microcosm the current state of the Hungarian economy, poised at the transition from extensive to intensive economic development but seemingly unable to make the leap decisively. On the one hand, the partnerships resemble the extensive model of development in which growth is premised on the quantitative increase of factor inputs such as capital and labor: the VGMs are an undisguised extension of the working day. And the statements above have shown, it is this facet that exhausts and infuriates the work partners. On the other hand, the partnerships prefigure an intensive model of economic development based on the qualitative improvement of factor inputs: the productivity gains inside the VGMs are possible because of qualitative restructuring of both the wage system and the organization of work. And as their statements also illustrate, it is the failure to incorporate these lessons into the official hours that so frustrates partnership members. Whether the Hungarian authorities decide to dismantle the VGMs, leave them in place, or expand and incorporate a partnershiplike form within the regular hours, to the VGM members one matter is clear, as stated by a technician who is a VGM representative:

This possibility has been given to the most important people in the factory and it can't be taken back without other possibilities. Because otherwise, there is a fear that people will leave these key positions. And if they would leave, the whole production would fall to the ground. They can't take it away— especially now after they have already given this.

As this statement indicates, whatever choice is made by the Hungarian leadership, it will necessarily have to contend with a sizable group of workers whose experience in a new organizational space has increased their confidence in their capacities and their strategic importance in the Hungarian economy.

Whether the authorities decide to step back, stand still, or move forward on the question of the partnership form, it is also clear that this decision will not be made in an atmosphere in which the general public is merely indifferent to, or ignorant about, the VGMs. On the contrary, the partnership form figures prominently in public opinion about economic reforms in Hungary. For broad segments of Hungarian society, the work partnerships are the most visible institutional change in recent years. This is not to say that the partnerships are the most important change in the Hungarian economy but that they have a salience within popular perceptions that far outweighs their objective impact on the Hungarian economy. That is, whereas the immediate economic significance of the partnerships should not be exaggerated, their political significance should not be underestimated.

This conclusion is argued most persuasively by Erzsébet Szalai, a reform economist working in the Ministry of Finance, who conducted an important study of popular perceptions of economic reforms in Hungary.[21] Szalai's study is based on in-depth interviews conducted with approximately sixty workers and intellectuals in late 1984. In her interview schedule, Szalai did not include questions about the VGMs. She was, therefore, surprised when almost all of her informants began to answer questions about the economic reforms with reference to the

work partnerships. Moreover, the study revealed not only that people were quick to voice opinions but that these views were strongly
held and expressed with considerable emotion. Szalai explains this
curious development by noting that the larger institutional changes
such as modifications of the banking system, import restrictions, and
reduction of the various industrial ministries to a single Ministry of
Industry are almost completely outside the field of vision of most citizens. What looms largest, because most proximate, in the topography
of reform measures are the work partnerships. Almost everyone can
see (or certainly hear about) partnerships working in their enterprises
or can talk with friends, in-laws, or neighbors who are partnership
members. And these private discussions about the partnerships within
enterprises, neighborhoods, and families can resonate with a public
discourse about the new form. Probably more than any other single
issue in the Hungarian economy, the debate about the subcontracting
experiment has been extraordinarily open, widely covered, and without taboos. The Hungarian media seem to have adopted a policy
toward the VGMs, unlike other measures, that allows any and all perspectives to be aired: detractors and advocates, skeptics and prosely-
tizers, each can have a say. It is because of these two factors, familiarity through everyday experience and the prominence of the topic
in the popular press, that the partnership experiment occupies a central place in public opinion about the reforms. Szalai reports that it
is as if the partnership issue serves as a device through which people organize and express their views on a wide range of topics, be it
stratification and inequality; personal income taxation; the problem
of overwork; the suppression, toleration, or legalized expansion of the
second economy; the meaning of entrepreneurship; corruption; or
enterprise management. It is through talking about the partnerships
that workers can voice views about these broader issues.

Moreover, although these views are strongly held, opinions about
the partnerships per se are highly ambivalent. Few respondents endorsed them uncritically and even fewer denounced them unquali-
fiedly. Most addressed the partnerships with a mixture of criticism
and praise, corresponding to the positive and negative features attributed (with considerable variability) to the innovation. Szalai argues
that the "outpouring of emotion" with which her informants discussed
the VGMs is directly related to this deep ambivalence:

What is really important from the point of view of this investigation is that the
people I talked with had an ambivalent relationship regarding this contradic-

tion-filled form. This calls forth vehement emotions because it brings close to hand and makes them aware of the contradictory nature of our whole socio-economic structure and the dual/divergent nature of the various proposed ways out of this. It serves as the embodiment of those contradictions which people suspect but do not consciously know. The various new phenomena such as a freer possibility of expression, enterprise autonomy, new forms of enterprises, small enterprises, etc.—all of these exist alongside the older forms. They are saturated with them, and it is impossible to determine whether they perpetuate the old relationships or whether they serve to pass beyond them.

Szalai concludes, "It is as if the VGMs were the symbol of some disquieting duality."[22] For Szalai, the ambivalence about the partnerships is simultaneously a deep ambivalence about the current state of reforms in the Hungarian economy. Indeed, what other single institution better embodies the contradictory character and bridled potential of the Hungarian economy than this curious form with its hybrid mixture of public ownership and private initiative, its markets hampered by bureaucratic regulations, its real but restricted autonomy, its location as a part of the socialist enterprise but holding up a critical mirror to it, its higher productivity but its longer working day, its benefits promised to all but limited to the few, and its alternative but subordinated forms of interest representation?

But where Szalai sees evidence of a disquieting dualism, other Hungarian economists regard the seemingly incongruous as signs of normalcy, or even of latent dynamism. János Kornai, for example, challenges the modernist assumptions of traditional socialist thought when he argues: "There are no 'pure' and perfectly 'consistent' societies. Every real system is built upon the practical compromises of mutually contradictory principles and requirements." Similarly, for István Gábor, the "antagonistic relationship" between the contradictory organizing principles of the first and second economies is not necessarily destructive but can play a fruitful and functional role. In a recent essay of theoretical and political importance he argues that the expansion of the second economy "is a process leading not to the 'degeneration' of socialism but to its advancement, to the release of its natural driving forces and self-correcting mechanisms fed by the two economies straining against each other, and thus, to the exploitation of the economic potential inherent in the socialist system."[23]

Thus, in contrast to many reform economists who could conceptualize a reformed economy only as a fully marketized economy and to hard-liners who could only envision a developed socialism in which the second economy would be unnecessary and hence easily eradicated, Gábor steps outside the unitarist bias of the old terms of debate. In effect, he calls on all parties to acknowledge a mixed economy as a viable hybrid form and not as inherently unstable and necessarily transitional. If there are good reasons to be ambivalent about the current course of the Hungarian reforms it is not because of economic dualism per se; the sooner the mixed character of the economy is openly and officially recognized, the sooner the contest between its diverse components can be a source of positive development.

Perhaps the distinctive contribution of the Hungarian experiment will be to demonstrate that the path to reforming a socialist economy lies less in promoting competition among firms than in fostering competition among organizational forms. Not simply decentralization of economic decision making but diversification of property forms might be the Hungarian lesson for reconstructing the centrally planned economies. A society in which not merely consumers' choices are expanded but in which producers have genuine options about investing their energies in state enterprises, worker cooperatives, individual ventures, or complex combinations of such endeavors might yet be the institutional legacy of Hungarian reforms. It is, of course, premature to make such an assessment, but we should not preclude the possibility of a socialist economy functioning on multiple principles, with a plurality of property forms. Collective intrapreneurial units—such as the partnerships could potentially become if incorporated directly into the official hours of the Hungarian firms—would be one property form (among numerous others) in such an economy. This form and other mixed property forms will provoke ambivalence, and even paralysis, so long as an economy is justified on the basis of a single universalistic principle, be it market-defined "self-interest" or bureaucratically defined "societal interest." An alternative is to step unambiguously on the road to a mixed economy and to raise the plurality of property forms from the status of the contingent and ambiguous to one in which diversity is itself a principle of justification. Hungary might yet take such a step. As analysts, our next step is to accept the challenge of comparing mixed economies not on the basis of the relative weights of "capitalist" and "socialist" elements but on the basis of the complex combinations of diverse and internally heterogeneous organizational forms.

FIVE

Peasant Entrepreneurship and the Politics of Regulation in China

Victor Nee

The progress of market reform in rural China has given rise to a new social group, peasant households that specialize in production of petty commodities for the marketplace. From the specialized households (*zhuanye hu*) a rural entrepreneurial elite is emerging that is rapidly acquiring experience and expertise in estimating market demand, using local resources to produce needed commodities, and opening up new markets for these products that frequently extend far beyond the boundaries of the local marketing system.

For most specialized households, the scale of production has remained at the cottage industry level, limited by the supply of raw material, capital, and market demand. Many entrepreneurial peasants are rapidly expanding their firms beyond the scope of household production, however, and have formed joint-stock companies or private cooperatives, pooling their capital, expertise, and labor power to produce and sell their products in both local and regional markets. Other households have built substantial family businesses that in organizational structure and scale of production resemble small capitalist firms. These peasant entrepreneurs are hiring labor from the large pool of surplus agricultural workers in the countryside and may become the major nonagricultural employer in rural China. Based in market towns and villages, peasant entrepreneurs constitute a new social force in the Chinese countryside, likely to play an increasingly important role in rural development. How do we explain the rise of elements of a market economy and the rapid emergence of peasant entrepreneurs in a state socialist society?

Markets and State Socialism

Past scholarship on developing countries has attempted to understand the underlying dynamics of economic development by analyzing the roles of households and markets. This emphasis is in part an outgrowth of the influence of neoclassical economics in development studies. An example is Sol Tax's study of peasant economy, in which the state is never mentioned as a significant unit for analysis.[1] In the neoclassical perspective the problem of rural development is primarily to reduce interference from the state and allow the market the opportunity to do its magic in providing peasants with incentives to be productive. As Theodore Schultz has claimed, "Once there are investment opportunities and efficient incentives, farmers will turn sand into gold."[2] The neoclassical perspective thus has been closely associated with microsocietal studies that show how peasants respond rationally to economic incentives.[3] When the state is mentioned, it is typically in reference to interventions that result in the redistribution of agricultural surpluses from producers to urban manufacturers and consumers.[4] This focus on state action versus market functioning, however, has deflected attention away from the critical issue of how states intervene in society to establish the institutional and normative context of market structures.[5]

There is a considerable body of scholarship that has shown how the Chinese state has sought to manage rural economic growth through nonmarket mechanisms.[6] Though these studies differ in their assessments of the effectiveness of bureaucratic allocation, they share a common assumption that the Chinese socialist state has been largely hostile to the allocative role of markets. Before the current market reforms, there was little reason to question this view. This assumption continues to color discussion of the Chinese state, however, even after the post-Mao reformers launched their program of economic reforms. To some degree, the analysis of state interventions to encourage market arrangements has been overlooked by analysts through force of habit: we have grown accustomed to thinking about the socialist state as inherently hostile to markets. This view is also an outgrowth of the tendency of the social sciences to ignore the explanatory centrality of the state, as Theda Skocpol has maintained.[7]

Institutional economist Douglass North argues that the rise of market economies in the West depended upon the establishment by the state of property rights that promoted economic growth and reduced transaction costs. According to North, the basic role of the state is to specify the fundamental rules of competition and cooperation that underlie the structure of property rights. Within this framework, the state's efforts to promote economic growth result in public goods and services that reduce the transaction costs of specifying, negotiating, and enforcing contracts in economic exchanges.

This paper argues, in similar fashion, that analysis of China's transition to a mixed economy must also view the state as a primary actor in establishing the institutional arrangements required for the growth of markets and the rise of entrepreneurship.* In state socialism, the introduction of mechanisms to regulate the market requires deliberate and sustained state involvement. In a state-dominated economy, not only are market reforms initiated by the state, but subsequent expansion and consolidation of markets require selective state interventions. The character and quality of these interventions determine the extent to which market coordination replaces state planning and allocation of resources. If state interventions continue to specify particular courses of economic action, especially at the local level, then markets are not likely to play a strong role in coordinating the socialist economy. For market reforms to be successful, there must be a shift toward indirect macroeconomic regulatory interventions.

According to the new economic sociology, rational pursuit of economic interests takes place within networks of ongoing social relations and not, as the utilitarian tradition suggests, in settings in which social structure is a residual factor. Mark Granovetter argues that "the anonymous market of neoclassical models is virtually nonexistent in economic life and that transactions of all kinds are rife with . . . social connections."[8] I argue in this paper that emergent market transactions are embedded in social networks in which rural cadres hold pivotal positions. Thus both reemergent and new market structures are embedded in peasant society, in the web of social networks that links the market town with village social structure, as G. William Skinner has argued,[9] and in the personal networks maintained by village cadres

---

*In China market forces were tamed by the state within the first decade of the communist regime. Even though the Chinese have weakened state control over peasants and rural markets through decollectivization, the state continues to be a dominant organization, defining the institutional parameters of household production and rural marketing. The return to household production was initiated by the state and is dependent upon continuing state support for the policy. The state controls basic factors of production such as land, access to credit and modern inputs, and primary labor markets, maintains production quotas, and sets the state purchasing price for key agricultural commodities. If the state is ever again committed to restricting rural market developments, it has powerful means at its disposal to accomplish this goal.

that reach beyond the village and penetrate state organizations. In this view, local cadres, defined as village, commune, and county officials, often act as brokers or middlemen in market exchanges, especially those involving economic transactions between private entrepreneurs and state agencies. The niches in which peasant entrepreneurs operate and compete are typically crisscrossed by patronage networks dominated by local cadres who can use their power and influence to pressure, bully, and squeeze entrepreneurs. Entrepreneurs themselves are local individuals who must mobilize social networks to gain access to capital, labor, raw materials, technology, and markets. These networks frequently are controlled by gatekeepers in the state structure. Peasant entrepreneurs sometimes seek favorable access to capital, raw material, and markets by bribing local cadres to gain access to scarce resources controlled by the state. This embeddedness of market transactions complicates state interventions to establish the institutional and normative requirements of a rural market economy.

This paper analyzes the intertwined processes involved in the evolution of rational, end-oriented bureaucratic institutions with higher levels of autonomy and the establishment by the state of the institutional framework of a mixed economy, including commercial laws that specify a new structure of property rights, ways of enforcing contracts in economic exchanges, and new market structures such as stock, commodity, and credit markets. Though at the risk of merging distinct issues, I argue that these processes are interrelated. They result from the socialist state's interest in promoting economic growth through market reforms and attempting to reduce the high transaction costs involved in integrating an emergent market economy within a state-dominated economy. Even more than in market economies, in socialist economies the state must assume a strong role in economic regulation to balance the contradictory dynamics of market and bureaucratic coordination of the economy. Simultaneous to the state's effort in setting up institutions of a market economy, it must defend the economic institutions of the still dominant state sector. To accomplish this, in China the dynamics of market reform have pushed the state toward increasing bureaucratic rationalization and societal autonomy.

Having stated my conceptual framework, I shall now present my theoretical argument in propositional form.

Proposition 1

When socialist states launch market reforms, they need to legitimize reform policies among the staff of the state apparatus and to intervene to create the institutional framework of a mixed economy in which the market assumes a greater role in economic coordination. Fundamentally this effort requires the state to specify a new structure of property rights and to reduce transaction costs associated with integrating market and bureaucratic mechanisms of economic coordination.

After decades of state allocation of resources, a return to a market economy requires major institutional change. First, reformers must gain the support and compliance of the state bureaucracy in the legitimization of reform measures. Because the socialist state is the primary organizational actor in initiating market reforms, the voluntary compliance of middle- and lower-level state officials and functionaries is necessary for the successful implementation of reform policies. Second, new market structures need to be established and old markets expanded and modernized. Labor markets need to be legitimized and regulated. New legal codes to regulate enterprises and market transactions need to be promulgated and enforced. Reliable access to capital, raw material, and markets has to be made available to entrepreneurs and firms. The proper uses of public property and resources need to be stipulated and enforced. More important, private property and the profits of business need to be safeguarded in communities where only recently the pursuit of profit was a political and social taboo. In short, the institutional requirements for markets and entrepreneurship have to be renewed, created, and legitimized by the socialist state. Moreover, the problem of legitimization and compliance with reform policies is politically more important to achieve among the staff of the socialist state than among social actors in society. In the reforming socialist economy, the state is the midwife of emergent market structures.

Proposition 2

The more open the organizational boundaries of state structures, the more susceptible are states to societal claims and the less bureaucratic they are in Weber's sense of a modern bureaucracy, and vice versa. The capability of the state to intervene in society is weakened when either latent or manifest opposition to reform policies emanates from social groups that have access to state power. To resolve this dilemma, reform leaders are likely to seek closure of the state's organizational boundaries in the sector where recalcitrance is centered.

The boundaries of state organizations vary in their degrees of permeability, at varying levels of societal interactions, and in different sectors of the state organization. As with other social boundaries, processes similar to osmosis regulate the flow of exchanges (including people) between state and society.[10] Organizational boundaries are called porous or "open" when state organizations are embedded in society through the existence of social networks that knit the state to society, whether they are "old-boy" networks linking officials to dominant classes or patron-client ties linking the state to subordinate social groups.[11]

Organizational boundaries are spoken of as "closed" when state organizations are unencumbered by exchange networks with social groups, either of the dominant classes or of the underclass. More open organizational boundaries are associated with lower organizational capability for autonomous action because they are more susceptible to claims or liens made on the state by social groups. The relative openness of organizational boundaries does not mean that the state is more open to participation, more equal in access to services or resources, or more responsive to the public interest. To the contrary, state organizations with open boundaries may be open to special interest groups, unresponsive to the public interest, inaccessible to subordinate social groups, and closed to participation by outsiders. Nor do more open organizational boundaries imply that the state is less selective or more inclusive in its recruitment procedure for officials and staff. A mobilizational state, with open organizational boundaries, may limit recruitment on strict ideological and class criteria. Moreover, open organizational boundaries may be associated with more internal closure if the state is controlled by an oligarchical elite. Relatively closed boundaries, on the other hand, may at times result in more openness within, in the conduct of day-to-day business and in the recruitment and retention of members. If organizational boundaries are relatively closed, there may be less need for secrecy in the handling of sensitive business or personnel decisions. Both the extent and the method of regulation and exclusion in relationship to society can vary considerably so that the transition from relative openness to more closure is gradual.

The relative openness of the organizational boundaries of the agrarian bureaucracy was a product of the Chinese revolutionary history. The Chinese Communist party won state power through its ability to mobilize the peasantry over the course of a protracted historical process which gave rise to the state's commitment to maintain a permanent organizational presence in villages. This made possible sustained mobilization extending from the Sino-Japanese War, through the civil war and revolutionary land reform, to the collectivization of agriculture and the creation of the people's commune. Franz Schurmann attributed the interlocking of the state organization with village social structure to the role of the rural cadre: "By creating a new Communist party and by training a new type of leader, the cadre, the Chinese Communists were finally able to achieve what no state power in Chinese history had been able to do: to create an organization loyal to the state which was also solidly embedded in the natural villages." [12] The mobilizational politics of the Chinese state required village cadres who were both subject to the state's organizational discipline and natural leaders within the villages, capable of mobilizing peasants to support and comply with state policies in agriculture. [13] Village cadres were typically leaders whose authority was based on their ability to command respect among fellow villagers. They acted within a moral order molded by village traditions and customs, but they remained in power with the approval of the commune administration and were the embodiment of the state in the village. Cadres lacking popular support in the village faced difficulty in exercising the power their government positions granted them. [14]

Complex and often subtle exchanges between villages and commune and county governments, mediated by village cadres, both facilitated the implementation of state policies and provided the village with access to state-controlled resources. [15] The exchange of material resources and services typically involved personal networks within the village and *guanxi* (personal connections) with officials in the commune and county governments in which village cadres played a pivotal role. In my own field study of Yangbei Village in Fujian Province, I found that village cadres assiduously cultivated *guanxi* ties with fellow villagers who served as powerful county cadres, and they drew on the influence and connections of these cadres to gain access to resources for Yangbei Village. The top cadres in Yangbei moved in and out of positions in the Xiangdong commune administration during the years preceding the post-Mao reforms (1974–81) and thus were able to open the organizational boundaries of Xiangdong commune to Yangbei interests more than in any other period of collectivized agriculture.*

*Surprisingly, the earlier literature on local government in China, based on interviews of refugees in Hong Kong, does not have much to say about informal social relationships in state and society interaction. This literature instead describes the functions of formal organizations of the party-state. See, for example, A. Doak Barnett with Ezra

We see in Richard Madsen's descriptions of Longyong how village cadres seek to build personal networks within the local government when they do not have direct access through fellow villagers: "Longyong spent much of his time going to the commune and county seats making friends and securing 'connections'—exactly the type of corruption that he righteously abhorred within his village—in order to get priority for the village in the allocation of scarce building resources: cement for new grain-drying yards, lumber and nails for new buildings." In Madsen's description of the basis of Qingfa's power, we have an illustration of why village cadres developed exchange networks as a basis of power and influence within the village:

> The brigade administration had no economic leverage to enforce compliance with its policies. As a cadre in another part of southern China is reported to have complained at this time: "If there is not rice in your hands, even the chickens will not come to you." Since Qingfa could not exert any regular economic leverage over the village, it was very useful to him to have the loyalty of a corps of kin and friends whom he had helped, when given the opportunity, with small favors. He could count on the members of production team no. 6 to back him up if he proposed a mildly controversial program for village economic development. Here were people who might support him if he had to call a meeting to criticize political offenders in the brigade. Here were people from among whose ranks he could recruit new Party members who would be loyal to him.[16]

When Maoist mobilizational politics, the increasing allocative role of the state, and the decentralization of administrative power came together, as they did in the Great Leap Forward and the Cultural Revolution, local cadres gained considerable discretionary powers. As long as local cadres appeared to support the policies of the state, they could use their positions to accumulate social and political capital by building and extending their networks in both local society and the state organization. As the state expanded its control over social

Vogel, *Cadres, Bureaucracy, and Political Power in Communist China* (New York: Columbia University Press, 1967). Michel Oksenberg wrote on informal processes and social relationships in party and society interaction, but his study was based on interviews with seven cadres, only one of whom, a village accountant, was from a rural area. The study provides suggestive evidence but little that is useful for the analysis of social structures and networks developed in this essay. See Oksenberg, "Getting Ahead and Along in Communist China: The Ladder of Success on the Eve of the Cultural Revolution," in John W. Lewis, ed., *Party Leadership and Revolutionary Power in China* (Cambridge, Eng.: Cambridge University Press, 1970). A paper by Jean Oi, "From Cadres to Middlemen: The Commercialization of Rural Government," presented at the Annual Meeting of the Association of Asian Studies, March 21–23, 1986, however, emphasizes the importance of *guanxi* ties in the middleman role played by cadres after market reform.

and economic life, and as market transactions were displaced by the bureaucracy in allocative processes, *guanxi* and other exchange networks assumed greater importance. When allocative decisions are concentrated in a status group, rather than in market transactions, personal connections become critical in economic activity. They help to reduce the uncertainties and friction associated with bureaucratic allocation in providing a framework for trust and predictability. Stable, ongoing personal relationships lubricate economic transactions involving multilevel bureaucratic hierarchies. For these reasons, in state socialism economic transactions become embedded in social networks that parallel the vertical integration of economic units with the state, giving rise to vertical social segmentation. The Maoist bureaucracy thereby fostered an organizational style that emphasized personal relationships, factional loyalty, and the interpenetration of state and society by *guanxi* ties or networks of social relationships.

Proposition 3a

If market reforms are sustained, and private markets expand rapidly, market action is likely to provoke state regulatory interventions. The organizational dynamics of regulatory intervention will likely result in increased rationalization of the state bureaucracy.

Proposition 3b

The organizational dynamics of the new regulatory approach may be generating pressure for the transformation of the Maoist mobilizational state into a regulatory state.

In the rise of the market economy in the West, "the road to the free market was opened and kept open by an enormous increase in continuous, centrally organized and controlled interventionism," argued Karl Polanyi. "Administrators had to be constantly on the watch to ensure the free workings of the system."[17] In Polanyi's view the unregulated market threatened to destroy society, and efforts to protect society from its ravages necessitated sustained regulatory interventions by the liberal state. North, on the other hand, emphasizes the reduction of transaction costs resulting from regulatory interventions. The establishment of the federal regulatory agency to regulate the American meat industry, for example, promoted the export of meat in world markets by reducing uncertainties about the quality of American meats. In state socialism the impulse to regulate private markets has been even stronger and more encompassing than it was in the rise of market economies in the West. Indeed, in the initial period following the revolutionary takeover of power, the state intervened in the economy to bring markets firmly under state control with the long-term objective of eliminating private markets altogether. China in the Cultural Revolution almost succeeded in accomplishing this goal, as Martin Whyte's essay in this volume points out. By contrast to the Maoist period, the new regulatory approach seems to allow firms and entrepreneurs some measure of autonomy, and it attempts to regulate indirectly through manipulation of prices and therefore relative profitability, as opposed to directly through state interventions specifying particular courses of action. The intent to use macroeconomic regulatory levers is explicit in many Chinese policy statements since 1978. Moreover, regulations are not only to constrain markets but, more important, to reduce transaction costs of specifying, negotiating, and enforcing contracts in a socialist mixed economy.*

Effective state interventions to shape and maintain regulated markets require a public bureaucracy akin to Weber's ideal type of the legal-rational bureaucracy, capable of stable, methodical, rule-governed action based on written documents and files, strict subordination to higher bureaucratic levels, and the separation of the office from the personal interests of the officeholder.[18] These qualities were greatly weakened in the Maoist mobilizational state, which stressed the importance of the moral and ethical orientation of cadres, their leadership qualities, and their ability to make decisions case by case, based on a generalist understanding and commitment to Maoist ideology. Maoist *kadijustice* proved inadequate to the new regulatory demands imposed on the state in its quest to establish regulated markets.

The data for this study were gathered from an intensive survey of the Chinese press from 1980 to 1986 and a selective reading of Chinese economic journals during this same period. The research effort focused on collecting accounts describing the progress of market reforms and decollectivization. The newspapers included the leading national paper, the *Renmin Ribao*, and a provincial press, *Fujian Ribao*. Selective use of the *Foreign Broadcast Information Service: China Report* and the *Joint Publication and Research Service* provided access to a national sample of Chinese presses and journals, including the provincial press and radio broadcasts. When applicable, observations are drawn from interviews I conducted with rural cadres and peasant entrepreneurs and from the village and household data from a survey research project based on a random sample of thirty villages and

*The current approach may well have been contemplated during the 1950s or early 1960s, but certainly not during the Great Leap Forward and after 1965.

634 households. The research was conducted from April to August 1985 in Longhai, Tongan, and Wuping counties in Fujian Province under the joint sponsorship of Xiamen University and the University of California at Santa Barbara.

Crisis of Legitimacy and State Ideological Intervention

The rapid rise of peasant entrepreneurship in response to market reforms preceded the state's legitimization of entrepreneurship. Without legal norms and legitimacy, new peasant entrepreneurs were vulnerable targets for the hostility and suspicion of rural cadres and villagers.

When the Chinese state launched its current market reforms, it sought to stimulate economic growth and productivity by linking material incentives to economic performance. It is doubtful that reformers possessed a blueprint for the economic reform they introduced between 1978 and 1984. Once market reforms were introduced, a dynamic process began in which the more the state relied upon direct household incentives, the less the people's commune, brigade, and team were involved in a managerial capacity in agricultural production. The progress of market reforms quickly eroded the organizational basis of collective agriculture. As the state backed away from its hegemonic control over agricultural production, it had to rely increasingly on the market mechanism to play the allocative role formerly assumed by the state's agrarian bureaucracy.

The rapidity with which the Chinese state implemented its market reforms was startling in light of the decades of institutional investment in stabilizing and consolidating the people's commune system. Even as late as 1980, the production team was still the dominant organization of agricultural production, and it managed all but 5 to 7 percent of the arable land. From 1978 to 1981, various models were experimented with that tinkered with the collectivist organizational form, but none of these proved satisfactory.* By 1983, the collectivist forms

---

*I was doing field research in China during this early period of experimentation in 1980, and I remember many mornings when peasants stood outside of their front doors, listless and confused about the reform models then under experimentation in Yangbei Village. The array of models introduced in the village all sought to retain the basic framework of the production team, while approaching as closely as possible the conditions of individual household production. The new systems of accounting and remuneration were so complex and subtle that even the team accountant had difficulty in explaining them to me. For a detailed account of this field experience see Victor Nee,

were displaced by a variety of models based on individual household production.[19]

The pace of change did not slow down. Market reforms encouraged households to produce for the market rather than the state once they fulfilled their contracted quotas. Many households began to specialize so as to gain competitive advantages in the emergent market economy. Many specialized in a single cash crop,* but increasingly they left agricultural production to specialize in one or more lucrative lines of commodity production.† A diversity of peasant enterprises quickly sprang up to enter the competitive fray of the marketplace. These included private cooperative ventures that pooled capital and labor and households that specialized in transport, construction, and commerce.‡ According to Dong Fureng, the peasants' enthusiasm for

"Post-Mao Changes in a South China Production Brigade," *Bulletin of Concerned Asian Scholars*, 13 (Apr.–June 1981): 32–39. For general accounts of the early period of agricultural reform see *Jingji Yanjiou* (Journal of Economic Research), 1982, no. 3; and Tang Tsou, Marc Blecher, and Mitch Meisner, "The Responsibility System in Agriculture: Its Implementation in Xiyang and Dazhai," *Modern China*, 8 (1982): 41–103.

Renmin Ribao [People's Daily], Nov. 3, 1983, p. 5. The *chengbao zhuanye hu* operated on the same principle as the household contract system. In a common variety, households specialized in grain production by aggregating land from relatives and friends. These arrangements were approved by the state as a means to overcome the extreme fragmentation of landholdings that emerged after land was divided among team members.

†*Zhongguo Shehui Kexue* [Chinese Social Science], 1984, no. 4, pp. 72–75. These households, the *ziying zhuanye hu*, form the base of the new stratum of peasant entrepreneurs, who withdrew from the production team. They are independent family businesses that own their means of production and assume all the risk associated with running a business. Bankruptcy has been high, but it is unclear how many of the households that failed in one business later started up other lines of business (*Renmin Ribao*, Nov. 7, 1983, p. 1, May 19, 1983, p. 5, Sept. 10, 1984, p. 1, Nov. 7, 1983, p. 1, Oct. 19, 1983, p. 2). In many cases of bankruptcy, a household might begin to produce a commodity anticipating strong market demand for it, yet by the time its products arrive on the market, the market is saturated with the product, or the product is not competitive enough (*Renmin Ribao*, Nov. 7, 1983). Other unanticipated problems also are responsible for failure. For example, in Hunan Province many households began to breed poultry, but a shortage of forage resulted in an epidemic, forcing many poultry-breeding households out of business (*Renmin Ribao*, Nov. 7, 1983).

‡*Renmin Ribao*, Apr. 26, 1984, p. 2, May 5, 1984, p. 2, July 20, 1984, p. 2, Feb. 1, 1983, p. 2. To gain a strong competitive position and to meet growing demand, many specialized households have pooled their capital, labor power, and expertise to form joint-stock cooperatives (ibid., Jan. 20, 1984). These cooperatives usually are small enterprises made up of three to five households. Profits are distributed as dividends to stockholders, and those who work are paid according to their contribution of labor. If the scale of production increases to a point that household labor no longer is sufficient, the joint-stock cooperatives can hire laborers on a contractual basis (ibid., Apr. 26, 1984). The emergence of joint-stock cooperatives has enabled peasant entrepreneurs to overcome the limitations imposed by individual household production and to launch private enterprises that can produce for both local and regional markets. The pooling

the state-initiated reforms was expressed in the virtual explosion of market activity and in the diversity of new organizational forms. In his view, the state assumed the role of encouraging, legitimizing, and popularizing new organizational forms that were in accord with its reform agenda.[20]

It has been estimated that up to 14 percent of rural households are specialized, although after a national conference on specialized households in October 1986, a figure of 2.3 percent or 4.5 million peasant households was given.* In part the wide range in estimation may result from a definitional problem: because virtually all peasant households engage in marketing activity, the *zhuanye hu* classification is to some degree arbitrary. In my 1985 village survey, I was struck by the pervasiveness and intensity of the entrepreneurial spirit among peasants I interviewed. Many said that their primary object was to make more money from their household sideline production. Sideline income made up slightly over 50 percent of total peasant household income; indeed, the dramatic increases in peasant household income in recent years can be largely attributed to its rapid growth. In the village survey, specialized households made up 3.7 percent of the households in the sample, slightly higher than the current national estimate, as might be expected in periurban counties. If other categories of peasant enterprise are included, peasant households that operate business enterprises in market towns (3.2 percent) and those that engage in commercial activity only in the village (1.8 percent), then the proportion of enterprising peasant households is closer to

---

of capital has facilitated capital accumulation and investments needed for expanding the scale of production in a competitive market environment. The availability of surplus wage labor has provided a ready source of cheap labor for the peasant entrepreneurs. And joint-stock cooperatives may be in a better position to gain credit from the state rural development bank than single household firms.

To meet the expansion of commodity production, households began to specialize in marketing products. The transport and marketing households (*yunxiao hu*) began to expand from local marketing systems to reach interprovincial markets (ibid., May 5, 1984). Their profit comes from playing the role of middleman between producer and consumer. These proto-merchant households have had problems with a negative public image, having inherited both the prejudices of traditional Chinese culture against merchants and the antimercantile bias of socialist China. Yet, like the other independents, if successful, their profits are frequently many times greater than if they specialized in agricultural production.

*Specialized households have been defined by the state as those households in which family members spend at least 60 percent of their time in specialized commodity production and sell at least 80 percent of their products on the market. Specialized grain-producing households must sell at least 60 percent of their products. The income of specialized households is typically about three times higher than that of other peasant households (Xinhua News Service, Nov. 4, 1985).

8.9 percent. The village survey was based on village cadres' estimates of private household firms. In the household survey (N = 634) 19.7 percent of peasant households reported having invested in some form of private enterprise in recent years, with capital investments ranging from 8 to 20,000 yuan (mean = 1,355 yuan). The discrepancy between the cadres' estimate and the household data reflects differences in the scale of peasant household enterprises. The cadres' estimate points to household firms that have left agricultural production to specialize in commodity production for the market, whereas the household data can be interpreted as the percentage of households that have invested capital in commercial activity since 1978. The official estimate of 2.3 percent probably understates the scope of peasant entrepreneurial activity in China, and as the Fujian household survey data suggest, the earlier estimate of 14 percent of peasant households engaged in some form of private sector entrepreneurship is closer to the mark.

In a rural economy in which marketing atrophied during the decade of agrarian radicalism in the Cultural Revolution, the upsurge of so much new entrepreneurial activity in a brief span of years gave rise to widespread uncertainty and confusion. When societal changes outpace the emergence of clearly defined statements of what is acceptable behavior in a given context, social transactions become problematic because people do not know what behavior to expect of others.[21] Numerous accounts were published in the Chinese press which documented this breakdown of consensus and the lack of legitimacy and a normative framework for market activities. In many areas the informal political discourse among rural cadres and peasants was whether to classify the new specialized households as "socialist" (*she*) or "capitalist" (*zi*). Local cadres warned villagers not to stick their necks out lest they get their heads blown off (*qiang da chutou niao*). A common saying among peasants was that "some people have gone too far in getting rich." In Hebei, one peasant entrepreneur was reported to have earned 32,000 yuan in 1983. Villagers envied his success, noting that his earnings were several times greater than those of the landlords of the past. Some commented, however, that he should not be congratulated for his new-found fortune because his wealth probably would be liquidated in the future.[22] Middlemen entrepreneurs appeared the most vulnerable to biting social criticism, probably because of the traditional cultural bias against merchants. These entrepreneurs were frequently characterized as immoral for profiting from others' efforts without producing anything themselves (*tao bieren yaobao, buwu zhenye, bu zou zhengdao*).[23] Another commonly heard characterization of the new entrepreneurs was "If a person gets rich, there must have been something that he did that was underhanded." Negative stereotypes of entrepreneurs were widespread, and according to one report, this made entrepreneurs feel that they were victims of "discrimination, sarcasm, and even attack." These stereotypes characterized entrepreneurs as "complex or mixed elements," "shady characters," "people who engaged in crooked ways and dishonest practices, in gambling and speculation, and in making ill-gotten gains."[24]

Their vulnerability to social criticism left many peasant entrepreneurs exposed and insecure about their status within the community. Reflecting this sentiment, one entrepreneur confided, "People in the village talk a lot about me, and I have a heavy mental burden. Some people have even said that specialized households will be repudiated. I am a little afraid."[25] Entrepreneurs worried that they might be attacked by jealous neighbors in a future political campaign.[26]

The lack of a normative framework to support entrepreneurship also fueled widespread speculations about a possible reversal of agrarian policy. Entrepreneurs wondered whether, as in past periods of liberalization, market-oriented policies adhered to in times of economic difficulty would be abandoned when the economy improved. Such uncertainty and anxiety worked to erode the confidence necessary to make long-term investments. From a cost-benefit standpoint, the risks for many appeared very high, as reflected in the following statement: "My family has made considerable investments on contracted land and we harvested nearly 20,000 jin of grain last year. But we always fear that some day the policy will be changed, and the land will be taken away from us, and our efforts will be wasted."[27] This perception tended to encourage the pursuit of short-term profits, often in fly-by-night or speculative ventures, rather than to make the long-term investments that the state sought.

To counter the social criticism and negative stereotypes of entrepreneurs, the state mounted a major propaganda campaign to encourage peasant entrepreneurs. The campaign to demonstrate official approval for entrepreneurship lasted for several years and filled the national, provincial, and local media with upbeat images of the new entrepreneur.* Typical of the tone of the state's effort to provide ideological support for entrepreneurship is the following editorial:

*The international presses were also fed the new line on the positive socioeconomic role of entrepreneurs by the Chinese state, as witnessed in the many articles that surfaced in U.S. newspapers and magazines describing visits and interviews with China's "10,000 yuan households," new millionaires, and other enterprising entrepreneurs.

It is only natural that they [entrepreneurs] have become rich first on the strength of their superior features of being adept in technology and in business dealings. . . . It must be admitted that in the countryside today . . . it is hardly sufficient in doing things to rely sheerly on arduous and hard work, or on exertion of manual labor, or on taking advantage of traditional methods and old experiences. . . . [Instead] the ability to study and learn scientific knowledge and technical know-how, to be adept in absorbing various kinds of information and intelligence, to improve business management methods, and to dare to try out new ventures without fear of bearing the risks involved [are necessary for success]. Only the sum total of all these capabilities provides the main road for the new type of peasants to become rich in the 1980s.[28]

The slogan "to be rich is glorious" permeated the Chinese media in news accounts that described in glowing terms the success of entrepreneurs who developed new products and firms, in documentary films highlighting the visits of high-level state cadres to bestow social honor to successful entrepreneurs, and in television features that projected an image of entrepreneurs as modern, enterprising, and efficient. The conferring of social respectability to entrepreneurship was pursued with single-minded tenacity by the state's propaganda machine. It helped to create a new climate of legitimacy for the market activities of aspiring entrepreneurs among cadres, the primary readership of the party-controlled newspapers. The creation of a public ideology supporting entrepreneurship and the pursuit of profit is an especially important form of state intervention when previous to the market reforms legal norms regulating and safeguarding market transactions and property rights were lacking.

Local Cadres and Market Reforms

Many rural cadres initially viewed decollectivization as a threat to their control over local resources.* The opposition of local cadres to decollectivization was probably widespread, and in some areas county governments used heavy-handed measures to force brigades and teams to decollectivize.[29] In my 1985 survey of three agricultural counties in Fujian, a clear pattern emerged whereby peasants expressed overwhelming approval for decollectivization and market reforms, but many rural cadres expressed skepticism and in some cases continued opposition. In one village I visited, cadres described the many meet-

---

*Those in positions of bureaucratic power have a vested interest in maintaining bureaucratic allocation over economic resources. See János Kornai, "Bureaucratic and Market Coordination," *Osteuropa Wirtschaft*, 29 (Dec. 1984): 306–19.

ings they organized in 1981 when they were being pressured to de-collectivize by the county government. Through their mobilization of peasant opposition and refusal to comply, this brigade succeeded in warding off decollectivization until finally the pressures from the county government proved too strong, forcing the rural cadres to ca-pitulate. By this time the former model brigade was among the final holdouts for collective farming in Tongan County.

According to Elizabeth Perry, "Rural violence—of both the religious and secular varieties—has undergone a resurgence in recent years."[30] Perry argues that the resurgence of rural conflict and violence was often led by rural cadres who sought to mobilize discontent and un-rest in the countryside. Why were local cadres more apt to oppose decollectivization, while peasants were more likely to prefer individual household production? First, in collectivist agriculture, the state acting through rural cadres controls the allocation of resources and man-power in the village. Under household production, allocative power is shared by the market and the state, and peasant households take con-trol of agricultural production into their own hands. Decollectiviza-tion thus weakened the organizational basis of the rural cadres' power. Second, as the functional roles of rural cadres in agriculture were reduced through decollectivization, their political and social power was also threatened. Peasants complained about having to support rural cadres, their lifestyles, and their leisure, viewing them as "free riders."[31] Though local cadres often sought to mobilize their political capital to take advantage of new market opportunities,[32] many lacked the work experience to farm efficiently, not to mention starting up new enterprises in a competitive market economy.

A survey of 20,989 households in Ying County, Shaanxi Province, revealed that rural entrepreneurs came from varied backgrounds, but in general they tended to possess some technical expertise. Ac-cording to the survey, entrepreneurs came from the following social backgrounds: urban-educated youths who settled in the countryside, urbanites who returned to their villages, demobilized soldiers, pro-duction team cadres, artisans, and "honest" businessmen.[33] Former production team cadres made up 43 percent of the specialized house-holds, whereas educated youth, demobilized soldiers, and craftsmen constituted the majority at 51 percent. In light of the relatively high rate of participation by peasants in former cadre positions within pro-duction teams, one should not put too much weight on their former cadre status. Moreover, team cadres participated directly in agricul-tural production, working in the fields next to ordinary peasants, and were not principally involved in bureaucratic coordination as were brigade-level cadres. The sampling procedure for the Shaanxi survey was not specified, and therefore it is difficult to interpret the findings. In the Fujian household survey, which was based on a probabilistic sampling technique, only 1.12 percent of the peasant entrepreneurs (N = 123) were currently cadres, whereas 1.92 percent were former production team cadres, and a mere .48 percent were former brigade cadres. Clearly, few local cadres in Fujian were able to mobilize political capital to become entrepreneurs in the newly expanded private sector.

As enterprising peasants rushed in to take advantage of new marketing opportunities, whether as brokers or entrepreneurs, increasingly they encroached on the power of rural cadres. Though some new peasant entrepreneurs came from cadre backgrounds, especially those who became middlemen or brokers, most entrepreneurs who ventured into nonagricultural commodity production did not. Entrepreneurs who start up household businesses in the production of handicrafts, food products, cash crops, and light industrial products often need prior work experience and technical expertise. Local cadres are apt to be experts in the management of human relations, possess administrative experience, and have access to organizational resources, all qualities that enhance entrepreneurship in state-controlled economies. The commercialization of the rural economy opened up new opportunity structures for entrepreneurial peasants whose competitive advantages were typically based upon technical expertise and access to appropriate technologies, rather than political capital. Competition between local cadres and emergent entrepreneurs thus set the stage for new lines of social cleavage and conflict in rural communities.

We have little reliable data on how well cadres have fared while they are still in office. There may well be former cadres in the new rich peasant elite, but most are no longer cadres in the sense of currently holding an official position. In my 1985 rural survey, I interviewed current village cadres who complained that there was a widening gap between their own earnings and those of their more prosperous neighbors. Indeed, reports of growing incidents of corruption among cadres may be an indication that cadres are experiencing difficulty in making ends meet on their official salary. The sharp increases in recent years of malfeasance among cadres can be interpreted as an indicator that as a group, cadres have fallen behind economically relative to the new rich peasant elite and have sought to compensate the relative decline in economic status through illegal means. There is scattered evidence of a decline in the status and prestige of village cadres in reports of violence committed against them that go unpunished. For example, the *Hubei Daily* reported several instances of violence against a village party secretary, which left him with a brain concussion and injury to his right cornea, and an attack on a party member in another village that resulted in facial disfigurement and loss of memory owing to a brain concussion. The letter to the editor urged protection of lower-level cadres: "Both Chen and Deng were injured while on duty. In the first case, the injured man has not been able to pay his medical bill. And his assailant does not feel sorry and has not been punished. In the latter case, the victim was compensated for only half his loss. Though arrested, the attacker was released as 'not guilty.' "[34]

Though decollectivization weakened rural cadres' organizational base of power, they still retained their middleman role, mediating exchanges between state and society, which, in turn, helped to prop up their social power in the community. Though the village government no longer has responsibility for managing agricultural production, it retains ultimate control over the allocation of land and other remaining collective assets, decides on the allocation of state production contracts, and is responsible for the collection of taxes and other fees. Village cadres have the power to negotiate production contracts between the state procurement agency and peasant households, setting the quota that households must meet before they can sell surplus products on the free market. They have the power to grant extensions to contracts and licenses and to terminate contracts if it is determined that a household has violated the terms of its contract or has not fulfilled it within two years. Their power to issue licenses and negotiate contracts for the lease of collective property and enterprises gives cadres the final say as to which households in the village will have the opportunity to develop the major productive assets of the village for private gain. This and their power to negotiate the terms of the leases and contracts have redistributive implications within the village.

To illustrate the contractual power of rural cadres, I cite the case of Zhejiang Province, where four households contracted with a brigade to grow peaches for three years, agreeing to pay the brigade 5,200 yuan for the right to manage the brigade's peach orchard. In the first year of the contract, the four households fulfilled their contract and derived a handsome profit of 2,000 yuan per household. Their profit, however, incurred the jealousy of cadres and neighbors, who argued that it was gained at the cost of the brigade. The brigade cadres contended that they had set the contract fee too low and subsequently withheld the profits. The four households then brought the case to the county court for arbitration. The court ordered the brigade to hand over the profits to the four households. Shortly after the arbitration, the brigade abruptly terminated the contract with the four households and transferred it to another group of households.[35] In another case, peasants were unable to meet their quota because of natural disasters in the area. Local cadres forced them to compensate for their quotas and debts by handing over their horses, cattle, pigs, carts, sewing machines, and grain. They also threatened to take away land assigned to households that refused to comply with their requisitions.[36]

In promoting market reforms, state managers sought to create an environment favorable to the development of entrepreneurship in rural communities. Not only did the state seek to extend credit to aspiring entrepreneurs, but it worked hard to persuade peasants that the new market policies were genuine in encouraging them to enrich themselves through their entrepreneurial activities. The state sought to assure peasants that their properties and profits were not at risk as they had been in the past because the new policies represented stable, long-term commitments by the state. Safeguards also were provided for private investments in public property, especially in arable land.*

Simultaneous to the state's effort to stimulate rural entrepreneurship, frequent reports of hostility and abuse of entrepreneurial peasants by rural cadres appeared in the Chinese press. The number and frequency of these reports, published in the official news media read primarily by cadres, indicate the dimension of the problem. In general, the reports of cadre opposition were most frequent in the early stages of market reform, when many cadres opposed decollectivization. But once it became clear that the reform policies were stable and were backed by the national leadership, many rural cadres sought to use their power and access to public resources to benefit from market reforms. Thus reports of malfeasance among cadres grew dramati-

---

*In the early phase of decollectivization, households were assigned land only on a temporary basis. But because peasants were reluctant to make investments on land that might be taken from them to be reassigned to their neighbors, the contracts awarded to households to farm a plot of land were extended to two to three years. Even this extension proved too temporary for peasants. Eventually, the period of land assignment was extended to ten to fifteen years. In many provinces peasants now have the right to inherit the rights to land from their parents. Specialized households may lend their land out to neighbors and kinsmen, and in return they receive a portion of the harvest to meet their consumption needs. The state furthermore stipulates that peasants are to be compensated for investments and improvements they make on their land if the land is taken away from them to be reassigned to another household (*Renmin Ribao*, July 25, 1983, p. 2).

cally and outnumbered reports of their opposition. But whether it was opposition or malfeasance, both forms of deviance were interpreted by the state as detrimental to the successful implementation of its reform policies. The reporting and discussion of cadres' opposition and malfeasance in party newspapers reflects the seriousness of the problem. It also implies that the party regarded such incidents as deviant behavior, not so pervasive and intractable that solutions could not be found.

Malfeasance among cadres was more apt to incur state sanctions when it threatened to undermine the institutional context required for the growth of peasant entrepreneurship or when it interfered with the workings of the market as an efficient allocative mechanism. There were many reports describing how cadres squeezed entrepreneurs by imposing unauthorized local taxes and levies.[37] In Jiangsu Province, for example, rural cadres imposed extraordinary levies on peasant entrepreneurs, forcing them to pay for the repair of the brigade's truck, for a new local water conservation project, and for banquets held by the brigade cadres. Numerous accounts described how rural cadres took advantage of their social power by freeloading off entrepreneurs, dropping by their homes and shops for free meals and banquets.[38] There were other stories about how rural cadres used their power to wrangle from entrepreneurs partial ownership of new firms;[39] to withhold profits made by households that sold their produce to the state so as to augment their own salaries; to take from peasants a portion of their crops over and above what was stipulated by their contracted quota; to threaten to cancel arbitrarily leases and contracts held by peasant entrepreneurs to public land or properties; and to rake off huge profits by playing a middleman role in the sale of peasant products.[40]

Not only did some rural cadres use their power to squeeze peasant entrepreneurs, but there were many reports of cadre-led social conflict directed against entrepreneurs. A typical account describes how, in Hubei, the village (*xiang*) and district (*chu*) cadres forced their way into a private restaurant, smashed the furniture and dishes, and forced the restaurant to close after they learned that the restaurateur had filed complaints that he had lost 1,500 yuan to forced requisitions for free meals by rural cadres.[41] The vulnerability of peasant entrepreneurs to the power of rural cadres was heightened by the existence of jealous neighbors in the village community. Some reports described how jealous neighbors stole entrepreneurs' crops, vandalized their property, and slaughtered their animals under cover of night.[42] Some accounts described how rural cadres mobilized crowds of jealous neighbors to vandalize, attack, and intimidate peasant entrepreneurs.[43] For example, in Gansu Province, a peasant who opened a bran mill discovered one day that her electricity had been cut off by village cadres. She complained to higher-level authorities, and her story of harassment by village cadres was picked up by the provincial newspaper. Angered by the exposé in the provincial press, the cadres threatened to retaliate, but she continued to expand her business. One day, the brigade's electricity was shut off by the county power plant because of the brigade's negligence in paying the village electric bill. The incident triggered a minor riot in the village when the village cadres led a hostile mob of villagers to cut the household's power line, forcing her out of business.[44] The outcome of such harassment, hostility, and social conflict was to discourage, isolate, and in some cases drive out entrepreneurs from their businesses.[45] At the very least, the mere threat of mobilizing jealous and suspicious neighbors against them perpetuated a climate of worry and insecurity among peasant entrepreneurs.

Though rural cadres were hostile toward the emergence of autonomous economic power, they have not shirked from using their political power to take advantage of new economic opportunities for themselves, their relatives, and friends. Some local cadres have sought to take advantage of the effort to solve the problem of overfragmentation that resulted from the land distributions carried out during decollectivization. In some areas where only recently 70 to 80 percent of households farmed, the reconcentration of land has reduced the proportion of households engaged in farming to 20 to 30 percent.[46] Some cadres have used their power to transfer to their own households a disproportionate share of arable land.[47] In Jiangsu, rural cadres were reported to have forced peasants to contribute free labor to farm their fields and to use the brigade's fertilizer without paying for it.[48] Cadres in the administrative village (*xiang*) have used their power to obtain business licenses for their relatives and friends, ignoring the applications of others. They have also engaged in illegal speculation by using their power to purchase commodities from the state marketing agency to sell locally at marked-up prices.[49] Local cadres have used their power to market excess household products to state purchasing agencies.* The most common example of malfeasance, however, appears to be the acceptance of bribes for official favor.

---

*For example, in Jiangsu Province, a commune party secretary sold 5,000 gloves to the commune for 75 cents a glove, which his household manufactured at a cost of 30

In describing these major areas of cadre deviance, opposition, and malfeasance, I am not arguing that rural cadres have not played a supportive or positive role in market reforms; they have done so or the market reforms in agriculture might have stalled, or at least would have been less successful. Nor am I arguing that "grass-roots" cadres are doing better in the reform era compared with peasant entrepreneurs. Despite the rise of cadre opportunism and malfeasance, on balance village cadres have experienced a decline in power relative to the peasantry.* Instead, I have described cadre deviance to show how emergent markets are embedded in social structures in which cadres play a pivotal role and how this embeddedness often distorts the allocative mechanism of the market and impedes the role that peasant entrepreneurs might play in economic development. Finally, I argue that the deviance of rural cadres poses an incorrigible problem for the state as long as local cadres can draw on exchange networks built on personal connections within the state organization, enjoy relative immunity to state sanctions against malfeasance, and perpetuate their middleman role in the allocation of public resources. As long as the organizational boundaries of the agrarian bureaucracy remain relatively open, the state cannot effectively curtail cadre malfeasance; in short, its capacity to intervene to perform the regulatory roles required to sustain the development of a market economy is reduced.

Reorganization of the State Structure

How did the Chinese state resolve the dilemma of organizational recalcitrance? The subterfuge played by many village cadres in seeming to support reform policies, and yet in their actions undermining them, posed a difficult dilemma for the state. The very people whom the state relied upon to serve as functionaries in the implementation of policies intended to establish market structures and norms were instead frequently the source of the state's difficulties. Not only were many village cadres deeply involved in venal pursuit of private gain by drawing on their positions in networks that gave them privileged access to both public and private resources, but they posed an obstacle to the rise of a new entrepreneurial stratum that could serve

cents, even though there was little market demand for these gloves (*Renmin Ribao*, July 17, 1984, p. 5).

*See Victor Nee, "A Theory of Market Transition: From Redistribution to Markets in State Socialism," *American Sociological Review*, forthcoming.

as a dynamic agent of technical innovation and economic growth in the state's new market-driven rural development strategy. Entrenched in both the organizations of local state power and social power, village cadres proved difficult for the state to bypass. Unlike recalcitrants within the state bureaucracy, who can be dealt with through established bureaucratic procedures such as lateral transfer, retirement, expulsion, and purge, village cadres posed a dilemma that required a different solution.

Earlier in the paper I pointed to the lack of clear organizational boundaries between the state and local society. This condition grew out of the need for deep penetration by the state to carry out land reform and collectivization. In both periods of social change, the state needed to maintain a permanent political and organizational presence in village communities. In both cases, the penetration of state power into villages required the recruitment of village leaders into formal organizations which state managers sought to use as a means to maintain control over social and economic processes in the village. Relatively open organizational boundaries were implicit in the very concept of the people's commune, which sought to unify within a single state organizational system activities of the state, economy, and society as part of the Maoist strategy to promote the eventual merging of state and society. The Maoist attraction to the Paris Commune ideal probably reflected not so much a sympathy for its democratic vision as the recognition of its status as symbol in the Marxist lexicon of the possibility and desirability of a local government in which state and society were fused into one sociopolitical entity.

What was striking about the people's commune system, made up of the commune administration, the production brigade, and the production team, was the lack of clear organizational boundaries between the state and society. Although the commune administration was formally the lowest level of state organization, the actual boundaries of the state could not be so sharply drawn. Formal and informal ties linked the commune administration with village organizations—the people's militia, party branch, brigade, team, peasant association, women's association, and youth league. These organizations were not indigenous to the villages; but they were put there by the state to secure its control over the villages. The quasi-military organizational form of the people's commune system followed the logic of state power as it penetrated rural society. During the Cultural Revolution, the expansion of bureaucratic controls over spheres of social and economic life fostered an organizational culture that emphasized personal connections, factional loyalty, and the "gift economy" in the allocation of state resources and services, the net result of which was to embed the state even more deeply in society.*

From 1983 to 1985 the Chinese state rapidly dismantled the people's commune system and in its place established the township government. Whereas the people's commune integrated the management of commune enterprises and agricultural production with the responsibilities of local government, decommunization has sought to take the state out of the business of economic management. To accomplish this, the commune has been reorganized into the township government to handle civil affairs and routine state administration. The responsibility for overseeing the commune enterprises and other economic concerns appears to have been entrusted to new corporate entities—vertically integrated corporations (*yitiao long*), horizontally integrated corporations (*nong gong shang lianhe gongsi*), and joint-stock companies (*lianheti*) or other shareholding arrangements.

It could be argued that the demise of the people's commune was a response to the vacuum left after decollectivization, which sharply cut back the commune's economic responsibility in overseeing agricultural production. According to this view, without collective agriculture to supervise, there was no longer a need for the people's commune. But this argument does not explain the commitment to get the state out of economic management, nor does it explain why decommunization was accompanied by a sustained state effort to upgrade the quality and professionalism of the township bureaucracy, which replaced the people's commune. Why would the state invest its resources in building a modern, more professional bureaucracy after dismantling the people's commune system? Getting the state out of the economy to eliminate sources of economic inefficiency is certainly consistent with the thrust of market reforms in agriculture. Nevertheless, its critics' association of the people's commune system with ineffective local government and weak state capacity and the state's new commitment to building a professional local government bureaucracy, staffed by younger and better-educated bureaucrats with technical expertise in specialized areas, points to another interpretation.

*For an in-depth analysis of the gift economy, *guanxi*, and state redistributive economy see Mayfair Mei-hui Yang, "The Art of Social Relationships and Exchange in China" (Ph.D. dissertation, University of California, Berkeley, 1986); and Thomas Gold, "After Comradeship: Personal Relations in China since the Cultural Revolution," *China Quarterly*, 104 (1985): 657–75.

In the many editorials and reports published in the party's news-paper and journals that emphasized the need for "sound government" staffed by "full-time" professional bureaucrats we see the outlines of a new regulatory state replacing the Maoist mobilizational state.[50] De-communization, in the words of Vivienne Shue, "is involved both in the institutional transformation and in the transformation of values entailed in any commercial revolution."[51] This transformation, I con-tend, is likely to result in the gradual closure of the organizational boundaries of the rural state structure, in bureaucratic rationalization, and ultimately in enhanced state capacity. Already this was evident in remarks made in 1985 by village cadres who complained to me that the new township government had become more inaccessible and less approachable through personal connections.

The initial evidence of bureaucratic change at the village level ap-pears consistent with the direction of administrative change espoused by the Chinese state. In the village survey, we can see trends that point to change in the quality of village cadres. Table 5.1 shows that the number of cadres with a primary school education has declined from 55.9 percent in 1978 to 47.8 percent in 1984, while there has been a steady increase in the number of village cadres with junior middle school education, from 17.8 percent to 33.3 percent, and senior mid-dle school education, from 4.6 percent to 15.5 percent, and a slight increase in the number of village cadres with higher education, from .3 percent to 1.5 percent during the same period. Table 5.2 shows a decline in the size of village government after decollectivization (1981–82) from 11.9 to 9.2 cadres per village. There has also been a notice-able trend toward younger village cadres with the mean age dropping from forty-one years in 1978 to thirty-eight years by 1984. I do not have systematic data on changes in the composition of cadres in the township government, but impressionistic evidence from my survey suggests that a similar trend toward a new professionalism reflected in younger and better-educated township cadres has been in progress since decommunization.

The Rise of a Regulatory State

In state socialism market reforms require the state to assume new responsibilities for creating market structures and for regulatory in-terventions. There are striking parallels in the forms of interventions required by both the capitalist and socialist state in creating and main-

TABLE 5.1
Mean Educational Attainment of Brigade Cadres

Educational level	1978	1980	1982	1984
Primary school	55.9	57.6	59.2	47.8
Junior middle school	17.8	17.9	17.8	33.3
Senior middle school	4.6	4.6	4.4	15.5
Technical school	0.3	0.3	0.3	1.5

NOTE: The mean was standardized for a cross-year comparison.

TABLE 5.2
*Percent Change in Mean Number of
Brigade Cadres for 29 Villages*

Year	Mean^a	Percent change
1978	11.9	—
1980	11.7	−1.7
1982	11.7	0
1984	9.2	−22.4
1978–84	—	−22.7

^{a} The mean of the number of brigade cadres per village (29 villages surveyed).

taining what in essence are regulated markets. I shall first illustrate the role played by the socialist state in creating new market structures through two case studies: the creation of new rural market towns and the establishment of capital markets. Then I shall analyze the organizational dynamics of regulatory intervention that pushes the state toward bureaucratic rationalization.

STATE INTERVENTIONS TO CREATE NEW MARKET TOWNS

From 1982 to 1984 the number of people living in rural market towns increased by 25 percent. Much of this increase resulted not from village-to-town migration but from state policy and interventions to reclassify entrepreneurial villages into market towns. As market towns, these centers of peasant entrepreneurship become entitled to state services denied them as villages. More important, they can more readily be encouraged to develop new market structures that can assume a central place in the state's economic strategy for promoting rural industrialization and rural-urban trade. In Zhejiang Province, which has prospered enormously through the market reforms, there has been a 2.55-fold increase from 1978 to 1983 in the volume of trade between cities and rural market towns and a 70 percent increase in the number of rural markets. Chinese state planners believe that the trends toward rapid expansion of market towns and rural enterprises will continue, and they estimate, for example, that in Zhejiang Province, 70 percent of the rural work force will leave farming to work in enterprises located in market towns. In the emergence of the rural market towns as major commercial and production centers, we can see the close interaction between natural economic growth and state policy. Since the Third Plenum of the Eleventh Chinese Communist Party Central Committee in 1978, the Chinese state has actively intervened to encourage the development of rural towns as centers of industrialization and commercialization, absorbing surplus agricultural labor power and thus stemming growing pressures for rural migration to the cities.[52]

STATE INTERVENTIONS TO ESTABLISH NEW CAPITAL MARKETS

My second case study focuses on the formation of new capital markets, the culmination of which has resulted in the creation of a new security exchange in Shanghai and in other urban centers. The establishment of the Shanghai stock exchange addresses the problem of capital formation for urban industries; a more widespread problem, however, has been the issuance of securities in rural enterprises. From 1978 to 1985 the number of registered private businesses in China grew to 11.2 million, employing over 16.6 million people.[53] Most of these businesses have been rural enterprises established by peasant entrepreneurs in villages and market towns.* Issuing securities is still uncommon in rural areas, but in recent years there has been a sharp increase in interest in this form of capital formation; in 1984 alone, capital raised through stocks and bonds in China amounted to about 5 billion yuan.

The rapid increase in the use of securities as a means of capitalization for new firms has caused concern within the state about regulating this method of capital formation. Once again we see a complex interaction between state policy, market action, and state interventions.

---

*According to my village survey, the most common forms of capitalization for peasant household businesses have been personal savings, bank loans, personal loans, and joint-stock arrangements.

The market reforms legitimated private sector production, especially in villages and rural market towns, which in turn gave rise to demand for capital to finance new enterprises. As entrepreneurs and firms turned increasingly to the issuance of securities as a means to raise capital, the problems created by an unregulated free capital market provoked state intervention. We can see the state's interest in establishing the normative and institutional framework for a security market in the following statement by reform economist Liu Delin:

The norms of raising capital are incomplete and the convertibility of stocks and bonds into cash is not strong enough. Those (individuals and units) who organize the raising of capital in society usually do not have clear-cut and concrete rules formulated beforehand. The powers and the economic responsibilities of the shareholders are not stipulated. In some cases, only verbal agreements prevail and the necessary formal procedure is lacking. The share certificates issued do not show whether they are stocks or bonds or the kind of securities purported. Attractive terms, such as keeping the share capital intact, regular payment of interest and dividends, permission to withdraw midway from participation, and so forth, are offered to attract capital funds. Regarding the issuance of share certificates, some of the companies do not actually print and issue the share certificates; rather, they merely register the names of the shareholders, issue receipts to them, and on this basis pay them the share interest or dividends when due. Certain regions have gone so far as to resort to noncompensatory or irrecoverable capital-raising or compulsory levies and assessments, arbitrarily asking subordinate enterprises to subscribe to the sharers, or ordering their staff members to buy the shares or bonds. In addition, our country has no stock market facilities and the banks do not discount shares or accept them as securities for loans. As a result, the convertibility of the securities into cash is extremely low or is nonexistent. All this not only brings confusion to the raising of capital in society, but also restricts the scope of the issuance of share certificates and bonds and hinders the raising of capital funds. This is definitely harmful to those enterprises which have bright prospects and are under capable management and to the relevant departments in rapidly raising large amounts of capital funds.[54]

Clearly the logic of this line of reasoning pointed to the establishment of regulated capital markets.

From 1979 to 1985, ministries and commissions under the State Council have issued more than four hundred regulations concerning agriculture alone that have included regulations on forestry, protection of aquatic resources, marketing of farm produce, labor market, land, and taxation. There are many other general regulations that also affect agriculture. According to the Ministry of Agriculture, Animal Husbandry, and Fisheries, additional regulations will be required to meet the explosion of litigations and disputes over land, water resources, forests, orchards, bankruptcy, and the legal rights of peasant entrepreneurs and rural firms.[55] As in the case of capital markets, the initial surge of economic activity within unregulated free markets created the demand for regulation. For example, in mountainous areas, specialized households, responding to market demand for forest products, harvested timber so intensively that forests were rapidly denuded.[56] In agricultural areas, water conservation facilities formerly maintained by the brigade administration fell into disrepair and were vandalized and equipment stolen. Farmland was lost to private housing construction and became the sites for new plants and shops built by peasant entrepreneurs in villages and market towns.[57] Disputes between peasant entrepreneurs and the township government over contractual terms of leases for orchards, land, and enterprises require impartial litigation in local courts. The proliferation of fake and shoddy products in diverse rural industries generated demand from consumers and producers for regulation to protect the brand names of established enterprises and consumers' rights.[58]

Demand for regulation of the market economy can be generated by investigative reporting, which exposes new social problems. For example, in a report filed on abuses of child labor in Zhejiang, we learn that Wenzhou City and Cangnan County sent a cadre work team to Jinxiang Township to investigate 284 rural factories that employed 483 child laborers ranging in age from 10 to 16 years. The following summary of the work team's investigation illustrates how demand for state regulation is generated by social problems created by an unregulated market. The work team reported that the age distribution of child laborers in Jinxiang Township ranged from 10 years to 16 years, with the mean age of 13.6 years; 83 percent (405) were young girls, and 94 percent (454) came from surrounding villages to work in the factories and were not residents of the township. The illiteracy level of the child laborers was high at 30 percent. Only 20 percent of the total group had completed the first and second grades of primary school, though 4 percent had graduated from junior middle school before starting to work in the Jinxiang factories. Child laborers worked from eight to eleven hours a day, with some working extra night shifts. The wage scale was based on a piece-rate system, which yielded daily earnings from 1.2 yuan to 3 yuan. The report, however, emphasized that poor working conditions in the factories were harmful to the child laborers' health:

The child laborers are engaged in more than 20 different types of work in production, including lacquer paint touchup, gluing, platemaking and plastic platemaking which uses xylene, cycloketone, and banana oil as the major solvents. These chemical raw materials are toxic, endangering the physical and mental health of the child laborers. The high-frequency machines commonly used by the small factories are also subjecting the working child laborers to the danger of radiation. The working conditions for the child laborers are often poor, with several types of work taking place in crowded workshops, and there is no special ventilation and lighting equipment in the factories and the employers do not issue any protective gear for work. We learned that the child labor problem is not confined to Jinxiang Township, it also exists in Qianku, Yishan, Bacao, Lupu and other places in Cangnan County in varying degrees.[59]

Similarities between the working conditions reported above and those of child laborers in the Industrial Revolution in the West are striking. This investigative report on the plight of child laborers shows how the demand for regulatory interventions might arise from reactions to the ravages of an unregulated market. As Polanyi wrote, "the introduction of free markets, far from doing away with the need for control, regulation, and intervention, enormously increased their range."[60]

Another dimension in the state's intervention to establish regulated markets is its interest in protecting its own monopoly position in key commodities and industrial products against private competition. This interest can be seen in the State Tobacco Bureau's fight against the virtual explosion of unregulated tobacco production and new tobacco factories. To eliminate this source of competition, the State Tobacco Bureau worked to get the State Council to promulgate the "tobacco monopoly regulation," which made illegal the production of tobacco leaves and cigarettes outside of the state monopoly. To gain control over the illegal production of tobacco leaves, the State Tobacco Bureau issued 2 million new tobacco permits to small growers. To eliminate private competition in the manufacture of cigarettes, it pressured local governments to close down tobacco factories operated by private entrepreneurs or lower-level administrative units producing outside of the state plan. With a profit rate of up to 500 percent, cigarette production is a natural target for entrepreneurs, who can easily undersell state monopoly units and still make a large profit. When the bureau failed to shut down local tobacco factories, it sought to block the flow of raw material and equipment to the factories and have their products confiscated. In spite of these efforts, which included appeals for a coordinated attack through price controls, tax policy, public security interventions, and the cooperation of the railway and telecommunication departments, the deputy director of the State Tobacco Bureau, Ma Erchi, acknowledged that after two years of fighting the illegal manufacture of cigarettes, "tobacco factories not included in the state plan have not yet been completely closed down, the tobacco market is in disorder, and there is a very serious problem of counterfeit and black market cigarettes."[61]

The weak link in the State Tobacco Bureau's fight against private competition apparently was the reluctance of local governments to shut down highly profitable tobacco factories in their localities, which is consistent with proposition 2, which predicts lower state capacity because of open organizational boundaries and societal penetration of the lower levels of the state apparatus. Entrepreneurs of new privately owned cigarette factories can use personal connections with local officials to seek protection for their businesses. Moreover, plant managers of nonstate collective tobacco firms can use personal ties to persuade officials in the county government to protect the local tobacco industry from the central tobacco ministry. Local government, I have argued, is rife with *guanxi* networks that interpenetrate state and society and is the center of the "gift economy" characterized by the exchange of gifts for official favor. Regulatory interventions cannot be effective without the strict subordination of local administrative bureaus to higher levels of the state bureaucracy, and this realization, I contend, pushes the state toward bureaucratic rationalization.

To illustrate the complexities of market reform, in which state allocation and market forces interact to create structural sources of cadre malfeasance and market distortions, I shall examine the problem of the allocation of motor vehicles to rural areas in the aftermath of market reforms. Before the market reforms, vehicles were allocated by the State Bureau of Supplies only to state agencies and enterprises; in recent years, however, private demand for trucks and cars has increased dramatically because of the rapid increase in peasants' buying power. In the spirit of the market reform, private individuals and enterprises now can purchase motor vehicles and compete with public agencies for the quota of vehicles allocated by the state to rural areas each year. In 1985 the quota of vehicles allocated for sale to rural areas by the State Bureau of Supplies and the China Motor Vehicle Company was slated at 76,500, far short of the demand. Because demand has far outstripped supply for the past several years, vehicles sold by the state could be resold to newly rich peasants at windfall profits. For this reason, the vehicle market attracted speculators who used *guanxi* ties to secure favored access to the limited supply of vehicles and credit from the People's Bank to purchase the vehicles, which they could then quickly resell at several times the purchase price. Similarly, cadres who worked in the county government, either in the state allocation bureau or with personal connections to someone in the bureau, could profit from speculation in motor vehicles through the gift economy, outright bribes, or directly sharing in the profits through so-called "trading companies."

To stem the speculation in vehicles and to ensure that vehicles could be purchased at reasonable prices, the State Council issued a ruling in 1985 that 70 percent of all vehicles must be sold to cooperative enterprises, with the remainder available for individual consumers. Only firms or individuals who were issued vehicle-purchase permits were eligible to buy a vehicle from the state.[62] Temporary county allocation groups were created to review applications to screen out speculators. As a further safeguard against speculation, permits were made nontransferable, and the county allocation group was forbidden to receive any fees other than those covering the cost of handling the vehicle-purchase permit. It was also stipulated that cadres who "practice favoritism, engage in fraudulent activity, accept bribes or sell vehicle-purchase permits for profit" were to be prosecuted if caught. According to proposition 2, it is doubtful that the state's effort to maintain its monopoly position will succeed in stemming private speculation in the sale of motor vehicles as long as organizational boundaries remain open in the county government and a Maoist organizational culture remains strong, especially in light of what we know about the economics of shortage.[63] This case study also illustrates how market reforms provoke regulatory interventions and helps us to understand further the organizational dynamics that are pushing the state toward bureaucratic rationalization (proposition 3b). Even in attempting to impose monopolistic constraints on market exchanges, in a mixed economy legal-rational bureaucratic discipline and state autonomy are required.

In partial reforms by which the socialist state seeks to develop a market economy within a socialist economy, market dynamics can generate powerful incentives for cadres to use their power and position for personal gain in market transactions. The acceptance of bribes can result in prosecution, and the gift economy in *guanxi* relationships typically yields a smaller payoff to the cadre than the value of the official service or resource. Direct participation in market transactions by cadres, however, can be highly profitable, and until recently it was legal. For this reason many cadres established or became shareholders in private "trading companies" or "trade centers," which bought from the state and sold to the public. Recent scandals involving illegal activities by trading companies such as smuggling foreign imports, speculation, and profiteering have provoked vigorous state interventions to investigate trading companies for conflict of interest and illegal activity, to force the resignation of cadres from private enterprises and businesses, and to close down trading companies that operate as fronts for cadres wheeling and dealing in the marketplace for personal profit, or to reregister the trading companies as part of the state organization.

According to Ren Zhonglin, the director of the State Industrial and Commercial Administration, in the first nine months of 1985 the state had uncovered more than twenty-seven thousand illegal firms, involving more than sixty-seven thousand state cadres, and was in the process of investigating over two hundred thousand private trading companies,[64] many of which were established in rural county towns and townships. Bank offices in rural areas now also prohibit their officials and staff from holding concurrent posts in private businesses.[65] The renewed effort to impose sanctions against profiteering and speculation by cadres and to police the organizational boundaries of the state as a means to curb malfeasance, I argue, is similar to the intent of decommunization. It is part of the larger effort to achieve organizational closure; for without a greater degree of organizational closure the state has little hope of intervening effectively in a regulatory capacity.

In recent years the State Council promulgated an ambitious agenda of new regulations that specified the legal norms for the new market economy. It is impossible to review all of these State Council documents because they cover diverse aspects of the market economy; I shall instead make general observations about them. First, these regulatory codes reflect a decisive move away from the prereform system of Maoist *kadijustice*, based on the case-by-case review and personal discretion of state officials, toward a legal-rational basis of authority. The norms are clearly stated, in abstract, universalistic terms, and are highly specific. They are based on individualistic assumptions about the rational interests of participating parties, defining and specifying legal rights and liabilities. Though there continues to be a noticeable tendency to subordinate the interests of individual and private enterprise to that of the state, nonetheless, the new regulations specify limits to state power and the rules and normative framework within which individuals, firms, and the state must act, and thus seek to eliminate the arbitrary and unpredictable quality of Maoist *kadijustice*. Second, the regulations assume legally binding contracts, specify the rights and obligations of parties to the contract, the liabilities for breach of contract, the use of mediation or arbitration at a higher administrative level to settle disputes, and the right to press suit in the people's court. Third, to be legally binding, all contracts must be written documents, not oral agreements. Fourth, the regulations are written in legal and technical language, are impersonal and objective, and are based on legal-rational discourse, rather than the political rhetoric of the Maoist era. The responsibility for interpreting the regulations is entrusted to the appropriate ministries and the people's court. If there are areas of ambiguity which require further refinement or if more detailed regulations are required, the responsibility to formulate them is entrusted to the appropriate state ministries. Fifth, all levels of the state organization must maintain files and documents. Sixth, officials and staff must have specialized knowledge and training, and the development of specialized administrative bureaus to implement the regulations is encouraged. Finally, the content of specific articles of the regulations reflects the attempt by the state to solve problems arising in implementation of market reforms and to define and enforce the legal and normative framework of a market economy operating side by side and interacting with a dominant state sector.

I shall summarize briefly two sets of regulations, the loan contract regulation and income tax regulation for collective enterprises, as examples of the scope and content of the new state regulations.

The loan contract regulation specifies the legal norms governing loans made by banks to private firms and individuals. The document is organized into five separate chapters and contains twenty-four articles, which specify the rights of lender and borrower in making and implementing loan contracts, the terms for alterations and termination, and the liabilities for breach of contract and violation of the law. It states that loan contracts are legally binding as soon as they are signed and that both parties must observe the terms of the contract. The loan contract must specify the type, purpose, amount, interest rate, repayment schedule, method of repayment, terms of security or guarantee, and liability for breach of contract. The collateral offered to guarantee the loan must be sufficient to repay the loan. "Lenders have the power to check and examine the use of loans," and borrowers "must provide lenders with information related to plans, statistics, financial, and accounting statements and data." The loan contract may be altered or terminated only under conditions specified in the loan contract regulation. And liabilities for breach of contract are carefully defined and specified.[66]

The income tax regulation for collective enterprises contains twenty-one articles specifying the conditions for tax exemptions and reduction, the accounting records to be kept by firms for tax purposes, the

right of tax organs to investigate for possible tax evasion, the dead-
line and guidelines for submitting income tax returns, the timing and
method of quarterly or monthly tax payments, the penalties for delin-
quent payment and for tax evasion, the rights and avenues for appeal
by the taxpayer, and the rights and procedures to be used by the state's
tax organs to investigate and enforce tax laws. The income tax regulation also specifies a progressive tax schedule of eight grades with tax
rates from 10 percent to a high of 55 percent. It entrusts the Ministry of Finance with the responsibility for interpreting the twenty-one
articles and formulating more detailed regulations for their implementation. Taxes must be paid to local tax organs, which means in
rural areas that the county or township tax offices must maintain detailed files and have the capacity to audit firms' accounts, the expertise
to interpret tax rulings, and the organizational discipline to enforce
tax rulings without partiality to personal considerations, methodically,
continuously, and on a routine basis.[67]

The normative basis of bureaucratic rationalization and its link to
market reform are clearly evident in the State Council's new regulatory code. If the Chinese state is ultimately successful in building a
modern bureaucracy, staffed by professional bureaucrats recruited for
their specialized knowledge, increased state autonomy and capacity
can be expected to develop over time. The more bureaucratic the state
organization, in Weber's sense of the legal-rational bureaucracy, the
greater the degree of state autonomy, and the more likely its organizational boundaries will be closed to societal encroachment or penetration (proposition 2). The central features of the modern bureaucracy
—rule-governed action, strict subordination of lower levels to higher
levels, the separation of the office from the officeholder, and the impersonal task-orientation of the modern office—tend to generate an
organizational culture hostile to the pervasive use of *guanxi* to gain
official favor or services.

The future of China's ambitious market reforms remains open-
ended, dependent on the outcome of the politics of succession that
will inevitably follow Deng Xiaoping's death. The student protests in
Shanghai and other urban centers in December 1986, reminiscent of
the May 4th Movement of 1919, may have augured the opening stage
of the politics of succession, when competing visions of the future and
political factions position themselves for the succession. If the reform
faction led by Deng Xiaoping is able to survive the politics of succession and retain its control over the higher levels of state power, we

can expect that the market and organizational dynamics I have analyzed in this paper will most likely continue to propel China toward an economy in which the market plays an increasingly important allocative role. If so, China may well emerge by the twenty-first century as a mixed economy bearing important similarities to such East Asian economies as Taiwan, South Korea, and Japan, with perhaps a stronger and more dominant state sector. In this case, the social processes I have analyzed will mark the early stage of China's transformation into "Asia's next economic giant," as forecast by Dwight Perkins.[68] If, however, market reforms are derailed after Deng's passing from the scene, I am inclined to think that the Chinese state may evolve in a manner more similar to the contemporary Soviet Union, albeit governing a poor, underdeveloped economy, with deepening social divisions. Thus the political faction that gains control of the levers of state power, whether reformers or conservatives, will have the decisive say in what becomes of China as it enters into the twenty-first century.

When socialist states launch market reforms, they need to legitimize reform policies among the staff and intervene to create the institutional framework of a mixed economy. Fundamentally this effort requires the state to specify a new structure of property rights and reduce transaction costs both within the market sector and especially between the market and state sectors (proposition 1). Without the state's intervention to initiate market reforms in the first place, the events I have written about simply would not have taken place. Yet I have also pointed to the limits of the state's capacity for autonomous action imposed by its embeddedness in *guanxi* and other exchange networks that interpenetrate the state and society, especially at the lower levels of the Chinese state. According to proposition 2, state structures characterized by relatively open organizational boundaries are likely to be susceptible to societal penetration and claims and are therefore less likely to be potent organizational actors in Weber's sense of a modern bureaucratic organization. Thus the capacity of the state to intervene is weakened when opposition to its policies emanates from social groups that have penetrated the state. To resolve the dilemma of organizational recalcitrance, state managers are likely to resort to restructuring the apparatus of power to close the organizational boundaries of the state, reducing the likelihood of penetration by problematic social groups.

In this paper I pointed to the problem posed by the opposition and malfeasance of cadres as indicative of the extent to which emergent market transactions are embedded in social structures in which cadres play a pivotal role. And I documented how the state's capacity to implement its market reform was frustrated by rural cadres whose opposition and malfeasance posed an incorrigible problem to the state. Only by restructuring the organization of state power (decommunization) and policing its organizational boundaries (sanctions against malfeasance), I argue, can the state achieve greater closure of its organizational boundaries. The extent of openness and closure of these boundaries, however, is relative, because the social boundaries of organizations are always to some extent permeable. Nonetheless, the flow of informal exchanges between the state and society through exchange networks can vary considerably depending on the extent to which boundaries are defended.

Where market coordination of the socialist economy has expanded in scope, increased horizontal relationships between buyers and sellers are likely to reduce the extent of vertical segmentation characteristic of command economies. Thus although in some sectors relative closure of the organizational boundaries of the state may result in a gradual decline in the importance of exchange networks between the state bureaucracy and social groups, this does not imply that economic transactions will become less embedded in *guanxi* and personal connections. The continued growth in the scope and volume of market transactions in rural areas, where 80 percent of the population resides, and in rural-urban trade will most certainly stimulate the formation of horizontal linkages or *guanxi* relationships within society. To the extent that hierarchical forms of economic coordination remain dominant, however, personal connections between state organs, firms, and households will continue to provide critical informal linkages. This is especially true in urban society, which has few sources of employment outside of state enterprises and bureaus and in which progress in market reform had all but stalled in 1988.

If market reforms are sustained and there is a rapid expansion of private markets, market action is likely to provoke regulatory interventions by the state, according to proposition 3a. Unregulated markets provoke state interventions to regulate their action, as illustrated in the case studies on child laborers, capital markets, the state tobacco monopoly, the motor vehicle market, and private trading companies. The promulgation of hundreds of new regulations by the State Council in recent years has laid the legal foundations of a new regulatory state and is defining the institutional and normative framework for a mixed economy (proposition 3b). The essence of regulation, to enforce rule-governed action, requires the establishment of legal-rational authority. The dynamics of (indirect) regulation may involve a retreat from the particularistic microinterventions to macroeconomic regulation. China is just beginning this transition.[69]

The Hungarian experience of partial reform, however, points to the seemingly intractable difficulties of balancing market coordination and bureaucratic regulation in the state sector of the socialist economy. The dilemma analyzed by János Kornai of "dual dependence," in which markets are emasculated and dominated by bureaucratic microregulations, may prove to be inherent in any partial reform effort. But in both Hungary and China, the nonstate sectors, agriculture and the private economy, have experienced the greatest success in market reforms. In China, peasant entrepreneurs, disciplined by hard budget constraints and driven by the profit incentive, have demonstrated the dynamism of market coordination. However acrimonious the debate over the future of market reform may grow in China, the relative success of the agricultural reforms is likely to serve as a reference point for renewed reform efforts.

SIX

Eastern Europe in an Epoch of Transition: Toward a Socialist Mixed Economy?

Ivan Szelenyi

The 1980s are a time of crisis and reform for Eastern Europe. In this paper I explore the nature of the current crisis of state socialism, analyze the reform strategies of the last decade, and speculate about alternative scenarios for the future.

In discussing three different theories of the socialist economic crisis, the theories of cyclical crisis, of the general crisis, and of the crisis of transition, I hypothesize that Eastern Europe today is in a crisis of transition. The current economic recession is deeper than past cyclical crises were, but it still may not be severe enough to qualify as a general crisis. State socialism may still be capable of adapting to the challenges of the intensive stage of growth.

I distinguish two ideal types of past reform strategies: the strategy to rationalize the redistributive economy and the strategy to open up opportunities for the second economy. After initial successes, by the mid 1980s both strategies proved inadequate to resolve the ever-deepening crisis.

My conclusion is that Eastern Europe is most likely to become a socialist mixed economy. Such a transformation presupposes the radical expansion of the second economy from a consumption-oriented, part-time, secondary activity to investment-oriented private enterprise. In the socialist mixed economy, bureaucratic-redistributive integration remains dominant, but its failures are increasingly compensated by a vigorous network of private enterprises.

The Current Crisis of State Socialism

Two decades ago most East European economists believed that crisis was an exclusive characteristic of market capitalism. During the last decade it became obvious that cyclical movements in the economy and recurrent periods of stagnation or even decline in production are as inherent to socialism as they are to capitalism. Thus one fascinating new task of political economy is to develop the theory of socialist economic crisis.

THE THEORY OF CYCLICAL CRISIS

Michal Kalecki and András Bródy discovered during the 1960s that the socialist reproduction process has its own cycles. Tamás Bauer was inspired by their ideas, and in one of the most fascinating East European books of recent times he developed a full-fledged theory of the cyclical crisis in socialist economies. Bauer analyzed a wealth of statistical data on economic growth and investment patterns from different East European countries for the last three decades. He demonstrated that the economies of virtually all East European countries experienced cyclical fluctuations, periods of overheated growth followed by periods of slowdown or outright recession.[1]

These cyclical movements were analogous to but very different from Western business cycles. To explore these differences as well as similarities, Bauer compares Western capitalist and East European state socialist economies with "the method of mirrored comparisons" recently articulated by David Stark. Whereas in the West economic crises tend to result from overproduction, in Eastern Europe the major cause as well as indicator of crisis is overinvestment. The two systems are indeed mirror images of each other: overproduction and the lack of sufficient demand for goods cause crisis under capitalism; the reproduction of the economy of shortages, a tendency toward overinvestment, and excessive demand for goods cause crisis under state socialism.[2]

This theory has elegance and power, and it is obviously useful to explain many state socialist economic phenomena during the last two decades. But how much can we learn from it about the present economic crisis?

In a lecture delivered at the Institute of Economics, Hungarian Academy of Sciences, in June 1982 Wlodzimierz Brus asked a few penetrating questions about the validity of the cyclical crisis theory. Brus agreed with Bauer that the socialist economy indeed grew in a cyclical manner during the 1950s and 1960s, but he found that in 1975 Eastern Europe began to experience unique economic difficulties. The current crisis has lasted too long; it is too deep and broad to qualify as just another cycle in socialist economic growth.

The long socialist depression of the 1970s and 1980s has several unique features:

1. It has been exceptionally long. Earlier socialist crises lasted for one or two years. The present one started a decade ago and has not yet ended.

2. During earlier cycles, growth rates were low and living standards stagnated at the bottom of the cycle. During the current crisis, several countries produced zero growth rates. The Polish economy collapsed in the same way the most severely hit capitalist economies did during the Great Depression of the 1930s. Living standards are not only stagnating, they are declining.

3. The current crisis is so severe that socialist countries are falling behind core capitalist countries and may even be sliding from the semiperiphery toward the periphery.[3]

While socialist economies have been moving deeper into crisis, the capitalist world economy and particularly the core countries began to emerge from their own recent long recession. Since 1982 most core capitalist countries brought inflation under control, interest rates came down, and growth rates increased. For the first time in the history of communism, East Europeans, laymen and experts alike, admit to a widening gap between East and West. Since the Bolshevik revolution communist regimes have claimed that they are more dynamic than capitalism. And indeed there have been signs of such dynamism since 1917 in Russia and since 1949 in Eastern Europe. The gap in economic development between advanced capitalist countries and formerly peripheral or semiperipheral state socialist countries appeared to be narrowing. This situation changed in the mid-1970s, however, and today most East Europeans think their economies are becoming more backward every year.

Many Hungarian economists whom I have interviewed during my frequent trips to Hungary compared Hungary, Poland, and Romania with such Third World nations as South Korea, Taiwan, Brazil, and Mexico. They argued that though all these countries had their share of problems during the last decade, particularly during the great international debt crisis, at least some of them used the crisis to restructure their economies. Hungary, Poland, and Romania borrowed from the core countries as excessively as many developing countries did, but socialist planners invested the borrowed capital ineffectively and reproduced a backward, internationally noncompetitive industrial structure. Korea now exports computers and other high-tech products to the United States and Western Europe, but Hungary is known for its wine and salami, Poland for its cucumbers, and Romania for its jam and honey. My Hungarian economist friends did not fail to remind me that Hungary did much better during the 1930s. During the interwar years Hungary was on the semiperiphery, but it could export some fine industrial products, including radios, electrical goods, trains, and buses. Today the Council for Mutual Economic Assistance (COMECON), or at best the Third World, remains a market for such Hungarian goods. In COMECON, communist countries exchange their mediocre industrial products, which are not marketable for hard currency, and their hard currency revenues depend on the export of agricultural goods, raw materials, and semifinished industrial products.

The current crisis in Eastern Europe is not limited to the economy. It is simultaneously a political and a legitimation crisis. Until the early 1970s in all countries of the region there was a large and articulate communist minority, which superimposed an ideological hegemony of socialism and Marxism over the majority. During the last decade this hegemony has withered away. Marxism ceased to be the normal social science discourse, and even the word *socialism* was devalued. Bourgeois democratic, nationalist, and religious values have been gaining ground. Until recently Poland has been the only country to develop a full-fledged political and legitimation crisis, but now signs of increasing legitimation problems are present everywhere.

THE THEORY OF THE GENERAL CRISIS OF SOCIALISM

Many of the younger Hungarian economists whom I interviewed agreed with Brus. They regard the current crisis as a qualitatively new phenomenon, more serious than just another cycle in socialist reproduction. But they are even more pessimistic than Brus. On the basis of discussions with young economists from the Institutes of Economics, Sociology, and World Economy of the Hungarian Academy of Sciences I put together the sketch of an alternative to the cyclical crisis theory, which I call the theory of the general crisis of socialism. I am particularly indebted for the ideas presented here to Kálmán Mizsei, Gábor Kertesi, and Gyula Pártos, but since the present formulation of this theory of general crisis is mine I have to accept responsibility for its inaccuracies and inconsistencies.

In listening to these young economists I could not help but think of the idea of the general crisis of capitalism, which was fashionable among certain wings of Marxism during the 1930s and 1940s. The notion of general crisis in these circles was counterpoised to the concept of cyclical crisis. It was argued that with the Great Depression, the decay of capitalist world hegemony, and the emergence of a socialist world system, capitalism had entered a general crisis. Past cyclical crises were normal features of capitalist growth. They were normal in the sense that they were inevitable, but they did not threaten the repro-duction of the capitalist mode of production. On the contrary, they served the purposes of such a reproduction. But in a general crisis, the final disintegration of capitalism had begun and lasting recovery could not be expected.

My young economist friends in Hungary seem to think analogously about state socialism. They believe that state socialism exhausted its growth potential and this situation is aggravated by the loss of legiti-macy of the communist regime.

The exhaustion of growth potentials thesis has a softer and a harder version. Those who believe in the softer version claim that state social-ism was a reasonably successful strategy of extensive industrialization, but as this task was achieved it became redundant. The more radi-cal economists formulated a harder version of this thesis: they kept asking me whether the task of extensive industrialization had been achieved. True, the agricultural population was reduced, and a large industrial labor force was created at an accelerated rate, but is this a goal in itself? It is possible to perceive extensive socialist industrializa-tion as quasi-growth, as growth for the sake of growth. The result was inefficient industry, which cannot be integrated in the world market and which produces mediocre products in an unprofitable way. It is indeed not unreasonable to argue that Eastern Europe might be bet-ter off today without the heavy industry created during the 1950s and 1960s. Sztálinváros-Dunaujváros, Nowa Huta, and other new "social-ist towns" and major industrial complexes of the first decade of state socialism are probably not assets today and may even be handicaps for future growth. According to those who believe in the hard version of the exhaustion of growth potentials thesis, state socialist economic growth was never real, not even in the extensive growth stage. The economy was kept afloat in a parasitic way. Its growth was fueled by appropriation of private wealth and by depressed living standards of the population, but no real productive capacity upon which future growth can be built was created. As these sources became exhausted, the economy collapsed.

The general crisis of socialism theory does not imply the automatic or inevitable collapse of state socialism. None of the young economists I interviewed thought that such a collapse is just around the corner.

They believed in a Gouldnerian dark dialectics, in the likelihood of a gray future rather than in the Apocalypse of the negative dialectics.[4] The economy can settle at a low level, locked into the vicious circle of low productivity and the low quality of the COMECON trade. In a world divided into two nuclear spheres, a new socialist isolationism may evolve. Communist countries may decide to continue exchanging products with each other. After all, their products have "use-value" too. The East German car, for instance, takes you from point A to point B; the only problem is that it cannot be sold on the world market for hard currency. The gray economy of technical mediocrity can go on virtually indefinitely as long as technical innovation is guaranteed in the one area of military industry.

Since Mikhail Gorbachev came to power, those factions of the Soviet elite are gaining influence who do not want to settle for a gray economy of stagnation and who may believe that the long-term military balance must be based on a more dynamic civil economy. As a result, they seem to be ready for reform and compromise. Still, the gloomy picture presented above cannot be dismissed. Who knows how thick the ice is upon which Gorbachev is skating? Can Gorbachev's task be accomplished? Does he have the will and power to carry out deep enough reforms? It is too early to answer these questions. There is a great deal of bureaucratic opposition to Gorbachev's cautious reforms in the Soviet Union and elsewhere in Eastern Europe, even in otherwise reform-minded Hungary. After a short adventure with reform, the Soviet Union may return to the practices of the Brezhnev years. The stagnation and grayness of Russia under Brezhnev and Czechoslovakia after 1968 may be the normal state of affairs of state socialism.

THE THEORY OF THE CRISIS OF TRANSITION

The distinction between extensive and intensive growth stages played a formidable role in the debates about socialist economic policy during the late 1960s in Eastern Europe, and particularly in Hungary and Poland. The focus of the debates has since shifted, but I still find the pair of concepts insightful, and I will try to develop here, inspired by Ferenc Jánossy's work, what could be called a theory of the crisis of transition.[5]

The term *extensive growth* was often used as a synonym for socialist industrialization or socialist accumulation of capital. Such an extensive growth lasted from the end of World War II until the late 1960s, or in the less developed countries of the region until the mid-1970s.

Right after World War II there was a substantial surplus agricultural population in Hungary, Poland, Yugoslavia, Romania, and Bulgaria and in the Slovak regions of Czechoslovakia. The reduction of this agricultural population through the transformation of former under-employed peasants and rural proletarians into industrial workers generated an impressive growth in industrial output. Since the basis of growth in this period was the expansion of the numbers of industrial workers during the extensive stage, dynamism was concentrated in the production of means of production, or what Marxists call Department I. High growth rates could be achieved, and levels of personal income and consumption were kept down.

As the surplus agricultural population was absorbed into the industrial work force, the strategy of extensive growth had to come to an end. Now the economy could grow only by increasing productivity and developing new technology. The intensive stage of growth began. There were, of course, productivity gains and technical innovations in the earlier epoch, but for an ideal-typical distinction of the two phases the emphasis on increasing the absolute number of industrial workers in the first epoch and increasing productivity in the second was justified.

In Eastern Europe, Czechoslovakia and the German Democratic Republic (GDR) were the first countries to complete the extensive stage and begin to confront the task of transition during the 1960s. They were followed by Hungary and Poland a few years later. By the mid-1980s virtually all socialist countries seemed to be struggling with the task of transition. Today some of the socialist countries, primarily China, and to a lesser extent the Soviet Union, still have large agricultural populations, thus in principle they could keep growing intensively. But they face a military challenge from the West, which is increasingly based on high technology, and they try to integrate themselves into a world economy in which technological change plays a far greater role than ever before. Under such circumstances it is not surprising that they may feel forced to try to achieve faster technological development, thereby entering the intensive growth stage somewhat prematurely.

The transition from the extensive to the intensive stage is a traumatic experience. It requires the basic restructuring of the economy. The importance of Department I is likely to decline, and pressures are likely to build to increase real wages, increase the production of consumer goods, and move toward a mass consumption society. Even the system of economic management may require fundamental changes. Central planning in the extensive stage involved a few thousand agents, but now it has to predict and influence the behavior of millions or hundreds of millions of consumers. Clearly old planning methods are unsuitable; the entire system of central planning might have to be scrapped.

A similar transition proved to be traumatic for the capitalist world in earlier years. Extensive industrialization in core capitalist countries ended just around World War I. After the postwar reconstruction period, the impossibility of continued extensive growth became obvious, and the capitalist world began to slide into the Great Depression. The Great Depression was a unique crisis, not just another turndown in the world economy. It was a structural crisis, the crisis of transition from the extensive to the intensive stage, and it could have been resolved only by fundamental modifications in the nature of the capitalist economic system.

Around 1930 capitalism was at its breaking point. It was not obvious that capitalism could survive the challenge of transition and learn how to grow when surplus labor was no longer available.

The New Deal, or to put it more generally, Keynesianism, the establishment of the social democratic welfare state, turned out to be a successful strategy to cope with the problem of transition. One essential feature of this strategy was that private business accepted an unprecedented degree of state intervention in the reproduction process. Market failures were compensated for by government redistribution, but the market remained the dominant mechanism of economic coordination. State intervention played a particularly important role in the maintenance of high levels of employment and retention of stable incomes. Under such circumstances the production of consumer goods became the major driving force of economic growth. Capitalism entered its mass consumption stage. In a mass consumption economy labor became expensive and the economy moved away from labor-intensive to capital-intensive forms of production. Technical innovation and increases in productivity gained importance when the economy entered the intensive stage of growth.

The socialist long depression of the 1970s and 1980s is analogous to the capitalist Great Depression of the 1930s. I call the present crisis a crisis of transition in that sense. Those who believe that Eastern Europe at present is in such a crisis do see the socialist system at its breaking point, and they may not be surprised if in the long run it stagnates or even disintegrates. But unlike the advocates of the general crisis of socialism theory, the crisis of transition theorists think that a structural reform of state socialism is still possible. The general crisis theory assumes that socialism cannot grow intensively because all intensively growing economies are based on private ownership. These theorists give socialism the benefit of the doubt. Nineteenth-century bourgeois economists made an error by suggesting that capitalist economies are the only ones capable of capital accumulation and industrialization. Soviet-style economies proved them wrong. The USSR and Eastern Europe did industrialize and proved that there is an alternative road to industrialization. Analogously, why not give the benefit of the doubt to state socialist economies in the crisis of transition? Why not assume that socialism may learn how to function in a stage of intensive growth if it undergoes a deep enough transformation, one that is as radical and far-reaching as the one capitalism experienced following 1930?

Past Reform Strategies

From the reform experiments of the last two decades I construct two reform scenarios: rationalization of the bureaucratic-redistributive coordinating mechanism and reliance on the second economy. The essence of the second strategy is to allow greater freedom to part-time private activity, primarily in agriculture and in the tertiary sector, but to integrate these activities through the first economy, the bureaucratic-redistributive coordinating mechanism.

What I am going to describe are pure or ideal types, so no concrete historical case will fit them perfectly. Still I use East Germany to illustrate the first strategy, Hungary to illuminate the second. This example inevitably oversimplifies the richness of empirical reality. East Germany tolerated a fair amount of small private business, and there are rationalizers among the Hungarian cadre, even among the reformers. These anti-market ideologues had an important influence at various times on Hungarian economic policy.

RATIONALIZATION OF THE BUREAUCRATIC-
REDISTRIBUTIVE COORDINATING MECHANISM

During the late 1950s and early 1960s criticism of Stalinist economic policy emphasized the voluntarism of the planning practices of the earlier epoch. With de-Stalinization the achievements of Soviet economics of the 1920s were rediscovered. It was a widely held belief among economists in the Soviet Union and Eastern Europe that many of the earlier failures of the economic policies could be corrected by drawing on more sophisticated planning methods that were developed by scholars such as L. Kantorovich, V. V. Novozhilov, and S. Strumilin.[6] The application of mathematical methods such as linear programming and input-output tables was perceived by many as an alternative to the introduction of market mechanisms and increased managerial autonomy. In the Soviet Union during the early 1960s a lively debate took place. E. Liberman represented the views of decentralizers, those who would reform the market system, and L. Kantorovich was regarded as the representative of the rationalizers, who believed that good econometric models could do whatever the market could. There is no real need even in a mass consumption economy to let the anarchic forces of the market loose; with proper modeling not only the behavior of a few thousand firms but also the anticipated action of hundreds of millions of consumers can be predicted.

The idea of scientization of economic management and the program of social and political engineering were popular in all of Eastern Europe, particularly in Czechoslovakia and East Germany, during the 1960s. Radovan Richta's book *Civilization at the Crossroads*, a manifesto of the scientific-technical revolution, became a best-seller in the region before 1968.[7] Even in Hungary, where market reform had been the hegemonic ideology among economists since the mid-1950s (Antal Máriás, Tibor Liska, György Péter, and others were advancing such ideas before 1956), the vision of socialism as a scientifically planned rational order held attraction.

During the last years of Nikita Khrushchev's rule it was unclear which camp would be victorious, but by the late 1960s the Libermanites were losing ground in most countries as a result of the political counterattack of the bureaucrats. The reform experiments in Czechoslovakia were crushed in 1968, and the Soviet Union was sliding into stagnation under the bureaucratism of the Brezhnev epoch. Neither market reformers nor rationalizers had much influence in these countries; rather, a sort of neo-Stalinist restoration was under way.

In contrast to the stagnation in Czechoslovakia, East Germany emerged during these years as the leader in the scientific-technical revolution, claiming that with more rational planning methods the socialist economy could work even in the epoch of high technology and perform well in competitive world markets. The history of East Germany during the early and mid-1970s is fascinating. Those of us who at that time lived in Eastern Europe followed developments in East Germany with great skepticism. I remember on my own trips to East Berlin, Dresden, and Leipzig around 1970–72 the long lines in front of restaurants, the hopeless fight for taxicabs, which were in short supply, the boring displays in department stores, the stupidity of *Neues Deutschland*, the central party newspaper, and I have to confess that I was never impressed, not for a minute. Still, the East Germans claimed to be among the great economic powers of the world. They claimed to be catching up fast with West Germany, and though their industrial products may not have fared extremely well on the world market, they at least harvested an extraordinary number of gold medals in the Olympic games and world championships. They claimed that these achievements, including their success in sports, were the consequence of the superiority of their scientific methods of management.

East Germany thus achieved some domestic legitimacy (even the young Rudolf Bahro, for instance, was an enthusiastic socialist technocrat). I was amazed when sometime during the late 1970s a leading Swedish Marxist sociologist told me the GDR was the best example of socialism, and he was not alone in such views among the Western Left.

During the 1970s East Germany was often compared with Hungary, the ideal type of the second economy reform. Those who favored the East German road argued that East Germany had achieved as dynamic an economy and probably more affluence than Hungary but without inflation and increases in inequality, which were the early characteristics of the Hungarian economic policy.

But in the mid-1980s few people maintained their enthusiasm for East Germany. There are empirical and theoretical reasons why one should not be overoptimistic about the rationalization strategy as the method to adapt to the conditions of intensive growth. The East German economic miracle, if there ever was one, no longer looks so promising. First, East Germany may have produced impressive statistics about its economic performance, but it does poorly on the world market and it is not competitive with any of the core capitalist countries in marketing its industrial products. Second, although East Germany still maintains stable prices and full employment, its economic growth is slowing down. Some of my East European economist friends have expressed doubts about the accuracy of these statistics. Last but not least, many East European experts believe that the relative economic well-being of the GDR is the result of trade within the Germanies. Through West Germany the GDR participates in the European Common Market and receives major financial support from the Federal Republic of Germany (FRG).

But one can also question on theoretical grounds whether an attempt to make a socialist economy work with a rationalized bureaucratic-redistributive system is viable. János Kornai's contributions to the political economy of state socialism are of importance in this respect. Since the late 1950s Kornai has been trying to explain the reasons for the inefficiencies in the socialist economy, in particular the shortages, which are the main reason for the failures of all modern socialist economies. In his first book, *Overcentralization in Economic Administration*,[8] he identified overcentralization as the primary cause of economic inefficiencies. But by the early 1970s he began to see that decentralization of economic decision making will not resolve the problem of recurrent shortages. In two important volumes, *Rush versus Harmonic Growth* and *Anti-Equilibrium*, he expanded his analysis.[9] He demonstrated that socialism has an inherent tendency toward accelerated growth and overinvestment. He also showed that changes in the price system, especially the introduction of equilibrium prices, do not eliminate shortages and guarantee efficient, profitable, high-quality production.

But what causes the tendency toward overinvestment and the reproduction of shortages regardless of the price system adopted? His fourth book, *The Economics of Shortage*, offers a persuasive answer to this question.[10] In this book he proved that publicly owned firms always operate with soft budget constraints because of the willingness of the bureaucratic-redistributive center to bail out firms if they are in trouble, thereby producing exaggerated demand, particularly for investment goods.[11]

In *The Economics of Shortage* Kornai does not draw policy conclusions, but I will try to do this for him now. The softness of budget constraints and the reproduction of the system of shortages cause cyclical movements in economic growth in the extensive stage but do not prevent the economy from achieving the tasks of extensive industrialization. In the intensive stage, however, the systematic occurrence of shortages is fatal. As Kornai proved with great eloquence, if shortages occur, firms will try to find substitutes for raw materials that are not available in order to continue production. The tendency toward such substitution decreases quality and lessens competitiveness in a world market oriented toward high technology.

If I read Kornai accurately, in *The Economics of Shortage* he gives up hope of the possibility that a bureaucratic redistributively coordinated economy can work in the intensive stage of growth. Rationalization of the redistributive-bureaucratic coordinating mechanism is not a viable strategy to resolve the socialist crisis of transition and to integrate into competitive world markets, which are based on high technology.

In my reading, Kornai is the theorist of the socialist mixed economy. Socialism may still be reformable, but it will be able to interact with a high-tech world market only if it allows the emergence of firms with hard budget constraints, that is, private enterprises. The state sector may remain dominant, but it has to be supplemented by a vigorous private sector.

EXPERIMENTS WITH THE SECOND ECONOMY

Over the last ten to fifteen years the Hungarian regime began to show increasing tolerance for small-scale, part-time private business, normally referred to as the second or secondary economy. This trend began in agriculture. By the late 1960s restrictions on the crops that could be produced on one-acre family plots were lifted, and an impressive growth in food production resulted.[12] Hungary became the first communist country that did not suffer from food shortages. Its markets were full of fresh fruits and vegetables, meat, and dairy products. Encouraged by the success of this small-scale, part-time farming, Hungary began to open up similar opportunities, first in the tertiary sector and to some extent in industry. An impressive boom in private housing construction occurred, a reasonable service industry was created, and cities were well served with restaurants and small shops. Hungary was on its way to becoming a mass consumption society in which personal consumption becomes the driving force in economic growth. By the mid-1980s 70 percent of the households in Hungary earned incomes from the second economy, and about a fifth of the income earners received a third or half of their incomes from private business activities. As a result, by the mid-1980s Hungary appeared more affluent than the GDR or Czechoslovakia. East German and Czechoslovak statistics may have claimed differently, but the objective observer who visited East Berlin, Prague, or Budapest in recent years undoubtedly found Budapest not only livelier but also more affluent than the neighboring capital cities.

The Hungarian experiments with the second economy proved to be successful socially too. The tolerance toward part-time private activities produced a model of complex class compromises, which allowed Hungary to maintain a relatively high degree of political stability even during the early 1980s, when under world market pressures the Hungarian economy began to crumble and a political crisis began to shake most countries in the region.

As a part of these class compromises the Hungarian bureaucracy made certain concessions both to the technical intelligentsia and to the working class. The origins of these compromises, the willingness of the bureaucracy to grant concessions, and the readiness of the intelligentsia and the working class to accept them can be traced back to the 1956 revolution. With a touch of irony, Hungarian intellectuals frequently claim that 1956 was the only successful revolution in their history. Indeed, many of the economic demands, though not the political ones, of the opposition movements of 1956 were met by the mid-1970s. The Hungarian bureaucracy learned the lesson of history. The generation of the *apparatchicks*, which came to power in 1957–58, is still in power. They have vivid memories of 1956, and they want to avoid the recurrence of revolutionary upheavals. This cohort of bureaucrats was willing to give up some power in exchange for stability. The intelligentsia and the working class similarly learned the lesson of history. They learned that excessively radical demands for reform will be met by coercion. By the mid-1960s they were also ready to compromise. To the intelligentsia the bureaucracy made mainly political and ideological concessions, to the working class mainly economic ones.

After 1965 the bureaucracy demonstrated some willingness to share some of its power with the technical intelligentsia.[13] The power of technocrats, particularly at the enterprise level, was increased. Reform committees were set up. The reform-minded intelligentsia (the majority of the university-trained intellectuals belong to this category) was invited to join these committees.

The composition of the bureaucracy, both in the state and in the party apparatus, began to change. Some of the "old-line bureaucrats" were replaced by technically highly skilled though politically loyal technocrats.[14] The ideological intelligentsia was also rewarded for loyalty by an impressive degree of political liberalism, some freedom of speech, and almost unlimited right to travel abroad.

By the second half of the 1970s a significant proportion of the Hungarian working class, particularly the peasant-workers, learned that they could have a relatively prosperous life, despite the inefficiencies and low wage levels in the redistributive sector of the economy. As the second economy expanded, many workers began to regard the time spent in government-owned firms as a compulsory labor service delivered to the "state-lord" in exchange for freedom to engage after hours in highly productive and profitable private activities.

This system was the outcome of a decade-long class struggle, not a master plan by a political genius such as János Kádár or the reform intelligentsia. Through a silent revolution from below, workers and peasant-workers gradually carved out greater freedoms for themselves, not through collective political action but through everyday economic practices. This silent revolution dissolved class conflict at the point of production and eased class antagonism between redistributors and direct producers. The Hungarian workers, unlike their Polish counterparts, lost interest in trade unions. Even the level of their wages declined in importance for them. Whatever happened to them in the state enterprises was of diminished significance. For them life began after they left the gates of enterprises. Workers rewarded the liberalism of the regime and decreased government interference in their private lives with some loyalty and a certain degree of legitimacy.

Around 1968 the Hungarian bureaucracy, with the cooperation of most of the technical intelligentsia, attempted to implement a new system of economic management to reform the statist economy. During the past two decades precious little happened along these lines. The relative success of the Hungarian economy during the 1970s was not the result of an effective reform of the state sector from above, a reform by design. Rather, it was a reform by default. To compensate for its failure to implement its reform design for the statist sector, the Hungarian bureaucracy gradually withdrew its restrictions and allowed people to act as they wanted to act. In a way, the Hungarian peasant-workers taught their new masters a lesson: if they are left alone they can resolve many of the problems the bureaucratic sector is unable to cope with.

The Hungarian workers accepted at least for the time being their dependent status within the sphere of bureaucratically organized production because they gained substantial autonomy as consumers and producers within the second economy. Relative material affluence and de facto autonomy as part-time petty commodity producers compensated for the lack of autonomy in state industry and for limited political and civic liberties.

From the early 1970s onward a process of socialist embourgeoisement began in Hungary.[15] In the process of creating a civil society, former proletarians, peasants, and peasant-workers became part-time entrepreneurs. They gained some economic autonomy from the "state-lord," but at this stage without a clear conception or guaranteed institutions of citizenship. In this Hungarian socialist embourgeoisement process, somewhat paradoxically, former proletarians are transformed into bourgeois first, citizen second.

The notion of civil society received a great deal of attention among East European dissidents, particularly in Poland, during the last decade. But the concept of civil society has not been clearly defined. It is, after all, an ambiguous notion, which refers simultaneously to civic liberties and political freedoms usually associated with bourgeois democracy, but it also connotes private economy, capitalism, and private property. Can these two meanings of civil society be separated from each other? Can one have civil society without a bourgeoisie in the economic sense of the term, or can one at least begin this process with the development of civic culture and political reform?

Poland during the late 1970s and early 1980s experimented with an extraordinarily innovative alternative that those of us who share socialist values found particularly attractive. The Solidarity movement was a bold attempt to build civil society without private ownership, to renegotiate the state-society relationship within a fundamentally statist economy. The Poles conducted a struggle at the political level in which they tried to create citizenship without entrepreneurship.

The Polish case was unusual, and the Hungarian strategy of embourgeoisement more closely resembled what we know from the history of Western Europe. Under Western feudalism burghers gained economic autonomy first, establishing their rights to private ownership of the means of production before they developed institutions of bourgeois parliamentary democracy. At least in the past, capitalism appeared as a necessary though not sufficient condition for democracy and civic liberties.

It would be a historicist error to conclude that therefore the Solidarity experiment was inevitably doomed to failure and the Hungarian strategy will work. Solidarity was defeated under a specific historic conjuncture. The international situation, and in particular the domestic political situation of the Soviet Union, may have been in part responsible for the tragic outcomes of 1981. Furthermore, by the mid-1980s the Hungarian economic and social miracle had ended. I will briefly summarize the unfolding economic and social-political crisis in Hungary today.

The emergent economic crisis. Since late 1982 the weaknesses of the Hungarian economy have become increasingly apparent. The statist economy's failures were so severe that the highly restricted secondary economy was unable to compensate for them. What were the signs of these failures of the bureaucratic-redistributive sector? First, the statist sector was stagnating; it had produced almost no growth since the late 1970s. Real wages were declining, and living standards increased only because incomes were generated in the secondary economy. Second, the bureaucratic-redistributive coordinated industry was unable to produce enough high-quality consumer goods to absorb the incomes generated through the secondary economy. The Hungarian bureaucracy borrowed heavily from international markets (by mid-1987 the Hungarian debt was by the most conservative estimate $12 billion), and about a third or half of the borrowed capital had to be spent to buy Western consumer goods so as to balance supply and demand. Hungary was spending about half a billion dollars more every year than it was producing. Third, the rest of the borrowed capital was not used much more efficiently. As I noted earlier, Hungary, like Poland and Romania, also failed to restructure its economy. It invested the borrowed hard currency poorly, and its competitiveness on the world market has been deteriorating rather than improving.

Failure of the severely restricted private activities to solve the crisis of the statist economy. It is not surprising that the Hungarian second economy could not bail out the increasingly bankrupt statist sector. Severe limitations were imposed on private economic activities, as follows.

1. Most private activities are part-time. The proportion of full-time entrepreneurs is small, 2 to 3 percent of all income earners, and it is not growing rapidly.

2. Private business is almost exclusively based on self-employment. Employment of wage labor is rare and is discouraged.

3. Capital accumulation in private firms is insignificant. There are few bank loans available for private investors. Business confidence is also low. Entrepreneurs often feel that they are overtaxed, and they are concerned that they may be nationalized again if a new generation of conservative bureaucrats comes to power. Consequently, the second economy is oriented toward conspicuous consumption.

4. Most private business is in agriculture or in the tertiary sector. In those economic activities, in which firms with hard budget constraints are particularly necessary (development of high technology, for instance), the statist sector tolerates little private competition.

5. There are few horizontal links between private firms. Most second economy activities are "integrated" by the bureaucratic sector. Statist companies provide raw materials and semifinished products and purchase products or services. The second economy is therefore segmented by the bureaucratic-redistributive sector and cannot form a system of its own.

Indeed, how could one expect such a highly restricted secondary economy to rescue a mismanaged national economy? It is a miracle that such a secondary economic operation was sufficient to produce the economic prosperity and social stability of the late 1970s and early

1980s. But one cannot expect that part-time farmers, who produce tomatoes or lettuce after working hours on one-acre family plots, will integrate the Hungarian economy into the world market. The relative tolerance of the Hungarian regime toward private incentive gave an exceptional boost for a few years, but by now its energies have been exhausted.

The emergent social and political crisis. As the economic contradictions of the economic strategy to resolve the crisis of transition with a highly restricted secondary economy became more obvious, the broad social coalition upon which Hungarian social stability was based began to disintegrate.

During the happier years of the Hungarian experiments with the secondary economy, the prospect of embourgeoisement gave hope for upward social mobility and increased economic autonomy for the majority of the working class and peasant-workers. Market reform and increased autonomy of enterprise management brought the technocratic intelligentsia into the market-reform coalition. The technocratic wing of the cadre elite, the emergent new petty bourgeoisie and those fractions of the working class who earned significant incomes from the second economy, formed the core of the great coalition of the Hungarian model.

This great coalition was never unopposed. As early as 1972 a group of conservative trade union and party bureaucrats began to form a countercoalition, which I labeled elsewhere the counteroffensive of the ruling estate or the ouvrierist opposition.[16] This conservative opposition (Western Marxists may call these conservatives "left wing," though in the East European context they are "right wing," authoritarian, antireform reactionaries) began to accuse the Hungarian party leadership of being too lenient toward the peasants. They claimed that the working class–peasant income ratio altered in favor of the peasants as a result of the 1968 reform. The conservative forces succeeded in implementing legislation that limited family production. This ouvrierist counterattack against the secondary economy collapsed around 1975–76, partially as a result of infighting within the party and partially because of a strike conducted by peasant-workers. Part-time farmers responded to the reintroduction of administrative regulations of their second economy activities by decreasing their production. As family agricultural production fell back, prices of food on urban markets jumped. The demagoguery of the ouvrierists became obvious: the working class did not benefit from antireform measures. The political climate turned against the ouvrierists. Their main representative in the Politburo lost his position, and the conservative opposition moved into the background.

Since the early 1980s there have been signs of revitalization of the conservative opposition. The ouvrierists may have learned the lesson of their earlier defeat. During the early 1970s they used a pro-working-class, anticapitalist rhetoric, but they had little grass-roots support. The new breed of ouvrierists tries more consciously to create an alliance between those fractions of the working class that were left out of the benefits of the second economy and the conservative, nontechnocratic party and trade union bureaucracy.[17]

One important weakness of the Hungarian experiment with the second economy is that a sizable proportion of the working class does not have access to private incomes. Ideologues of the Hungarian model promoted the idea that everybody is in the second economy, that access to private incomes is similar to access to bureaucratic wages and salaries.[18] This is far from true. About a third of the population has no private income. Furthermore and even more important, different social strata have differential access to the private sector.[19]

There are at least three important groups that have little or no private income.

1. A significant fraction of the state and party elite, particularly middle-level party bureaucrats, earn lower incomes than peasant-workers or small entrepreneurs. At the same time, they think they are losing political power as a result of decentralization of decision making.

2. An important fraction of the urban-industrial proletariat, particularly those employed in heavy industry, highly skilled workers who were well rewarded during extensive industrialization, are losing their relative advantages.

3. The retired, the disabled, and the nonworking poor are especially badly hurt by the inflation of recent years. A political coalition between (1) and (2) could become a formidable political force, which could lead to a policy of recentralization.

One interesting development is that even some of the intellectuals are losing enthusiasm for the reform movement. I repeatedly heard intellectuals speaking against the nouveau riche, the new petty bourgeoisie. A great deal of dissatisfaction is expressed about the low income levels of professionals, teachers, and academics. Even engineers and doctors complain often that small entrepreneurs with little education earn incomes far greater than their own. Some intellectuals, who were wholeheartedly free-marketeers just a few years ago, are now rediscovering the beneficial aspects of state redistribution. They are beginning to defend state subsidies for high culture, higher education, and research, though somewhat paradoxically they are vehemently opposed to the recently proposed personal income tax.

The popular appeal of the second economy may be weakened too. For the first few years it appeared that state socialism was a paradise for the petty bourgeoisie. In this economic system everybody could start a business, high profits could be realized quickly, and the possibility of bankruptcy was minimal. As the number of people who tried to become entrepreneurs increased, this situation changed. Despite the disincentives, some accumulation did take place, and the new entrants did not have the chance to compete successfully with those already in business unless they had capital. Bankruptcy began to spread. The state socialist petty bourgeois dream that in this system everybody who works hard enough will get ahead is rapidly losing credibility.

The Hungarian experiments with a bureaucratically fragmented, highly restricted secondary economy as a compensatory mechanism to redistributive failures are heading toward what appears to be a major economic and social crisis. There is an intense sense of crisis in Budapest today. Not only critical intellectuals but also the ordinary people and even the party cadre are talking about the possibility of an economic and social collapse, which may be as severe and lasting as the one that occurred a few years ago in Poland and Romania. How can Hungary, or the rest of Eastern Europe, learn how to function in the intensive stage of growth?

Toward a Socialist Mixed Economy? Key Issues in Current Reform Debates in Hungary

Despite the increasing influence of the ouvrierist, conservative opposition and the spread of general antireform sentiments, the hegemonic ideology in Hungary remains one of market reform. Return to a monolithic bureaucratic-redistributive economy and recentralization seems unlikely. This strategy did not work in the past, and it does not work in Czechoslovakia or East Germany at present. Even the Soviets seem to be moving away from it.

During 1987 in Hungary two important scenarios are shaping the reform discourse, one prepared by a group of leading economists and other social scientists, the other a document prepared by leading dissidents.[20] The Communist party is on the defensive. Two recent party responses to these initiatives indicate that the party elite does not have an alternative and is ready to accept many of the radical reform proposals.[21] I end this paper with a short review and assessment of these four statements. All four are complex and with the exception of the dissident political reform proposal not particularly lucid, but with more or less reservations they all seem to express the desire to move toward a socialist mixed economy, to radicalize past market reforms, rather than to return to a centralist model. In these reform proposals I see two new elements: they treat the question of diversification of ownership as the central issue, and they realize that such a diversification, and in particular the acceptance of private property as equal to public property, is intimately linked to the need for some political reform. All four statements agree that economic reform cannot proceed without certain legal-political changes.

The first scenario, "Fordulat és reform," which translates as "Turnaround and Reform," initially signed by some fifty economists and other social scientists and finally published under the names of five researchers in the Ministry of Finance in abbreviated form in the major academic journal of economics, makes a distinction between short-term and long-term solutions to the present crisis. The document begins with an analysis of the crisis, which, very much in harmony with the earlier arguments in this paper, links the current recession to the extensive growth period. To adapt to the requirements of intensive growth and a competitive world market, a period of stabilization, a "turnaround" from the present stagflation, is needed. The authors believe that this will require a restrictive monetarist policy. The recommended monetary restrictions will have three components. They require (1) a reform of the taxation system, the introduction of a personal income tax, and a new system of appropriation of revenues from the state enterprises, in the form of value-added tax; (2) liberalization of imports and devaluation of the domestic currency; and (3) increasing reliance on monetary measures of planning. But restrictive monetary measures and the best monetary planning are not sufficient to achieve the long-term solution. To adapt to the stage of intensive growth the system of ownership must be transformed. The main problem with the current system is that economic actors currently lack interest in increasing the wealth of the firms; they wish merely to maximize yearly incomes.[22]

According to the authors of "Turnaround and Reform," "While the solution to the question of ownership will require a long-term reform process one already can begin to build a structure which reflects long-term interests more than the current system [by basing this new structure] on the already existing dualism of state ownership and private ownership."[23] In somewhat opaque language, the document seems to be proposing that the gap between large-scale state firms and small-scale, primarily part-time private firms be filled with a variety of forms of ownership. This would imply that more investment in private firms should be allowed to open up private enterprises to outside investors, including foreign investors, and also to transform some of the state enterprises into joint stock companies (and presumably allow private individuals or foreign investors to own stocks and not just bonds in such firms). "Turnaround and Reform" ends with a call for political reform, more concretely with a call for constitutional regulation of the role of the Communist party, and a stronger government, which is responsible to a democratically elected parliament.

The second scenario, "Társadalmi szerződés. A Politikai kibontakozás feltételei," or "Social Contract. Preconditions of Political Rejuvenation," focuses on questions of political reform. The authors call for reform because they believe that "reform is our hope to catch up with the developing regions of the world. Sabotage of reform is to keep sliding down toward the stagnating nations of the Third World." "Social Contract" names some seven conditions, which are necessary to catch up. The first is "to assure equal rights to all forms of property in the market sphere of the economy. Legal security is required for the creation of private firms and for the investment of private capital. All kinds of economic organizations, all firms have to have identical conditions in taxation, in the credit system, in domestic and foreign trade." This can be achieved only if the following radical changes take place within the political system: (1) the rights and duties of the Communist party must be regulated through legal, constitutional means; (2) the parliament must be given sovereignty to create a stronger government, but one controlled by a popularly elected parliament; (3) freedom of employment must be guaranteed so that citizens are free to choose whether they want to seek employment and where they want to be employed. They also must have the right to form organizations to express their collective interests.[24]

The Economic Subcommittee of the Central Committee of the Hungarian Socialist Worker's party prepared a response to "Turnaround and Reform," which acknowledges that "Turnaround and Reform" gave a "basically correct" diagnosis of the situation and which blames the problems on the antireform tendencies of the ouvrierist opposition between 1972 and 1978. The Economic Subcommittee takes an even stronger pro-market-reform stand than "Turnaround and Reform," which it attacks for attaching too much importance to monetary measures. The statement by the Economic Subcommittee emphasizes instead the importance of the reform of ownership. It rejects the call for the transformation of any of the state firms into joint-stock companies, but it gives strong, though at crucial points qualified, support to the expansion of private business. According to the document: "If we want private entrepreneurs to invest their incomes in the expansion of their businesses, then we have to give institutional guarantees that, within certain limits, they can grow. We have to work out arrangements, which would gradually shift the growing private firms —to the satisfaction of the private owners—toward a social form of ownership."[25] The language is more than cautious; it is obscure. Still, I find it interesting that the Economic Subcommittee of the Communist party favors the expansion of private business over the transformation of government-owned firms into joint-stock companies. During the summer of 1987 the Central Committee of the Hungarian Socialist Worker's party made a statement about economic and social reform, which also underlines the newly won legitimacy of the private sector: "The second economy and the private sector are integral parts of the socialist economy. All initiatives which contribute to the increase of the national income and to the amelioration of the living standard of the population should be encouraged."[26] Both party documents, of course, avoid the real issues of political reform, and they frequently use the phrase "leading role of the party,"[27] which of course is incompatible with the separation of state, economy, and society that is necessary for the establishment of a genuinely mixed economy under socialism.

How much attention should one pay to such reform talk? Certainly not too much. As I pointed out earlier, following 1968 little happened along the lines of the scenario prepared by reform committees. Genuine and lasting reforms are not reforms by design but by default, the products of invisible, everyday struggles, which are fought below the political surface.

Still, Hungary and the rest of the region are in lasting and deepening crisis; they are at a crossroads. Which way will state socialism move? Will it slide into a permanent stagnation, will elites attempt a new wave of recentralization, or will the system move beyond the limited experiences with the secondary economy and allow a full second system of the economy to develop? Will Hungary, or even the Soviet Union, and following their examples, the rest of Eastern Europe become a socialist mixed economy?

In my assessment the most likely future for Hungary and for the rest of Eastern Europe is to move toward a socialist mixed economy. During the next few years I anticipate an increasing differentiation of forms of ownership, experiments with new forms of cooperative enterprises and self-managing firms, and a further and significant expansion of the private sector. I anticipate much more investment in private firms, a rapid increase in full-time self-employment from 2–3 percent to 10–15 percent, with an increase in the number of employees in private businesses. This outcome is not likely to be the doing of the planners. The reform proposals are restricted mainly to changing procedures within the statist sector. But I assume that in the next few years the experiences of the post-1968 epoch will be repeated. Reformers write and talk about new methods of management, new parliamentary committees, and so forth, but as these methods fail they will fall back to the built-in potentials for dynamism—to private incentives. As "Turnaround and Reform" puts it: "With small firms simply by lifting regulations we could produce dynamism and expand the market."[28] Indeed, all other reform measures have higher costs and put pressures on the government budget. Reprivatization requires only paperwork, the elimination of regulations, and changes in laws. This is exactly why during the stagnation of the statist sector the second economy began to blossom, and this is why I expect, according to the logic of reform by default, the mixed economy to develop in the future. Such a reform by default is likely to lead to measures such as elimination of any limits on private investment to allow private individuals to deduct business investments from taxable income; elimination of limits on the number of employees a firm may hire, which also implies the right of individuals to choose employers freely or to decide not to seek employment without any penalties; the right to trade, including the right of private firms to trade with foreign firms and the right to own hard currency accounts and to use hard currency revenues for business purposes; elimination of all restrictions of horizontal ties between private firms; and equal treatment of private and nonprivate firms in matters of taxation and credits.

I am also sure that such developments will have political implications. Proper incentives to the private and semiprivate sectors will require legal regulations of the authority of the Communist party; legal, constitutional guarantees of the sanctity of private property; and security of private investment and of inheritance without prohibitive inheritance taxes. As the private economy expands and the civil society strengthens, political interference in the functioning of the economy must be reduced. The separation of state and society, party and economy, will be slow and gradual. In a way the transformation of state socialism from a monolithic bureaucratic-redistributive economy and a totalitarian political system into a socialist mixed economy with certain democratic institutions is analogous to the transition from a feudal society and absolutist state to a constitutional monarchy with an autonomous civil society and private economy.

My prediction about the economic and social future of state socialism is cautiously optimistic. I think it is possible that a socialist mixed economy will emerge, which may be dynamic enough to stop further deterioration of the international standing of these countries. But in the absence of a drastic break, the statist sector will remain dominant and, even in its self-managing or cooperative forms, moderately dynamic, state socialism still will lag behind the core of the world economy. Diversification of forms of ownership, guarantees of free employment for both employees and employers, and guarantees of private ownership necessarily imply certain civil liberties, but they could fall far short of the fully developed institutions of Western "bourgeois" democracy. With some good luck, what we can expect is more, but still modest, dynamism with more, but still limited, democracy in the new socialist mixed economy.

One could present a gloomier scenario too: East European bureaucracies with ideological stubbornness may resist the development of the mixed economy as a "restoration of capitalism," and they may oppose even a limited increase in civil liberties and limited separation of civil society from the political state as concessions to bourgeois democracy. But in this paper I elaborated several reasons why I think the movement toward a mixed economy is more likely than a bureaucratic recentralization: pragmatism undermined the ideological firmness of these regimes, as the Gorbachev phenomenon indicates even in the USSR. Thus after two decades of decay the window of opportunity may open up one more time in this part of the world.

SEVEN

Who Hates Bureaucracy?
A Chinese Puzzle

Martin King Whyte

A primary aim of reforms in state socialist systems is to reduce the problems of bureaucracy. Bureaucratic evils, sometimes referred to as "bureaucratism," are seen by observers both inside and outside of these societies as endemic to them. Bureaucrats who are arrogant and yet overly cautious while amassing power for themselves and privileges for their families, and subordinates who are alternately sullen and unproductive and obsequious in currying favor seem to proliferate in Leninist systems. They are a far cry from the "new socialist men" who should be emerging to serve society selflessly. Yet the exact sources of bureaucratism and the changes that might reduce or eliminate them remain far from clear. Indeed, there is the possibility, even the fear, that reforms that are introduced may increase, rather than reduce, the problems of bureaucracy in socialist societies. In this essay I hope to contribute some clarity to the discussion of this issue by considering some interesting aspects of the struggle against bureaucratism in the People's Republic of China (PRC). The Chinese case is of special interest because, in a sense, it has displayed not one but two different attempts to deal with the bureaucratic tendencies of Soviet-style societies—one initiated by Mao Zedong after 1958, and especially during the Cultural Revolution decade (1966–76), and another presided over by Deng Xiaoping since his return to power in 1978. By considering each of these efforts, we may be able to reach greater understanding of successful and unsuccessful ways of dealing with bureaucratism in state socialist societies.

The conceptual background for considering these two separate attacks on bureaucratism in China involves the question of how many alternative ways of organizing a socialist society exist. In a recent and thought-provoking book of essays, Dorothy Solinger and her co-authors argue that there are three alternatives.[1] These are mass mobilization (as advocated by Mao Zedong and his radical supporters), bureaucratic rule (as stressed by Liu Shaoqi, but also perhaps by Deng Xiaoping in earlier times), and market distribution (advocated by no Chinese leader in a pure form, but by Deng Xiaoping and others around him recently in a partial sense).* Edward Friedman, one of the contributors to the Solinger volume, refers to these as the Maoist, Stalinist, and Titoist paths to socialism. The import of this claim is that Maoist-style mass mobilization might be able to depart from centralized bureaucratic allocation and the bureaucratism that it generates without opting for market reforms and all of the insecurities and inequalities such reforms may produce.

An alternative view, that there are only two ways of organizing a socialist society, or indeed, any modern society, is stated most forcefully by economist Alec Nove in his work *The Economics of Feasible Socialism*: "In a complex industrial economy, the interrelation between its parts can be based in principle either on freely chosen negotiated contracts (which means autonomy and a species of commodity production [and thus markets and money]), or on a system of binding instructions from planning offices. *There is no third way*."[2] In Nove's view, what is central is not the mode of production, as in orthodox Marxism, but the mode of distribution. And if distribution is carried out through centralized bureaucratic allocation rather than through markets and contracts, mass mobilization or other participatory devices can make little difference in checking bureaucratic power. As he notes later in his book, marketless socialism "can only have as its counterpart the hierarchical and bureaucratic organisation of politics."[3] By implication, Nove is arguing that problems of bureaucratism arise only in the structure of bureaucratic allocation. So in Nove's view, unlike that of Solinger and her co-authors, the Maoist alternative is not a real alternative. A complex society, such as China's, has to employ some combination of bureaucratic allocation and market distribution in order to operate, and for solving the problems of bureaucratism the exact combination is crucial.

*This posing of three alternatives is presented as a challenge to the prevailing depiction in the China field of a "two line struggle" between radicals and conservatives/revisionists. The authors note, for instance, that the Maoist policies of the Cultural Revolution have in recent times been attacked both by advocates of orderly bureaucratic rule and by champions of market reforms, groups that are at odds with each other. A somewhat similar tripartite distinction was used earlier by Charles Lindblom in his book *Politics and Markets* (New York: Basic Books, 1977).

In the pages that follow I will comment on the applicability of these two competing views to the realities of post-1949 China. First, however, I need to consider whether China's various leaders have differed in their attitudes toward the problems of bureaucracy and what to do about them. And that brings us around finally to the topic that provided the source for the title of this paper.

How China's Leaders Have Viewed Bureaucracy

Various public figures in China have made statements vigorously opposing the evils of bureaucracy. Most well known is Mao Zedong's animus toward that organizational form, as conveyed most bluntly in his 1967 listing of "Twenty Manifestations of Bureaucracy." A few excerpts convey Mao's tone:

2. They are conceited, complacent, and they aimlessly discuss politics. They do not grasp their work; they are subjective and one-sided; they are careless; they do not listen to people; they are truculent and arbitrary; they force orders; they do not care about reality; they maintain blind control. This is authoritarian bureaucracy. . . .

9. They are stupid; they are confused; they do not have a mind of their own; they are rotten sensualists; they glut themselves for days on end; they are not diligent at all, they are inconstant and they are ignorant. This is the stupid, useless bureaucracy. . . .

18. There is no organization; they employ personal friends; they engage in factionalism; they maintain feudal relationships; they form cliques to further their own private interest; they protect each other; the individual stands above everything else; these petty officials harm the masses. This is sectarian bureaucracy.[4]

Many analysts have argued that Mao launched the Cultural Revolution in 1966 primarily as an effort to combat bureaucratic tendencies and purge bureaucrats so that China would not become a society like the Soviet Union. Soviet "revisionism" was, in Mao's eyes, essentially a dictatorship of entrenched bureaucrats.

But Mao was not alone in denouncing bureaucratic evils in this fashion. In fact, it now appears that Mao may have taken much of his list from Zhou Enlai, who developed his own list of twenty evils in a report he delivered in 1963, entitled "Oppose Bureaucracy." Here, for comparison, are the same traits as listed by Zhou:

2. To be arrogant and conceited and swollen with pride; to be one-sided and subjective and crude and careless; to indulge in empty political talk and fail to grasp professional work; to be arbitrary and refuse to listen to others'

opinions; and to command recklessly in spite of reality. This is the bureaucratism which resorts to coercion and commandism. . . .

9. To be muddleheaded and ignorant, echo the views of others, drift along, and be sated with food and remain idle; and to say "I do not know" to every question and work hard for 1 day and do nothing for 10. This is muddleheaded and useless bureaucratism. . . .

18. To disregard organizational discipline, willfully employ one's favorites, form a clique to pursue selfish interests, and shield each other; to establish feudal relationships and share interests in light of factions; and to make private interests overstep everything and let the interests of a small public encroach upon the interests of the larger public. This is sectarian bureaucratism.[5]

Zhou's style is perhaps less colorful and pithy than Mao's but the message is much the same. Not to be outdone, Deng Xiaoping has voiced similar sentiments on several occasions. One example would be his important August 1980 speech on the reform of the party and state leadership systems, in which he offers a truncated listing of bureaucratic evils:

Bureaucratism remains a major prevailing issue that tarnishes the political life of our Party and state. Its harmful manifestations consist mainly in standing high above the masses; abusing power; divorcing oneself from the reality and the masses; putting up a facade; indulging in empty talk; sticking to a rigid way of thinking; following conventions; overstaffing administrative organs; being dilatory, inefficient and irresponsible; failing to keep one's word; passing documents round without solving problems; shifting responsibility on to others; and even assuming grand airs as bureaucrats, reprimanding others all too often, attacking others in revenge, suppressing democracy, deceiving one's superiors and subordinates, being arbitrary and despotic, practising favouritism, offering bribes, participating in corrupt practices in violation of the law, and so on.[6]

Similar sentiments were even voiced on occasion by Liu Shaoqi, China's chief of state until he became the foremost victim of the Cultural Revolution. Liu, denounced at the time as "China's Khrushchev," has been seen by most Western analysts as the leading champion of a bureaucratic style of rule within the communist leadership.* Yet some of his statements are similar to those already quoted. In his major 1945 report, "On the Party," Liu stated:

The tendency to bureaucracy was shown by some comrades who did not work on the basis of serving the people and who lacked responsibility toward the people and the Party. Typical examples are those who loafed around all day long, doing nothing but issue orders. They did not investigate, study or learn

---

*Lowell Dittmer, in his major study of Liu, summarizes his assessment: "In a word, Liu was a bureaucrat." See his *Liu Shao-ch'i and the Chinese Cultural Revolution* (Berkeley: University of California Press, 1974), p. 182.

from the masses. They rejected criticism from the masses, ignored the rights of the people, or even demanded that the people serve them. They did not scruple to sacrifice the interests of the people for their own benefit. They became corrupt and degenerate and lorded it over the people.[7]

Or, to quote a 1957 speech of Liu's, "Anti-bureaucracy is a long-term campaign. There will be a struggle against it so long as it exists. It will gradually vanish. If we do not fight it, it may become more and more serious until one day we will have to mount a big drive against it."*

What is going on here? One is reminded of the old television quiz show "To Tell the Truth," in which three contestants try to convince the panelists that they are the *real* person whose history and characteristics the moderator reads out. Upon reading such similar, vehement denunciations of the evil of bureaucracy in China, one may feel like the panelist trying to sort out who *really* has opposed bureaucracy in post-1949 China.[†] Of course, a skeptic, having also perused the speeches at the Twenty-seventh Party Congress of the Communist Party of the Soviet Union (CPSU), may be suspicious that this is all hypocritical cant and that seeming to be opposed to bureaucracy is just one of those rituals that leaders of Leninist systems have to perform periodically. (Parallels to denunciations of big government by American presidents might be noted.)

*Liu Shao-ch'i, *Collected Works of Liu Shao-ch'i, 1945–1957* (Kowloon: Union Research Institute, 1969), pp. 423–24. Of course, it can be admitted that the methods recommended by Liu for dealing with bureaucratic problems, predominantly moderate criticism within the party organs, were different from those that Mao came increasingly to favor. One might also note that Zhou Enlai in the spring of 1957 made a similar statement giving an eerie premonition of the Cultural Revolution. When meeting visiting Soviet diplomats arriving at an airport in Hangzhou, Zhou turned and pointed at the two children who had come to present flowers to the Russians and stated, "If, ten years from now, there is still bureaucracy in the leadership, you should oppose it" (cited in Roderick MacFarquhar, *The Hundred Flowers Campaign and the Chinese Intellectuals* [New York: Praeger, 1960], p. 31).

†One needs to take into account a translation problem here. In English the term *bureaucracy* can be used in a relatively neutral sense to refer to a particular organizational form, as I will discuss shortly. As such it can be distinguished from a less widely used term, *bureaucratism*, which refers to the specifically negative aspects of this organizational form. In Chinese, however, the term normally translated as bureaucracy, *guanliao zhuyi*, always entails a strong negative sense and might therefore be better translated as *bureaucratism*. The term came into frequent use in the 1930s and 1940s to refer to the harmful aspects of imperial bureaucratic traditions that had carried over into the Republican period. See, for instance, Wang Ya'nan, *Zhongguo Guanliao Zhengzhi Yanjiu* (Research on Chinese bureaucratic politics) (Shanghai: Contemporary Culture Publishers, 1948). Some scholars in China have recently advocated the use of a different term, *kecengzhi* (literally "section-level system"), as a way of conveying the neutral, analytical sense of the term *bureaucracy*. See Han Mingmo, "Cong guanliao zhuyi dao kecengzhi" (From bureaucratism to bureaucracy), *Shehui Kexue*, 1984, no. 6, pp. 36–41. So far, however, this new term has not come into general usage.

Still, it would be an error to dismiss this antibureaucratic rhetoric as unimportant, since both under Mao and in the post-Mao period fairly vigorous measures have been adopted that, unlike those taken in the Soviet Union, seem to have made a major impact on how the system operates. And in the literature on the PRC we do find an answer to our quiz show question about who is the real antibureaucrat within the Chinese elite. The conventional wisdom is that Mao Zedong should be accorded that recognition. Mao, it is argued, attempted to make the Chinese system less bureaucratic. Leaders such as Zhou Enlai and Deng Xiaoping, and especially Liu Shaoqi, in this view, have protected bureaucrats and restored the bureaucratic systems attacked by Mao, and thus we would be wrong to be misled by their antibureaucratic statements into picking them as genuine opponents of bureaucracy.

One influential analysis of this topic, *Organizing China*, by Harry Harding, develops an argument somewhat along these lines.[8] In Harding's view Zhou, Deng, and Liu as well as Mao could probably be counted as having genuine concern for the problems of bureaucracy. Zhou, Deng, and Liu advocated moderate means for improving the functioning of China's bureaucracy, which Harding terms rationalization and remedialism. Mao, in contrast, was in favor of more drastic solutions, "radicalism," in Harding's terms, that involved tearing down bureaucratic structures so as to rebuild them on a new, nonbureaucratic basis.

An earlier argument along similar lines was advanced by Richard Solomon in his book *Mao's Revolution and the Chinese Political Culture*.[9] Although Solomon is not so exclusively concerned with organizational problems as Harding, he sees most Chinese Communist leaders as imbued with a long-standing Chinese cultural fear of *luan*, or chaos, if strict authoritarian rules are not used to control the population. Mao was distinctive within this elite, in Solomon's view, in having a very non-Chinese view of the virtues of disorder and of being willing to foster disorder as a way of constructing a less bureaucratic social order.

In this paper I will reject this conventional argument and offer instead what may appear to be almost the opposite view—that in certain respects Mao should be seen not as the true opponent of bureaucratization but instead as its most vigorous champion. By contrast, although the post-Mao regime under Deng Xiaoping was composed mainly of rehabilitated bureaucrats, it appears in my view to be countering some of the trends toward bureaucratization that Mao set in motion. In the end I shall not wish to argue in a simple-minded fashion that the "prize" for opposing bureaucracy be taken away from Mao and given to Deng, but to make my revisionist argument clear, I need to introduce some important conceptual distinctions.

Two Aspects of Bureaucratization

To clarify the basis for my argument, it is necessary to sort through some of the confusion that surrounds the terms *bureaucracy* and *bureaucratization*. I contend that, in the writings of Max Weber and many others, there are two distinct aspects of these phenomena that are mixed together. These can be considered most easily if we concentrate upon the term *bureaucratization* in reference to Weber's writings. In one sense, bureaucratization refers to a process by which more and more of social life comes to be governed by large, hierarchical, non-kinship-based organizations, and through this transformation less of social life is left to the autonomous action of individuals, families, kin groups, religious sects, and local communities. As a result of this change, more and more the distribution and consumption of resources in society are carried out not by self-sufficient individuals and communities or through the market mechanism but are instead subject to hierarchical allocation and coordination. This I would refer to as bureaucratization in form or structure. This sense of the term does not specify the nature of the roles and norms within such large organizations; it simply specifies that members of the population are having an increasing share of their activities subject to management or control by such organizations. This sense of the term also does not specify how centralized or decentralized the power is within such large organizations. Both organizations in which a single manager or set of managers at the top makes all the decisions and ones in which much authority is delegated to those at lower levels would be considered at the high end of the scale of bureaucratization, as long as most areas of social life were subject to regulation and control by these large-scale organizations.*

The other meaning of the term *bureaucratization* involves the extent

---

*Many of the post-1949 antibureaucratic efforts detailed in Harry Harding's book and in other works have taken the form of decentralization campaigns, in which "simpler administration" is pursued by cutting back the staffs of central ministries and delegating some powers to regional governments and even to enterprise administrations. But these lower-level agencies do not thereby become autonomous units and are still under hierarchical control from the center, and the center can and often has taken back powers that were delegated downward. But in any case, the point I wish to stress here is that such shifts in the powers of different levels of the bureaucratic hierarchy do not imply any real change in the degree to which the population is subjected to bureaucratic control.

to which an organization approximates the ideal-typical traits specified by Weber, for example, an organization based on legal-rational
authority, emphasizing formal rules and procedures and written files,
with selection by appointment based on universalistic competence criteria, with officials treating the job as a full-time occupation and given
a fixed money salary, and with the office separated from the officeholder, who enters it as a contractual obligation with specified duties
and rights, and so on.[10] This sense of the term, then, refers to the
extent to which various organizations in a society are coming more
and more to approximate the ideal type of bureaucratic organization
specified by such a list of traits. The other side of this process is the
extent to which organizations based on other modes, such as charismatic or traditional authority, decline in importance in a society or are
transformed into a more bureaucratic type. This second aspect I will
refer to as bureaucratization in content or functioning, as contrasted
to the bureaucratization in form or structure discussed above.

In reviewing various Western works written on the subject of bureaucracy, particularly for a popular audience, it seems apparent that
many are concerned with bureaucratization in one of these senses but
not the other. For example, works such as Robert Presthus's *The Organizational Society* and Henry Jacoby's *The Bureaucratization of the World*
are mainly talking about the first, or structural, aspect of the process.[11]
In other words, they are mainly concerned with what happens when
more and more of social life is governed by large-scale organizations,
rather than with how similar to Weber's typology of traits the internal
operation of these organizations is. The same could be said for George
Orwell's *1984*. No pretense is made that Big Brother presides over an
ideal-typical legal-rational bureaucracy, only that the organizations he
presides over have eliminated virtually all individual choice, market
alternatives, and human freedom.

In Weber's own writings he sometimes made the distinction I am
introducing here. In a statement that is particularly appropriate to the
subject at hand, Weber in 1913 parted company with those who felt
that socialism would introduce a new, less bureaucratic age: "Only by
reversion in every field—political, religious, economic, etc.—to small-
scale organization would it be possible to any considerable extent to
escape [bureaucracy's] influence. . . . Socialism would, in fact, require
a still higher degree of formal bureaucratization than capitalism."[12]
Here Weber did not assume that large organizations in a future socialist society would necessarily approach the ideal type of a legal-rational
bureaucracy, but only that even more of social life would be subject

to control by large-scale organizations under socialism than is the case under capitalism because of the former's preference for planning rather than market distribution. Weber did assume that in practice in modern societies these two aspects of bureaucratization would tend to develop together, with both more and more large-scale organizations and an increasing dominance of the legal-rational form of functioning within those organizations. Still, we can maintain the conceptual distinction and consider the possibility that these processes could occur separately. There could be only a very few large-scale organizations in a society otherwise organized in some nonbureaucratic way, but these few could be constructed upon a strictly legal-rational basis. Or there could instead be an increasing dominance of large-scale organizations in all of social life, but these could be based upon some other principles, such as charismatic or traditional authority, or perhaps simply coercion and fear.*

What does all of this abstraction have to do with China? By now the reader can probably see that I intend to use this distinction to cope with the "To Tell the Truth" puzzle. I would argue that Mao Zedong's opposition to bureaucratization was primarily concerned with its content or functioning, rather than with its structure. He did, it seems clear, want to avoid developing organizations that would be based upon legal-rational principles.[13] But at the same time he was a fervent advocate of structural bureaucratization. He abhorred private choice, market distribution, private enterprise, and other manifestations of individual and group autonomy, and he wanted to subject an increasing share of all human activity in China to state regulation and allocation. His "creative chaos" and attempts to attack organizational forms in the name of his "uninterrupted revolution" were not designed to produce a society in which the hand of large-scale organizations was less dominant; rather, he wanted to destroy organizational routines and construct new organizational forms that were even more bureaucratic in the structural sense but perhaps more charismatic in their internal functioning.

---

*In some earlier sociological writings others advanced a similar argument—that Weber "mixed together" two distinct aspects of bureaucracy. See, for instance, Helen Constas, "Max Weber's Two Conceptions of Bureaucracy," *American Journal of Sociology*, 52 (1958): 400–409; Stanley H. Udy, Jr., "'Bureaucracy' and 'Rationality' in Weber's Organizational Theory: An Empirical Study," *American Sociological Review*, 24 (1959): 761–65. Udy presents empirical data from a sample of work organizations in preindustrial societies that indicate that organizational traits involving bureaucracy in the structural sense and those involving bureaucracy in the content sense (which he refers to as "rationality") tend to be negatively correlated.

Since Mao's efforts to combat bureaucratization in the second, or content sense, are well known and widely commented upon, I will concentrate here on substantiating my more controversial claim that Mao was a fervent champion of bureaucratization in the first, or structural, sense. The period 1949–66 witnessed a major advance of bureaucratization, as Weber would have predicted. The state bureaucracy expanded massively, and socialist transformation made the entire economy and much of the rest of society (the educational system, health care, the mass media, culture and the arts, and so forth) subject to bureaucratic control. Resources that had been distributed by the market predominantly before 1949, such as jobs, housing, medical care, and schooling, began to be allocated instead primarily by bureaucratic agencies. Individual producers found themselves swallowed up by larger and larger organizations. For example, peasant families became members of mutual aid teams of five to eight families, but these gave way to agricultural producers' cooperatives (in two versions, with the "lower-stage" form rapidly giving way in 1956 to a larger, "higher-stage" form), and the latter were finally amalgamated in 1958 into rural people's communes that were designed to regulate the activities of several thousand families. I have discussed these trends toward bureaucratization before 1966 in more detail elsewhere.[14]

To be sure, China in the years before 1966 was guided by a form of collective leadership, and it might be argued that Mao even as first among equals should not be held responsible for organizational trends over which Liu Shaoqi or other leaders may have had more influence. Before 1966, however, the periods when Mao's personal vision was most predominant were characterized by novel changes in the direction of structural bureaucratization. It was during the Great Leap Forward (1958–60) that major efforts were made to eliminate the remaining vestiges of private enterprise activity and market exchanges and thus to subject social life more uniformly to bureaucratic regulation. This was also the period in which China, although setting out to pursue its own road to socialism, seemed most infected by the Soviet penchant for "gigantism." This phenomenon was particularly visible in the early communes, which in a few cases were made so large that they embraced an entire county.* Also during the

---

*Ezra Vogel details the creation of a county-commune in Guangdong Province that had a population of more than 275,000. See his *Canton under Communism* (Cambridge, Mass.: Harvard University Press, 1969), p. 248. Even in much smaller communes, the shift from peasants making their own decisions about farming and marketing, through

Great Leap the central leadership made vigorous efforts to eliminate local autonomy and traditional customs in realms such as religious and festival behavior, to advocate cremation and simple and secular "memorial meetings" in place of traditional funerals, and to promote the round of new patriotic holidays. I would argue, then, that a major push toward further structural bureaucratization of Chinese society was launched during the period of Mao's ascendancy during the Great Leap Forward. By the same token, the collapse of the Great Leap, which placed Mao on the defensive for a time, led to a partial retreat in the level of structural bureaucratization. During the period 1961–63, for example, restrictions on private enterprise and marketing activity were lifted and experiments were even carried out with restoring the peasant family farm, presaging the dramatic shift in this direction after 1978. During the same years attempts to have the state regulate all cultural, leisure, and other realms of social life were relaxed.

It might be argued that in the years 1958–60 China's break with the Soviet Union was only just beginning and Mao's ideas on what China should be doing differently were still in the process of formation. Perhaps it was only during the Cultural Revolution years that we can see Mao's antibureaucratic impulses fully unleashed. I would argue, however, that it was precisely during this latter period, a time most observers have seen as representing the pinnacle of Maoist attacks on bureaucracy, that structural bureaucratization reached its fullest extension. To substantiate my revisionist argument, therefore, I need to deal with the developments of the Cultural Revolution era in somewhat greater detail.

The Cultural Revolution Reforms

The initial consequence of China's Cultural Revolution was to immobilize and damage the existing state and party machinery. Large numbers of bureaucrats were purged, and many segments of China's Leninist apparatus (such as trade unions and women's federations) essentially disappeared. For those involved in the Red Guard movement, and even for many bystanders, it became a period not only of considerable chaos but of unprecedented freedom. Local rules and

---

small cooperatives and finally to a central commune leadership trying to direct everything created severe problems, as can be seen in the account of this period provided in William Hinton, *Shenfan* (New York: Random House, 1983), p. 3.

rulers were rejected, required political indoctrination meetings were
no more, and young activists were free to travel around the country,
publish their own unofficial newspapers, search and raid homes and
temples, and do battle with authority figures and factional enemies.
Some would argue that the sudden change from having rigidly controlled lives to near-total autonomy was a major ingredient in the fre-
netic energy and violence displayed by the Red Guards.[15] In any case,
I would acknowledge that the initial stages of the Cultural Revolution
produced a dramatic reduction in bureaucratization in the structural
sense.

At the time it appeared that Mao Zedong was presiding over the
demise of the Leninist party/state structure that his regime had constructed, and there were some intriguing hints of ideas for developing
different and less bureaucratic organizational forms. In particular,
wide-ranging study and discussion of the Paris Commune model as
an alternative to Soviet-style bureaucratic rule was undertaken and an
attempt was made in Shanghai to rebuild authority in early 1967 on
the basis of a Shanghai Commune.[16] But Mao squelched this effort by
pointing out that the Paris Commune had been too weak to defeat its
enemies and that with the commune form there would be no place
for the party. And as organizations were reconstructed after the Cultural Revolution, they took a form that was not only largely familiar
but even, in important respects, more bureaucratic (in a structural
sense) than before the Cultural Revolution. Mao was thus able to do
for China's bureaucratic Humpty Dumpty what all the king's horses
and men had not been able to do in the nursery rhyme—to put it back
together again, and then some.

In what sense did China emerge from the Cultural Revolution more
bureaucratized than before? Several elements were involved. First,
both in the cities and in the countryside, new attempts were made to
eliminate the remaining vestiges of private enterprise activities. For
example, private craftsmen and peddlers were suppressed, peasants
were no longer allowed to come and market extra produce in urban
"free markets," attempts were made to eliminate private plots in the
countryside, and the remaining owners of private housing in cities
were forced to turn over their deeds and begin paying rent on their
premises (if they were able to remain living there at all). The limited
amount of personal choice that had been allowed earlier in matters
such as job assignments and university enrollments, based on lists of
preferences filled out by applicants, was eliminated, and all were expected to serve at the pleasure of the state. In the countryside attempts

were made to shift the unit of farming and remuneration from the production team of twenty to fifty households to the brigade of two to five hundred households and to dictate what crops could be grown locally, changes that eliminated much of the relative autonomy that the teams were supposed to enjoy within the commune structure. In cities these changes coincided with a tightening of the ration system, with many items formerly available for sale (such as pork and sugar) becoming available only to those who had the necessary ration coupons.

In general the Cultural Revolution reforms discussed here seem to display intolerance for the complexity and impurities of Chinese society and a desire to hasten the transition to a unified form of state socialism in which planners would dictate production, education, employment, consumption, and other goals and paternalistically allocate goods and services to citizens without relying on markets and personal choice. In this image the countryside would merge with the city, as collective forms of ownership would be raised up from team to brigade and then to the commune level, and finally commune collective ownership would be transformed into state ownership, the dominant form in urban China.

How Mao and those around him came to this vision is unclear. In many respects the formula for how to achieve a fuller form of socialism seems to come right out of Stalin, as manifested particularly in the latter's *Economic Problems of Socialism in the USSR*, published in 1952, which envisioned a future that included the gradual raising of collective ownership in the *kolkhozy* to state ownership and the eventual elimination of commodity production and market exchanges for money. In the wake of the Great Leap Forward, Mao, in commenting on Stalin's work, displayed a preference for similar changes but a recognition that they could not occur until the distant future.* Somehow

*See his *A Critique of Soviet Economics* (New York: Monthly Review, 1977). Mao, however, differed from Stalin in arguing against the "full consolidation" of collective ownership. He feared that such consolidation would become permanent and wanted immediately to begin taking small steps toward the distant goal of unified public property. It could be argued that the vision of socialism as one internally coordinated bureaucratic machine goes back much further than Stalin. In 1917 in *State and Revolution*, Lenin portrayed the future communist society as follows: "*All* citizens are here transformed into hired employees of the state. . . . *All* citizens become employees and workers of *one* national state 'syndicate'. . . . The whole of society will have become one office and one factory, with equal work and equal pay" (V. I. Lenin, *State and Revolution* [New York: International Publishers, 1932], pp. 83–84). Radoslav Selucky argues that Lenin here was following Marx, who in his fascination with the efficiency of modern industry and his distaste for "chaos" of the market, envisioned the future communist society as a factory writ large. See his *Marxism, Socialism, Freedom: Toward a General Democratic Theory of Labour-Managed Systems* (London: Macmillan, 1979).

over the next decade or so Mao lost his patience and tried to bring these changes into being. He attempted not only to extend state allocation and control over more areas of social life, but also to begin to eliminate the money economy. For instance, in 1974 Mao revived the idea that Zhang Chunqiao had advocated during the Great Leap Forward of eliminating the state wage rank system and reverting to the supply system used before the revolution (in which cadres did not have salaries that became discretionary income but received such supplies as the authorities felt they needed), and he was reportedly angry when the Ministry of Finance told him that this scheme was not feasible.[17]

Also during the Cultural Revolution decade bureaucratic regulation of the private lives of citizens reached its highest point. Large numbers of customs and leisure pursuits, including ones as innocuous as raising crickets or goldfish, were suppressed or driven underground, as were a wide range of religious activities, forms of cultural expression, and styles of dress. The display of pictures of Mao on the walls of every home and office became obligatory, and for a time work units organized their employees for ritualized sessions of reciting Mao's quotations and taking part in "loyalty dances" to Mao. The attempt directly to regulate reproduction as well as production also began at this time. From 1970 onward new regulations decreed the maximum number of children families could have (at the time, generally two in the cities and three in the countryside), and work organizations and communes began to make decisions about which members could be granted places in their quota of birth rights for that year.*

As a result of all these changes, individuals throughout Chinese society found themselves more totally dependent upon bureaucratic gatekeepers and superiors at the time of Mao's death in 1976 than they had been in 1966. There was less room for personal choice, market selection, or reliance on their own efforts, and there was also a much smaller "zone of indifference" within which to engage in behavior that higher authorities would ignore. The result was thus intriguingly dialectical—an antibureaucratic mass movement, the Cultural Revolution, resulted in China becoming an even more Orwellian society through the further extension of bureaucratization in the structural sense.

*Regulation of these areas of social life was not predominantly carried out through secret police terror but through the normal grass-roots organizational network in work organizations and neighborhoods. Even though this regulation of social life was carried out by a different part of the bureaucratic machinery, and with more organizational finesse than in Stalinist Russia, it still involved a heightened degree of structural bureaucratization.

At this point it might be objected that I am oversimplifying by ignoring how Mao and his radical followers tried to alter structures in ways that worked against, rather than fostered, bureaucratization. In particular, what about his regular stress on decentralization, mobilization, and mass participation? It might seem that decentralizing certain decisions to lower levels than before and allowing or even requiring the masses to criticize and supervise their superiors would promote debureaucratization in the structural sense. I would argue that these changes are part of Mao's attempt to change the internal functioning of organizations and not to reduce the structural dominance of large-scale organizations. As Arnold Tannenbaum and others have argued, participatory schemes may, in fact, increase bosses' control over their subordinates, rather than increasing subordinate power or autonomy, and Andrew Walder argues that this is exactly what occurred in Chinese factories in the Cultural Revolution decade.[18] Decentralization schemes within organizations do not reduce structural bureaucratization when those organizations are gaining an increasing hold over all corners of social life.

In retrospect it would appear that, however Mao's dialectical mind may have perceived the situation, in reality the combination of structural bureaucratization with content debureaucratization did not work. In the increasingly totally state-dominated China of Mao's last years the organizational problems Mao feared most, such as elite arrogance, abuses of power, pursuit of personal and family advantage, currying favor, and aversion to making decisions and taking risks, only got worse. As a consequence, corresponding forms of undesirable behavior by subordinates also increased—alienation, low productivity, seeking patrons among superiors, and so forth. Mao's various mobilizational techniques were not able to offset the behavioral tendencies generated by this structure. Indeed, it might be argued that these techniques even made matters worse because they undermined the rules and regulations that had placed some limits on bureaucratic power and made it even more necessary to seek patronage and protection from superiors.[19] So Mao's cure for the problem of bureaucracy in many ways made the disease even worse.

The results of Mao's assault on bureaucracy during the Cultural Revolution thus lead me to side with Nove rather than with Solinger et al. on the issue of whether there are two or three "paths" to socialism. Mao clearly did not admire bureaucracy, and I believe he sincerely wanted to overcome the many manifestations of bureaucratism in the society he had helped create. But as often happens, the consequences of a leader's actions were quite different from those he intended. Mao ignored the importance of the bureaucratic system of allocation as a source of bureaucratic evils, and in practice he presided over a significant extension of bureaucratization in China, in the structural sense of the term.* He assumed that the main sources of bureaucratic evils were to be found in bourgeois ideology, hostile class influences, markets, and the rules and regulations of organizations that were bureaucratized in content. Although he attacked the latter through various favored devices designed to make organizations less bureaucratic in content and more charismatic, political study rituals, decentralization measures, stimulation of class struggle, and mass labor mobilizations, for example, these measures left the fundamental sources of the problem untouched and even aggravated them.†

The Post-Mao Reforms

If we use this conceptual framework, what are we to make of the policies and preferences of Deng Xiaoping and others in his post-Mao reform group? It seems that the reforms pursued under Deng are designed to move away from Mao's preferences in both aspects of bureaucratization. Bureaucratization in the content or functioning sense is advocated in place of the more charismatic forms stressed under Mao.‡ At the same time some limited but dramatic steps have

*One of the authors in Dorothy Solinger, ed., *Three Visions of Chinese Socialism* (Boulder, Colo.: Westview Press, 1984), Carl Riskin, has noted that Mao's "model" of socialism lacked any clear alternative mechanism for carrying out distribution other than bureaucratic allocation and markets. (Mass mobilization and class struggle do not, after all, distribute goods, jobs, or services.) Thus from the viewpoint of the Solinger volume, Mao ended up being as much a Stalinist as a Maoist by reinforcing bureaucratic allocation as the basic principle of distribution.

†Images of Maoist China in the literature have altered dramatically in recent years from a view of a highly participatory, mass-oriented system described in many works in the early 1970s to a more or less totalitarian dictatorship portrayed in writings in the 1980s. I would argue that this is not simply a case of the field overcoming its delusions and recognizing the truth (or of substituting one delusion for another). Rather, both pictures are in some sense real but partial because they represent two sides of the effort in the Maoist years to deal with the problems of bureaucracy.

‡The current leadership argues that what Mao was creating was not so much charismatic as traditional or feudal forms of rule. This argument is advanced by pointing out the parallels between organizational life in Mao's final years and feudalism. Perhaps it could be said that the charismatic forms that Mao favored rapidly decayed and became "routinized" in quasi-traditional forms of organizational authority. Or perhaps Mao's initiatives ended up producing the worst of both worlds, with negative features of traditional Chinese bureaucratic institutions and centralized Leninist institutions reinforcing each other.

been taken that reduce the level of structural bureaucratization of Chinese society. If successful, these reforms will make China both less bureaucratic structurally and more bureaucratic in organizational functioning.

The efforts by the reformers to promote more legal-rational modes of organizational functioning are fairly familiar. Criteria of technical competence are supposed to be increasingly stressed in appointments and promotions, rather than political attitudes, seniority in the party, or loyalty to the leader.* Offices are supposed to be increasingly separated from officeholders, and a system of regular promotions and retirements is supposed to replace the lifelong tenure of the Maoist "iron rice bowl." Campaign mobilizations within organizations and officially stimulated class struggle are now denounced, and instead orderly procedures based upon reasonable rules and regulations are supposed to guide organizational behavior. A hierarchy of monetary salaries, with extra incentive payments added on, is now viewed positively as the key way to motivate members of such organizations, and "moral incentives" are less often stressed, or noted only as supplements. Managerial autonomy within Chinese organizations is also being advocated at least to some extent, with party committees directed to withdraw from active management into a supervisory position.† Of course, all of these are policy preferences, not reality, and the Chinese press reveals that the changes in many organizations have been marginal to date. It is fairly clear, however, that the reformers are pushing toward creation of a society in which large-scale organizations are at least somewhat closer to the legal-rational ideal type that Weber described.‡

In terms of structural, rather than content, debureaucratization,

---

*This last proviso is at least debatable. Loyalty to the leader of a particular organization is not being stressed. But loyalty to the reform effort, which implies at least in part loyalty to the cause being championed by Deng Xiaoping, is surely an important criterion in personnel selections.

†Of course, some trends are visible that do not fit neatly with the Weberian trait list of legal-rational organizations. For example, in some factories experiments with elections of managerial personnel are being carried out, a departure from Weber's insistence upon appointment from above as the mode of personnel selection. This measure, however, may be viewed as necessary to advance the cause of selection according to competence, if superior officials are too "infected" with Maoist viruses to make appointments on that basis.

‡Chinese leaders do not refer to Weber's writings and ideas in advancing their reforms, and they are probably unfamiliar with his views. Some scholars in China are beginning to cite Weber's writings on bureaucracy with approval, however, which shows that his ideas are beginning to become known in that country. See, for example, Han Mingmo; and Zheng Yefu, "Shilun guanxixue" (An exploration into relying on connections), *Shehuixue yu Shehui Diaocha*, 1984, nos. 2–3, pp. 52–56.

the most dramatic change in the post-Mao period has been the decollectivization of agriculture and the reemergence of family farming. Although peasants are still in many ways more subject to state controls than they were before the revolution, or even during the early 1950s, the increased ability of peasant families to make their own decisions about how to farm, whether to leave farming, and how to handle their income still constitutes a clear reduction in the scope of bureaucratic controls.* These changes have unleashed a tide of changed behavior in the Chinese countryside, with peasant families producing new crop mixes, making contacts in distant markets, undertaking new forms of nonagricultural activity, sending family members off to the cities to supplement family income, and engaging in a buying spree of consumer durables, such as televisions, washing machines, and in a few cases even trucks and automobiles. At the same time many traditional peasant customs seem to be reemerging, such as lavish wedding processions, elaborate funeral rituals, and even in some cases rural salvation cults and would-be emperors.[20] Although the changes in structural debureaucratization in the Chinese countryside are much more dramatic and real than the bureaucratization in content discussed earlier, there is at least one important realm that constitutes an exception to this pattern. That concerns birth control. The state effort to regulate fertility has been heightened in the post-Mao period, and it is only since 1979 that the controversial one-child-family policy has been imposed on the population. In this realm, but not in others, the grasp of

---

*Vivienne Shue has advanced a contrary interpretation of this change, arguing that these reforms increase the direct controls of the state over the peasants. See her recent book, *The Reach of the State: Sketches of the Chinese Body Politic* (Stanford: Stanford University Press, 1988). She argues that the commune system provided a source of insulation from direct state controls that is now removed, making peasants more vulnerable to state decisions on prices and other matters. I see this argument as intriguing but misguided. The use of organizational power to control individual behavior is clearly more constraining than the setting of laws, prices, taxes, and similar items by the state and then allowing those individuals to make choices within the framework offered by the items that have been set. After all, prices, tax quotas, and other items were set by the state even in the era of the communes, and the state's inability then to control peasant behavior perfectly does not mean that now peasants are subject to more controls than in the past. Of course, this is not to deny that competing on revived markets introduces insecurities into the lives of peasants that some would prefer to avoid, a phenomenon Erich Fromm, Karl Polanyi, and others commented upon long ago. See Fromm's *Escape from Freedom* (New York: Rinehart, 1941), and Polanyi's *The Great Transformation: The Political and Economic Origins of Our Time* (Boston: Beacon Press, 1944). Polanyi's argument that commercialization fosters state control is more plausible than Shue's because he is dealing with stateless cultures and relatively autonomous villages that lose their autonomy because of world market penetration, not with Leninist organizational hierarchies experiencing market reforms.

state bureaucratic agencies has been extended, rather than contracted, in the post-Mao period.

Although the clearest reductions in structural bureaucratization have occurred in the Chinese countryside, more modest shifts in the same direction can be seen in urban areas. For example, there is less effort under Deng than under Mao (and Jiang Qing) to see that all leisure activities and cultural pursuits fit a narrow definition of socialist propriety, and a wide variety of proscribed activities, from raising songbirds to engaging in religious worship, adopting Western styles of dress, and listening to foreign radio broadcasts, have been allowed or even encouraged. The limited revival of private enterprise activities, proposals for cooperative building and financing of apartments, the revival of urban free markets, reductions in the scope of rationing, and experiments with allowing people to change jobs all provide urbanites with somewhat greater options and make them marginally less than totally dependent upon goods and services allocated to them by bureaucratic superiors. Most urbanites, to be sure, are still employed and housed by fairly all-encompassing work units that regulate many aspects of their lives, and for them the changes to date have been minor. But again at least the direction of the reforms seems clear—to reduce the extent to which the state attempts directly to organize and control all areas of social life and to foster instead individual competition and ingenuity in operating in urban markets that will form an increasingly important supplement to state allocation through bureaucratic channels.

China in the late 1980s was, to be sure, very far away from any form of market socialism, and even if the urban reform program introduced in 1984 makes more substantial headway than it appears to be doing to date, China will still be a very different place from, say, Yugoslavia. In 1980 there were signs that Deng and some of his close followers were toying with the idea of dismantling parts of their Leninist legacy and reducing the role of the bureaucracy in more dramatic ways.* But in subsequent years no direct assaults on Leninism were made in China, and it is not clear whether this is because Deng

---

*See Deng's August 1980 speech; and Liao Gailong, "Historical Experiences and Our Road to Development," trans. in *Issues and Studies*, 17 (1981): 89–90. Both documents blame the overconcentration of power in Mao's last years not simply on Mao and the "gang of four" or on China's feudal heritage but on wholesale adoption in China of Leninist organizational forms (or Stalinist versions of them). For a particularly biting commentary along similar lines, see Liu Binyan, *People or Monsters?* (Bloomington: Indiana University Press, 1983). For a related critique, see Chen Erjin, *China: Crossroads Socialism* (London: Verso, 1984).

and his followers did not dare or did not care to pursue the matter. The former possibility is at least suggested by the fact that political reforms were put back on the agenda for discussion in 1986 and again in 1987, with Deng's 1980 remarks prominently republished. Accompanying commentaries suggested that, whereas the time was not ripe for dealing with reforms of the political system in 1980, by 1986 the economic reforms had progressed far enough so that the obstacles posed by the unreformed political system had finally become serious and obvious, making it clear that they finally had to be confronted. But the political turmoil that occurred at the end of that year and in early 1987 made it clear that there was substantial opposition to any major reforms of the political system and thus of the structure of bureaucratic allocation that continues to dominate Chinese society.

Conclusion

Who can we say, then, *really* hates bureaucracy in China? From the evidence reviewed here, we would have to conclude that everyone and no one does. The Chinese communists created one of the most bureaucratized social systems known to man. In certain important ways it is significantly more bureaucratized, in the structural sense, than is the Soviet Union. In particular, from the 1950s onward the authorities endeavored to limit or eliminate entirely any labor market and also any migration into urban places (large or small), thus creating a society in which people would be assigned by bureaucratic agencies to jobs and residences and then stay put, unless those agencies decided that they needed to be reassigned somewhere else. The limitations on job changes and migration in the USSR under Stalin seem much less comprehensive and effective. Mao championed this extension of state bureaucratic power, but he tried to create new modes of organizational functioning that would not be bureaucratic. This effort failed or was counterproductive, and Mao's successors have attacked bureaucratic problems in a different way. Their solution is both modestly to restrict the structural reach of bureaucratic power and to adopt more conventional legal-rational procedures to try to get bureaucrats to act in more desirable ways.

Neither Mao nor Deng is consistently antibureaucratic, in the sense that we might judge an anarchist, syndicalist, or Milton Friedmanite laissez-faire capitalist as antibureaucratic. Both remain fundamentally Leninist in their orientations, and they want to maintain the centralized bureaucratic system without the evils of "bureaucratism." Where they differ is in their analysis of the source of those evils. For Mao that source was mainly in bad class influences and poor ideology affecting bureaucrats, problems that should be combated through various normative influences and social pressure devices. In this approach Mao was less a Stalinist or Weberian than a Confucianist, since in the Confucian framework it is good ideas and good men, more than good structures, that are important.* For Deng, in contrast, bureaucratic problems are seen as at least partly caused by structural factors and not simply by the defects of the individuals who staff those structures. To improve the situation it is necessary to allow organizations to operate closer to an ideal, legal-rational manner and to place some limits on the realms that bureaucratic authorities try to regulate. In this sense Deng Xiaoping is at least somewhat more of a Weberian than Mao Zedong because he has a greater appreciation of the dynamics that flow from the organizational form.

Deng Xiaoping's Weberian inclinations can be seen particularly in the following passages from his 1980 speech on reform of the political system:

Of course, bureaucratism is also related to one's way of thinking, but this cannot be solved without first reforming the systems themselves. That is why we achieved little in spite of our repeated struggle against bureaucratism in the past. . . .

It is true that the various errors we made in the past had something to do with the way of thinking and style of work of some leaders. But it had even more to do with the problems in our organizational and work systems. Sound systems in these respects can stop bad people from running unbridled while poor ones may hamper good people in performing good deeds to the best of their ability or, in certain cases, may even cause them to go in the opposite direction.†

I have argued that Mao's efforts to combat bureaucratism were flawed in conception and a failure in execution. What can we expect

---

*In his final years Mao did repeatedly move in the direction of a Djilas-like "new class" argument, in which the structure itself would be seen as the problem. But he always shied away from taking the final steps to this argument and returned to state his faith in Leninist structures. See, for example, Harry Harding, *Organizing China* (Stanford: Stanford University Press, 1981); and Richard Kraus, *Class Conflict in Chinese Socialism* (New York: Columbia University Press, 1981).

†*The Selected Works of Deng Xiaoping* (1983), pp. 19, 21. This contrast between Mao's "Confucian" approach and Deng's "Weberian" approach to the problem of bureaucracy parallels the differences Erik Wright sees in how Lenin and Weber explained the sources of the evils of bureaucracy. For Lenin it was "bad ideology" rooted in class origins, rather than bureaucratic concentrations of power, that led to bureaucratism. See Wright, *Class, Crisis, and the State* (New York: New Left Books, 1978), chap. 4.

of Deng's quite different approach? On the one hand, that the analysis of the current leadership seems much more sociologically on the mark than Mao's might seem to indicate that the current reforms can have some success in reducing bureaucratic evils. On the other hand, that Deng is only slightly a Weberian, and very much still a Leninist, and that much of the bureaucratic system constructed in the 1950s is still in place, point to a more pessimistic conclusion. I would argue that only if a more substantial reduction in what I have called structural bureaucratization were carried out would it be likely that the built-in problems that Mao and Deng and all the rest have inveighed against would be substantially reduced. Unless Deng Xiaoping and those who follow him are both willing and able to make fundamental changes in the Leninist organizational system they preside over, we can expect only superficial and cosmetic changes to take place. If this pessimism is borne out, we can anticipate that China's future leaders, like their predecessors, will be ardent and perhaps eloquent, but also ineffective, champions of the antibureaucratic cause.

EIGHT

Evolution of the Communist Economic System: Scope and Limits

Wlodzimierz Brus

The aim of this paper is to present some tentative results of the author's attempt to assess institutional developments in the economies of communist countries. In one way or another I have been involved in these issues for over forty years, and since the mid-1950s I have participated in or closely observed the process of systemic changes (economic reforms). This experience may justify the personal approach taken here, which is reflected in the almost total absence of direct references to the vast literature, both in the countries concerned and in the West, devoted to the subject.

What Evolution Has Occurred?

The answer to the above question depends on the point of reference. If we compare the present shape of the economic system in communist countries with the prerevolutionary concepts derived from (or attributed to) Karl Marx, or with some initial attempts to implement them in practice (Soviet "war communism," Maoist communes, Castroist crusade against incentives, and the like), the distance covered is substantial indeed. The dream of a marketless and moneyless economy equally distributing the fruits of freely associating and harmoniously coordinated labor not only has given way to a much more pragmatic setup but has also disappeared (or at least is fast receding) from programmatic documents concerning the future (compare, for instance, from this point of view the three programs of the Communist party of the USSR).

If, however, our point of reference is the economic system that emerged after the transitional period in the Soviet Union in the early 1930s and that was imitated as a model by most of the communist countries after World War II, the actual evolution has been modest, to say the least. I do not mean to underestimate changes that took place after Stalin's death, but I should like to draw a clear distinction between what I regard as the model features (or principles) of the system and the deviations that were so numerous and so important in Stalinist practice. Thus, all the well-known restrictions on the market for consumer goods (consumers' freedom of choice) and on the labor market (the right to choose one's job) cannot be treated as elements of the model, and hence their gradual lifting does not signify a move away from it. The same applies, in my view, to the greater practical recognition of the differences between the state and cooperative enterprises (as reflected, for example, in the improved terms of trade between the state and the *kolkhozy* in the USSR), or to many organizational changes in the hierarchical structure of management (for example, the *Kombinate* organization of industry in the German Democratic Republic [GDR], or the recently promoted agroindustrial complexes in the USSR). The principles involved in regulation of the economy, which I described in my 1961 book (English edition, *The Market in the Socialist Economy*, 1972) remain in place in the USSR and in most of the other communist countries (with exceptions that will be mentioned below): obligatory output targets, physical allocation of producer goods, and the passive role of money within the state sector, which together form the model of a command economy (or, in my own terminology, the "centralistic model").

The changes that either mean a move toward a different regulating principle (what I like to call "economic reform") or substantively modify the existing principle have to be divided between those within the (dominant) state sector and those outside. Within the state sector, the two outstanding cases are Yugoslavia since the early 1950s and Hungary since 1968; in both these countries the formal structures of the command model have been dismantled and new regulating principles officially proclaimed. In Yugoslavia, especially after 1965, it was to be basically the market (as the appropriate allocating mechanism for self-management socialism); in Hungary, a combination of central planning on the macroscale with the market as an instrument of regulation on the microscale (again, using my own terminology, a system close to the model of "central planning with a regulated market mechanism"). I shall have more to say about the success (or lack of it) of these two reforms later, particularly with regard to Hungary;

whatever the evaluation, however, they represent the most decisive departure from the command model of the state sector so far. China has taken some steps along a similar road but still retains strong elements of the old system in the main state industrial sector. The 1982 Polish reform project has been bogged down by the interaction of political and economic disequilibria and only in 1987 have new attempts been made to regain the lost momentum. In other countries, the command model still stays in place, and its practical modifications amount mostly to reduction of the number of obligatory plan indicators, with the financial ones gaining in importance (Bulgaria is a case in point here, as is the so-called "complex economic experiment" in the USSR), to streamlining of the supply system (this seems to be one of the benefits of the reorganization in the GDR), and to some relaxation of the traditional form of the foreign trade monopoly. The degree of autonomy of lower-level economic units is perhaps also increasing as a result of the introduction (albeit slow and hesitant) of collectivist incentives linked to final results, which in consistent application may resemble a "contracting out" system (as in the idea of the "full-khozraschet" brigade in some Soviet experiments). The real implications for the evolution of the communist economic system of the concept of "radical economic reform" launched by Gorbachev in the USSR cannot, obviously, be assessed at this stage.

Outside the state sector systemic evolution shows significant differences between agricultural and nonagricultural activities. In agriculture the evolution took a peculiar form of retention of or return to some form of individual farming. In Poland private farms are dominant (although the share of state farms increased in the 1970s at a considerable social cost); in Yugoslavia they still hold the majority share of total output but not of the marketed one. A dramatic change occurred in China, where earlier ambitions to implant a communistic system have been replaced by "production responsibility devolved to the households," that is, by some sort of leaseholds with surpluses traded freely on the market. In Hungary a successful combination of collective and individual farming has developed within the framework of agricultural producers' cooperatives, which gained much greater autonomy as a result of the overall economic reform, and in which the individual component has come to be larger and to be treated more as a partner in the division of labor than as a barely tolerated remnant of the past. The latter attitude, for a long time predominant, is gradually receding in other countries as well with the development of more favorable conditions for individual plots in Bulgaria, the USSR, and elsewhere, but is still far from matching Hungary. In nonagricultural activities changes are on the whole less pronounced. In Hungary and Poland the number of establishments privately owned (or contracted out to private entrepreneurs) has grown, including the controversial "workers' partnerships" within state firms. Private enterprise in various forms exists more freely in tourism industries in several countries (not only Yugoslavia and Hungary, but also Bulgaria) and receives encouragement in handicrafts and services in general. Attempts were made to attract foreign capital investment without much success. In China, where the weight of agriculture is so enormous and where the production responsibility system with its market implications demands greater flexibility from industry and services dealing with agriculture, the tendency to extend the scope for private and small collective enterprise is gradually gaining momentum. I leave aside here the entire field of the "second economy"—understood as economic activity outside the formal structure, illegal or semilegal—not because I underestimate its significance, but because I find it difficult to establish any particular trend in its share and structure.

When one lists the changes by themselves they may loom large, but obviously they have to be related to the overall systemic developments, which in my view have been modest. Except perhaps for agriculture in China and some areas close to it, there is hardly anything in the evolution of the communist system so far that would warrant putting it in one league with the Russian New Economic Policy (NEP) of the early 1920s. If we take, for instance, the specific weights of the state and nonstate sectors even in a country like Hungary, the clear front-runner in reforms within the Soviet bloc, the share of the former in national income (NMP) has grown over the last quarter of a century from around two-thirds to around three-fourths of the total; it is difficult to get overall figures for the other side of the spectrum—the private and quasi-private sector (including activities counted officially as part of the socialist sector, such as individual farming within agricultural cooperatives, auxiliary farms of those employed in socialist enterprises, leaseholds and franchises, and workers' partnerships), but its share seems not to have increased even after 1970, despite the recovery since the late 1970s following an earlier slump. Of course, the same or a similar share means a substantial increase in absolute output of the private and semiprivate sector, particularly in agriculture, where it is estimated as about one-third of agricultural production proper.

To sum up the picture as I see it, a tendency is discernible in commu-

nist countries to move away from gauging the level of genuine socialism in their economic system simply by the scope of state ownership
of means of production and by the degree to which centralist planning eliminates the market mechanism; this tendency is significant,
especially because it appears not in the first (transitional) period of
socialist transformation as with NEP, but in the one claimed to be advanced. The impact it has made on the edifice of the economic system
in communist countries, however, is less than some observers (myself
certainly among them) would have expected a quarter of a century
ago: expectations notwithstanding, the economy is overwhelmingly
and firmly in the hands of a monoarchal* state, which still relies mainly
on administrative means of regulation.

The Possible Causes of Slowness

The changes have been slow, their scope has been limited. Why?
The first supposition would be that they simply might not be needed,
that the system performs satisfactorily. But this would clearly be an inadequate answer in view of the persistent and well-founded criticism,
not only by outside experts or a handful of domestic intellectuals, but
in a sense by the ruling elites themselves, which in one way or another
have for a long time tried to effect a change. Yugoslavia, initially the
most faithful imitator of the Soviet command system, began in 1950;
several countries of the Soviet bloc tried to carry out systemic reforms
in the second half of the 1950s (Hungary, abandoned after the bloody
Soviet invasion; Poland in 1956–57; the USSR since 1957 with the
Sovnarkhoz reform; Czechoslovakia in 1958). Then came what I call
the second wave of economic reforms in the 1960s: the New Economic
System in the GDR; the Kosygin reform and its Bulgarian imitation;
the economic component of the Czechoslovak Spring, suppressed with
only slight delay after the Soviet invasion; two clumsy Polish attempts
(the second ending with the massacre of the workers on the Baltic
coast in December 1970); and finally the Hungarian New Economic
Mechanism (NEM), introduced in January 1968. The 1970s were less
propitious for reform projects: in the GDR and Czechoslovakia they
were formally condemned, in most other countries tacitly abandoned.

Monoarchy is a term I use to describe a political system in which power is monopolized by a single group (upper echelons of the Communist party) without the possibility
of being contested by any outside groups, without freedom to form independent organizations, or freedom of expression; the opposite of *polyarchy*. Cf. Robert A. Dahl and
Charles E. Lindblom, *Politics, Economics and Welfare* (New York: Harper, 1953).

Nevertheless, there was another—unsuccessful—attempt in Poland (the so-called WOG reform, WOG standing for "large economic organizations"), and the Hungarian NEM survived despite mixed fortunes in the middle of the period.

The 1980s, to the contrary, display a strong, although not universal, revival of reformist attitudes, undoubtedly under the mounting pressure of economic difficulties and the collapse of the earlier import-led growth strategy, which also could have been perceived as an attempt to outmaneuver the need for systemic change. Apart from the sharpening of the reform tendency in Hungary and a more comprehensive blueprint in Poland, we witness another move in the same direction in Bulgaria. Moreover, the 1980s are marked by a resolute move to reform the economic mechanism in the major centers of the communist world: China and the USSR. The Chinese economic reform began first and, if not for other reasons, for its sheer scale must be regarded as of paramount importance. It should be noticed that as an expression of criticism of the Soviet model, the earlier Maoist commune drive and "cultural revolution" were also relevant regardless of all the aberrations involved. That the Maoist move away from the Soviet model proved futile (as did Khrushchevian ideas in the 1960s) makes the concept of reform of the economic mechanism more unequivocal. Reform means moving toward economic decentralization, breaking the monopoly of vertical lines of information and stimulation, using market mechanisms within the state production sphere, and other means, with appropriate consequences for relations outside the state sector. The alternative is not another kind of reform, but retention of the old model with or without corrections of its modus operandi (the GDR since the beginning of the 1970s is a case in point of the former).

Thus I see the past thirty years as a long series of attempts to change the economic mechanism, and this in itself should be considered an important element of evidence of perceived shortcomings of the existing system. In the course of that period some peculiar convergence of ideas about the possible direction of reform has emerged, despite all the differences with regard to the scope and role of the market mechanism in a socialist economy. And yet, the results are meager, which in my opinion indicates that reasons other than needs (and awareness of them) are to be sought.

There are numerous hypotheses concerning these reasons. I see them in the interaction of three groups of obstacles: political, vested interests of various social groups, and substantive difficulties in combining plan and market on the basis of public ownership. I do not

mention here a fourth possible source of resistance to change, ideological—a market-oriented economic reform as a direction opposite
to the traditional image of communism—because its actual role in the
behavior of communist elites can hardly be established, even approximately (if pressed, I would venture to say that the importance of this
factor is diminishing). In the remaining part of this section I shall
briefly sketch what I mean by the first two groups of reasons, devoting
the entire next section to the third one, including its interactions with
the former two.

Political obstacles are rooted in the fear of the ruling elites that
an economic reform presents a threat to the political system of communist monoarchy. It is by no means certain that there is a straightforward and simple relationship between evolution of the economic
and of the political systems, but in all instances of political struggle
around the issue of economic reforms in communist countries such
a relationship seems to have been recognized both by the supporters
and the opponents of the power monopoly, and some features of the
centralistic model of functioning of the economy are virtually inseparable from the way power is exercised: *nomenklatura* at all levels of
management, ability to direct and redirect resources by commands in
order to achieve chosen political priorities, control over both the price
and the wage sides of income distribution, and so on. The domestic political dimension has been obviously discernible in all individual
reform attempts, in none perhaps more than in Poland, where the
sequence of forward and backward movements repeated itself time
and again resulting in a characteristic pattern: under economic and
political pressure, resistance from above would periodically turn into
reluctant acceptance of reform; directly political aspects of reform
(among other things, meaningful workers' self-management) would be
eliminated; the scope of changes in the economic mechanism would
be narrowed; gradualistic tactics of implementation would then be
adopted, with particular attention to preservation of the institutional
setup at the center and of the *nomenklatura* principle in appointments;
finally, all avenues promising to overcome economic difficulties without reform would be given priority, and the preserved institutional
structure would provide the fallback framework for a return to the old
system, perhaps with slight adjustments. The external political dimension is linked with the special position of the USSR within the Council
for Mutual Economic Assistance (CMEA or COMECON). The Soviet
Union's Warsaw Pact and the interests in preserving the internal cohesion of the bloc on the basis of its own brand of socialism are inter-

locked with Soviet interests as a global power. In my view the overall role of the political factor as an obstacle to economic reform has, so far, been greater in the Soviet Union than elsewhere for the following reasons:

1. Since the introduction of NEP in a political emergency, Soviet leadership has not been confronted with the same pressure for reforms experienced in several other communist countries. This does not mean that such latent pressure is absent (that material aspirations of the people are lacking), but that the room for maneuver for the Soviet leadership remains much larger, as is the degree to which the reform process depends on initiative from above. Under such conditions political attitudes of the ruling elite carry correspondingly greater weight.

2. The Soviet Union is a multinational state, with a formally federal structure. An economic reform, entailing decentralization of some elements of the market mechanism, may pose a threat of centrifugal tendencies in non-Russian areas.

3. Economic reform in the USSR encourages reformist tendencies in the "people's democracies" with possible political consequences in more than one sense. In Eastern Europe the link between economic and political change is closer, threatening Soviet political interests within the countries in question. An additional problem is the impact of an economic reform on the cohesion of the Soviet bloc.

4. The Soviet Union is a superpower not by virtue of her overall economic might but by her ability to mobilize a greater share of resources for global military purposes than other members of the bloc. Insofar as this ability is ascribed to the properties of the centralistic system, the Soviet leadership may see an overriding political interest in maintaining it. All this has added to the endogenous obstacles to reform in the "people's democracies" an exogenous one: the threat of Soviet opposition, sometimes genuine (as in Czechoslovakia, when economic reforms formed a part of a broad political change), sometimes used by the local elites as a kind of bogey.

It would be wrong to perceive the political factor as acting only in the direction of anti-reform. Provided an economic reform is effective, it should bring obvious political dividends too. An often cited example is the political gain from Hungarian economic reform as opposed to the huge political losses in unreformed Poland. From a purely military viewpoint, it may be increasingly difficult to continue to maintain a superpower position based on an economic system that is not conducive to innovation and is wasteful in use of labor and materials. On balance, however, the political factor must be counted, in my view, as a serious obstacle to economic reform. Moreover, even in cases when this obstacle has been surmounted (as in Hungary), or when political interest demanded an economic reform (as in Yugoslavia after the break with Stalin), the ruling elites tried their utmost to isolate the reform as narrowly economic, preventing its spread to the political sphere. Whatever the signs of liberalization in areas regarded as of secondary political significance (I use the term "political indifference zones"), the monoarchal polity in all the countries reformed or reforming economically has remained firmly in place (a touch of irony: Yugoslavia and Hungary do not even have any of the noncommunist parties that exist in other countries without a real role in normal times, but sometimes capable of springing into life in moments of crisis). This is not merely a statement of fact that economic and political change do not necessarily go together, but also an indication of a fundamental problem: what is the impact of such unchanged monoarchy on the consistency and effectiveness of economic reform? I shall return to this question in the next section.

The role of vested interests of various social groups in hindering economic reform is most difficult to ascertain, let alone to measure. "Interest" in a general sense is not a well-defined category, especially—as in the case we are concerned with here—when political and directly material interests are intertwined, and not only for the ruling elite and its supporting apparatus but also, on the other side of the spectrum, for a substantial part of the population at large, which—as could be seen a number of times in the "people's democracies"—may expect economic reform to result in both improvement in living standards and extension of political freedoms. Another complicating factor is the power of habit, which makes individuals and entire social groups wish to conserve the customary ways of doing things, and which again overlaps with concrete material interests insofar as change may demand qualities never possessed or irretrievably lost in operating or simply working in the existing system. The difficulty is increased by lack of systematic and reliable evidence from research, particularly in the Soviet Union, where the official ideology has been for a long time based on the assertion that under socialism there are no meaningful social groups interested in preservation of obsolete relations of production, and the current political leadership is by definition always the most progressive. Nevertheless, I think, on the basis of my own observations and pieces of evidence that can be gathered from sociological works published in the West and in some communist countries, that the following proposition can be accepted: there is a constituency *for* economic reforms in all countries, but at the same time there are considerable social forces *against* them, not only among the upper strata close to the seats of power, or in the middle levels of party and state apparatus (often the strongest resisters), but also among the rank-and-file workers, especially the less skilled, who are frequently wary of the promise of greater efficiency and earnings if reform is linked to higher labor productivity and the possibility of losing the familiar cushions of absolute job security, overmanning, and a take-it-easy atmosphere. Even among the managerial stratum, regarded in the conventional wisdom as the most ardent supporter of economic reform ("technocrats want to be rid of bureaucratic tutelage"), attitudes are by no means uniform, especially in the USSR, where the centralistic system has operated for over half a century and in conditions of stricter isolation than elsewhere, alternatives look more alien for the third or perhaps even the fourth generation of managers raised under this system, selected by criteria containing a strong political component and unused to risks connected with independent decision making.

Again, as in the case of political obstacles, resistance engendered by vested interests might significantly influence the consistency and effectiveness of economic reform even if it went ahead. Hence the feedback between the first two groups of causes of the slowness of change and the substantive difficulties of combining the plan with the market.

Substantive Difficulties of Reform: The Compatibility of Plan and Market

An assessment of the substantive difficulties facing economic reform in communist countries requires that the notion of economic reform be better defined. As indicated in the first section of this essay, I understand an economic reform in the strict sense to be a change from one principle of regulation of the economy to another. But this in turn calls for clarification of the meaning of the principle. Because this is a discussion of the evolution of the communist economic system, we can hardly stretch the change of a regulating principle to include replacing the dominant position of public ownership of means of production with the dominance of private ownership. Within these limits, however, there can be different proportions of mix between various forms of ownership (including private) and—what the experience of communist countries proves of particular importance—different relations between the regulating (coordinating) role of administrative agencies on the one hand and that of the market on the other. The latter are usually presented as relations between the plan and the market, which is not fully precise (some forms of central management hardly deserve the term *planning*, some forms of planning may be conceived as working through the market) but can be accepted for the sake of simplicity. An administrative mechanism of regulation is, as a rule, tantamount to centralization of economic decisions (although some decisions may be delegated to lower levels of the administrative hierarchy); a market mechanism of regulation requires decentralization of decisions. Now, let us schematically divide economic decisions into three broad categories: (1) macroeconomic decisions concerning main lines of development of the national economy (including the rate of savings and the balance between savings and investment), as well as broad issues of social policy; (2) current microeconomic decisions at the level of the firm or amalgamation of firms; and (3) individual decisions taken by households in the sphere of consumption and employment. Using "centralized" to denote the administrative mechanism of regulation (command planning, physical allocation of resources) and "decentralized" to denote the market mechanism, I arrange the historically known systems of functioning of a socialist economy in the following pattern of models:

War communism: centralizes (1), (2), and (3).
The command ("centralistic") model: centralizes (1) and (2) but decentralizes (3).
The model of a centrally planned economy with a regulated market mechanism (sometimes called the "decentralized model"): centralizes (1) but decentralizes (2) and (3).
Market socialism: decentralizes (1), (2), and (3).

Needless to say, all this is terribly schematic and oversimplified, but it helps to clarify my understanding of an economic reform in the strict sense of the term. It is a change from one of these models to another, as distinct from modifications within each of them. According to this classification, the objective of the 1968 Hungarian reform was to go over from the command model (which approximates the Soviet-style system operating since the beginning of the 1930s) to a system close to the model of a centrally planned economy with a regulated market mechanism. By the same token, the objective of the 1965 Yugoslav reform was, on the whole, to arrive at a system corresponding to market socialism. In both cases there was sufficient will from above to go

ahead with the reforms (within limits indicated earlier), as well as—
to the extent it can be assessed on the basis of mostly impressionistic
evidence—rather widespread support from below. And yet both reforms have encountered serious difficulties and—so far—have failed
to reach the form of regulation envisaged and the economic effects
expected. I shall try now to examine the issues involved, concentrating
mainly on the Hungarian case, with the Yugoslav experience brought
in only occasionally (among other things because of the peculiarities
of the Yugoslav system connected with the federal structure of the
country).

The idea of the Hungarian NEM was to retain the benefits of
planned regulation on a macroscale—adjustment of the distribution
of national income to a full employment level of output over time,
taking care of externalities in long-term structural changes, and the
like—while simultaneously to remove the informational and motiva-
tional deficiencies of central planning in its command form: the growing inability of the center not only to achieve efficiency but even consistency in the plans, the systemically determined tendency of each
level of the economic hierarchy to press superiors for lower targets
and greater resources (János Kornai's "soft budget constraint" leading
to the all-pervasive "shortage economy"), reluctance to innovate, and
import hunger combined with low capacity to export, particularly to
competitive markets. For this purpose the market was to be assigned
an active role not only in relations between the state and the households (with restrictions appearing often in practice of the Soviet-style
system consistently removed), but also within the state production sector. Abolishing obligatory output targets and administrative allocation
of production factors was to free enterprises from commands and ex-
pose them to self-regulatory mechanisms in the market. With profit as
the main criterion of success and the source both of incentives for the
work force (wage rises dependent on financial viability plus a profit-
sharing fund for bonuses) and of self-financing for autonomous investment activity, enterprises were supposed to be subjected to the discipline of the market ("hard budget constraint," again using Kornai's
terminology). The price system was to meet the requirement of market clearing both in the consumption and production spheres and at
the same time to remain parametric, that is, independent of the interested parties (enterprises as price-takers only), by distinguishing between three categories of prices: freely fluctuating (with competition
to be judged as sufficiently effective), moving within an established
range, and fixed by state bodies (the most important items with strong

probability of monopolistic price making; this category was supposed to shrink along with the development of competitive conditions).

Coordination of the market-regulated activity of the enterprises with the general provisions of the plan was supposed to rest on (1) the macroeconomic framework created by fundamental decisions of the central planner with regard to the distribution of national income (including principles of remuneration) and allocation of the main bulk of investment funds among sectors, areas, and large individual projects; (2) determination of the rules of behavior for enterprises (success criteria and their incentive consequences) in such a way as to direct local interests onto a converging path with the general ones; and (3) fiscal, monetary, and price policies which would effectively support (1) and (2). Thus the macroeconomic plan should remain effective in setting the economy on a broadly delineated course, but without exercising direct control over economic actors in the microsphere, even relinquishing central control altogether in matters outside well-defined social preferences (recognition of broad economic "zones of indifference"). The interaction between an effective central plan so conceived and a market mechanism was to be made possible by, on the one hand, providing the central planner with the right to issue binding rules, but, on the other, making these rules general (except for major investment projects) so as to create the necessity and the room for both the planner and the enterprises to adjust.

Why have the almost twenty years of experience of the Hungarian NEM failed to provide an unequivocal confirmation of the expectations connected with the model of a centrally planned economy with a regulated market mechanism (which, I am bound to say, happened to be my own favorite idea)? There were factors both external (operation of NEM was affected by the unreformed CMEA and the adverse impact of developments on the world market, stronger than anywhere in Eastern Europe) and internal (an antireformist backlash between 1972 and 1978) which prevented the consistent implementation of some essential features of the concept. Nevertheless, and notwithstanding some improvements in many aspects of the performance of the economy, the general opinion of Hungarian economists is that the systemic changes failed to live up to expectations not only because of deviations from the 1968 blueprint but also because of deficiencies in the blueprint itself. When one reads Kornai's *Economics of Shortage*, many chapters of which contain sections dealing specifically with the post–1968 Hungarian economy, it becomes clear that although in his view the introduction of NEM has somewhat improved the operation of the system, it has not eliminated the fundamental ills of the soft budget constraint and its consequences. To him the Hungarian economy under NEM is not coordinated by the market but still remains administratively coordinated, differing from the Soviet one more in form than in substance (indirect instruments as distinct from direct ones). The main manifestation of this incomplete reform for the state sector (in the cooperative sector the situation is different) is seen in the failure to apply to state enterprises the general rules discussed above and through them to subject these enterprises to the rigors of the market. Instead, the widespread practice has been to tailor financial norms in such a way as to keep every enterprise afloat, replacing the former bargaining with the higher authorities over output targets and input allocations with new forms of bargaining over financial conditions.

To what extent are these failures (or weaknesses, if one wants to be kinder to the effects of NEM) attributable to the very idea of grafting a market mechanism on a fundamentally planned (centrally managed) economy, albeit in principle mainly on a macroscale? This is the crucial question that needs to be discussed.

Having rather carefully monitored and scrutinized the working of NEM, I can see now better than previously the pitfalls of such grafting. The exigencies of central control (even genuine exigencies, untainted by vested interests) inevitably generate tendencies at variance with conditions propitious for the operation of the market. Among these tendencies is the desire to retain a strong center of economic administration, supposedly for overall control purposes, but with an obvious inclination to extend its activities to general management. The reverse of the same coin is the preference for organizational concentration of enterprises: it is easier to control from the center a smaller number of larger units. In Hungary mergers on an exceptionally large scale preceded the transition to NEM, and analogous processes were taking place elsewhere as well whenever an economic reform was contemplated (the Polish WOG reform was the most conspicuous case in point, but similar phenomena occurred in Bulgaria, Romania, and East Germany). Needless to say, whatever the merits of concentration for the purposes of control, it threatens to undermine a number of premises for an effective market: (1) it creates obvious—oligopolistic, or even straightforward monopolistic—barriers to competition, especially because counting on foreign competition quickly proves futile in view of balance-of-payment difficulties (this is also the Yugoslav experience); (2) it creates powerful pressure groups for the tailoring of financial rules mentioned above, and particularly for state support of

overambitious investment plans; and (3) it makes less probable a refusal by the state to bail out a huge concern in trouble because of the
scale of economic and social consequences, a phenomenon well known
also in Western economies, not only with regard to nationalized industries but also to private corporations. In other words, the objective of
maintaining central control seems not easy to reconcile with one of the
basic assumptions of the model of a centrally planned economy with
a regulated market mechanism requiring enterprises to work under
firmly applied (and stable) rules of behavior.

This problem is, as it turns out, connected with another fundamental assumption of the model, namely the distinction between long-
term investment decisions (largely assigned to the center) and current
operations left to autonomous decisions of the enterprises. The latter
are not deprived of investment initiative entirely. They can, out of
their own accumulated funds supplemented by borrowing, modern-
ize their equipment and even expand productive capacity. What they
cannot do within this model, however, is to undertake on their own
a wide-ranging diversification program, let alone branch out into a
completely new field of activity, if more substantial capital outlays are
involved. In a situation when an enterprise is stuck in its old mode
and no more promising line of activity arises, the only choice is often
between complete closure and subsidization, and the latter course is
usually taken. Apart from the negative consequences for the strength
of market pressure on efficiency, this situation increases the dependence of enterprises on their administrative superiors. Then there is
the question of responsibility for poor-quality investment decisions
taken by the center which adversely affect conditions of current operations (this is again a frequent case in Yugoslavia, where complaints
abound about "lame ducks" created by political decisions).

Here we come to the interaction between the consistency and effectiveness of economic reform and the lack of change in the political
system. In the past, when arguing the need to combine economic with
political reform, I emphasized mainly the indispensability of plural-
ization of the polity for eliminating the arbitrariness of central decisions (uncontrolled, without genuine consideration of alternatives
under monoarchy), as well as for increasing the involvement of the
population at large in national economic matters, thereby making the
link between common and personal interest more tangible and giving
self-management initiatives a better chance. What was stressed less,
if at all, was the importance of the political change for the functioning of the market component in the combined model. Meanwhile, the

practice of Yugoslavia and Hungary (and in a fledgling form also that of China) shows how great a hindrance a system of monoarchy is for the use of market parameters. Credit policy, for instance, cannot work properly without a degree of independence of the banking system in determining the size, conditions, and sureties of a loan; but if the local bank manager is on a *nomenklatura* list of the local party committee, which is likely to be interested in expansionary spending or in bailing out underperforming enterprises, he can hardly be expected to resist a "suggestion" from the authority empowered to appoint and dismiss him. This example is particularly relevant for the situation in Yugoslavia, where the power of local authorities often makes impossible coherent national monetary and fiscal policies (some provincial and municipal authorities in China have also shown their capacity to force banks to act against both commercial judgment and central policy guidelines). But the problem is not limited to local subordination or to bank managers; it is equally, and sometimes maybe even more, acute on a national level or with regard to the managers of industrial enterprises. Of course, the dependence of banking and industry on government administration is ubiquitous nowadays, with nationalized industries and institutions especially so. But any comparison of communist with Western countries in this respect must take into account not only the difference in degree, but first and foremost the difference in political system, which is the point here: communist countries depend on the hierarchically structured apparatus of a single party not exposed to public scrutiny and to electoral verification. It would perhaps be premature to assert without separate detailed examination that the communist monoarchy makes operation of any kind of market outright impossible, but it certainly creates serious difficulties.

The last point on my list of major substantive obstacles to an economic reform concerns the ownership structure. I have touched upon this issue in the first section when sketching the picture of actual systemic evolution, but now I should like to look at it a bit closer, again mainly with reference to the experience of the reformers—Hungary and Yugoslavia and perhaps also China. It is clear that (1) reforms outside the state sector are by far easier and more successful, and (2) the dominant state ownership of means of production appears in a single traditional form of property rights vested fully in state institutions. Even in Yugoslavia, where the term "state ownership" has been purged in favor of an ill-defined concept of "social ownership," the self-managing collective does not own the assets (thus it is not a cooperative) but is a trustee of the society as a whole, which somehow tends inexorably to institutionalize itself in state bureaucracy on various levels, despite the ample rhetoric about all authority emanating from self-managed communities. The link between (1) and (2) seems not hard to trace: introduction of the market outside the state sector, genuine cooperatives included, finds here a ready-made motivation syndrome linking personal (or personal through group) interest with business performance and—even more important—interest in current gain with interest in growth (or at least preservation) of assets; whereas within the state sector such a motivation syndrome properly reacting to market stimuli has yet to be created, a complex enough task for the link between current performance and remuneration of various categories of employees (including managers), but particularly difficult (some would say impossible) with regard to long-term development requiring a fine balance between present and future, as well as between risk and responsibility. I was always aware that the solution to the conflict between long- and short-term interests would present particular difficulties in a state-owned enterprise, but I hoped that employees' self-management would help to achieve it by strengthening the collective, which in itself is a factor of continuity. This was the reason for my critical attitude to the omission of self-management in the Hungarian NEM. The Yugoslav experience, however, does not seem to have confirmed my point about self-management solving or at least significantly alleviating the above conflict. That the workers' share in the results of enterprise is based not on any form of personal property rights but exclusively on employment, the loss or change of which means disappearance of the stake in assets, generates a strong tendency to maximize the personal share and minimize the collective share in current distributable income of the enterprise (often accompanied by inflation-fueling pressure for development funds from outside). It is interesting in this context that the tendency in question is by no means a reflection of low propensity to save as such, but of low propensity to save collectively (a considerable part of current incomes may be turned into private savings). This shows that it is was wrong to underestimate the question of property rights in the blueprints of economic reform, which focused on the new relationship between the plan and the market without posing the question of how the existing ownership structure would fit into the new situation. I still do not subscribe to the view that private ownership is the only possible environment for the operation of the market, but a mixed economy, both in the sense of a larger share of nonstate enterprises and in the sense of greater diversification of ownership relations within the state sector, seems to me much more conducive to a market-oriented economic reform than the structure that has evolved so far.

Apart from the problems discussed above which relate to the shape of the reformed system, there are also numerous difficulties connected with the transition from the old system to the new one. Experience shows that the hardest to manage is the change in the field of pricing, in which it is necessary to move from passive, demand-insensitive, often heavily subsidized prices to flexible indicators of real alternatives of choice. Under prevalent conditions of market disequilibria (if not always in the aggregate, at least in many important markets for particular goods), such a change must lead either to an overall increase in the price level or at least to substantial alterations of price relativities. The effect on income is obvious, and attempts to compensate losses—strongly differentiated by social groups and family circumstances—may be either futile or very costly because of the unavoidable overpayment on the aggregate scale. Not only the danger of an inflationary spiral but also the imminent damage to the incentive system has to be kept in mind, especially as one of the elements of the reform is strengthening the role of incentives linked to the performance of enterprises. This complex of issues becomes even more daunting in view of the obvious circumstance that systemic changes cannot normally produce quick spectacular results, which brings us again to politics. The population's readiness to swallow bitter medicine is no doubt a function of the degree of trust in and support for the leadership, and the leadership's resolve to go for painful but effective surgery is dependent on the same conditions. Depoliticization of an economic reform is in itself a sign that these conditions are lacking, which does not augur well for the ability to overcome the substantive difficulties, and this in turn reduces the desire to reform both from above and from below: a true vicious circle.

A Few Thoughts on Prospects

The inevitable conclusion from all these deliberations is that the success of the reform project depends heavily on the ability to push the boundaries of change forward. This seems to be the prevalent opinion among academic economists (and other social scientists) in those communist countries in which a debate about reform is going on: Hungary, China, Poland, and Yugoslavia (although in the last case the open debate is still confused, probably for ideological and political reasons, i.e., of the untouchability of the existing self-management concept on the one hand and the complexity of the national question on the other).

Hungary, where the orderly experience of a reformed system is available along with an admirable intellectual effort to use it, is already in the course of tackling at least three out of the four groups of problems discussed in the previous section.

1. The overconcentrated industrial organizations are being split up.

2. Attempts are being made to diversify the institutional status of state enterprises and their relationship with administrative agencies by distinguishing among three categories: infrastructural enterprises directly subordinated to government departments; commercially run enterprises with conventional management supervised by boards representing the interests of the state, the employees, and outside interests such as financial institutions and consumer organizations; and smaller enterprises organized fully on self-management principles with management elected by the work force.

3. Rudimentary forms of the capital market are being introduced by entitling state enterprises (along with cooperatives and local authorities) to issue bonds, with a perspective to try equity shares as well; a complementary banking reform with the aim of establishing commercial banks is under way. At the same time the process of improving the conditions for the nonstate sector, particularly for cooperatives and all forms of partnerships, is in progress (not without the usual hiccups).

Similar ideas, and practical moves, can be observed in the nonstate sector in China. In the Chinese state industry, some of the old command methods are still present, but important elements of what may be called a dual system of planning and regulation are emerging on a scale not witnessed elsewhere. Only part of an enterprise's production capacity is being covered by obligatory targets with corresponding state-allocated inputs (both output and input at government fixed prices), and the use of the remaining part (as a rule substantial) is left at the discretion of the enterprise itself (including flexible pricing of sales), with the proviso that inputs are procured from the market. Although this duality cannot be a lasting phenomenon, it indicates the direction of change and probably helps in the gradual transformation of the system in state industry. It is a strategy that has its dangers, but it is regarded by many as the only realistic one in Chinese conditions.

It is not my purpose here to discuss the details of these and similar measures. What is essential is to note the coincidence of the moves

toward diversification of the status of state enterprises and enlargement of the mix element in the economy with the attempted new forms
of financial intermediation in the investment sphere. The intercon-
nection is clear: the recognition of the need to open up significant
room for horizontal capital flows must go hand in hand with further emancipation of state enterprises from administrative tutelage,
including financial responsibility ("full responsibility for profits and
losses," as the appropriate Chinese phrase goes), while at the same
time wider application of commercial criteria in allocation of funds
(genuine credit) must force these enterprises to prove their financial
viability in competition with each other and with claimants outside
the state sector. It is also clear that what we are seeing cannot be
regarded as a conceptually (let alone practically) closed stage. In particular, the concept of public (or social, as I prefer it) ownership of
the means of production is a prime candidate for serious reconsideration, which must include such questions as whether public ownership
(in communist countries but elsewhere too) should be identified with
outright and exclusive ownership by the state without any room for
equity participation by individuals (both employees and the public at
large), financial institutions, voluntary organizations, and others. The
matter is discussed with increased intensity in all countries engaged in
economic reform and struggling with the problem of how to achieve
its expected effects. Such discussion is most active in Hungary but is
also occurring in China and Poland and even in Yugoslavia (in the
latter case, however, without clearly relating it to critical examination
of the universal self-management structure). Practical steps are, so
far, few, and those that are being taken (such as reorganizing state
firms or institutions into joint-stock companies) seem rather to shift
the problem than to solve it. The shareholders are mostly designated
bodies whose behavior hardly resembles that of a proprietor striving
for business gains and forcing entrepreneurship; cases of individual
or group shareholding playing a more substantial role are not known
to me. This is hardly surprising in view of the obvious difficulties in
accommodating reconsideration of property rights with fundamentals
of the orthodox socialist doctrine, but the very fact that such reconsideration begins at all in a pragmatic way says something about the
awareness of the depth of the changes needed.

Can anything be said about economic limits to this evolution of
the communist system? This is a most pertinent question from the
point of view of the limits which I tried to define in the model of a
centrally planned economy with a regulated market mechanism, par-

ticularly with regard to the lines of division between the centralized decisions and the decentralized current ones, as well as with regard to the fundamental question of the relationship between the plan and the market. Even if the concept itself assumed some interaction between the plan and the market, between central decisions and those of the enterprises and households, the emphasis on the instrumental role of the market as merely a tool of the plan (an institutional structure in which resources are allocated *through* the market but not *by* the market, to paraphrase Andreas Papandreou's formula from the preface to his *Paternalistic Capitalism*) was too strong. It is difficult to say to what extent this conceptual flaw has actually influenced the practice of reforms, which was obviously affected by more powerful factors, but even in the cases when market institutions actually did emerge they were as a rule reduced to basically an instrumental role. Hence the conclusion formulated at the beginning of this section—the success of the reform depends on the ability to push forward the boundaries of change—has to be understood, in terms of my own theorizing, that reform should go beyond the model of a centrally planned economy with a regulated market mechanism.

Having said this, I must stress, however, that I do not regard the need for reconsideration of some of the limits recognized in the past as tantamount to acceptance of unlimited marketization of the system, even for reasons of pure efficiency. Enough is known about market failures, particularly in providing information for long-term investment decisions under conditions of technological and structural change, and about the problem of external costs and benefits, to excuse me from developing the argument here. The only thing that may be useful to recall in this context (I am wont to repeat it on every occasion) is the unlikelihood that market regulation can sustain full use of resources, particularly human resources, on a macroscale, because of fluctuations and the persistent tendency of profit maximizers in a market economy to hamper distributional adjustments that would assure an adequate level of aggregate effective demand. If the sustenance of reasonably full use of productive resources, and hence removal of the main source of waste, should be regarded as a legitimate objective of a socialist economic system (for me this is a rhetorical question the answer to which is an emphatic "yes"), then the following elements of effective central control, clearly beyond Keynesian fiscal and monetary macromanagement, must be retained:

1. Control over the investment process not in the sense that the state is the only or even the predominant investor but because it holds

a sufficiently strong position to be able to fill a possible ex-ante gap between the level of savings and the level of actual investment activity and to influence the shape of future productive capacity by its own investment initiative, if necessary.

2. Control over income distribution (price-wage relationship) on the macroscale, both for satisfying the conditions of macroequilibrium emphasized above and for achieving well-defined social objectives (the equity aspect).

(A third element should be added—control over external economic relations, by no means through the monopoly of foreign trade characteristic of the command system, which isolates the domestic economy from the outside world, but effective enough to filter the impact of the external environment. The international aspect, however, has been left out of this paper.)

These two (or three, including the international aspect) areas of effective central control were regarded by Michal Kalecki as indispensable conditions for planning in a mixed economy with a Popular Front form of government. He distinguished in 1964 between this kind of effective planning and planning in a socialist economy, which could rely on direct methods of control. It seems to me, however, that the main line of the reasoning is also applicable to a reformed socialist economy such as is discussed here. If this is correct, there is still a substantial scope for moving beyond the concept that underlay the Hungarian NEM without abandoning the essentials of socialism. Obviously, this extended version of central planning with a regulated market mechanism is bound to generate frictions and conflicts threatening failure to reconcile full use of resources with a hard budget constraint for the economic actors and to combine development along an equilibrium path with propensity to innovate. It looks more promising, however, to provide room for maneuver, to engender more flexible forms of conflict resolution, and in this sense on the whole more viable economically not only than the orthodox command system but also the reformed systems that have been tried.

The catch is once again in the political sphere—the one out of the four groups of problems discussed in the previous section which has not yet been mentioned in this section. NEM, the Yugoslav attempt at "market socialism," and the Chinese reform endeavors all suffer from monoarchy, which prevents the economic actors from exercising the necessary degree of independence. Our extended version of the reform model requires even greater independence for them. Let us assume that there is the political will to go ahead with a capital market, diversification of public ownership, and increased mix of different ownership sectors (in itself a bold assumption!). Does this mean that at the same time the political elite and its supporting apparatus are prepared to give up the *nomenklatura* principle of appointments and dismissals, to recognize the autonomy of popular organizations (trade unions) and institutions, to enter into corporatist negotiations? There are analysts who think that such a prospect is not excluded because it amounts to a compromise, to political pluralism of a limited nature, which does not challenge the dominant position of the Communist party through demands for a multiparty electoral system. I personally am skeptical because it is hard to envisage the degree of independence required being compatible with the leading role of the party, at least as it has always been interpreted in practice—as full monopoly of power. Resolution of this difference in opinions cannot be taken up here. What deserves to be stressed again, however, is the proposition that a coherent perspective on an evolution of the communist economic system toward a viable combination of plan and market must include political change.

In sum, the experience hitherto seems to indicate that to stand a chance of success, the evolution of the communist economic system needs to widen its scope substantially—not without *any* limits to marketization, but clearly beyond those that were previously thought sufficiently broad, including the political ones. The assessment of the likelihood of such widening, as well as of the alternative to a satisfactorily consistent economic reform, is a matter for separate discussion.

NINE

Dilemmas in the Pattern of Resource Allocation in China, 1978-1985

Nicholas R. Lardy

Beginning in the mid-1970s a profound debate occurred in China concerning the character and purposes of the socialist economic system. The range of opinions was diverse, the role of ideology was muted, and the political leadership was receptive to proposals for a broad range of alternative institutional arrangements. The ensuing implementation of reform policies was evolutionary and, lacking a detailed model of a reformed economic system, the leadership was willing to experiment and make corrections.

The liveliness of the debate and the boldness of the new policies would lead an observer to conclude that the post-Mao reforms have been profound. Distinctions must be made, however, between rhetoric and reality and among different sectors of the economy. A detailed study suggests that in certain critical respects China's resource allocation system changed but marginally by 1985. To be sure, the long-term consequences of the reforms remain uncertain. Nonetheless, almost eight years after the leaders committed themselves to substantial reform of the resource allocation system, the actual changes, except in agriculture, fell far short of announced objectives. The ownership and incentive structure in farming have been transformed almost completely, but in some other areas the reforms seem only to rationalize the administrative planning system rather than substantially to replace bureaucratic forms of allocation with market relations. In this respect the Chinese reforms to a significant degree paralleled those in the Soviet Union, the German Democratic Republic, Poland, and Romania, rather than those in Hungary, and earlier in Yugoslavia, which were oriented toward market economy conceptions.[1]

The inability to substitute markets for bureaucratic allocation in a larger sphere of the urban economy, particularly in state-owned industry, stems in part from China's industrial price structure. The fixed price system adopted in the 1950s over time became increasingly divorced from the underlying cost structure. Costs of producing raw materials rose, squeezing profit levels. For manufactured goods economies of scale and marginally increased productivity frequently resulted in declining costs as output expanded. The disparity between costs of production and prices for different items thus tended to rise over time, making incremental reform of the urban economy difficult to accomplish. Because prices rarely gave the appropriate signal to enterprises or other agents, newly freed from centralized controls, the bureaucracy all too often had to intervene to ameliorate the unanticipated negative consequences of the previous relaxation of bureaucratic control. Thus the centrality of the bureaucracy has endured, seemingly immune to the attempts of the reform-oriented leadership to break out of the encrusted system.

Resource Mobilization

The neglect of comprehensive balance in the Maoist era was among the most salient criticisms made by the reformers during the late 1970s. The attack focused on the appropriate rate of gross investment, or "accumulation," as it is called in Soviet and Chinese accounting of net material product. Accumulation, the share of output devoted to investment, averaged 24 percent during the First Five-Year Plan and rose to more than 30 percent during 1966–78 (Table 9.1). Despite that increased rate of investment the growth of national income had declined somewhat from 8.9 percent per annum in the 1950s to 5.8 percent in 1966–78.[2]

In 1977 an important debate developed over the underlying purpose of economic growth. Some Chinese criticized the rising investment rate and the high priority attached to producer goods as compared to other sectors; they condemned the emphasis on "production for the sake of production."[3] These critics noted that the improvement in the welfare of the population, as reflected by the growth of per capita income and consumption between 1957 and 1978, was remarkably modest for an economy in which per capita national income had doubled. Per capita output had been growing at more than 3 percent per annum, but consumption had risen by less than half that rate. The per capita consumption of food grains, and almost certainly total ca-

TABLE 9.1
Accumulation as a Percent of National Income, 1953–1985

Period	Rate	Period	Rate
1953–57	24.2%	1979–83	30.6%
1958–62	30.8	1984	31.2
1963–65	22.7	1985	33.7
1966–78	31.2		

SOURCE: *Chinese Statistical Abstract, 1986* (Beijing: Statistical Publishing House, 1986), p. 7.

loric intake per capita, had declined.[4] The high rate of investment was accompanied by a profusion of investment projects. But the competition for scarce construction materials and machinery led to significant increases in the time required to complete projects. That meant that more and more capital was tied up in projects not yet producing goods, resulting in a further decline in the productivity of capital.

By 1978 a consensus apparently favored a substantial cutback in the rate of investment to facilitate an increase in personal consumption and living standards. Xue Muqiao, China's preeminent government economist, for example, spoke of the need to "repay a twenty year debt to the people's livelihood" and supported a reduction in the rate of investment to less than 30 percent. Others suggested that a rate of about 25 percent, the same as in the First Five-Year Plan, would be appropriate.[5]

Although substantial support existed for a lower rate of investment, the data in Table 9.1 show that that outcome was not achieved. The rate of investment in 1979–83, 30.6 percent, in nominal terms was not significantly lower than the 31.2 percent prevailing before the onset of reform, and the rate in 1985 rose to exceed the prereform level.*

*Chinese data on accumulation are calculated in current prices. Because there is some evidence that prices of consumer goods have risen more rapidly than those of producer goods since 1978, it is possible that the investment rate measured in constant prices would be higher than that reported. Since the Chinese State Statistical Bureau does not publish separate indices of prices of producer and consumer goods this tentative evaluation is based on indices for categories of commodities that are believed to be approximations of the underlying desired indices. Between 1978 and 1983 the national retail price index rose by 14.5 percent or 2.8 percent annually and the worker and staff cost of living index rose 16.9 percent or 3.2 percent annually. The index of ex-factory prices, however, which includes producer goods as well as consumer goods, rose by only 2.1 percent in total or .5 percent annually between 1978 and 1985, implying that the index of producers' prices probably actually fell (State Statistical Bureau, *Chinese Statistical Yearbook, 1983*, p. 455). Unfortunately, the State Statistical Bureau has discontinued publishing the index of ex-factory prices so it is not clear whether relative price changes continued after 1983.

The period 1979–85 thus differs from a seemingly similar period of readjustment in 1961–65, when the investment rate fell by more than half compared to the preceding years of the Great Leap Forward, 1958–60.

In large part that difference arose because the reform shifted the locus of investment decisions away from the central government toward enterprises and provincial governments, both of which, because of profit- and revenue-sharing systems introduced in the early stages of reform, had considerable incentives to undertake their own investment initiatives. Moreover, that hunger to expand investment was not curbed by realistic pricing of capital. Less than one-quarter of investment in the first half of the 1980s was financed by bank loans bearing any interest charges. Most investment continued to be financed by budgetary grants, for which no interest was paid and no repayment of principal was required, or from retained earnings. From the point of view of enterprises and ministries that controlled the bulk of these funds the rational strategy was to convert them to new machinery or expanded factories. In the absence of capital markets, retained earnings could not be used to purchase financial assets nor, of course, could they be used, as they might in a system characterized by private equity ownership of firms, to pay dividends. Moreover, the initiative of the early 1980s to institute an interest charge on the value of an enterprise's fixed assets met widespread resistance and was not implemented. Thus expansion cost enterprises very little.

Local governments frequently sought to invest in sections of the economy in which high rates of profitability (frequently assured by the fixed price structure) and provisions of fiscal decentralization allowed them to retain a significant share of the profits to finance their expenditures. The most obvious examples were in processing industries. Provinces that earlier had sent raw materials to major industrial centers established their own processing facilities even though this frequently led to excess capacity in existing centers.

Finally, peasants, who were experiencing real income growth for the first time in two decades, allocated a large share of their additional income to build new and enlarged private houses.

The combination of rising investment demand on the part of firms, local governments, and farm households on the one hand and underpriced capital on the other inexorably resulted in a rising share of output going to investment, despite the initial reform goal of reducing the rate of accumulation. Thus the actual rate of investment far exceeded the 29 percent target included in the Sixth Five-Year Plan (1981–85).[6]

Thus, except in agriculture, which showed evidence of substantial growth of total factor productivity, the resource mobilization characteristic of the Chinese economic system was not altered significantly. In the mid-1980s, with an investment rate approximately twice that prevailing in market-oriented economies at comparable levels of development, growth still was achieved in large measure through a massive accumulation of fixed assets rather than through substantially greater efficiency in resource use. In this respect China's continued reliance on resource mobilization to achieve extensive growth rather than successfully raising the efficiency of resource use, that is, shifting to intensive growth, parallels that of the Soviet Union in the years following Stalin's death. In the Soviet Union the investment burden placed on the consumer did not decrease from 1950–55 through 1980.[7]

Sectoral Allocation

The allocation of investment between agriculture and industry was a second critical component of comprehensive balance. The seeming consensus of the late 1970s was that industry's historical share of investment funds had been so high that agricultural growth had been significantly depressed. Fixed assets per agricultural worker in 1978 were only a tenth the level prevailing in state industry, a gap that had widened substantially since the 1950s.[8] Moreover, many collective units had inadequate internal working capital and were unable to borrow sufficient funds from the state to finance the purchase of modern industrial inputs such as fertilizers and electric power that are crucial to agricultural modernization.

One of the few quantitative goals set forth at the December 1978 Third Plenum was an increase over a period of three to five years in agriculture's share of state investment from its then current 11 percent to 18 percent. Noninvestment outlays, which the Chinese refer to as current expenditures, were also to rise, but more modestly, from an existing 7 percent to 8 percent of state expenditures.[9]

Yet such a redirection of state resources was not achieved. As shown in Table 9.2, absolute investment outlays for agriculture from state funds rose moderately in 1979 but still comprised only 11 percent, nowhere near the 18 percent goal. More surprisingly, beginning in 1980 agriculture's share of state investment fell continuously to only 3.4 percent by 1985, the lowest share in any year since the beginning of the First Five-Year Plan in 1953. The share of the budget devoted

TABLE 9.2
State Budgetary Flows to Agriculture, 1978–1985

Year	Investment outlays[a]		Current expenditures[b]	
	Billions of yuan	Percent of state investment	Billions of yuan	Percent of budget expenditures
1978	5.334	10.6%	7,700	6.9%
1979	5.792	11.1	8,990	7.1
1980	5.203	9.3	8,210	6.8
1981	2.921	6.6	7,370	6.6
1982	3.412	6.1	7,990	6.9
1983	3.545	6.0	8,670	6.7
1984	3.712	5.0	9,440	6.2
1985	3.694	3.4	10,156	5.6
1986			11,790[c]	5.5[c]

SOURCES: State Statistical Bureau, *Chinese Statistical Yearbook, 1984* (Beijing: Statistical Publishing House, 1984), pp. 306–7, 424; *Chinese Statistical Abstract, 1986*, p. 74; Wang Bingqian, "The Implementation of the State Budget for 1985 and the State Budget for 1986," *Beijing Review*, 1984, no. 20, pp. vi, ix.

[a] Includes investment in fixed assets and increases in working capital.

[b] Includes the two budgetary subcategories, "current expenditure," which largely supports non-investment expenditures by the state bureaucracies responsible for water conservancy, state farms, fisheries, and meteorology, and "support for communes and brigades."

[c] Budgeted, not actual, amount.

to current expenditures for agriculture increased for an equally brief period, rising only in 1979 before falling to a share just equal to or below that of 1978 in each of the years 1980–86.

Moreover, during these years other sources of agricultural investment did not rise to offset the decline in state investment. Collective investment, undertaken by brigades and teams from their retained funds, fell precipitously as collectives were dismantled and the "responsibility system" was introduced. By 1982 and 1983 collective investment had fallen by about 4 billion yuan or almost half that of the late 1970s. Private investment in farming, though perhaps rising, was inhibited by peasants' uncertainty about the durability of the new agricultural system. Higher procurement prices had led to sharply rising income, but this was allocated to increased consumption, to improved housing, and to increased savings deposits. In 1983, for example, private investment in farming was only 6.79 billion yuan.[10] By comparison, rural household savings deposits in rural credit cooperatives rose more than 9 billion yuan, private investment in rural housing was 21.5 billion yuan, and consumption expenditures for food, clothing, and other items but excluding housing rose by more than 18 billion yuan.[11]

The Chinese Communist party's concern that private investment would be insufficient to sustain adequate agricultural growth underlay the decision in early 1984 to extend to a minimum of fifteen years the period in which peasant households had exclusive use of fixed farming areas. The decision was an attempt to convince peasants that the new system would endure long enough for them to be able to realize the increased incomes that might be generated by private investment in farming.

Although the higher share of investment once envisioned for agriculture was not realized, industry's share of investment resources was curtailed. From an average share of 55 percent in 1966–78, it fell to an average of 48 percent in 1981–82 and to 46 percent by 1984.[12] Several long neglected sectors of the economy, however, did enjoy substantial infusions of investment funds: services, science, education, health and welfare, municipal construction, including residential housing, and, beginning in 1983, transport and communication.

The interindustry allocation of investment also changed, but only for a brief period. In the initial years of the reform, light industry received a larger share of industrial investment, rising to a peak of 20 percent in 1981, then falling toward its prereform share by 1984.[13] This brief rise reflected primarily a short-term increase in investment in food processing and textiles. The traditional emphasis on heavy industry or producer goods was modified, at least in the short run, with its share of industrial investment falling from about 90 percent during 1966–75 to about 80 percent in 1981–82. But heavy industry's share began to rise after 1981, exceeding 82 percent in 1982 and 88 percent by 1984, above the 85 percent share of the First Plan. Most of the temporary reduction in this sector's share of investment resulted from a sharp drop in the machine-building branch and a modest decline in investment in the metallurgical industry.

Foreign Trade and Investment

One of the most striking changes in economic policy in the late 1970s was China's decisive turn outward to seek international markets in goods and capital. Traditional constraints on the use of long-term commercial borrowing, on acceptance of government-to-government loans and foreign aid, and on direct foreign investment in China were eased. In 1979 Chinese authorities signed a large number of loan agreements, including commercial export credits and long-term low-interest loans extended by foreign governments; promulgated a law on Chinese-foreign joint ventures; and established the China International Trust and Investment Corporation. The following year they formally approved the establishment of special economic zones on the southeast coast to attract direct foreign investment and became members of the International Monetary Fund and the World Bank. These and other changes were part of a systematic effort to accelerate flows of both trade and investment to increase the contribution of advanced Western technology to China's economic development.

These policies produced significant changes in resource allocation. China's total trade turnover (imports plus exports), shot up from $20 billion U.S. in 1978 to $69.6 billion U.S. by 1985.[14] By the measure of trade turnover to national income the Chinese economy became substantially more externally oriented than that of the Soviet Union.* Although imports outpaced exports by a wide margin by 1985, export performance, the nemesis of centrally planned economies, was particularly strong through 1984. Exports grew from $9.75 billion U.S. in 1978 to $27.36 billion U.S. in 1985, an increase of almost 200 percent. That marked acceleration in export growth was all the more remarkable because it was achieved during a period of worldwide economic slowdown and stagnant worldwide trade.

In summary, the major indicators of resource allocation showed elements of both continuity and change between 1978 and 1984. In agriculture, reforms led to enormous short-term productivity growth, but otherwise growth continued to be generated by a high degree of resource mobilization. There was little evidence of a significant decline in the overall rate of investment, still among the highest in the developing world. Some changes occurred in the allocation of investment resources. Although, for reasons discussed below, agriculture was not the beneficiary of the promised increase in state funding, the share of investment resources allocated to the producer goods industry was reduced somewhat in the short run and the share going to light industry, services, health, science, education, and urban development increased significantly. Similarly, there was a substantial increase in the ratio of imports plus exports relative to national income.

---

*Precise calculation of trade ratios is difficult because Chinese foreign trade data reported in yuan are dollar figures converted to Chinese domestic currency at the official exchange rate. The value of the yuan fell by more than 50 percent between 1978 and 1985 so the trade ratio calculated in yuan introduces a substantial upward bias in this measure of the degree of outward orientation of the economy. The alternative, carrying out the entire calculation in U.S. dollars, is also problematic because there are no reliable measures of China's national income in U.S. dollars.

Constraints to Reform

Although much of the reform in the late 1970s appeared to reflect a desire to replace China's bureaucratic planning system with a system of market socialism, several constraints were not overcome, and at least through 1985 the outcome, outside of agriculture, fell short of the market socialism ideal. I will focus on four such constraints: (1) the continuing undervaluation of agriculture and the preeminence of the producer goods sector of industry in the thinking within dominant circles of the government and party; (2) the nature of the prereform industrial price structure, which predictably undermined attempts to allow enterprises significant autonomy in decision making; (3) the inability or unwillingness of the political leadership to institute unpopular price increases for some of the most important consumer goods purchased by the urban population, necessitating ever-escalating price subsidies and vitiating the prospects for substituting market-based prices and incentives for bureaucratically determined rewards; and (4) an unwillingness to relate directly international and domestic prices for traded commodities to allow a substantial reduction in the monopoly position of the state foreign trade corporations and to increase the power of enterprises to deal directly in imports and exports.

UNDERVALUATION OF AGRICULTURE

The continued undervaluation of agriculture posed an enormous constraint on market decentralization. The latter implies a rate and pattern of investment that is quite different from that prevailing in recent years. Market decentralization would imply that, as in Hungary after the introduction of the New Economic Mechanism (NEM) in 1968, the state would replace artificially low farm-level prices with negotiated or market-determined prices that would be sufficiently high to elicit voluntary deliveries to the state of the required quantities of cereals and other farm products without use of compulsory procurement targets.[15] Until the unprecedented harvests of 1983 and 1984, the market prices for most cereal crops subject to compulsory procurement remained at least twice the level of quota procurement prices. Even after the introduction of the contract system for state grain purchases in 1985, the state purchase price was fixed and frequently below prices prevailing in the market. The state, in short, remained reluctant to eliminate purchases at fixed prices and to purchase all grain required in the market because such a policy either would reduce substantially the financial resources directly controlled by the state or would compel the state to raise retail prices for wheat flour, rice, and edible vegetable oils for urban consumers, neither of which had, by the mid-1980s, been accepted by the party leadership.

Market decentralization also implies, as in the case of Hungary and Yugoslavia, that the state would abandon its position as the monopoly supplier of industrial inputs to the agricultural sector.[16] Allowing competition in the supply of chemical fertilizers, machinery, diesel fuel, and so forth to peasants, however, might substantially lower the prices of some of these commodities and thus reduce the degree of implicit taxation on agriculture.

China never introduced decentralized pricing of industrial inputs purchased by peasants. Moreover, although price reductions of from 10 to 15 percent during 1979 and 1980 for machinery, chemical fertilizers, pesticides, and other agricultural producer goods were endorsed by the party at the Third Plenum in 1978 and included in the "Decisions of the CCP Central Committee on Some Problems in Accelerating Development (draft)," that provision was deleted when the final version of the document was approved at the Fourth Plenum in the fall of 1979.[17] Most prices for producer goods purchased by peasants have remained high. The price of nitrogen relative to that of rice in 1981 was about two and one-half to three times the world price. The excess profits accruing to the state from these sales at above world prices were 8.0 to 8.8 billion yuan, almost three times state investment in agriculture that year.[18]

Not only did prices paid by agricultural producers remain high, but some prices were raised significantly after 1979. The state increased the price of diesel fuel used in agricultural machinery by 25 percent when the subsidy of 120 yuan per ton, in existence since 1956, was eliminated overnight on November 1, 1982.[19] In 1980 the value of this subsidy to peasants was 800 million yuan. Similarly, in 1980 and again in 1982 the state raised prices for hand tools and semimechanized implements, and in 1984 the prices of tractors, irrigation equipment, and other agricultural machinery rose as well.[20]

The stunning success of agricultural production in the early 1980s, resulting from decollectivization, the reopening of rural private markets, and price increases for agricultural products purchased by the state, allowed state resources to be diverted to other purposes. As so many times in the past, many leaders thought organizational change in agriculture could substitute for a commitment of state resources. The critical difference, of course, was that after Mao's death the ideological commitment to collectivized agriculture gradually eroded. A dominant coalition that still advocated the Stalinist principle of priority for producer goods was willing to reintroduce private farming in the countryside if, at least in the short run, it yielded more resources for urban and industrial development. Thus, as agricultural liberalization led to higher rates of growth, state commitments of resources to agriculture were curtailed. Moreover, despite dramatic change in the collective structure of rural China, the potential mechanisms that the state had relied on for decades to extract resources from agriculture, compulsory procurement or advance contracts to purchase farm products at fixed prices and the monopoly sale of modern inputs, remained in place.

INDUSTRIAL PRICE STRUCTURE

The transition from central planning to market socialism requires the elimination of compulsory output targets set by higher-level administrative authority for each enterprise and the granting of considerable authority to enterprises to determine their own product mix and output levels. Such reforms were introduced experimentally in Sichuan in 1979 and subsequently on a wider geographic basis. Yet the most important lesson of the Eastern European reforms of the 1960s and 1970s, the necessity for the prior rationalization of the industrial price structure, was largely ignored in China.[21] The result was profound problems in implementation, which may ultimately undermine the reform.

In the absence of prices that reflect social costs, inevitably some activities that are financially profitable from the perspective of the producing enterprise will reduce social welfare while other activities that may be socially desirable will be feasible only if the enterprise's losses are subsidized by the state. For example, an enterprise that uses heavily subsidized and underpriced raw materials may expand its output so as to increase its profits. But those profits, though real in financial terms from the perspective of that enterprise, may be achieved at the expense of increased losses elsewhere that more than offset the enterprise's increased profits. Economic reform that encourages enterprises, through retention of profits and bonus schemes and an easing of compulsory output targets, to maximize profits will quite likely reduce social welfare substantially. These problems are only compounded when investment decisions are simultaneously decentralized and put on a self-financing basis. Investment may increase in socially low-priority but financially profitable sectors while shrinking in socially desirable but unprofitable sectors.

The Chinese industrial price structure in the late 1970s appeared to embody defects as severe as or more so than the prereform price structure of other centrally planned economies. These problems stemmed from two distinct sources. First, the price structure established by the Chinese government in the 1950s embodied substantial indirect taxation on manufactured consumer goods, which tended to keep prices for those goods relatively high. The prices of industrial raw materials, fuels, and minerals were set relatively low, on the grounds that a large share of the output would be purchased by other state units. Agricultural products also were underpriced so that state procurement agencies could profitably resell them to the nonagricultural population.

Problems of the initial price structure were compounded by the failure to undertake periodic adjustments to reflect changing costs. Since the costs of producing agricultural products and fuels, mining products, and other industrial raw materials rarely decline significantly and commonly rise as output expands, initially low levels of profit are further reduced. Costs of manufactured goods, on the other hand, tend to fall as output expands because of economies of scale, substantially increasing initially high profit levels. Thus over time the disparity between prices and costs in different sectors of the economy grows.

The problems of the industrial price structure were recognized almost immediately. As early as 1955 the State Council approved a recommendation of the State Planning Commission to undertake, over a period of from two to three years, an overhaul of the relative prices of goods manufactured in the various branches of the producer goods sector of industry. The first step in this process was taken in 1956, when the price level of producer goods was reduced by 9.35 percent, with almost all the reductions concentrated in the products of the Ministry of Heavy Industry and the First Machine Building Ministry.[22]

For reasons that still remain unclear, however, the process of adjusting relative prices was thwarted after the first round of adjustments. Even in the more liberal period of the early 1960s, when discussion of the allocative role of prices in a socialist economy was revived, no significant adjustments were made in the pricing of producer goods. This pattern differentiates China from Hungary, where a major price overhaul, particularly for producer goods, was pushed through in 1959, an overhaul that helped lay the groundwork for instigating the New Economic Mechanism in 1968.

The State Price Commission, reestablished in 1962 under the direction of Xue Muqiao, devised a five-year plan for fundamentally realigning the domestic price structure, which except for minor adjustments in 1956 had been unchanged since the onset of the First Five-Year Plan.[23] The major objectives of the plan, which was approved by the State Council in 1965, were to raise the prices of agricultural and mining products and other industrial raw materials, to readjust the relative prices of many manufactured consumer goods (without changing the overall price level), and to reduce the prices of machinery, chemicals, and some other producer goods. The plan was to reduce the index of producer goods prices by 20 percent in two or three stages within a period of five years. The plan included much more dramatic changes in relative prices within the producer goods sector. Since the prices of industrial raw materials, which are included within producer goods, were to rise, the prices of machinery, chemicals, and other finished producer goods obviously would have to fall by far more than 20 percent if the overall objective were to be achieved.

Only the first stage of the 1965 price reform plan was implemented. Procurement prices for agricultural products were raised substantially.[24] Retail prices for flour and polished rice were raised slightly for the first time since 1952, to eliminate the need for price subsidies.[25] The price of coal and perhaps some other minerals was raised, and the prices of machinery, metallurgical products, and electronic products were reduced. But the multistage adjustment process was abruptly terminated in August 1967, when the Chinese Communist party Central Committee and the State Council jointly promulgated a directive calling for strict price control. That action all but froze prices for a dozen years although underlying relative costs of different product categories continued to change. The only significant change in industrial prices between 1967 and 1978 was a reduction in prices of chemical products in 1969.[26]

The price reform of 1978–80 resembles that of 1965–66, with procurement prices for farm products and prices for some fuels and minerals increasing. The state raised the price of coal 30 percent in 1979, the price of iron ore by 20 to 50 percent in 1980, and the price of phosphate rock by 30 percent in 1980. There were some reductions in state-fixed prices of machinery and electrical and rubber products. But these changes were not part of an overall strategy of rationalizing the relative prices of industrial products. Rather, as is made clear in the discussion below on coal, the object was simply to raise prices to cover costs of some major raw materials and intermediate goods. There was no systematic reduction in the prices of producer goods such as chemicals, machinery, and steel products. Xue Muqiao, the architect of the 1965 price reform, pointed out the desirability of a thoroughgoing reform but admitted in 1980 that such a reform was extremely difficult because each price adjustment affected the distribution of profits and led to fierce conflict between center and localities, between industry and commerce, between government and enterprises, and between different enterprises. Every price change influenced the distribution of profits and was fiercely resisted, especially since various forms of profit retention had been initiated.[27]

Despite the conflict, in the summer of 1980 the State Bureau of Commodity Prices and the relevant departments of the central government agreed to an ambitious price reform for producer goods. The two major objectives were to reduce substantially the varying rates of profitability in different branches of heavy industry and to allow world market prices to serve as a guide to relative domestic prices. But this effort was significantly modified in the beginning of 1982, when the State Council, in a move parallel to that of August 1967, terminated any further adjustment of state-fixed prices for producer goods.[28] As will be discussed below, that action did not preclude introducing flexibility for some producer goods at the margin or freeing up consumer goods prices, but it did postpone adjustment of state-fixed prices for most producer goods.

The starkest evidence on the failure of the modest price adjustments undertaken in 1979 and 1980 to create a price structure that would provide meaningful information for Chinese enterprises to make autonomous decisions is the persistently high share of state-owned industrial enterprises that operate at a loss. In 1979, 1980, and 1981 these enterprises constituted 23.7, 23.3, and 27.1 percent, respectively, of all state industrial enterprises.[29] Some of these enterprises may have been poorly managed, burdened with outdated equipment, or compelled to spend heavily to provide housing for workers or pensions for retired workers, which are paid from current enterprise income and therefore would raise their costs. But many of these enterprises ran at a deficit because their products were underpriced. One reason so few money-losing enterprises were closed down, despite repeated calls, was the difficulty of differentiating between poor management and underpriced output or other factors largely exogenous to the firm as the ultimate cause of deficits.

One of the clearest examples illustrating problems in the prices of producer goods was coal. As shown in Table 9.3, the initial margin

TABLE 9.3

Costs, Prices, and "Profits" in the Chinese Coal Industry, 1952–1979

Year	Average product cost (yuan/ton)	Taxes (yuan/ton)	Ex-factory price (yuan/ton)	"Profit" (yuan/ton)
1952	9.00	.86	11.46	1.60
1957	10.90	.90	12.05	.25
1965	15.77	1.44	18.00	.79
1978	16.12	1.44	18.00	.44
1979	17.78	1.77	22.10	2.55

SOURCE: Xü Yi, Chen Baosen, and Liang Wuxia, *Socialist Price Issues* (Beijing: Finance and Economics Publishing House, 1982), p. 164).

of price over cost set for the coal industry in 1952 was 1.60 yuan per ton, which allowed an operating profit of 27.8 percent of non-capital costs.[30] Capital was provided from non-interest-bearing grants through the state budget.* As production costs and taxes rose and the ex-factory price rose more slowly, operating profits were squeezed. By 1957 profits had shrunk to .25 yuan per ton. An increase of about one-third in the price of coal raised profits slightly in 1965 and for a few years thereafter, but the freeze on industrial product prices during the Cultural Revolution, combined with steadily rising operating costs, squeezed profits. In 1974, 1976, and 1977, the industry actually lost an average of .25 yuan for each ton of coal produced. In 1978 profit was .44 yuan per ton or 2.7 percent of cost (again, not accounting for capital), and the rate of return on capital in the industry was a mere .3 percent, compared to 16 percent for all industry (and 70 percent for petroleum, 19 percent for electric power, 37.1 percent for textiles, and so forth).[31]

The consequences of that pattern of underpricing the major source of energy in the economy became profound when an attempt was made to introduce some degree of market decentralization to make enterprises responsible for their own current profits and losses and their own expansion. Most critically, the industry was unable to finance its own expansion. As shown in Table 9.4, in 1957 state investment in the coal industry was almost twenty times operating profits and in 1978 about ten times profits. That was not necessarily a critical shortcoming before 1979, when most investment was financed from nonreturnable,

---

*This percentage of profit, except for an unrealistically low rate of depreciation, ignores capital costs and thus overstates the real economic rate of return in the industry. Since the industry did not have to pay capital charges, however, the profit rate reflects the extent to which revenues could cover the costs actually incurred.

TABLE 9.4
Comparison of Profits and Investment in the Chinese Coal Industry,
1957, 1978, and 1979

Year	Unit profit (yuan/ton)	Output (million tons)	Total profit (million yuan)	Investment (millions of yuan)
1957	.25	131	33	597[a]
1978	.44	618	272	3,180
1979	2.55	635	1,619	3,186

SOURCES: Unit profit, Table 9.3. Output, State Statistical Bureau, *Statistical Yearbook of China, 1981* (Beijing: Statistical Publishing House, 1982), p. 227. Total profit, calculated as unit profit times output, State Statistical Bureau, *Chinese Statistical Yearbook, 1985* (Beijing: Statistical Publishing House, 1985), p. 425.
[a] Average annual investment, 1953–57. Annual data not available.

non-interest-bearing budgetary grants. But it was a critical constraint to a reform that sought to shift investment financing to a different basis, namely, enterprise profits or interest-bearing loans.[32] Even after an increase of almost 25 percent in the price of coal on May 1, 1979, the rate of return on capital was still only 2 percent and operating profits could have covered no more than about half of all investments. Moreover, that somewhat more favorable situation deteriorated rapidly as costs continued to rise, partly because wages rose considerably and the ex-factory price of coal was frozen. In the industry as a whole losses in 1980 were 10.9 percent of operating costs and the rate of return on assets was a negative 5.5 percent, whereas state investment in coal mining had risen to 3.3 billion yuan. In 1980, 54 percent and by 1982, 65 percent of the largest state-run coal mines were in the red.[33] Thus moving to a system of profit-financed investment for the coal industry was infeasible.

Over the long run the relatively low price of coal also contributed to inefficient use of energy resources. According to the analysis of World Bank economists, in 1978 China's energy use per unit of gross national product was two and one-half times the average for all low-income developing countries and one and a half times the average in other centrally planned economies.[34] Most of this inefficiency was attributable to wasteful use of energy in industry. Although energy was used somewhat more efficiently following the major price increase in 1979, the price of coal remained relatively low and the efficiency of its use far below that of other countries at comparable levels of economic development.

The relative prices of alternative fuels also reflected the irrationality of the interindustry structure of prices. In 1980 coal exchanged for

TABLE 9.5
*Chinese and World Parity Price Ratios
of Energy Sources, 1980*

Energy source	Chinese ratio	World ratio
Coal : crude oil		
(ton : ton)	4.25 : 1	2.4 : 1
Coal : electric power		
(ton : 10,000 kw)	55.9 : 1	5.16 : 1
Crude oil : heavy fuel oil		
(ton : ton)	1 : .41	1.1 : 1

SOURCES: Rows 1–2, Ye Ruixiang, "Studies on Issues in China's Energy Pricing," *Price Theory and Practice*, 1983, no. 5, p. 16. Row 3, World Bank, *China: Socialist Economic Development* (Washington, D.C.: International Bank for Reconstruction and Development, 1983), 2: 196.

crude oil in China at almost twice the ratio in world markets and coal exchanged for electric power at ten times the world ratio. In short, relative to other energy sources coal was substantially underpriced in China compared to the world market. Consequently the rates of profit in electric power and in petroleum were a manyfold multiple of that for coal mining. The price of heavy fuel oil, however, was inexplicably far less than that for crude oil whereas in world markets the price differential is modest and favors crude oil by about 10 percent (Table 9.5). The lower price indirectly and inappropriately encouraged the use of heavy oil instead of coal in electric power generation.[35]

Rather than reforming the structure of state-fixed prices for producer goods, which would have wholesale redistributive effects, the center sought to introduce selective price adjustments in some branches of industry and to allow the freeing up prices of a portion of the output in other branches. The latter approach became known as the "dual channel system" (*shuanggui zhi*) of prices and was applied to a growing share of output in some branches of industry. For example, though unwilling to change the state-fixed price of coal, in the early 1980s the state allowed state-owned mines to sell all or most of their above-plan output on the free market. In 1985 the dual channel system was extended to a broad range of producer goods.[36]

This approach had several advantages. First, and probably most important, it was politically feasible. The state agreed to continue to supply coal at the low state-fixed price for electric power generation, steel making, and railroads, thus buying off powerful domestic ministerial bureaucracies, which opposed wholesale adjustment of state-fixed prices but would accept a partial reform that vested their rights of access to underpriced inputs. Second, the free market price served as a signal of relative scarcity and, in principle, led to a more efficient allocation of output. Firms at the margin of their overquota output would allocate resources purchased at free market price to produce goods that could be sold most profitably. This possible source of efficiency gain, by comparison with the Soviet Union and Eastern Europe, may be particularly important in China, where plans are relatively less taut, allowing most enterprises to overfulfill their output targets.[37] Third, in principle the relative disparity between the state-fixed price and the free market price could provide an indication of the degree of distortion entailed in state-fixed prices and thus provide important information to be used in price adjustments.

To continue the example of coal, the market provides a way of simultaneously distributing overquota production, a source of profits for coal mines that can be reinvested to expand output, and a more realistic signal to users of the real cost of energy. By 1984 only half of all coal production was distributed by the state at fixed prices. Purchasers of market-distributed coal paid a substantial premium over the price of coal distributed through state channels, providing incentives to use energy more efficiently and more profits to reinvest in the coal industry.*

The introduction of the dual channel system for producer prices has not diminished the controversy over price reform. Advocates of market pricing see the dual channel system as a means of moving toward market determination of the prices of all but a few commodities. They tend to stress the distortions that will be introduced if the multiple price system persists too long. The large gap between state-fixed quota prices and free-market above-quota prices creates enormous incentives for corruption because moving goods from state-controlled channels to the free market can produce huge windfall profits. Advocates of the primacy of planned pricing, however, appear to believe that the share of output sold at market prices should be limited and that as long as there is pervasive excess demand and the persistence of strong monopolistic elements in important markets decontrolling prices too rapidly would be a mistake.

In addition to freeing up the prices for overquota output of almost

---

*In Anhui Province in 1985 coal in the market sold for as much as 128 yuan per ton early in the year and for 103 yuan near the end of the year. By comparison, the price of coal supplied through the state distribution system in Anhui was about 75 yuan per ton.

all producer goods by 1985, several other important price reforms were undertaken. Unlike producer goods, for which vested interests precluded across-the-board reform, prices of many consumer goods were either changed or freed up altogether. The process began in 1980–81 with upward price adjustments for bamboo, wood, and metal products, pottery and porcelain products, leather products, and alcoholic beverages and downward adjustments for televisions, watches, and so forth. In 1985 prices for vegetables and pork were decontrolled, and in the fall of 1986 similar decontrol was instituted for several consumer durables, notably bicycles, televisions, washing and sewing machines, refrigerators, and electric fans.[38] Adjustments were also made in 1983 and 1985 of railway freight and passenger transportation prices.[39]

PRICE SUBSIDIES

Although the evidence is not clear-cut, a reduction in the significance of price subsidies in the consumer goods sector appears to have been a prerequisite to the successful implementation of reform along market socialist lines. For example, since initiating the New Economic Mechanism the Hungarian government reduced or narrowed consumer subsidies for a number of basic commodities. The price of bread, which at one time was so highly subsidized that large quantities were used as animal feed, was raised in 1980 (the first price increase in twenty-eight years) to the point that no subsidy was required.[40] Residential rents and the prices of milk, coffee, sugar, and meat all underwent sharp upward revisions so that prices more closely reflected production costs. Although price subsidies were not eliminated, the ability of the Hungarian leadership to reduce disparities between production costs and consumer prices contrasted with the less successful reform in Poland, for example, where price increases met enormous popular resistance and subsidies burgeoned.[41]

Price subsidies, as shown in Table 9.6, skyrocketed in China after 1978. Total subsidies paid out of state budgetary funds tripled to reach 48 billion yuan by 1985. The share of state budgetary income absorbed by these subsidies rose from 14 percent in 1978 to 38 percent by 1982 and then fell somewhat. These funds covered the financial losses of enterprises running in the red and rapidly rising food subsidies for the urban population. Subsidies for grain and edible vegetable oil sold to the permanent urban population were only 3.6 billion yuan annually in 1978 but more than quintupled to 18.3 billion yuan

TABLE 9.6
State Subsidies, 1978–1986
(billions of yuan)

Year	Total[a]	Grain and edible vegetable oils[b]
1978	16.4	3.63
1979		7.33
1980		10.81
1981		13.48
1982	43.0	14.72
1979–82[c]	150.0	
1983		18.3
1985	48.025	
1986	55.336[d]	

SOURCES: Mao Tianqi, "Rationalizing Economic Relations," *Economic Research*, no. 9 (1984): 42; Zhang Xiangwen, "A Discussion of Reform of the Price and Financial Systems," *Bulletin of Hubei Finance and Economics College*, 1985, no. 2, p. 81; Wang Bingqian, "The Implementation of the State Budget for 1985 and the State Budget for 1986," *Beijing Review*, 1986, no. 20, pp. v, viii.

[a] Subsidies paid out of state budgetary funds.

[b] The numbers in this series vary slightly from those published in other sources but are used because they constitute the longest time series from a single published source and thus are presumably calculated on a common methodology.

[c] Cumulative.

[d] Budgeted, not actual, amount.

by 1983. Part of that increase was the result of increasing losses on the resale of imported grain to the urban population.

Price subsidies inhibited economic reform in several ways. Most obviously, sale of commodities at prices far below cost invariably leads to excess demand, which is reflected in either rationing or widespread shortages. In China, of course, most highly subsidized consumer goods and housing are rationed or allocated bureaucratically. Because the value of subsidies, most of which are available only to the nonagricultural population, grew enormously after 1978, the state was compelled to devote increasing bureaucratic resources to control access to subsidized goods. As a result, the power and role of the administrative bureaucracy grew rather than contracted from 1978 to 1984, as one would anticipate under market socialism.

Subsidies, especially of staple foods (grain and edible vegetable oils) for the nonagricultural population, were linked closely to the undervaluation of agriculture. Food subsidies were so large that they came to constitute almost an independent argument against paying higher prices for cereals and oil-bearing seeds procured by the state. Finally, the underpricing of basic food commodities at the retail level led to substantial financial losses on the domestic resale of imported cereals, notably wheat.

INTERNATIONAL AND DOMESTIC PRICES

The absence of any effort to relate domestic and international prices again sharply differentiated reform in China from that in Hungary. A major objective of the Hungarian reform was to align domestic prices more closely with international prices, at least for tradable commodities. Such an alignment is an essential prerequisite for transferring decision-making power from state-controlled foreign trade corporations to individual producing enterprises.

Before the economic reform of the late 1970s in China almost all trade was carried out by a small number of foreign trade corporations, which were responsible for foreign trade in specified product lines. The disparity between world and domestic prices usually necessitated massive cross subsidies among these corporations. The low domestic prices of agricultural products, mineral products, and raw materials made their export highly profitable for the responsible foreign trade corporations. These products were purchased from Chinese producers at prevailing domestic prices and sold at higher international prices, resulting in huge profits when the foreign exchange earnings were converted to domestic currency at the prevailing official exchange rate. But because domestic prices of most industrial and manufactured products were relatively high, the export of these items required massive subsidies. Goods purchased by foreign trade corporations at high domestic prices would not be competitive on the international market when sold at a dollar price determined by dividing the domestic price in yuan by the yuan per dollar official exchange rate. That is, when the foreign exchange earned from the sale of the product at the world market price was converted to yuan at the official exchange rate, the proceeds were less than the domestic price of the good. The inverse pattern, of course, applied to imports. Imports of agricultural products generally required subsidies whereas imports of manufactured goods were profitable for the foreign trade corporations.

Two inherent difficulties arose from the situation outlined above. First, there was a disparity of interest between the foreign trade corporations and domestic producers and users of tradable goods. Domestic producers of agricultural goods had little interest in expanding their output to increase exports because foreign trade corporations purchased their goods at relatively low and sometimes unprofitable domestic prices. Foreign trade corporations, on the contrary, profited from increases in their international sale of such goods. For imports of machinery and equipment, the reverse applied. The foreign trade corporations handling these products had an extra incentive to import such products because they could be resold at enormous profits whereas domestic users faced no such incentive because the domestic price of imported machinery and equipment was pegged to the price of similar domestic goods.

From a purely accounting point of view, a state monopoly on foreign trade makes it feasible to balance losses from the export of manufactures and the import of agricultural products with profits from the import of manufactured goods and the export of raw materials and agricultural products. That was precisely the strategy followed in China between 1953 and 1979, during which time the cumulative profits of the foreign trade system were 16.3 billion yuan.[42] The producers of export goods, however, had little incentive to increase foreign sales. Agricultural producers faced low domestic prices, not world prices. And manufactured goods generally were not salable on the world market if domestic prices were converted to dollar prices at the official exchange rate.

A more profound problem is that of determining the optimal pattern of import and export goods. A country with a market economy would export goods in which it had a comparative advantage in production. That advantage would be signaled by the price structure. But in China, because the domestic price structure did not generally reflect domestic costs, high profits earned from the sale of a good in the export market may have reflected the underpricing of the product on the domestic market, not comparative advantage in a meaningful economic sense. An increase in the volume of high-profit exports thus actually would decrease social welfare because the price received would be insufficient to cover the true opportunity cost of all inputs used. In theory, foreign trade corporations could make export decisions on the basis of shadow prices that reflect the opportunity costs, but this was not carried out on a significant scale.

China's economic reform changed the situation described above only marginally. A crisis arose by 1980 because of the increasing disparity between domestic and world prices and the changing composition of China's imports and exports. Over the long run, as world prices rose and internal prices remained fixed, profits on the domestic sale of imported machinery shrank. Simultaneously the share of exports of manufactured commodities rose, necessitating increased subsidies, and the share of agricultural and primary products fell, cutting profits of foreign trade corporations. On the import side, the share of foodstuffs rose, requiring increased subsidies, and the share of industrial products fell, cutting profits. In 1980 the foreign trade system sustained its first significant financial loss. The state trading corporations suffered a cumulative deficit of 3.18 billion yuan on trade turnover of 56.4 billion yuan.[43] The magnitude of the budgetary subsidy allocated to the state trading system to cover these losses was particularly troubling because it reversed a long period in which net profits from trading contributed to state revenues and it came during a period of substantial government budgetary deficits.*

In 1981 the state sought to alleviate these problems through several reform measures. The government effectively devalued the exchange rate by introducing an internal settlement rate. This rate, which was used by the Bank of China in its transactions with Chinese exporters and importers, initially primarily foreign trade corporations, was 2.8 yuan per U.S. dollar, representing an effective devaluation of more than 50 percent from the prevailing official exchange rate of 1.8 per U.S. dollar. Like any devaluation, it discouraged imports because their cost in domestic currency went up by half and encouraged exports because foreign exchange earnings could be converted to domestic currency at a much more favorable rate.

Simultaneously, the government allowed some enterprises to engage directly in import and export transactions.[44] Rather than selling to a foreign trade corporation at the fixed state price, those enterprises were allowed to sell their products directly at the prevailing world price and convert their foreign exchange earnings to domestic currency at a more favorable internal settlement rate. Many manufacturers would not have been interested in trading directly at the official exchange rate because the conversion of foreign exchange to domestic currency would not yield an amount sufficient to cover costs and they would have sustained substantial losses selling on the world market. The internal settlement rate made it possible to export a broader range of manufactured goods profitably.

Unfortunately, changes in the exchange rate are a very crude instru-

*The budget of 1980 had anticipated a deficit of 8 billion yuan, but the realized deficit was 12.1 billion yuan (Shan Qingnang and Chen Baosan, "China's Financial System," in Xue Muqiao, ed., *Almanac of China's Economy 1981* [Hong Kong: Modern Cultural Publishing Co., 1982], p. 644).

ment and did not resolve the fundamental problem of the disparity between Chinese domestic and world relative prices. China's domestic prices for manufactured goods tend to be high relative to those for agricultural products and raw materials such as fuels and minerals, and domestic retail prices for rationed foodstuffs sold to urban consumers are relatively low. Thus although effective depreciation of the exchange rate reduced the need for subsidies of industrial exports, it substantially increased the need for subsidies of imported foodstuffs. Moreover, although the internal settlement rate of 2.8 made possible some decentralized exports of industrial goods without subsidies by the foreign trade corporations, a broad range of high-priced domestic manufactures, many of which may well have been comparative advantage products, still could not be exported without subsidies. In Shanghai, China's most dynamic manufacturing center, two-thirds of all exported industrial products still required subsidies even at the more favorable rate of 2.8 yuan to the dollar.[45] One-third of all industrial exports from Kwangtung required subsidies at the higher rate. Thus though a portion of the industrial sector responded to export opportunities (particularly those created by changing world prices), most export trade was still channeled through foreign trade corporations with the result that firms still had little interest in exports and were unaffected by changes in world prices.[46]

Subsidies for exports may have been reduced by the introduction of the internal settlement rate, but subsidies for imports of agricultural products and raw materials, which were still sold at very low domestic prices, soared. In the 1970s resale of imported cereals, sugar, and perhaps edible vegetable oils was still profitable and helped to offset the subsidies that were required for exports of manufactured goods. Financial profits on imports of consumer goods, for example, were 4.1 billion yuan in 1971. By 1981 world prices of these commodities had risen substantially, but domestic prices remained unchanged. But beginning in 1981 the foreign trade corporations dealing in foods had to pay 2.8 yuan per dollar foreign exchange and the subsidies required to sustain imports, particularly of consumer goods, skyrocketed. In 1981, when imports totaled 34.6 billion yuan, subsidies of imported cereals, sugar, cotton, chemical fertilizer, and crude steel reached 8.73 billion yuan.[47] Wheat provides the best example. The world price rose from $64 U.S. per ton in 1971 to $223 U.S. per ton in 1981, yet the domestic price of rationed wheat flour in urban areas was unchanged. By 1980 profits on the domestic resale of wheat of the early and mid-1970s had been displaced by enormous losses. The subsidy required for each ton of imported wheat in 1981 was 400 yuan.[48] Thus total subsidies borne by the foreign trade system on the import of 12.66 million tons of wheat in 1981 were 5.064 billion yuan. Relief from this enormous financial burden came only later, when in response to huge increases in domestic agricultural output over several years, China's imports of wheat and cotton plummeted.

Despite the introduction of the internal settlement rate in 1981, financial losses on China's foreign trade continued to grow, necessitating further devaluations of the yuan, particularly in 1983–86. Thus the rapid rise in China's foreign trade in the first few years of reform is less impressive than the trade figures alone would suggest. In part, trade growth was sustained through a growing burden of budgetary subsidies.[49] The most critical problem, the divergence between domestic prices and product cost for a wide range of domestic goods, remained. In the absence of a close correlation between price and cost, there was no basis for judging whether increased exports, though profitable for the enterprise or foreign trade corporation, were desirable from a social perspective. As two research economists from the Shanghai Academy candidly put it, "some products incur losses because taxes and profits are too high, but these losses in reality are profits. Other products, because their raw materials are subsidized by the state incur profits, but these profits in reality are losses."[50]

Conclusion

The general impression among foreign observers is that major reforms occurred in the Chinese economy from 1978 to 1984. Certainly this is the image Chinese leaders have attempted to convey. A hard look at the data reveals greater continuity in practice than the rhetoric suggests. Moreover, for six years, the leaders took only partial and somewhat ineffectual measures to remove the most persistent and fundamental economic constraint to their reforms, namely, the structure of prices. This problem was manifested in four separate areas: low prices for agricultural products sold to the state; an irrational interindustry price structure; massive and growing subsidies of the basic consumption goods purchased by a relatively small number of nonagricultural households; and the lack of congruity between world and domestic prices for many traded commodities. These areas were closely interrelated. If price stability in urban areas were sacrosanct, subsidies of urban consumers needed to be increased if compulsory procurement of farm products at low prices were abolished, as was suggested by Sun Yefang in 1978. Overpriced industrial goods could not be sold on the international market at a profit except at an exchange rate that necessarily entailed accounting losses on important imported commodities. The constraints posed by the price structure on any effort to increase the role of the market in resource allocation almost certainly surpassed those existing in any other centrally planned economy that had sought to institute far-reaching economic reform.

The critical need for a thoroughgoing price reform has long been apparent to relevant government officials in Beijing. Three separate, seemingly well-planned reform proposals were worked out. Yet in 1957, 1967, and to a certain extent again in 1982, the party intervened to terminate each of these price reforms after only a few modest steps had been taken. The reasons for this pattern remain poorly understood, but a few hypotheses may be offered.

Price reform was massively complex, particularly by the late 1970s, for at least three reasons: China's relatively low initial level of economic development in the early 1950s, when the basic price structure was fixed; the pattern of growth in the first three decades of Communist party leadership; and the long period of time during which few major adjustments were made in the structure of prices. It has long been observed that in industry the relative costs of production of initially scarce commodities tend to fall most rapidly during the process of economic growth.[51] In China this phenomenon was particularly important because modern economic growth began from a very low level of industrial development and industrial growth was characterized by unusually large disparities in sectoral rates of expansion.* That combination accentuated the need for frequent relative price adjustments. The failure to undertake such adjustments on a periodic basis resulted in the need for massive relative price changes that have substantial secondary considerations.

The underlying complexity of the price structure was reinforced by the large number of commodities for which prices were centrally determined. By 1980 the central price authorities were unilaterally determining the procurement prices of 113 agricultural commodities,

---

*For example, with 1952 = 100 the indices of heavy and light industrial output (measured in comparable prices) in 1978 were 2,778 and 968, respectively. Rates of expansion of output within the heavy industrial sector were equally disparate. For example, output of steel products rose more than twenty times between 1952 and 1978 whereas output of timber products barely tripled in the same period.

the retail prices of 138 major consumer goods, and the ex-factory prices of 1,086 producer goods, including raw materials, sources of energy, and motive power.[52] The large scope of central price determination made reform massively complex. Adjustment of any single price necessarily influenced the distribution of industrial profits. As suggested by Xue Muqiao's comment quoted earlier, price adjustments were fiercely contested because they redistribute profits among enterprises, ministries, cities, provinces, and so forth. Price adjustments undertaken after profit- and revenue-sharing systems are in place are particularly complex because they inevitably lead to the need to renegotiate profit-retention rates for individual enterprises and revenue-sharing rates between different levels of government administration.

One example of the difficulties encountered in such adjustments followed the increase in the procurement price of raw cotton instituted in 1978, 1979, and 1980, taken in part because the declining profitability of growing cotton over time had led to stagnation in production. Although the cotton textile industry was among the most highly profitable of all branches of industry, it successfully resisted any increase in the price paid for raw cotton. Profits expressed as a rate of return on capital in the textile industry were more than twice the average of all industries in 1978. Thus the 30 percent increase in the procurement price for raw cotton drove the state procurement agencies into a position of sustaining massive losses that, in turn, were subsidized by the central government.*

The nature of Chinese bureaucratic politics intensified the inevitably difficult task of altering patterns of earnings through price reform. Ministries that were major revenue earners for the central government had accumulated political clout through the years. Such sources of financial support as the Ministry of Chemical Industry or the Ministry of Electric Power had earned considerable credit as a result of their contributions to the central treasury, and they had sufficient influence and incentive to temper reforms that would adversely affect their position. Further, already plagued by mounting budget deficits, the top leaders were naturally reluctant to unleash changes that threatened their proven revenue sources on the gamble that the lost revenue would be compensated through increased revenue from unproven, previously chronic deficit ministries.

Price adjustments necessarily changed the distribution of income among consumers, even when changes in retail prices were accompa-

---

*Subsidies for cotton in 1981 were 3.56 billion yuan (Liang Wu, *Research on Finance and Economics*, 1982, no. 3, p. 60).

nied by wage supplements or other payments that in the aggregate offset the increased outlays entailed by the price increases. The five yuan monthly wage supplements initiated in the fall of 1979 following price increases for meat, eggs, and other nonstaple foods had such distributive consequences because of the variation in the number of dependents per worker in the modern sector.[53] Similarly, the increase in the price of cotton goods in 1983 was accompanied by a subsidy fund of 100 million yuan in an attempt to mitigate the adverse consequences of the price rise on particularly poor peasants.

Sensitivity to the implications changes in the level of retail prices might have for income distribution highlights another major obstacle to price reform—the threat it appeared to pose to price stability. China's leadership, with seemingly few exceptions, shared a strong aversion to upward price pressure. Price adjustments initiated during the late 1970s were accompanied by upward price pressure that was significant by Chinese standards. Between 1978 and 1982, for example, the official index of retail prices rose by almost 13 percent, exceeding the cumulative increase in the preceding twenty years.[54] This rise occurred despite a massive increase in subsidies that were instituted in large measure to break the link between changes in industrial and procurement prices on the one hand and retail prices on the other.

Finally, price adjustment was inhibited by the apparent reluctance of the highest levels of the political leadership to reveal fully the extent to which China's development strategy was biased in favor of industrial and urban development. The burden on the agricultural sector entailed by artificially low procurement prices and the siphoning off of rural personal savings to finance industrial and urban development was far less obvious than a comparable level of direct taxation would be. Declining real prices paid by urban consumers for foodstuffs and housing and the provision of a broad range of goods and amenities to urbanites at no cost simultaneously enhanced the personal power of the bureaucrats responsible for such nonmarket forms of distribution and partially obscures the real differences between urban and rural living standards.[55] In the absence of a change in such underlying values, the progress toward market-based forms of resource allocation in the urban and industrial sectors of the economy was likely to continue to be sporadic and limited.

TEN

Imperial Dilemmas: Soviet Interests and Economic Reform

Walter D. Connor

World powers face different opportunities, risks, and perhaps constraints than states that may become world powers but are not yet, or those lacking the resources to aspire to such status. The concerns of the USSR as a world power, and, in relation to its multinational internal makeup and its East European client states, an imperial power, provide the frame here for an inquiry into prospects for economic reform in the Soviet bloc.

Though this topic may seem tangential to a discussion of the consequences of economic reform, it should be remembered that economic reforms involving the market structure become especially controversial in light of the political responses they evoke. Responses may vary in many ways depending on the current alignment of domestic political forces in a given state and, with respect to the East European states, to the alignment and direction of Soviet political forces as well. They can run the gamut from promotion of further reform as a remedy for the problems of a period of adjustment to new forces and rules, to a cancellation of reform where under way, or to a blocking of proposed reform in response to vicarious experience of its results elsewhere. The interaction over the last two decades of reformers and antireformers in (and among) the USSR, Hungary, Poland, and Czechoslovakia provides examples of each of these patterns. In them, the USSR has been a major force. Its role in the near and middle-term future is, at present, uncertain. The reformer Gorbachev represents a break with the past, wherein the USSR has been an obstacle to market reform. Will Gorbachev retain his office—by no means a certainty—and win through? Then, perhaps, both the Soviet Union and Eastern Europe will confront the consequences of reform. But, if he fails, the absence of market reform will have its own effects, and these too will be important problems for Soviet and East European domestic and intrabloc politics in the next decade.

Scale, Timing, and Sovereignty: Perspectives on Reform

The USSR, China, and the states of Eastern Europe are vastly different in size, history, and material and cultural endowments. Obvious as this diversity is, the question of reform in these currently (or one-time) "Soviet model" economies may turn to a significant degree on the impact of some of these "obvious" differences. At least, the link between some of these general properties and the decision for or against reform provides a useful starting point for discussion.

SCALE: PROBLEMS AND POSSIBILITIES

Basic endowments, including territory, population size, and level of economic development at the time of onset of communist rule, have surely affected economic policy making and decisions for or against market reform.

China's economic backwardness, size, and overwhelmingly peasant population made impossible thoughts of a transformation to an industrial society in any policy-relevant time period after 1949. The "backyard smelting" of the Great Leap Forward provides, in this context, a bizarre chapter, but even more rational planning, aiming at labor-intensive nonagricultural employment, would seemingly have foundered in the rapid growth of an already immense population. Aid from more developed states was, obviously, no way out because politics determined that the only source of such aid could be the USSR. Its postwar economy, however, was neither of the scale nor in the condition to render sufficient aid to transform China's economy. Nor, politically, was there any will to do so: Stalin surely found reasons to regard Mao's 1949 victory as bittersweet.

The difficulties facing China in any move toward a truly mixed agrarian-industrial or industrial economy left it, by the mid-1970s, still rooted in the countryside and farming. Economic reform, when it came, could and should mean first a reversion to more appropriate organization and techniques in the countryside, where motivation and the quality of human effort would be decisive factors. The industrial sector, organized more on the basis of a Soviet model, was a different matter, but comparatively small as a sector of the PRC's economy.

The experience of the USSR was in many respects very different, with a large population but not overlarge considering the land endowment, regional and climatic diversity greater than China's, and a level of development as of 1928—on the eve of Stalin's industrialization drive—on the whole superior to China's in 1949. A Bolshevik "urbanist" bias in long-term political and ideological perspectives combined with successive events that generated heavy loss of life (since November 1917, civil war, collectivization, mass purges, and World War II) to reduce what might have been a rapidly growing peasant base and to create in effect a population shortage to meet the aims of greater and greater industrialization, well into the period of the late 1950s to mid-1960s when, statistically, the USSR became a predominantly urban-industrial society. The architecture for planning, production, and control that developed during these years—the core of the Soviet model—grew in size and dominance as the nonagricultural sectors of the economy grew. For these reasons alone, market reform in the Soviet economy would, as history has shown, be a daunting task.

Eastern Europe presented no consistent pattern. Territorial and population ranges among this group of medium to small states were great. Developmental levels ranged from Czechoslovakia's essentially industrial economy to the Balkans' backwardness. Economically, these states were far from any of the possibilities of relative autarky possessed by the USSR and China; politically, their fates after World War II consigned them (with the exception of Yugoslavia) to the imposition of the Soviet model. The model had effects not only on their domestic economies but on their foreign trade capacities as well, tying to the Soviet market economies more advanced, or similar to, that of the USSR, and in the case of Czechoslovakia, reversing the orientation of an economy that had traded westward.

Over the years, these developments generated a mixed picture, which has weighed heavily in East European approaches to (and retreats from) economic reform. Given the differential unfitness of the Soviet model to the East European economies, the period of diminishing returns manifested itself at varying times, earlier in better-developed, later in less-developed economies. The responses, reform or trade openings to Western markets, have aimed at making good some of the losses generated by the Soviet model. But East European moves in this direction remain hampered by problems related to their political and economic scale. Political independence remains limited. Economically, the noncompetitiveness of the East European economies means a continued reliance on the USSR as taker of many goods unsalable in the West, and as supplier, on barter terms that have varied over time, of oil and other fuels these economies cannot afford to purchase on the world market. East Europe needs the USSR. Its continuing need will limit the progress East European economies can make, although it is not at all clear that East Europe's economic weakness in this respect adds in any meaningful sense to Soviet economic strength. Had it been the Marshall, rather than the Five-Year, Plan that came to Eastern Europe at the end of the 1940s, the Common Market rather than the CMEA, the meaning of political and economic scale for these states would be quite different. So, however, would be the postwar political history of the continent.*

SOVEREIGNTIES, FULL AND PARTIAL

Countries in control of their affairs, and not the clients of others, are in a different position to face decision making involving economic reform than are states that are clients or "satellites."

China is fully sovereign. It need not concern itself with the feelings of other states about whether economic reform should be tolerated at all, or how far: it is not a Soviet satellite with leaders in any way ultimately beholden to the Kremlin to keep them in power or the system in place.[1] Beyond this obvious point, two others merit notice. China is not encumbered with a system of satellites that must adhere to (or cope with) the "Chinese model"; it need not fear effects of reforms it undertakes in a set of reluctantly allied states. Nor need China yet fear that internal economic reorganization and the attendant difficulties of adjustment compromise a military superpower status (which it does not possess) or weaken it militarily (I presume that the objectives of reform in the PRC include a more solid base for increased military power).

In contrast, the USSR has satellites about which it worries and is a superpower surely concerned that its military might—its major foreign policy asset—may be compromised over the (short? medium?) run by any market reform and the resulting internal political, social, and economic consequences. No external power has a veto over a Soviet leadership that might choose to move in a reform direction. But

*Paul Marer has estimated the "unrequited flow of resources" from Eastern Europe to the USSR between the end of World War II and Stalin's death in 1953 at around $14 billion—the same order of magnitude as U.S. transfers to Western Europe under the Marshall Plan. See Marer, "East European Economics: Achievements, Problems, Prospects," in Teresa Rakowska-Harmstone, ed., *Communism in Eastern Europe*, 2d ed. (Bloomington: Indiana University Press, 1984), p. 287 and source cited.

for the USSR as well as the PRC, should the feared overspill of reform result in severe social and political destabilization, no power will
intervene to save the leaders or the system.

To a larger degree, Eastern Europe is spared the risk, along with
the sovereignty. Soviet pressure can, and has, moderated, stalled, and
vetoed reform programs. The USSR sets political and military limits.
Within these limits, however, countries that are satellites and lack the
military clout to be otherwise can move, and in some cases have moved,
further in a reform direction (Hungary the obvious case; the GDR
and Bulgaria less notably) than the USSR does at home. As in the
Czechoslovak experience of 1968, and in another sense the Polish
crisis of 1980, the USSR is present to contain the overspill if attempts
at, or demands for, reform threaten to go too far.

Sovereign or not, leaders in all three varieties of state socialism face
some similar concerns: unspecified, but looming, political effects of
moves in a market direction; the social effects of increased inequalities
(and different forms of inequality) as the winners and losers differen-
tiate themselves under market reform conditions; and the economic
effects on political managers as they see fixed salaries and perquisites
lose some of their value to the private enterprisers newly affluent in an
economic context that breeds inflationary pressures as well. Reform
leaves many issues to ponder; the choices for or against it are fraught
with perceived and real political consequences.

TIMING AND EXPERIENCE

Habituation over time breeds resistance to change. On this basis
alone, the Soviet economy will prove resistant to market reform. Almost sixty years separate us from the end of the New Economic Policy (NEP) and the launching of the "plan era." The 1930s saw the
USSR left alone to build what became the Soviet model, to construct
the heavy industry that is its hallmark, to collectivize agriculture (and
along the way liquidate the most prosperous, market-oriented farmers), to preside over the decline of the service sector and the rise of a
huge planning and control apparatus staffed by a new breed of politi-
cal/economic bureaucrat. The World War II experience proved the
validity of the institutional recipe; the commitment to extension of the
model in Eastern Europe probably terminated any possible postwar
rethinking of its elements.

Generations have grown up within this economy. Virtually *no one* in
the USSR knows what an economy on Soviet territory operating with-

out Gosplan, the ministerial bureaucracy, and so on, looks like. There are those—including leaders—who "know" that other economies manage to produce and exchange food, goods, and services without such institutions, at prices set by markets. But they do not know, really, *how* this happens. Nor, one can presume, are they confident that anything so alien could work in the USSR.

China, in this respect, has been more fortunate. Several factors made the move to reform in the late 1970s possible. First, 1949 was a far later start—not enough years intervened, despite a violent and eventful history, to erase memories of a pre-Mao system, with its positive and negative aspects, in countryside and city. Demographic scale and a "backwardness" that retarded communication and bureaucratic control in the countryside slowed the process whereby old practices and methods, and the possibility of returning to the best of them, could be extirpated by purposeful *action* as well as time.

Nor was the system a demonstrated "success." No world war, no massive invasion, tested the system and found it solid. For the post-Mao leaders led by Deng, critical benchmarks were more likely the Great Leap Forward and the Cultural Revolution, two paroxysms hailed at the time as proof of China's revolutionary authenticity, but which set back economic progress markedly. For those leaders, it has been possible to read history more critically because the history gave them more to be critical of. If it did not determine the decision for reform, history's feedback nevertheless made that decision easier to reach.

For Eastern Europe, there was obviously no lack of people who, into the 1960s and 1970s, remembered prewar economies, though their number is constantly declining. More important, there were those who could remember that the postwar economic restoration of 1945–49 was generally achieved before the imposition of the fully articulated Soviet system, that the long overdue land reform in Poland and Hungary came under coalition governments, but collective farming began in the post-coalition period of Sovietization. This consciousness, and the fact that these smaller economies, moderate in their resource endowment and dependent on external suppliers and markets, showed the effects of systemic abuse more rapidly than the USSR, tended to telegraph those effects into the political sphere, increasing pressures for reform. In various ways, the 1956 concession of private agriculture in Poland, the Czech economic reform plans of 1968, and the 1968 Hungarian NEM all were reactions to such building pressures. But alterations in the political relationship between the USSR and the East European states, the move from Stalinist prescription of detailed

compliance with Soviet institutional patterns to the looser proscrip-
tion of certain major deviations, have not sufficed to open the path
to reforms, which would be justified by local economic conditions.
The time is surely not past when East European reform of a broader,
deeper nature than yet seen is possible. But time has been running
against the chances of moving toward reform free of large costs and
dislocations, and the USSR and its imperial policy must bear a certain
responsibility for this.

Reform, Interests, Autonomy: The Soviet Debate

Characterizing the Soviet stance on economic market reform at
home, with its implications for Soviet attitudes toward reform in Eastern Europe, is rather like trying to paint a fully detailed portrait of
a moving object. Since Leonid Brezhnev's death in 1982, under the
short-lived successions of Iurii Andropov and Konstantin Chernenko,
and into the first year and a half of the Gorbachev era, the fitness
of Soviet economic institutions and practices to the task of generating adequate economic growth and technological advance along a new
path of intensive development was called into question repeatedly and
sharply. In the debate, attackers and defenders of standpat policies
and central Soviet economic institutions have emerged. Rendering a
coherent account of some of the areas critical to the debate involves
examining elements of a scholar's debate in the period up to and after
the Gorbachev succession and looking as well at some of the indications of Gorbachev's priorities as they emerged in 1986 and early
1987.

HISTORY'S LESSONS?

In a *Voprosy istorii* article early in 1984, shortly after Andropov's
death and Chernenko's succession, Evgenii Ambartsumov, an advocate
of increased private enterprise in certain areas of the Soviet economy,
addressed the contemporary relevance of Lenin's 1921 New Economic
Policy to present and past crises in Eastern Europe (the GDR in 1953,
Hungary and Poland in 1956 and the latter in other times to the
present, and Czechoslovakia in 1968). Not unlike Western analysts, he
saw NEP, in its "strategic retreat" from direct state control to the economy's "commanding heights" and promotion of private agriculture
and small-scale private trade and manufacture, all regulated largely

by market mechanisms, as a corrective to both situational and policy-created disorders in the 1917–21 period. NEP was crisis management, and well-chosen at the time.[2]

This is heady stuff in that by implication the author criticized Lenin's 1917–21 War Communism policies, explicitly denigrating the destabilizing effect of foreign intervention or conspiracy and bureaucratic mistakes, save as these complemented the deep domestic causes of 1921's regime-society crisis. Tying this situation to the present, Ambartsumov raised implicitly a whole range of historical and contemporary issues: the alternate paths the USSR might have pursued after NEP, the meaning of Stalin's break with NEP and his creation of the USSR's enduring economic architecture, the possibilities of renewed NEP-line policies as a way out of Soviet and East European economic woes.[3] Raking over these coals can raise the ghosts of Nikolai Bukharin and others whose positions during the industrialization debate of the 1920s were far from Stalin's and promised more continuity with the gradualism of the NEP.[4]

Response, predictably, was not long in coming. An editor of the party's theoretical organ, *Kommunist*, attacked Ambartsumov's "strange position." Evgenii Bugaev rejected NEP's "contemporary relevance" on the base that Ambartsumov's historical cases, from the USSR in 1918–21 to Poland in 1980–81, were still in the phase of capitalist-socialist transition and condemned Ambartsumov for underestimating the power of foreign and "imperialist" influence on them at the time. Any advocacy of a move now toward expanded private enterprise risked damage to "collectivism" and the promotion of inequality and injustice. The use of Lenin's analysis of 1921's problems wrongly superimposed the founder's thought on the completely different situation of "developed socialism" today.[5] The editorial board of *Voprosy istorii* ate "humble pie,"[6] recognizing the "justice" of the criticism and leaving it to *Kommunist* to report the fact.[7] The exchange, addressed to the "fit" of NEP-style policies and institutions to the contemporary situations in both the USSR and Eastern Europe, seemed to end on a clear antireform note, evidence that reformers throughout the bloc might find their tasks as difficult in the future as they had in the past.

ENTER GORBACHEV: DIVIDED COUNSEL

With Gorbachev's accession in 1985, the discussion continued. For all the hopes that had been reposed in him as a vigorous leader with new ideas, his early economic statements were long on rhetoric, short on details. The prospect became even more bleak for reform with the June publication in *Pravda* of an article by the pseudonymous "O. Vladimirov," a harsh piece mainly aimed at Eastern Europe. The article's main thrust was a denunciation of nationalism, disparaging the "thesis of the special role of 'small' countries . . . as mediators in the formulation of compromises between the great powers" (backhanding thus the Hungarian-applauded moves by GDR leader Erich Honecker toward more independent diplomacy with the FRG in 1984) and decrying the continuing efforts of imperialist plotters to sow the seeds of disunity in the bloc. But "Vladimirov" reserved space for the condemnation of certain economic ideas and the reassertion of tried-and-true Soviet-model orthodoxies.

Attempts to interpret from a revisionist standpoint the problems of socialist ownership and of the correlation between social production and private production are appearing. Certain scientists advocate weakening state levers for the regulation of economic development, primarily centralized planning, propagating market competition, and increasing the size of the private sector. Such "quests" do not take into account the main point—the expansion of the private sector is fraught with serious economic, social, and ideological consequences, primarily a destabilization of the foundations of socialist economic management, the violation of social justice, and, as a consequence, an increase in social tension.[8]

Pravda's word, however, was not the last. Two articles in the July 1985 issue of *Kommunist* suggested another faction in high party ranks, or at least divided counsel. An article by Karoly Nemeth, deputy general secretary to János Kadar in the Hungarian party, explained and justified a number of Hungary's innovations against the backdrop of its specific needs and situation; notable especially was his frank language in discussing Hungary's economic problems, linking them to heightened international tension and its effects on a small, trade-dependent state.[9]

Oleg Bogomolov, head of the Institute for the Economics of the World Socialist System, provided in the second article a broader, programmatic endorsement of diversity in and among the East European states. Bogomolov discussed the reality and legitimacy of many different interests within socialist economies, but also among them: national interests and "internationalism" are not identical, nor would the first always give place to the second. Bogomolov, in effect, attempted to "normalize" the notions of the "specific interests" and "overriding preoccupations" of different states.[10]

The struggle of ideas continued through 1985, against the background of the drafts of a new Soviet party program and of the Twelfth (1986–90) Five-Year Plan. That the Soviets were concerned, for "imperial" reasons, with the economic health of both the USSR and Eastern Europe was not in doubt; that various combinations of hope and fear attached to divergent prescriptions of the appropriate means by which to promote economic advance was also clear.

The indications, at least through the first half of 1986, were that the USSR was not ready to embark on reform beyond a more vigorous, more intensified set of measures aimed at "perfecting" a centralized system. With respect to Eastern Europe (as one analyst suggested), Moscow could encourage reforms and adjustments (short of real "marketization") to produce healthier trading partners for a USSR that might thus fend off the need to reform itself.[11] Some, however, saw indications in Soviet statements (notably, the draft program of the CPSU) that tensions between the Soviet and East European states might be moderated by increased political maneuvering room for West-yearning Kadars and Honeckers, in return for a tighter CMEA integration that would reduce the real possibilities for substantial reform in the more fragile and vulnerable economies of the East European states.[12]

PRECEDENTS? 1968 AND BEYOND

The early 1980s were not the first time, obviously, that issues of reform, driven by perceptions of lagging economic performance, were raised across the Soviet bloc. As Sarah Terry has cogently observed, "cycles of permissiveness and retrenchment" have characterized the Soviet–East European relationship in the past and affected the reform-antireform dynamic.[13] Some examination of past history may illuminate the stakes, as they appeared in the transition to Gorbachev and the early period of his ascendancy.

From 1960, when a Central Committee plenum of the Czechoslovak party first used the term "developed socialism," to the fall of Khrushchev in late 1964 (and especially after the 1962 Twenty-second Soviet Party Congress), Soviet statements seemed to foster East European reform: good words about Kadar's (pre-NEM) alliance politics with the Hungarian populace and support for the reform plans of the GDR and Bulgaria (against the domestic background of *Pravda*'s publication of Liberman's modest reform proposals in 1962). Soviet plans for change seemed to focus on administrative decentralization, whereas the Bulgarian, and later the Czech and Hungarian, reform discussions moved closer to an economic decentralization with more room for the market and private enterprise. But the general trend seemed in favor of reform.

Khrushchev's ouster signaled, until the fateful August of 1968, "not a perceptible reversal in attitude, but the lack of clear warning signs of a pending change in the direction of Soviet policy.[14] A stalemate arose between moderate "re-Stalinizers" and reformers among the Soviet power elite and left the public discussion fairly open, with proreform elements seemingly dominant (Oleg Bogomolov praised Hungarian and Czech reform plans in 1966 in *Voprosy ekonomiki*.)[15] The Soviet discussions, however, were neither guidance for Eastern Europe policies nor evidence of authoritative political decisions. They were, for the most part, transactions among academic specialists. Soviet advocates of change may have felt, and may have had reason to feel, that events were moving in their direction; but their confidence misled East European advocates of reform, if not the political apparatus of the East European states.

The Czech invasion changed the terms decisively: discussions continued, but now, and until the later 1970s, emphasis on "socialist markets" gave way to "rationalization" and "streamlining" of central planning; the CMEA, as potential beneficiary of market reforms among its members, was instead placed in the role of a spur to greater efficiency and progress in the era of the "scientific-technical revolution," via greater plan coordination among the states. The Czech reform was aborted, Polish plans postponed, GDR and Bulgarian moves dutifully curtailed. The NEM survived but at decelerating speed until the halt (but not the reversal) of 1974. All this occurred against the background of an effective bureaucratic strangulation of the 1965 Kosygin reforms in the USSR, as "planners and bureaucrats began to react against 'undesirable' spontaneous enterprise actions."[16]

The stabilization of the early 1970s, a product of political fears, was dearly bought. But as economic indicators took an increasingly grim turn in the mid-1970s (despite some import-led growth in certain sectors in Soviet-bloc economies), and as debts to Western governmental and financial sources of those imports grew, a renewed, if moderated, discussion was again legitimated. This discussion, under conditions of economic crisis in pre- and post-Solidarity Poland, within the context of a renewed NEM running into inflation, slow growth, and trade deficits in Hungary, and generally negative indicators elsewhere save in the GDR, marked the transition period from Brezhnev to Gorbachev.

GORBACHEV: EMBATTLED REFORMER?

Whatever cautions the history of 1960s and 1970s seemed to offer, the "personal equation" emerged into even sharper relief in 1986 and 1987. Gorbachev, more and more, seems to "mean business," not only in the well-publicized loosening of control in belles-lettres and other aspects of Soviet high and middle-brow culture and in the greater openness (*glasnost'*) in the discussion of public issues, but also with respect to economic problems central to the shared dilemmas of the Soviet Union and the East European states. His rhetoric, from the February 27 Party Congress on, was heavy on the key words "acceleration" (*uskorenie*), "discipline" (*distsiplina*), and "restructuring" (*perestroika*). Speeches to the public increasingly saw him strike the tone of a leader whose program of renewal was being resisted at every turn by various layers of a bureaucracy, itself relatively novel as a gambit of the general secretary of a bureaucracy probably unmatched in the contemporary world. All of this would still be consistent with objectives well short of the radical reform Gorbachev called for at the Twenty-seventh Party Congress, with a program that sought to leave the central institutional framework unchanged but working better.

But indications were that he did, and does, intend more. A potentially important case in point is the question of even limited private enterprise. Though he was early thought an advocate of some expansion in this area, Gorbachev's direction seemed less clear when a Central Committee resolution and a Supreme Soviet decree of May 28, 1986, on the "struggle against unearned income" seemed to set a harsh tone against expansion of activities in which myriad Soviet citizens engage.[17] Yet a Supreme Soviet session of November 19, 1986, approved a decree that will, in fact, legalize twenty-nine different types of private activity[18] and bring earnings from them within the purview of a progressive income tax likely to rise quite a bit higher than the current 13 percent ceiling on earnings from state employment. Implementation of this new departure and benefits and social strains that may arise from it remain to be seen, but it is a departure, one the Soviet economy resisted for decades. Gorbachev is energetic, no doubt; whether he will turn out to be a reformer is more debatable and depends both on one's definition of reform and on one's assessment of whether he is likely, against the opposition he himself excoriates, to remain in power for anything like the sixteen years of Leonid Brezhnev.[19] These questions remain open.

"Spillover": The Risks of Market Reform

It seems appropriate, at this point, to explore at a more general level some of the specifics of Soviet domestic, and "imperial" East European, concerns in those areas of political and social relations which would bear the impact of moves toward a greater role for market forces and private enterprise.

Fears seem to center on the creation, via the market and possibly excessive privatization, of an unfamiliar environment, both difficult to control politically and new and divisive at the grass-roots level of Soviet society. Through all the maneuvers that have had as one of their stated objectives greater managerial independence, the "system" has closed in again, to restrict autonomy, to add to previously simplified sets of targets, and in other ways to prevent the managerial behavior that might be expected in response to market stimuli: concentrating on high-profit items, exploring demand hitherto unnoticed by the planners, and devoting resources to respond to it. Neither freewheeling Hungarian managers nor the Hainan Island scandal in the PRC in 1985 is likely to seem anything but alien and alarming to Soviet leaders. The inflation that seems to arise with reform is a deterrent to a leadership that has borne large-scale subsidies on basic foods and other products and habituated a population to ostensible price stability (along with shortages) in many areas. Soviet planners have, of course, allowed price rises, mainly on what are denominated luxury items, but their concerns are certainly reflected in the failure of rises to come near matching the pace at which unspent rubles accumulate. Price stability plus shortages is a pattern they, and the population, are used to, trading it for the risk of rising prices, but an increase in the supply and quality of certain goods and services would require a resolve missing in the past.

Income inequality is also a likely consequence of reform, as Yugoslav, Hungarian, and Chinese experiences have shown. Although the USSR has never been a spectacularly egalitarian society, even among the socialist states, the prospect of a resorting of large groups in the income hierarchy, transforming a fairly fixed Soviet social architecture, must be an impediment to reform. Hungarian and Chinese examples, where farmers' incomes have risen against those of industrial workers, must seem strange to Soviets used to the formers' permanent place at the bottom of the hierarchy. Beyond this, Soviet wage policy has long favored the workers in heavy and extractive industry over those in light and consumer production and the service sector. Readiness to offend this constituency by a combination of marketization and privatization (to allow assemblers of radios, TVs, and appliances to moonlight as repairmen and significantly increase earnings over those of the stamping-machine operators and foundry workers of heavy industry, whose skills and materials are less easily carried into the market) has yet to be shown.

Indeed, any significant opening to private enterprise must, in prospect, seem the source of many headaches. The November decree may signal the overcoming of some of the fears, but many questions raised in the past are likely to remain. How would privateers in small-scale trade or production acquire inputs? At what price to state users of the same? How much tax on private enterprise is appropriate, and how would it be collected? How many lines of endeavor would the state have to remain in to offer fixed-price alternatives to the market-priced goods and services of the privateers not all could afford to patronize? Such questions, and the difficulties of answering them to the satisfaction of the apparat, may still force the abandonment by the Soviets of their "best option" a "neo-NEP," in Joseph Berliner's words, which would permit the maintenance of directive target planning over the state-controlled "commanding heights" of the economy (now, as opposed to Lenin's time, the vast majority of the economy), while allowing a private sector, surely not impossible to control, to operate and grow. Such, however, is the risk of political choice of economic alternatives.[20]

There are also, it seems, deep-rooted convictions, frequently expressed in a Soviet press which leaders control but which may also represent broad public attitudes, that something is wrong with making a good deal of money in a market situation. Admittedly hard and efficient workers, like the roving brigades of construction workers (*shabashniki*) or odd-job repairmen who get the odd jobs done, are subject to surprisingly broad condemnation, a certain amount of it almost suggesting that not to be in a dependent, wage-earning relationship to a state employer is wrong. *Pravda* in a 1983 article focused its wrath on a crane operator and driver who, despite the generally good pay associated with these skills, went independent and repaired apartments and dwellings, dealing directly with his customers. "You work a little, then you are free again," he said. The newspaper observed that this "master craftsman" would not dream of taking a job in a state repair enterprise "because the latter maintains discipline."[21] Left unexpressed was the contrast between the quality of work done by independents and the generally sorry results of the socialist sector.

These issues cut deep into the prospects for more privatization and marketization (the latter not a major theme in the range of topics being widely ventilated). Articles in the press in the fall of 1986 by several scholars and commentators counterposed those who saw increasing income differentiation, if tied to work, as a positive stimulus, in no way contravening any principles of "socialist justice" to those for whom that quality would be strained by large differences in incomes and living standards, however legally achieved.[22] The egalitarian position would seem to partake of a populist notion of leveling down, a legitimation of the right to envy. One of its partisans cites as a correct understanding of "social justice" the comments of an office worker who lives modestly about a flashier friend: "I don't want to live like her; I want her to live like me."[23] If Gorbachev continues to back increased differentiation in the state sector and encourages private enterprisers, he may indeed be engaged in a battle for hearts and minds, with much of Soviet society, and not only a bureaucracy, to be won over.

The efficiencies a more marketized Soviet economy might bring would also raise the issue of redundancy and unemployment among workers now situated in inefficient enterprises or branches. There is evidence that the regime is girding itself for some of this, in any case, and thus setting itself toward possible modification of one of the most important strands in the Soviet welfare net—the guarantee of employment and effective tenure in job and workplace. Certainly, it has known for years that the inefficient "stockpiling" of workers by enterprises, and resultant low per-capita productivity, is one of the cardinal weaknesses of the system. The Shchekino "experiment" or system, which allows managers to divest themselves of unneeded workers while retaining some of the wage fund thus saved to reward the remaining work force, has been in effect since 1967 but never generalized to the entire economy, presumably because of the specter of adjustments to mass redundancy and reabsorption of released workers in an economy priding itself on its permanent solution to the problem of unemployment.

Thus when plans for transition payments and retraining were announced for the unspecified number of state bureaucrats to be made redundant by a merger of five Union-Republican ministries related to agriculture into one "supercommittee," the all but explicit news that the Gorbachev era might produce unemployment along with technological progress and heightened productivity was something of a sensation.[24] V. Kostakov, a frequent writer in professional journals and the press on labor issues, predicted early in 1986 that, if the ambitious targets for labor productivity increases were met through the year 2000, 13 to 19 million workers in manufacture would find themselves redundant.[25] But less than two weeks later, TASS quoted him as assuring workers that new technology would cause no unemployment problem because all released workers would receive wages and stipends while being retrained.[26] Would this leadership test the waters of a market determination of unemployment?

When one adds to all these sensitivities the (accurate) official perception that decentralization and more than marginal privatization would, in Soviet conditions, threaten to unleash the cultural, ethnic, and economic diversity of central Asia, the Caucasus, and the Baltic —a diversity the state has, since tsarist times, sought to control and contain—the likelihood of real reform seems all the more remote.

Instead, the current indications point to a strong option in favor of what Gorbachev has made a central theme—a technology-led increase in production and efficiency, within an organizational recipe stressing improved central planning and managerial autonomy (at the expense of intermediate bodies), a limited encouragement to private and (mainly) cooperative enterprise, and some carrots and sticks for the work force.

What, then, of Soviet attitudes toward reform alternatives in Eastern Europe? They need not be of quite the intensity or decisiveness as attitudes toward Soviet economic reform. Soviet control over Eastern Europe is not absolute, and willingness to tolerate departures from the Soviet model (which, in a true if somewhat trivial sense, are present in all the East European economies) probably depends on a calculus balancing Soviet economic gains to be anticipated from reformed East European economies against political and security losses from "spillover" in East European societies and intrabloc relations, as well as economic losses to the Soviets should reforms in the satellite economies raise the cost of doing business with them.

Economic gains to be anticipated are varied: more efficient use of energy and raw materials of Soviet origin; higher quality of exports to the USSR (incorporating, presumably, more Western content if reformed economies manage better relationships with the West), and in general lowered Soviet costs in its economic relationship with the bloc countries.

Negative contingencies include internal social tensions arising from price rises, widening of the gap between economic winners and losers under reform conditions, new patterns of inequality displacing workers in heavy industry as the favored top of the blue-collar majority, growth of unemployment, and other unfamiliar ills. Political weakening of the regimes, caused by the diminution of state economic power that comes with reform, is another clear concern, but here, at least, conservative elements in the East European regimes share a community of interest with the Kremlin. On the directly economic side, the Soviets have shown their sensitivity to the westward bending of East European trade policies, the tendency to ship high-quality goods to Western rather than Soviet markets. (Of course, some Soviet leaders must also realize that the lack of reform has, most spectacularly in the case of Poland, created its own negative feedback. The unreformed Polish economy generated massive social unrest, exacerbating political strains and putting the regime of the post-1976 Gierek, then Kania, into retreat. The debt burden Poland collected in the 1970s might not have been so large had it followed economic reform, and it could hardly have been handled worse by a reformed economy.)

This picture is, in all, very complicated. This fact should not be obscured by Gorbachev's travels in the first half of 1987 to push reform at reluctant leaders from Prague to Bucharest, which took on, notably in the Western press, the look of a missionary effort of *uskorenie* and *perestroika* (albeit by a missionary with great political clout). Economics were not the only item on the agenda; not with the political problems attendant on a number of forthcoming leadership successions in Eastern Europe, not with Gorbachev's certain conviction that he cannot afford to risk provoking social unrest in pursuit of economic policies and still keep a firm grip on his own Kremlin power. Backing reform courses in Hungary and Poland and pressing for measures to promote greater production, efficiency, and quality in East Berlin and Prague aim mainly at getting East European leaders to make their economies work, not to restructure whole societies, although Gorbachev seems willing to tolerate some greater degree of ambiguity in the social processes attendant upon reform than previous Soviet general secretaries.

Such a position accords with what Soviet leaders probably see as their mid-term interests. The shift in the mid-1970s to the "Bucharest formula" of pricing Soviet oil on a five-year rolling average of world market prices has for some time guaranteed the Soviets more favorable terms of trade than in earlier years. Whether one can, about an essentially barter relationship, say that East Europeans are paying some definite percentage of, or above, the dollar-denominated world market price is doubtful, but the USSR's leverage in this area is significant. As Charles Gati put it in 1974, "Hungary sold 800 'Ikarus' buses to the Soviet Union in order to purchase 1 million tons of Soviet oil. In 1981, it had to sell 2,300. . . . By 1984, the 'price' . . . may have reached 4,000 'Ikarus' buses."[27] Soviet concerns about getting a large share of East Europe's best technology are clear and also, under current circumstances, readily enforceable. These are hard times for the East European economies, made hard not only by their internal problems but also by slow West European recovery and hence lower receptivity to East European exports. Debt has forced Eastern Europe as a whole into an import-restriction, export-promotion situation and into an uphill struggle in Western markets. At such times more than ever, the tendency to lean on the Soviet economy, with its barter arrangements and huge market for East European manufactures, asserts itself. And in hard times, though the need to reform may manifest itself all the more clearly to those already disposed toward it, the practical problems multiply. No East European economy today faces the relatively benign international economic climate and domestic slack that Hungary did when it formulated the NEM in the middle 1960s. None will find it easy to concentrate on large-scale domestic reform when current internal political and economic and external pressures (to retire or keep current with hard-currency debt and export to the USSR to balance the imports of fuel and materials) force attention elsewhere.

Thus it seems unlikely that the Soviets need worry about forcing any rollback of the NEM or anticipate applying the brakes to similar reforms elsewhere. They will continue, in addressing Eastern Europe, to praise and criticize as they have done. They will stress, as they have done at home, technology as the answer to East Europe's problems in an age when the shift to intensive growth is on the agenda and further CMEA integration in the area of technology as an economically rational path to preserving socialist autonomy in the face of a threatened overdependence on Western technology.[28] Here they will face another contradiction between their announced goals and the methods they select. East Europe's earlier drive toward extensive growth required constant recourse to the energy and raw materials of the USSR. A centripetal force drove growth. The intensive growth that must depend on a massive upgrading of the level of socialist technology implies a search for the "best" technology, but such is not to be found within the bloc. Some progress, to be sure, is possible, but a continued search for world-class technology will drive its members, including the USSR, to look outside CMEA, subjecting the body to renewed forces.

Contemporary pressures on the USSR must, to some degree, conduce to a shortening of perspective. The reduced price of oil on the world market, the lower than anticipated West European demand for Soviet gas, and a downturn in Soviet oil output have hurt Moscow's hard-currency earnings, already strained by expenditures on grain imports and payments for the acquisition of Western technology. Added to evident Soviet anxieties over the Strategic Defense Initiative, born of a basic concern over the technology gap, these concerns work against any leap into a broad market reform at home or abroad. Fundamental reform might, indeed, offer the best prospect for a long-term resolution of these issues. But moving in that direction would involve a leap into uncertainty not to be expected from a leadership acculturated to risk aversion. If such reform is Gorbachev's ultimate intent, he has before him the necessity of a more thorough purge (nonviolent, to be sure) of resisters in the party and state bureaucracies.

Soviet Alternatives

It is important to understand that more can be gotten out of the Soviet economy without any substantial reform. The Gorbachev-Ligachev-Ryzkhov leadership's option thus far for a combination of discipline, streamlining, and the carrot-stick method of motivating workers, continuing from 1985 into 1987, has generated gains. The reason for these gains is that, whatever the logical relationship of current Soviet economic institutions to the desires of the leadership for intensive growth, those institutions have been very badly run for some time in the past.

Discipline, as it falls on the upper ranks, has seen the retirement in the last few years (since Andropov) of much "dead wood" in ministerial and party ranks and dismissals of many corrupt bureaucrats. Their successors, younger, better educated in technical and (perhaps) managerial skills, though not likely to be world-beaters, can scarcely do worse than many of their predecessors. They are likely, in a sense, to be younger versions of a Ryzkhov (whose career spans rising to the top of Uralmash, a machine-building complex that could stand as a symbol of the focus of Soviet industry, a top ministerial post in machine building, and the vice-chairmanship of Gosplan). They are successes within the current organizational framework of the Soviet economy. For the lower ranks of workers, a tougher discipline will work no wonders, but moderate progress does not depend on such. Reducing absenteeism, increasing sobriety, and some increase in workplace surveillance (against slacking, theft, and the like) may not contribute much to workers' morale. But, for a while, it can have effects.

Streamlining certain administrative processes, in a context of heightened discipline, can also help. Innovations in the service sector such as the experiment with television repair work in Estonia can be broadened with no great difficulties until the point at which higher earnings set up further inflationary pressures. The further generalization of the "Andropov experiment," which has already gone beyond the ministries in which it was introduced in 1984, can do no harm. Bottlenecks are many, but not all must be cleared simultaneously. Increasing transport capacity (better rolling stock and railway maintenance) may have positive effects, quickly felt.[29] In the potentially very important foreign trade area, a new policy encouraging joint ventures with Western partners may reap benefits, though, obviously, not immediately. Perhaps even more consequential, the freeing of some ministries and enterprises to deal directly with foreign partners rather than through Ministry of Foreign Trade bureaucrats could be a component of a reform that goes beyond structural streamlining. Here again, however, Soviet sophistication and quality control will be important in determining whether opportunities for profit may be realized.

With negative and positive incentives for workers added to a broad discipline and streamlined management, further effort can be evoked. Fear of loss of jobs and bonuses and the necessity of higher outlays for rent, utilities, and medical services (should the state go this far) can make even Soviet workers invest more effort. Should the regime intensify efforts in this direction, it will ready itself to deal with grumbling and discontent, but it will not tolerate much complaint. Fears of a Poland at home are surely moderated by the (accurate) conviction that Soviet workers know the USSR is not Poland and will act accordingly.

But the short- to medium-run success of such a program, measured in better output figures and higher growth rates, may bring on a point of maximum temptation, when the regime rejects deeper changes in the economic system in the conviction that early results constitute an indefinite trend. It is not likely that they will. The danger for Eastern Europe lies in a disinterest or lack of encouragement to its reformers at this point, or, worse, Soviet insistence that those economies adopt tactics of the Soviet sort to mobilize their own "hidden reserves" and follow the USSR into this new strategy.

This is, in sum, a moderately pessimistic treatment of prospects, as I am well aware. It may, indeed one hopes that it does, underestimate the degree to which the later Brezhnev years taught a lesson to the Gorbachev generation, providing evidence of the critical necessity of thoroughgoing change once they succeeded leaders too old, and too set in their ways, to move decisively. Similarly, it may underestimate Gorbachev's ultimate intentions, his political sophistication and that of the members of his leadership whom he has clearly chosen, as well as his luck, and thus fall short of an adequate appreciation of what he will mean for Soviet and East European history in the twilight of the twentieth century. It might be that the rest of this century will witness a Soviet rethinking of its own imperial concerns, their balance of costs and benefits, a coming to grips with the problems of institutional structures fit neither to Soviet nor East European long-term economic objectives. But those lines of thought remain speculative. The political resistance to reform certainly still exists, and it may defer the point at which it will be relevant to consider the social effects of reform to a time well into the future. Western analysts, and the citizens of the CMEA states themselves, are just as likely to confront further social effects of a rejection of deep reforms, as those of their adoption, over the coming years.

Afterthoughts: November 1987

Following Soviet affairs since Gorbachev's accession has continued to be an intriguing yet frustrating enterprise: nothing stands still. Yet more than halfway through his third year in power, Gorbachev would probably, in honesty, have to give himself and his policies mixed reviews. The economic fruits of any jolt to the economy from enhanced discipline and demands are not impressive. Long-term prospects from *perestroika* remain still in that long term. Programmatically the leadership forges ahead, but critical elements of the new economics, including a "rationalization" of the pricing system and a redefinition of employment security, have yet to be introduced as concrete policy, with effects on the rank and file which will surely be stressful. *Glasnost'* and "democratization" seemed to suffer some reversals in the fall, notably in, but not limited to, the ouster of Boris Yel'tsin: whether these are necessary for *perestroika* in the economy or not is a question over which Gorbachev may differ with some others in the leadership, but trimming in this area is unlikely to force the pace of economic renewal faster. In Eastern Europe, the diversity of conditions, economic and political, continues to impose itself on the Soviet and the domestic leaderships. The GDR and Romania differ vastly in the quality of their own economic performances, yet are similarly resistant to Gorbachev's recipes. Other countries, predictably, follow along at varying paces. Poland, where a certain economic realism forced upon the leadership by its own experience led to the referendum over a reform program wherein the bitter was much more pronounced than the sweet, has just witnessed the rejection of that program by the voters, and hence demonstrated that without political realism on both sides Poland will remain in an impasse. With the content and ingredients of the Soviet reform still less than certain, East European leaderships and peoples are likely to face a fair amount of maneuvering room for some time to come. Whether it will be well used is, as ever, the question.

ELEVEN

The Political Economy of Chinese Industrial Reform

Susan Shirk

China's experiences since 1978 are an important case for understanding the process of economic reform in communist countries. During this period the Chinese leadership introduced a series of policies designed to transform China from a system of Soviet-style central planning to a system of market socialism in which profits, competition, and markets played a larger role in economic life. When we examine the history of this post-1978 period, one pattern emerges clearly: the processes, inducements, and obstacles to change have varied by economic sector. The reform of agriculture has been implemented rapidly and smoothly, but the reform of industrial planning and management has been delayed by difficulties and reversals. Managing industrial reform and sustaining its momentum has required unusually adroit political leadership of the sort provided by Premier Zhao Ziyang.

The agricultural reform, which decollectivized agriculture and restored household farming, has been such a dramatic success that Chinese leaders have used it as a model to inspire industrial reform.[1] From 1979 to 1982, the value of agricultural production increased at an average annual rate of 7.5 percent, more than twice the 3.2 percent average of the previous twenty-six years. Even more impressive was the 130 percent rise of average per capita income of peasants from 133.57 yuan in 1978 to 309.8 yuan in 1983.[2]

The process of reform in agriculture has been comparatively smooth. When problems arose, national leaders addressed them by extending the scope of reform instead of by backpedaling. For example, when the incentive of farmers to increase production was limited by the monopoly of state-run supply and marketing cooperatives over rural commerce, the authorities broke the monopoly and gave farm households the right to engage in private transport and marketing of farm commodities.[3] When farmers preferred to invest in their own houses rather than in productive assets, the authorities clarified and strengthened their property rights over their land; leases were extended to fifteen years and made renewable and transferable.[4] When the dramatic increase in farm output overburdened the central treasury with price subsidies, the authorities eliminated state mandatory grain purchases (a fundamental feature of the command economy) and widened the commodity market to include grain.[5]

The industrial reforms, however, have been plagued with difficulties and have not improved the economic performance of factories.* According to a World Bank report, since 1978 labor and capital productivity have declined and inventories have not been reduced.[6] Product quality has not improved significantly, and waste of energy and materials persists. Generally speaking, economic results such as efficiency in the use of inputs to reduce costs and increase profits, which were an original objective of the reform, have been poor.† As of mid-1983, nearly 30 percent of all enterprises were operating at a loss. That proportion declined to 10.5 and 10.7 percent respectively for 1984 and 1985 but rose again to 17.6 percent during the first eight months of 1986.[7]

The central economic authorities reacted to problems arising from the partial reform of industry by limiting the autonomy of enterprises and local officials, not by extending the scope of the reform.‡ Although the goal of reform persists and Premier Zhao managed to sustain the momentum of reform after each recentralization, this hesitancy to expand reform and tendency to recentralize vividly contrasts with the spreading and deepening of reform in agriculture. For example, in 1980, when the loosening of central controls over industry stimulated local investment and caused massive state budget deficits, the central authorities' reflex response was recentralization. In 1984–85

---

*One proreform article does claim improved efficiency in the use of coal, a reduction in steel inventories, improvement of product quality, improvement of labor productivity, and increase in supply of consumer goods: *Banyuetan*, Sept. 15, 1982, *Foreign Broadcast Information Service (FBIS)*, Sept. 30, 1982, p. k8.

†For example, in Hunan Province during the first half of 1983, industrial investment in fixed assets increased by over 800 million yuan and employment expanded by 40,000 over the comparable period in 1982; during the same period, however, profits fell by 4.75 percent and profits delivered to the state declined by 22.22 percent (Hunan Provincial Service, June 17, 1983, *FBIS*, June 21, 1983, p. p6).

‡For Xue Muqiao's explanation why it was necessary to "slow down the speed of structural reforms" and "strengthen leadership by planning and administrative management" see his speech reprinted in *Shijie Jingji Daobao*, June 21, 1982, p. 3.

the authorities reacted to a serious inflation by strengthening central financial controls and delaying the critically necessary price reform.

This situation generates the two questions addressed in this paper: Why has industrial reform in China been more difficult to carry out than agricultural reform? What leadership strategies can sustain industrial reform despite its difficulties? Comparing the agricultural and industrial reforms illuminates the relationships between economics and politics during the stage of partial reform in China and other communist states.

The Soviet and East European Experience

The economic reforms in other communist countries provide a starting point for analysis of China. There, too, the leaders sought to transform their command economy, characterized by central planning, government-stipulated production quotas, centrally allocated supplies and deliveries, and administered prices and wages, into a system of market socialism. The transition from one system to another, inevitably a protracted process, can be labeled the period of partial reform.

The previous attempts at economic reform in the Soviet Union (1957 and 1965), Hungary (1968), Poland (1956), Romania (1967), Czechoslovakia (1968), and Yugoslavia (1950 and 1965) suggest that political leaders find the period of partial reform difficult to manage, especially in the industrial sector. In all these countries other than Yugoslavia (and even there to a certain extent), the increase in enterprise autonomy, loosening of central planning, and shifting of investment priorities were followed by recentralization. Only in the case of Hungary has the impetus of reform been sustained after each temporary recentralization, in large part because of the astute leadership of János Kadar.

In other communist systems, as we shall find with the Chinese experience, the partial reform of the industrial economy exacerbated economic problems in the short run. An expansion of local investment and construction, supply shortages, and inflation were the typical problems to emerge. Groups who viewed reform as detrimental to their interests then exploited these economic problems to discredit the reforms and forced a return to centralization. In some instances, the economic inefficiencies and dissatisfaction among consumers revealed the shortcomings of recentralization, and the reformers obtained another chance. In this way, economic and political forces interact to create a cycle of reform.[8] Chinese reformers recognize the existence of this cycle and are worried about it:

Introduction of the system of responsibility has opened an avenue for revitalizing the economy, but past experiences have shown on many occasions that "flexibility" usually brings about "disorder"—and we have witnessed the spectacle of "flexibility immediately followed by disorder, disorder immediately followed by control, control immediately followed by rigidity, and rigidity again followed by flexibility," in a "flexibility-rigidity-flexibility-rigidity" cycle.[9]

The Eastern European experiences also suggest that, in communist systems, agriculture is more amenable to reform than industry and that agricultural reform is a precondition of successful industrial reform. In 1956 Polish agriculture was decollectivized but industrial reforms were not implemented.[10] The Hungarians raised farm purchase prices, abolished compulsory deliveries of farm commodities, and increased incentives to collectivized agriculture before embarking on their New Economic Mechanism in industry in 1968. The Hungarian agricultural reform stabilized the flow of agricultural products to industry and, by raising rural living standards, strengthened rural support for the regime. The agricultural reform thereby enhanced the economic and political conditions for industrial reform.[11]

Constraints on Agricultural and Industrial Reform: A Comparison

The distinctive economic and political features of agriculture and industry constrain the ability of factory managers more than farmers to respond to the reforms as the leaders would wish. The nature of a command economy affects and constrains agriculture and industry differently. In both economic and political terms, as Premier Zhao Ziyang said in an interview, industrial reform "is a more complex matter" than agricultural reform.[12] Agriculture and industry differ in both their economic structure and their political context. These economic and political factors explain why the transition moved more rapidly in agriculture than in industry.

ECONOMIC FACTORS: THE STRUCTURE OF AGRICULTURE AND INDUSTRY

Many farmers and factory managers responded with alacrity to the economic opportunities and incentives which the reforms offered.

There are many energetic entrepreneurs among the ranks of both farmers and managers. The differing record of the two sectors is not owing to the personal attitudes or aptitudes of farmers and managers. When the central authorities cut the investments and planned output targets for heavy industry in 1980, the managers of some machinery plants began to sell products on their own, assessing market demand, diversifying products to meet demand, expanding their marketing operations, and servicing their customers. They even started to drum up business in the countryside, selling small tractors and trucks directly to individual farmers.*

The major differences between industry and agriculture, then, involve their internal economic structure (as well as their political environment) and as a consequence, the differential effect of the reforms on them. Agriculture and industry differ in their organization of production, their structure of competition and budget constraints, their prices, and their incentive systems linking effort and reward.

Organization of production. Industrial production is more complex and interdependent than agricultural production. A factory is more dependent on inputs produced by other enterprises than is a farm, whether collective or household. Because the supply of inputs is unreliable, especially in a command economy of the scale of China or the Soviet Union, factories tend to stockpile these inputs to make sure that they have the wherewithal to meet their output quotas.

Partial reform of the command economy exacerbates stockpiling and shortages of supplies in industry. The economic expansion which the reform generates increases the competition for construction materials and other supplies.† Allowing managers to market their above-

---

*See the case of the Shengyang Walking Tractor Factory in Peter Kwok, *Managing Enterprises in the People's Republic of China: Seven Case Studies* (Berkeley: University of California Institute of Business and Economic Research, 1981), p. 31. On the recovery of the machinery industry after the readjustment see Barry Naughton, "Economic Reforms and Decentralization: China's Problematic Materials Allocation System," unpublished ms., 1984; and Shigeru Kobayashi, "The 'Reality of Readjustment' in China, Part I, Machine Tool Industry Seeks a Role in Market Adjustment," *Metalworking Engineering and Marketing* (Nagoya, Japan), 3 (Nov. 1981): 22–31. The new demand for small tractors created by the agricultural responsibility system sparked an explosion of tractor production. In 1983, there were eighty factories producing them although only twelve were officially sanctioned by the Ministry of Machine Building, which had already planned to increase production by 120 percent over the previous year. The ministry was naturally pleased by the expansion of the market but was clearly displeased by the increase in competition (*Xinhua*, Apr. 19, 1983, *FBIS*, Apr. 25, 1983, p. k15).

†The press has frequently complained about local construction projects robbing building materials, manpower, transport, and energy from national projects. For example, see *Xinhua*, Apr. 17, 1983, *FBIS*, Apr. 21, 1983, p. k10. The unexpected recovery

quota production and retain a share of their profits increases their incentive to overfulfill their output quotas and to hoard supplies. This motivation has not yet been counteracted by any genuine increase in the cost of credit; despite the declared intention to shift from a system of administrative allocation of free investment funds to bank loans with interest charges, the charges for fixed and circulating capital are still much too low to constrain enterprise spending. The supply shortages, along with shortages of electric power, fuel, and freight transport, are a consequence of partial reform and limit the ability of factory managers to increase production.*

A farmer is less dependent on externally produced inputs and services. The increase in the division of labor associated with economic modernization does not necessarily apply to agriculture. As agricultural production becomes more technologically sophisticated, farmers in other countries have learned to adapt while preserving the family farm.[13] The Chinese farmer may want his own tractor, but he can continue to rely on human or animal labor. The farmer does not even require much electric power or long-distance transport, although he does need help to transport and market his crops locally.† Even the Chinese farmer who uses modern production methods is less prone to stockpile manufactured inputs because he cannot finance inventories through interest-free or low-interest capital, as a factory manager can.[14]

The relationship between degrees of interdependence and ease of structural reform is highlighted by comparisons within the agricultural sector. The household responsibility system spread more rapidly in the more backward regions of China, where farmers use fewer manufactured inputs, than in the more modern areas, which use more machinery and chemical fertilizer.[15] Reform has also proved to be more difficult to carry out in Soviet agriculture because it is more highly mechanized and dependent on manufactured inputs than Chinese agriculture; the 1982–83 Soviet "link" reform to establish spe-

---

and expansion of heavy industry also deprived light industry of the inputs it needed. Shortages resulted from a situation in which "capital construction squeezed out production and heavy industry elbowed out light industry" (*Guangming Ribao*, Apr. 24, 1983, *FBIS*, May 4, 1983, p. k8).

*During 1981–84, whereas industrial and agricultural production increased by 41.8 percent, freight capacity increased by only 19.4 percent and generated energy by 21.1 percent (*Renmin Ribao*, May 17, 1985, *FBIS*, May 24, 1985, p. k8).

†The relative independence of agriculture from centralized allocation of inputs helps explain why Chinese agriculture has always been less responsive to central control than industry. See Gregory Grossman, "Notes for a Theory of the Command Economy," *Soviet Studies*, 15 (Oct.1963): 118.

cialized agricultural teams responsible for their own profits and losses failed because without a reform of industry, teams that were unable to obtain farm machinery would be unfairly penalized.[16]

Because Chinese agriculture is a less interdependent process than industrial production, when the rural responsibility system gave farm households control over their own production and an incentive to increase output and cut costs, positive economic results occurred immediately. In industry, however, sluggish sectors and shortages of supplies, power, and transportation constrained the ability of managers to respond to the new incentives.*

Structure of competition and budget constraints. Chinese industry is more highly concentrated than agriculture, although compared to the economies of Eastern Europe, China has a large number of industrial enterprises and a preponderance of small-scale enterprises.[17] There are 437,200 factories, but less than 85,000 of them are state-run and only 1.5 percent of them (6,000) are large and medium-sized, producing 35 percent of total industrial output.[18] Whereas reform initiatives worsened the problem of monopoly in Eastern Europe, the number of Chinese factories has grown 25 percent in the reform period, with the addition of nearly 90,000 since 1978. Almost all the new enterprises, however, are in the collective sector.[19]

Despite the addition of many new small collective enterprises, Chinese state-run industry is moderately concentrated, certainly more so than agriculture, at the local level. In many cities and counties only a small number of enterprises produce the same product. The policy of local self-reliance, which was promoted since the late 1950s, inhibited interregional trade and forced enterprises to focus on local sales. Local officials have close ties with the managers of large local factories. Although these officials received a share of local industrial profits under the 1980 fiscal reforms, traditionally they have worried more about supplies and jobs than about revenue. The officials are always aware that if a local firm goes under, local shortages in its product and unemployment may result. This knowledge gives managers of large local factories considerable leverage in bargaining for loans, tax breaks, and other favors.

In other words, the budget constraints of industrial firms are "soft,"

---

*As Alec Nove says about reform and the interdependence of the industrial economy, "Piecemeal reform does not work, and one is driven back to the old system. The point is that the system has an inner logic which resists *partial* change. Thus if one frees an industry—say clothing—from central control, then what would happen to the industries which supply it with inputs?" (*The Soviet Economic System* [London: Allen & Unwin, 1980], p. 318).

not "hard." The reluctance to close firms in command economies, what Hungarian economist János Kornai calls the "soft budget constraint," limits the efficiency gains from economic reform of such economies. As Kornai describes it, the enterprise that suffers financial losses may react in two ways. It can face its difficulties by adjusting production. This might not be successful, and even if it were, it involves sacrifice. Alternatively, the enterprise can ask for financial help from higher authorities. By "crying" and lobbying, the firm bargains with the upper levels for price adjustments, tax cuts, and increased credit to help it continue operation. Personal connections often are used. Kornai says that the result of the second approach is that the firm that had been given autonomy by the reform subjects itself, almost voluntarily, to patronage. By asking for help it confirms its dependence on the central institutions that can influence its financial situation.[20]

Successful enterprises are those that cultivate relations with their bureaucratic superiors, not those that outcompete other firms. In the absence of any real pressure to make a profit, it is no wonder that many state factories, even after the reforms granted them more control over their own operations, remained dependent on government subsidies and uninterested in improving efficiency.[21]

The structure of agriculture is more competitive and more constrained by the bottom line than industry. In every county thousands of farm households produce the same crops. Unlike factory managers, who depend on industrial bureaus for survival, farmers are fully responsible for their own profits and losses. If an insufficient number of laborers or natural disaster puts them in the red, they must turn to relatives or village welfare funds. Rural bank credit is much less plentiful than urban investment funds, and there is no government bureau to bail out farmers. Farmers operate under hard budget constraints. Therefore, compared to industrial managers, farmers have a strong incentive to control their costs, shift production to the most profitable crops, and innovate.

Effects of price irrationalities. Chinese leaders have recognized the necessity to reform prices of industrial goods, but they have procrastinated because of the serious political risks entailed. Adjustment of the prices of fuel and power, raw materials, and machinery would create inflationary pressures, challenge the interests of the powerful manufacturing sectors, and throw many enterprises into the red by raising their costs.

For political and bureaucratic reasons explained below, the leaders were willing to adjust agricultural prices in 1978 and subsequently free them from central control. First they raised the plan purchase prices of the major agricultural commodities. Then, when farmers responded by growing too much grain and cotton, the authorities decided to let the pricing and sales of most agricultural commodities be regulated by the market. Beginning in 1985, grain and cotton were sold to the state by long-term contracts instead of by mandatory quotas. After meeting their grain contracts, farmers could produce crops for sale at market prices. The state purchase prices of nonstaple food products such as vegetables, meat, and fish have floated since 1985.

In industry, partial economic reforms in the absence of price reform created many perverse incentives.

1. Local officials built processing plants irrespective of supply and demand. Rather, they built plants where the administered price of the inputs was low and the fixed price of the produced commodity was high. The irrational price structure, for example, encouraged a proliferation of cigarette factories and wine distilleries, but other much needed commodities (blankets, daily use commodities) remained in severe shortage.[22]

2. Managers had little incentive to conserve low-priced inputs such as fuel and electric power. This waste of inputs inhibits improvement in efficiency.

3. Arbitrary prices impeded the effort to expand foreign trade. Producers have no incentive to export the many manufactured goods for which domestic prices are set higher than world price (machinery and electronics, for example), and they export excessive quantities of goods whose domestic price is below world prices, thereby generating domestic shortages (such as in tungsten and cashmere). Because of the price disparities foreign trade corporations find importing more profitable than exporting, and foreign trade subsidies place a heavy burden on the central government.[23]

4. Irrational prices precluded using profitability as a reliable or meaningful basis for evaluating the management or productivity of a firm. Profits largely reflect the price structure—the costs of inputs and the administratively determined value of outputs—rather than the efficiency of management and diligence of workers.*

5. In the absence of market prices, enterprise managers and their

*On average a worker producing coal, which is underpriced, generates 100 yuan of profits a year, but a worker producing chemicals, which are overpriced, generates 12,000 yuan of profit a year (Akira Fujimoto, "On Self Management of Chinese Enterprises," Japan External Trade Relations Organization, *China Newsletter*, no. 30 [Feb. 1981]: 5). Factories manufacturing products for agriculture and military-industrial products find it difficult to make a profit because of the low prices of their products (*Jingji Yanjiu*, Apr. 20, 1978, pp. 12–13). Because oil prices are high and coal prices are bureaucratic supervisors pursued their interests through bureaucratic strategies such as special pleading and particularistic bargaining, not through true economic competition.[24] Factories that consistently operate at losses defend themselves against the threat of closure or merger by claiming that their losses have "objective" (price) causes, not "subjective" (management) ones. Arbitrary administratively set prices make it difficult to harden the budget constraint of industrial firms and reinforce their tendency to bargain with the upper levels instead of competing with one another.

Price disparities create "false impressions," which lead to "wrong investment decisions."[25] Arbitrary prices prevent the center from allocating investment according to marginal return or some other objective economic standard. Therefore, enterprise representatives are able to "extort" investment funds from the authorities by claiming that it will be impossible for them to meet their targets without more resources.* Enterprises and ministries are natural allies in this effort.

Identifying this syndrome explains why without price reform the economic performance of Chinese enterprises continues to be poor and so few enterprises have actually been closed down.† The fear of failure (which Joseph Berliner calls the "invisible foot") is even more important than the positive incentive of profits in motivating firms' efficiency and productivity, and this fear has yet to be brought into play in the Chinese industrial reform.‡ As leading economist Xue Muqiao says, forcing enterprises to take full responsibility for their own profits and losses is more complicated in industry than in agriculture; so long as irrational prices affect profit levels, it is difficult to make enterprises independent economic entities.[26]

Thus administratively set prices, bureaucratic-style economic com-

---

low, railroads move into the red whenever they switch from steam locomotives, which run on coal, to diesel locomotives, which run on gasoline (*Guangming Ribao*, Apr. 8, 1979, *Joint Publications Research Service [JPRS]*, no. 73965, Aug. 6, 1979, p. 20).

*"A command economy is, at the same time, a demand economy; each ministry and department depends to a great extent on what it is able to extort from the planning organs and the units with funds and resources at their disposal" (Maria Hirszowicz, *The Bureaucratic Leviathan: A Study in the Sociology of Communism* [Oxford: Martin Robinson, 1980], p. 154).

†Thane Gustafson has noted the same phenomenon in the Soviet Union. Units appeal to the authorities for variances and exceptions, but when granted a reprieve, they do nothing to improve their situation or diminish their dependence on the authorities (*Reform in Soviet Politics: The Lessons of Recent Policies on Land and Water* [Cambridge, Eng.: Cambridge University Press, 1981], p. 110).

‡There are some exceptions: the heavy industrial plants, which were put under real pressure when their plan targets were cut during the readjustment of 1980–82, and township and collective enterprises, which bear responsibility for their own profits and losses.

petition, and particularistic bargaining go hand in hand in a command economy.* Of course, even in a market system with "real" prices, government and bank officials do not allocate investment on a purely financial basis. Social welfare considerations such as employment, geographic distribution, and environmental protection, as well as personal relationships and preferences, inevitably influence investment decisions. But a command economy is particularly vulnerable to the influence of such partial interests. The great irony is that the advantage of a centrally planned economy is supposed to be that it can transcend partial interests to promote the social good.[27]

These problems are more serious in industry than in agriculture. Industry is more capital-intensive than agriculture, and the modernization of industry is more costly to the state than the modernization of agriculture. There are also many more investors in the form of collectives and individual farmers in agriculture than in industry, where the largest share of the investment decisions, even under the conditions of partial reform, are made by the center. Without realistic prices the center is likely to make poor investment decisions in industry, and any mistake will be expensive.

The link between effort and reward. A clear link between effort and reward enhances the effectiveness of work incentives and the legitimacy of the pattern of income distribution. In agriculture most aspects of production can be organized at the household level, where work incentives and quality control operate effectively and the basis for reward is clear and legitimate. It is obviously impossible to subdivide most industrial production into family firms, although this is being done to some extent in the service sector.

In large-scale industrial organizations output is the result of the interdependent activities of many individuals, and payment systems rarely tie rewards to individual effort clearly and unambiguously. Recent Chinese reforms of industrial work incentives sought to move away from the seniority principle and reflect the socialist principle of "to each according to his work." Piecework, which provides a com-

---

*The pervasiveness of bargaining between enterprises and ministries and planning agencies, and between the ministries and the uppermost level of the party and government, has been analyzed in a thorough and sophisticated fashion by Hungarian social scientists. See, for example, T. Laky, "Enterprises in Bargaining Position," *Acta Oeconomica*, 22 (1979): 227–46. The Chinese case suggests that partial reform of a command economy does not eliminate particularistic bargaining but instead provides new issues for different levels to negotiate. The focus of bargaining shifts from plan quotas to the proportion of profits and foreign exchange retained, tax rates, and approvals for imports and joint ventures. Bailouts for deficit enterprises and allocation of investment continue to be subject to bargaining.

paratively clear, tangible link between output and reward, cannot be used in many types of production.* Even if piecework is appropriate, workers often object to it because piecework pay depends as much on the plan quota and the flow of work from other workshops as on their own performance. Use of work group discussions to distribute wages and bonuses created so much social conflict that many workers preferred equal distribution instead, nullifying the objectives of the new incentive policies.[28] When factory leaders participated in allocating wage increases and bonuses, employees suspected them of favoritism. Many managers therefore continually increased the wages and bonuses of all their workers.[29] As a result, bonuses became a part of the regular wage instead of a reward for special effort and lost much of their incentive effect. The reforms also allowed enterprises to use part of their retained profits to pay workers bonuses, but workers knew that the profits of their enterprise reflected the irrational price system more than their own diligence. This reform therefore did not increase substantially the incentive to work harder.†

The problematic link between reward and effort in industry evidently led many workers to perceive that the new pattern of income distribution was unfair. The reforms allow each factory latitude in allocating wages and bonuses, with a resulting increase in income inequality both among and within firms. The gaps caused discontent, especially among old workers in heavy industrial sectors, and constrain further experimentation in wage reform.‡ The wage contract system ending lifetime employment, when introduced in 1986, had a grandfather clause exempting veteran workers.[30]

In household agriculture the connection between effort and reward is less ambiguous. The output of the family farm is a clear, uniform,

---

*Piecework cannot be used for production in which quality requirements are high or work is done on a group basis (*Jingji Yanjiu*, Jan. 20, 1978, p. 62).

†In reformed Eastern European economies the workers and managers of low-profit firms complain that their lower earnings are "unjust"; they "put pressure upon higher authorities to equalize earnings." And the higher authorities themselves "often feel that it is wrong to tolerate any serious inequality, since that would contradict the egalitarian traditions of the socialist movement and the acknowledged principle of 'equal pay for equal work'" (János Kornai, "The Dilemmas of a Socialist Economy: The Hungarian Experience," *Cambridge Journal of Economics*, 4 [June 1980]: 150). For a similar analysis of Yugoslavia see Ellen Comisso, *Workers Control under Plan and Market* (New Haven, Conn.: Yale University Press, 1979).

‡David Granick notes that in Yugoslavia, the ideology of worker self-management has legitimated the situation in which workers' earnings differ substantially between enterprises depending on their market success (*Enterprise Guidance in Eastern Europe* [Princeton: Princeton University Press, 1975], pp. 470–71). Because the Chinese reform does not include worker self-management, resulting income disparities may be more politically troublesome.

tangible basis for income. Agricultural income depends on the number of able-bodied family members, their diligence and skill, and the crops they choose to grow. Of course, farm income also depends on factors beyond the control of a family, such as climate, availability of inputs, and market price. Nonetheless, the pattern of rural income distribution that emerged from the decollectivization of agriculture in China was probably considered fair, at least by the first generation of household farmers.[31] Future generations of farmers will have inherited family contracts and equipment and will not begin from equal starting points.

As nonagricultural activities (marketing, transport, cottage industries, and employment in local factories) have become an increasingly important source of rural family income, the link between effort and reward has grown more ambiguous and influenced by personal connections (*guanxi*). Already grumblings can be heard about the unfair advantages of cadres and their families in rural commerce; they can use their connections to gain access to lucrative business opportunities and avoid the extortionary license fees slapped on other rural businessmen by local officials.*

POLITICAL FACTORS: AGRICULTURAL AND
INDUSTRIAL BUREAUCRATIC ARENAS

Economic factors alone cannot explain why industrial reforms have been less successful than agricultural ones. Both encountered severe obstacles and constraints. Yet, when the top leaders encountered problems in agriculture, they persisted, whereas in industry they temporized and vacillated. There is no record in industry that compares, for example, to the 1983 decision to break the state monopoly over rural commerce, the 1984 decision to strengthen household claims on their land, and the 1985 decision to alter the twenty-two-year-old system of enforced grain and cotton deliveries to the state. In contrast, every

---

*The increase in extortion and other forms of rural corruption since the coming of the rural responsibility system is discussed in Thomas P. Bernstein's paper "Local Political Authorities and Economic Reform: Observations from Two Counties in Shandong and Anhui, 1985," presented at the Conference on Economic Reforms in China and Eastern Europe, Santa Barbara, California, May 8–11, 1986. Another potentially divisive issue is the intervillage income differentials, which have widened since the reform was implemented. These differentials are based on the quality of land and water and proximity to markets rather than on effort. The increase in these differentials puts pressure on rural authorities to permit migration from poorer villages to richer ones and to towns. Prohibitions on such movements will be viewed as more and more unfair to the poorer villages.

time the increased factory autonomy created pressures to alter other dimensions of the command economy, the leaders chose to retrieve their surrendered control. Their contrasting behavior is the result of political and bureaucratic considerations.

Bureaucratic politics of agriculture. Agricultural reform requires less redistribution among various bureaucratic entities and geographic regions than does industrial reform. Fewer central ministries are solely or largely concerned with agriculture (the Ministry of Agriculture, Animal Husbandry, and Fisheries; the Ministry of Grain; the All China Federation of Supply and Marketing Cooperatives; the Ministry of Commerce; the Ministry of Water Conservancy and Electric Power; and the Ministry of Machine Building [farm machinery]) compared with the approximately fifteen ministries responsible for industrial sectors; and only the ministries of Agriculture, Animal Husbandry, and Fisheries, Grain, and the Supply and Marketing Cooperative are focused entirely on rural agriculture. The decollectivization of agriculture did not threaten the existence of any of these agencies although the shift from mandatory purchases to long-term contracts of basic agricultural commodities drastically transformed the function of the Ministry of Grain, and the liberalization of rural marketing smashed the monopoly of the Supply and Marketing Cooperative. Still there appear to be fewer interagency conflicts among ministries in the agriculture arena than in the industry arena. And ministries such as Grain and the Supply and Marketing Cooperative, whose interests were directly threatened by reform policies, were unable to mount a strong resistance. Agriculture ministries in general appear to be comparatively weak. These ministries generate deficits rather than contribute revenue, they have less control over their collective farms than the industrial ministries do over state-owned factories, and they tend only to set broad policy guidelines over their subordinate provincial departments. All these are sources of weakness in bureaucratic politics as played in Beijing.

Moreover the Communist party continues to play a more active role in agriculture than in industry, as it has always done.* When a party leadership group committed to raising rural living standards attained dominance, it was able to sustain the reform drive without any significant bureaucratic opposition over a seven-year period.

---

*The party has a Rural Policy Research Center but no equivalent organization for industry. Whereas all important agricultural policy decisions are issued by the party Secretariat, many important industrial policy decisions are promulgated by the State Council instead.

Rural cadres in communes and production brigades provide the major source of opposition to the agricultural reform. Decollectivization removed many of their economic functions and undercut their political, social, and economic status by giving rise to a new class of rich farmers in the countryside. They are politically weak, however, especially because of the strong commitment of top party leaders to agricultural reform. Though some have harassed wealthy specialized households, they have not been able to obstruct the implementation of the responsibility system.[32] For one thing, since the reform freed farmers to buy their own equipment and market their own produce, rural cadres have less leverage over farmers. Most rural cadres apparently threw up their hands in frustration, no longer tried to control their villages, and opted to pursue their own family businesses instead.

Provincial-level bureaucrats, pivotal in the Chinese system, have also supported the rural reforms. Although initially the provinces that had prospered under collective agriculture resisted the rural responsibility system, they appear to have come to support it in recent years. Agricultural reform may redistribute economic benefits and social and political status within and among villages, but it has no major adverse redistributive implications for bureaucratic organizations or geographic areas. To the contrary, it arguably has reduced the burden of provincial and urban administrative units in the countryside while enhancing the revenue base. This fact has made the implementation of agricultural reform much smoother than in industry.

Agricultural reform also was unobjectionable from the perspective of the industrial ministries and the Ministry of Finance. Farmers have purchased more manufactured goods and contributed more revenue to the state since decollectivization. There was no contest when it came to allocating investment funds from the central budget; even though agriculture contributed more to the treasury, its share of investment was reduced.* In other words, rural reforms did not threaten the political or economic preeminence of urban industry.

Bureaucratic politics of industry. In contrast with agriculture, industrial policy involves many ministries competing for resources.[33] Economic policy making in communist states has been described by Jerry

---

*In the four years 1981–84 rural units paid a total of 41.65 billion yuan in tax payments, which was 3.1 times the total agricultural investment of 13.59 billion yuan made by the state during this period (*Xinhua*, Sept. 22, 1985, *FBIS*, Sept. 27, 1985, p. k6). Agriculture's share of investment declined to 6.1 percent in the Sixth Five-Year Plan (1981–85), lower than any other period (Nicholas R. Lardy, *Agriculture in China's Modern Economic Development* [Cambridge, Eng.: Cambridge University Press, 1983], p. 192.

Hough as "institutional pluralism." Policy making is dominated by bureaucratic institutions which contend for power and resources; policy is the outcome of bargaining among these institutions. Both Hough and Valerie Bunce have noted that the policy process in a system of institutional pluralism is characterized by incrementalism, that is, policy changes and shifts in investment priorities are undertaken, if at all, only gradually.[34] These insights, developed by scholars studying the Soviet Union, appear to apply with equal force in the Chinese case. Michel Oksenberg has noted the competition among Chinese government ministries for resources, and David M. Lampton has identified the consensus mode of decision making which prevails in the Chinese policy process.[35] Incrementalism and consensus-based decisions reflect the fierce competition among bureaucratic organizations, not basic harmony among them. With so many organizations having a veto over policies, it has been difficult to muster agreement on industrial reform policies.

Economic reform has intensified competition among bureaucratic agencies. Because substantial profits and tax revenues are now at stake, bureaucratic organizations have strengthened their sense of "ownership" over enterprises, and bureaucratic competition has become more heated. Moreover, industrial reform has clear redistributive consequences for different industrial sectors; the bureaucratic manifestations of these sectors, the ministries, resist policies that would threaten their relative position. The newspapers have recently criticized such bureaucratic infighting, which they call "economic wrangling," for interfering with economic reform.[36]

The history of economic reform in other socialist states suggests that this bureaucratic competition among ministries to protect their resources and prerogatives is the most severe political obstacle to reform.* Yugoslavia, the only socialist state that really abolished the central industrial ministries, is the exception that proves the rule: only when the central ministries are eliminated is it possible to expand enterprise autonomy and avoid the usual recentralization.†

---

*A confidential memorandum by a group of Soviet economists, which was leaked to the *New York Times* (Aug. 5, 1983), argues that the major opponents of economic reform are the economic ministries.

†Even with the dramatic reduction of central plan directives under the 1968 New Economic Mechanism in Hungary the central ministries remained intact. As a result "relationships of dependence" between the ministries and their enterprises continued (Laky, p. 231). At the end of 1980, the three industrial ministries combined into one, with one-half the total staff (Peter T. Knight, *Economic Reform in Socialist Countries: The Experiences of Hungary, Rumania, and Yugoslavia* [Washington, D.C.: World Bank, 1983], p. 68).

Predictably, the ministries that were most powerful under the pre-reform system, the heavy industrial ministries, have been the most effective in working at cross purposes to the reforms. Why is heavy industry so politically powerful? Its influence over policy originates in the structure of the command economy. All economic sectors are organized into vertical national bureaucracies headed by ministries in the capital. Each minister is similar to a division head in a huge conglomerate called "China Incorporated." (After all, Lenin conceptualized the national economy as one giant factory.[37]) The minister, sitting in Beijing, is able to articulate the interests of the industry he represents. In this way the structure of the system gives industrial sectors, heavy industry in particular, a powerful voice in policy making.

The extensive growth strategy which the Chinese adopted from the Soviet Union concentrated investment on the expansion of heavy industry.* The priority on heavy industry meant that when the central economic bureaucracy was established after 1953 at the start of the First Five-Year Plan, the most able cadres from the provinces were recruited into the heavy industrial ministries. From that time on, it has been widely recognized that the leadership of the heavy industrial bureaucracies is of superior caliber. Because workers and managers in heavy industry are paid more and have higher status than those in light industry (the managers of plants such as the Anshan and Wuhan Iron and Steel companies have a cadre rank higher than some provincial governors), heavy industry has continued to attract the most talented people.†

The preeminence of the heavy industrial ministries also stems from the nature of economic planning in a command economy. Planning by material balances puts the sectors that produce materials and equipment for many other parts of the economy in a pivotal position. The scale of the planning process forces officials, who have too many items

---

*Over the 1958–78 period, 52.8 percent of total state investment went into heavy industry (A. Doak Barnett, *China's Economy in Global Perspective* [Washington D.C.: Brookings Institution, 1981], pp. 19, 22). During the period 1949–78, gross value product of heavy industry multiplied 90.6 times, but agriculture and industry rose only 2.4-fold and 19.8-fold respectively (Dong Furen, "Chinese Economy in the Process of Great Transformation," in George C. Wang, ed., *Economic Reform in the P.R.C.* ([Boulder: Westview Press, 1982], p. 136). For a discussion of how the extensive growth strategy enhances the political influence of heavy industry see Radoslav Selucky, *Economic Reforms in Eastern Europe: Political Background and Economic Significance* (New York: Praeger, 1972), pp. 22–23.

†Jerry Hough has noted the same phenomenon in the Soviet Union; see *The Soviet Union and Social Science Theory* (Cambridge, Mass.: Harvard University Press, 1977), pp. 24, 47.

to handle, to identify some products as priorities.[38] Because so much of the economy requires coal, steel, and machinery to fulfill the plan, these industries are in a strong position when the bargaining over plan targets and investment allocations occurs.* And when the plan has to be revised (plans always have to be revised because they cannot take into account all factors), it is usually agriculture and light industry and not heavy industry that is cut. Heavy industry must be protected not only because its products are essential, but also because its labor force is larger and more influential.†

The reform line so dominates the Chinese political scene under Deng Xiaoping that the heavy industrial ministries have not raised head-on opposition to the reforms.‡ For the most part, the heavy industrial ministries have used their bureaucratic clout to get the best deal they could in the new economic environment rather than make a direct challenge to the reforms. They took a share of the lucrative consumer goods market away from the light industry departments; they provided newly built local factories with raw materials and (often technologically outmoded) equipment; they broke the monopoly of the Ministry of Foreign Economic Relations and Trade to establish their own trading companies (the light industrial departments had more trouble doing the same thing); they protected domestic industry by insisting that joint ventures use Chinese equipment and that purchases of foreign equipment be tied to licensing agreements; they reclaimed the lion's share of central state investment; and they supported the reemphasis on centrally funded large energy and transportation projects since 1983. The net result of these self-protective moves by the heavy industrial ministries was to increase their growth rates and retard the pace of structural reform.§

*For a critique of the Chinese planning process for beginning from steel and other key heavy industrial products instead of from the manufactured end products see *Jingji Yanjiu*, July 9, 1979, pp. 1–22.

†Hirszowicz, *Bureaucratic Leviathan*, pp. 156–57. Approximately 68 percent of workers are employed in heavy industry and 32 percent in light industry (*Statistical Yearbook of China, 1983* [Beijing: China Statistical Publishers, 1983], p. 128). In comparing the relative political influence of the heavy and light industrial work forces, it is noteworthy that light industry is feminized, that is, a large percentage of its employees are women. (See the percentages of female workers reported in ibid., p. 141.) Feminized sectors generally have lower social and political status.

‡Heavy industry was bolder in its opposition to reform at its early stages, in 1978–80. See Dorothy J. Solinger, "The Fifth National People's Congress and the Process of Policymaking: Reform, Readjustment, and the Opposition," *Issues and Studies*, 18 (Aug. 1982): 63–106.

§From 1979 to 1981, heavy industrial growth was outpaced by the growth of light industry, but in 1982, 1983, and 1984 the expansion of local factories caused heavy

The regional dimension. Reform of the industrial system also has redistributive consequences for various geographic regions. Industrial reform, combined with the new open-door policy and fiscal decentralization, benefited the coastal provinces more than the inland provinces. The coastal provinces (Liaoning, Hebei, Shandong, Jiangsu, Zhejiang, Fujian, Guangdong, Tianjin, Beijing, and Shanghai, along with inland industrial enclaves such as Wuhan and Chongqing) have regained the position of economic superiority they held before the communists came to power in 1949. The post-1978 policy weakened many central controls over the coastal provinces so they could take advantage of their natural strengths, their industrial plant and skilled manpower, port facilities, and ties to overseas Chinese capitalists who prefer to invest in their home provinces.* In the past political considerations led national leaders to redistribute economic resources in favor of the backward interior; their objective was economic growth that was equally balanced between the coast and interior.[39] Now the potential contribution of foreign capital has emboldened them to set out on the path of unbalanced growth.†

Officials from inland provinces recognized that the reforms put them at a competitive disadvantage. They demanded that the concessions granted to the Special Economic Zones be extended to them. Often they advocated recentralization measures for reasons of regional equity. For example, most of the industrial enterprises that depend on government subsidies because they operate in the red or just

---

industry to grow more quickly. See *Renmin Ribao*, July 6, 1983, p. 5, and Premier Zhao Ziyang's Government Work Report at the Third Session of the Sixth National People's Congress, Mar. 27, 1985, Beijing Domestic Service, Mar. 27, 1985, *FBIS*, Mar. 29, 1985, p. k3.

*"The coastal cities have industrial bases, technical forces and transport facilities. They are experienced in and have the conditions for doing business with foreign merchants. Their superior features should be brought into play in order to produce greater quantities of export goods" (*Shijie Jingji Daobao*, Feb. 7, 1983, p. 1). For a discussion of the regional impact of foreign trade and investment see Susan L. Shirk, "The Domestic Political Dimensions of China's Foreign Economic Relations," in Samuel S. Kim, ed., *Chinese Foreign Policy in the 1980's* (Boulder, Colo.: Westview Press, 1985), pp. 57–81.

†Albert O. Hirschman suggests that most governments are reluctant to concentrate their investments in a single region or sector when all regions and sectors are clamoring for help because "public investment decisions are easily the most political ones among the economic policy decisions taken by governments." The role of foreign capital often is "to enable and to embolden a country to set out on the path of unbalanced growth." The presence of foreign capital helps the local government "think in terms of development rather than in terms of the 'pork barrel' type of distribution of public funds." The foreign funds "can also be given the blame for departures from whatever standards of distributive justice are considered binding upon governments using their own funds" (*The Strategy of Economic Development* [New York: Norton, 1978], pp. 190 and 205–6).

barely break even are located in the interior, and the profit-making enterprises are concentrated along the coast. Therefore every reform that moves enterprises closer to responsibility for their own profits and losses represents a threat to inland provinces and their enterprises. Inland provinces argued for a major modification of the new tax policy in 1984 when they realized that the policy would increase the number of their enterprises operating at a loss. They succeeded in convincing policy makers to cut tax rates to protect their weak enterprises and make up the revenue shortfall with an extra tax, called the "adjustment" or "regulatory" tax, levied on high-profit firms in coastal areas. Although in policy disputes such as this one, the representatives of inland provinces have not been able to obstruct the industrial reforms, they have been able to delay and modify them.

Influential Chinese economist Xue Muqiao observed that there were serious contradictions among regions caused by "extremely uneven industrial development": "In general, the industrially developed areas wish to acquire greater independence and the underdeveloped ones prefer unified management and unified allocation of products by the central government. For these reasons it has been very difficult for the state organs of economic management to reach an agreement on changing the current system of planning and management."[40] It is not surprising that the economic sectors and geographic regions that see themselves as feeble in the face of international and domestic competition seek protection from the state and favor centralized control over the economy, while the sectors and regions that can compete successfully want to shake off the restraints of state control and favor decentralization.[41]

The political problems of regional unity and equity created by the reforms caused the leaders to consider new forms of national economic integration. In the past, regions were held together by their dependence on the center. The planners in Beijing allocated all economic resources, and except for some barter trade, there was little direct contact between provinces. Interregional trade declined as local self-sufficiency was promoted. Now that the center has lost much of its control over local finance, material supply, and production, economic integration through the center is no longer possible. Instead the center has encouraged local governments and enterprises to carry out direct bilateral transactions, including joint ventures as well as trade. Most interregional joint ventures, which are called "interprovincial cooperation," involved more advanced coastal provinces investing in the more backward inland provinces. This interprovincial cooperation can be seen as a "side payment" in the reform package to disarm the opposition of inland provinces by easing their shortages of capital and technology. Coastal provinces view such cooperative ventures as a way to improve their supply of raw materials and open markets for their manufactured goods.

Fiscal implications of reform. On another critical dimension, the industrial bureaucracies provide the financial base for the Chinese national state, which undoubtedly helps explain the caution of the top leaders in transforming institutional arrangements in industry. They must avoid inadvertently and irretrievably surrendering their own ability to rule. The strong financial interest in the performance of industry and the collection of industrial revenues also explains the extraordinary influence of the Ministry of Finance in shaping industrial policy.[42] The Ministry of Finance has taken a cautious attitude to the reform of the industrial and fiscal system and was an important factor in the decision to recentralize economic control and delay the progress of the reforms in 1980–82.[43] The Finance Ministry is less centrally involved in agricultural policy because from a public finance perspective it is less significant.* But on the other hand, reforms permitting enterprises and local governments to retain profits or determine their own prices must be challenged if they lead to deficits or inflation. The dispersion of funds caused by the industrial and fiscal reforms produced severe uncertainty for central financial officials. The ministry urged that extrabudgetary funds and local construction be brought under the plan and even that the percentage of profit retained by enterprises be lowered.[44] The policy requiring that enterprises pay taxes instead of remitting profits to the center (the *li gai shui* policy, which began in June 1983) was intended largely to guarantee a steady flow of revenues to the central treasury. The Ministry of Finance was also responsible for the establishment of treasury bonds (which local governments are required to buy with local funds) and a tax on locally funded extra-plan construction. The Ministry of Finance has used the issue of dispersion of funds to strengthen its bureaucratic position

---

*Agricultural reform, of course, does have some effects on the national accounts. Higher farm output requires the state to spend more money on purchasing agricultural commodities (13.2 percent more in 1983 than in 1982) but eventually may lessen the need for expensive subsidies. Increases in agricultural production generate more tax revenues from the rural areas. By increasing sales of manufactured goods to peasants the reforms raise state revenues from industry. If there are more locally generated funds in the rural areas, the center has to devote less money to rural expenditures. See *Beijing Review*, Apr. 2, 1984, p. 32.

vis-à-vis the State Planning Commission, State Economic Commission, and industrial ministries as well as to gain control over local finances.[45]

Though as a rule the central economic bureaucracies take a conservative attitude toward reform because their ideology and self-interest tell them that loss of central control over the economy will lead to chaos, there is one notable exception, the State Economic Commission (SEC).* The SEC views issues from the perspective of the industrial enterprises themselves. Because its function is to implement the plan (drawn up by the State Planning Commission [SPC]), it hears from enterprises about their practical problems in obtaining supplies and power, satisfying their bureaucratic masters, and so on. The SEC has fought energetically to increase the share of revenue enterprises may retain and to expand their autonomy by implementing an industrial *baogan* or contract system similar to the agricultural household contract system. The SPC and Ministry of Finance defeated the *baogan* plan, arguing that an industrial contract system would rob the treasury at a time when construction of infrastructure was a pressing need and that it would cause serious inequities between high-profit processing plants and low-profit raw materials and machinery plants. On many reform issues the debate has found the SEC on one side and the SPC and Ministry of Finance on the opposite side.

Urban attitudes. Industrial policy making is a predominantly bureaucratic process, with the main institutional actors being the industrial ministries, the State Planning Commission, the State Economic Commission, the Ministry of Finance, the Ministry of Foreign Economic Relations and Trade, and the provincial and municipal governments. The organized voice of mass interest groups is weak or nonexistent. Not even blue-collar workers have direct influence; labor union representatives are rarely included in policy deliberations at the central level.†

Nevertheless, policy makers in Beijing try to anticipate mass reaction to policy decisions. This task is more complicated with industrial reform issues than with agriculture because workers and managers are more ambivalent and divided among themselves about the reforms than are rural dwellers.‡ Workers and managers all want more

---

*Michel Oksenberg's interviews suggest that the People's Bank is another exception (personal communication).

†The weakness of the Chinese union contrasts with the situation in Hungary in which the union head sits on the party committee responsible for economic policy making.

‡This was also the response of workers and managers to economic reforms in the

opportunity to pursue economic rewards but only if their security is not threatened. The managers of large firms who bargained successfully for resources under the old centralized system are particularly apprehensive about changing the rules of the game.* Managers and workers are divided by sector, with those in light industry for which the markets are expanding and the profits are high naturally more enthusiastic than those in heavy industry, and by generation and technical ability. Younger and more skilled workers who are confident of their market capacity welcome the chance to earn more, whereas older, unskilled workers resent the reforms for eroding their security and social status.† Workers and other city dwellers also are sensitive to the price rises caused by the reforms; their protests over inflation, which came to a head in the summer of 1983, and their panic buying sparked by rumors about price rises at the end of 1984 have frightened authorities into delaying price reform. Communist officials remember the runaway inflation of the 1940s, which discredited the Guomindang and helped bring the CCP to power; they worry that they could suffer the same fate as the Guomindang if reform sets off inflation in the 1980s.

Zhao Ziyang's Political Strategy of Economic Reform

Given the complexities of and constraints on industrial reform, the analytical issue that emerges is to explain the strategy that has enabled the leaders to sustain the reform drive. Several times, the reforms appeared to have been derailed by a combination of economic problems and political opposition. Yet the recentralizations were temporary compromises and adjustments, not an abandonment of reform.

The interaction of economic and political forces created several mini-cycles of decentralization leading to economic problems and political opposition leading to recentralization. Central control over finance and construction was tightened during the 1981–82 readjust-

---

Soviet Union and Eastern Europe. See Alec Nove, *The Economics of Feasible Socialism* (London: Allen & Unwin, 1983), pp. 176–78.

*In Hungary the managers of large enterprises protested the shift from central investment grants to bank credits. They would favor full enterprise autonomy, including the right to dispose of capacities, profit, and development funds, but if that was not possible, they preferred the well-known and proved practice that had been advantageous to them to a partial change (Laky, p. 244).

†Hungarian workers in 1972 expressed discontent with the implications of the NEM for job security and income distribution. As a result there was a shake-up in the Party Central Committee and some recentralization occurred (Knight, p. 65).

ment, but this recentralization was followed by a major drive to institutionalize enterprise autonomy during 1984.* At the end of 1984 new economic problems arose. The economy became overheated as local officials competed to achieve high growth rates and local banks eager to boost local industrial growth extended too much credit. Managers gave workers unauthorized wage raises and bonuses, fueling consumers' demand for still scarce goods and creating inflation just when consumers' worries about price reform were building inflationary pressure. Government bureaus set up trading companies and other profit-making businesses, sparking complaints that public officials were taking advantage of the reforms to line their own pockets. The center's response to these problems was another recentralization, but this time with an explicit reminder that the temporary strengthening of central control did not mean a return to the "old road." As a major article in *Hong Qi* (Red flag) emphasized, "problems appearing in the course of reform can be solved only through continuing reforms."[46] In this instance, as in the previous mini-cycle of reform, the top Chinese leaders showed themselves willing to make compromises but determined to sustain the momentum of reform.

Their determination is critical in a political system that remains highly centralized. The political centralization of communist states like China creates the opportunity for leadership initiatives to reform the command economy. And although the process of implementing economic reforms is pluralistic, with bureaucratic institutions contending for power and resources, the highly concentrated power of a few top leaders to set the policy agenda, shape an ideology of reform through the party-controlled mass media, and resolve the conflicts between subordinate bureaucratic agencies gives them the tools to manage the implementation process.

The Chinese leadership has demonstrated acumen in meeting the political challenge of carrying out economic reform. Deng Xiaoping initiated the drive for economic reform and continues to guide the "high" politics of reform, controlling and transforming the military, which is a potential source of opposition to economic reform; design-

---

*The two most important policy statements of this 1984 reform drive were the "Ten Points" establishing the rights of enterprises ("State's Council's Decision on Further Expanding the Autonomy of State Industrial Enterprises," *Renmin Ribao*, May 12, 1984) and the Communique of the Third Plenum of the Twelfth Central Committee of the CCP ("Decision on Reform of the Economic Structure, Third Plenum of the Twelfth Central Committee of the CCP," ibid., Oct. 21, 1984). Also issued during 1984 were important decisions on the reform of the planning system (ibid., Oct. 11, 1984) and the reform of the foreign trade system (ibid., Sept. 20, 1984).

ing the reform of administration and personnel practices; leading the limited political decontrol over culture; making high-level personnel decisions; and charting the future role and character of the Communist party. Deng delegated the task of implementing the economic reform to Premier Zhao Ziyang and CCP Secretary Hu Yaobang (until January 1987, when Hu was fired). Hu was told to limit himself to the political realm, for example, party policy on culture, journalism, education, party rectification, and political education work to build support for economic reform. Although Hu did not exhibit any doubts about the economic reform (he was something of a "born-again reformer," eager to go further and faster than anyone else), the primary responsibility for implementing economic reform fell on Zhao's shoulders. Thus when we talk about the role of leadership in managing the political process of implementing economic reform we are really talking about Zhao Ziyang's strategy.

The term *strategy* does not mean that Zhao or anyone else has a well-thought-out long-term plan for economic reform similar to that which guided the Hungarian New Economic Mechanism in the 1960s. To the contrary, the Chinese reforms have been unplanned and have achieved a life of their own. Reform policies have been shaped by the actual consequences of previous policies, not by any long-term vision. For example, initially no one expected the agricultural household responsibility system to be universalized or to be such a success; the enthusiastic response of the peasantry and the dramatic economic results created economic and political pressure to extend the reform to urban industry. If the process had been rationally planned, the prices would have been reformed before the economic structure as they were in Hungary; instead structural reform has preceded price reform, causing terrible economic distortions but building political support for the reforms.

Although the leaders have not planned the reforms, the trajectory of their policies reveals a purposeful strategy. The following elements of this strategy help us understand how the Chinese may succeed in carrying through the reform of their industrial economy despite the economic and political complexities of the process.

CAUTION, COMPROMISE, CONSENSUS-BUILDING

The leadership style of Zhao Ziyang is cautious and consultative. He has subjected every major industrial reform decision to discussion and modification by meetings of ministerial representatives and provincial and municipal representatives. When bureaucratic conflicts emerge, Zhao hammers out a compromise that achieves a rough consensus. Even if the compromise means going halfway instead of all the way to the goal of market socialism, it institutionalizes new rules or practices without triggering major political opposition.

A good example of Zhao's economic statesmanship was the case of the second stage of the *li gai shui* policy replacing profit remission with tax payments in industry. A crucial part of the new tax system was a product tax, each product having its own rate, designed to put all enterprises manufacturing the same product on an equal footing and to narrow the profit differential among enterprises manufacturing different products caused by the effect of irrational administrative prices. The first draft proposal prepared by the Ministry of Finance had moderately high product tax rates. Inland provinces and some ministries such as Coal and Metallurgy objected because such high rates would have put too many of their enterprises into the red (a fixed asset tax, which had been successfully implemented on an experimental basis in Shanghai was also rejected for the same reason). But when the product tax rates were lowered, a simulation prepared by the Ministry of Finance determined that the treasury would suffer a shortfall in revenue. The only way to satisfy both the Ministry of Finance and the provinces and ministries with less profitable enterprises was to tack on a "regulatory" or "adjustment" (*tiaojie*) tax to collect enough revenue to meet the central government's requirements. This tax was to be levied only on the most profitable firms, over 90 percent of which are in coastal cities and most of them in Shanghai; the rate would be set individually for each firm (at a level guaranteeing each enterprise the same level of retained profits as it had in the previous year, 1983). Economists argued that the adjustment tax was an arbitrary ad hoc levy and not a tax at all, and officials from coastal cities complained that the Ministry of Finance was using the tax to continue to soak up the profits of the best firms, or as they put it, to drive the economy by "whipping the fastest buffalo" (*bianda kuai niu*). But the compromise made it possible to establish the structure of a fiscal system substituting tax payment for profit remission.

As this example illustrates, Zhao Ziyang understands that economic reform involves redistribution of power and resources. To implement reform, compromises must be made so that the agencies and regions that lose do not lose too much. The legacies of the previous system must be respected. Inefficient firms that could not possibly make a profit under true market competition must be given time to improve.

It would not be fair to destroy them with high tax rates. Neither would it be fair to penalize them with a fixed asset tax for all the capital plant they acquired in the past under conditions of free investment funds.* Whenever possible, conflicts over reform policies should be muted by preserving every unit's original level of benefits, at least in the short run. Adjustment tax rates, as well as allocations of wage funds to enterprises, credit funds to banks, and other specific amounts included in various economic policies, were set at levels designed to allow units to do at least no worse than the previous year under the new policy, thereby disarming their opposition to the policy.†

LET THE ECONOMY OUTGROW THE PLAN

The reform of the Chinese industrial economy has involved the gradual expansion of the share of economic activity outside the scope of the national plan.‡ The Chinese economy ever since the 1957 decentralization, and particularly since the Cultural Revolution weakened the central planning apparatus and encouraged localities to build their own factories, has been only partially and imperfectly planned by the center.[47] This legacy of weak central economic control distinguishes China from the Soviet Union and the Eastern European communist states and is an important background condition to the recent reforms.

During the post-1978 period of partial reform, control over material goods and investment funds continued to devolve to the local government and enterprise levels.[48] A high proportion of construction materials (30 percent of rolled steel, 40 percent of timber, and 70 percent of cement) were no longer allocated by central planners and were in local hands.[49] A parallel process occurred in the financial system as central budgetary control weakened and local governments and enterprises retained a progressively greater share of their revenues. After meeting their plan quotas, enterprises were permitted to sell their extra output on their own at prices 20 percent higher or

*This problem of legacies is particularly acute in China because under the command economy a higher percentage of its industrial enterprises operated at a loss and were dependent on government subsidies than is the case in the Soviet Union. Judith Thornton made this point to me.

†One problem with this approach to setting rates or allocating funds is that it gives units an incentive to spend more this year so that they get more next year (a phenomenon common to all incremental budgeting systems and hardly unique to China or communist economies). During the last quarter of 1984 banks granted excessive amounts of loans and enterprises excessive amounts of salary increases so that they would be allocated a higher level of funds during 1985.

‡The phrase that forms the subhead was suggested by Barry Naughton.

lower than the plan price (in a shortage economy the nonplan price is rarely lower than the plan price), and they were allowed to obtain the material supplies needed for this above-quota output on their own. A dual economy, within plan and out of plan, evolved and the actual price differential between the two increased, giving enterprises an incentive to expand their out-of-plan activity. Enterprises came to see profitable above-quota sales as their right.

The strategy of Zhao Ziyang is to expand the share of economic activity outside the central plan in order to transform the command economy into market socialism, or as one reformer put it, "to let the above-quota portion (*chao o*) squeeze out the within-quota portion (*ding o*)." By pursuing this strategy Zhao gave many industrial enterprises and local governments a stake in continuing and expanding the decentralization associated with reform. (Even the large heavy industrial plants, which under the dual system bear most of the burden of the mandatory plan quotas and adjustment tax payments, have demanded more autonomy from the plan, not a return to the old system.)[50]

Zhao also built political support for the reforms by placing new economic institutions and activities in the extra-plan part of the economy. New foreign trade and investment activity is largely beyond the reach of the central planners: the Special Economic Zones in both production and finance are exempt from the extractions of the center; the fourteen open coastal cities and Hainan Island have greater autonomy from central planners than ordinary cities; foreign joint ventures also can escape the plan. Even in the domestic economy, institutions, like the township enterprises, which operate outside the national plan, are the source of much of the dynamic growth attributed to economic reform. Regions such as Jiangsu and Zhejiang, with high concentrations of township enterprises and open cities, are enjoying an economic boom and are staunch supporters of the reform drive.

The strategy of letting the economy outgrow the plan even had the ironic effect of bringing the central planning and financial bureaucracies into the reform coalition from time to time. These bureaucracies watched their actual power and resources gradually seep down to the lower levels over the years. Therefore they were willing to go along with policies granting localities and enterprises more autonomy if the policies also codified the center's share of power and resources. As they saw it, a formal power- and resource-sharing reform could stem the de facto progressive deterioration of their position. The Ministry of Finance actually proposed the 1980 fiscal decentralization (the financial diffusion effects of the policy were later criticized by ministry officials) because it protected the center's share of revenues. The State Planning Commission favored a contract system allowing enterprises to sell their above-quota output because the SPC officials believed it would make it easier for them to collect the within-quota output. The SPC also supported the reduction of the mandatory plan (although not to the extent that can be found in the final decision) and creation of a guidance plan because its bureaucrats believed they would have greater overall control over the economy under such a system; under the dual economy that has prevailed with partial reform it has become harder and harder for planners to enforce the mandatory plan. The SPC also favors price reform because by narrowing the wide disparity between in-plan and out-of-plan prices, it will make their job of enforcing the plan less difficult.

At the same time the shrinking of the share of economic activity under the central plan and budget has weakened the ability of the central bureaucracies to impede or reverse the reforms. Zhao understands that central bureaucracies are major obstacles to economic reform in communist states because of their strong vested interests in the command economy. But he gradually weakened these bureaucracies so that they can eventually be merged or eliminated instead of confronting them head-on. The premier has established a small working group to propose possible schemes for merging or eliminating ministries. One element of this approach is to reduce the functions of the ministries by transferring the administration of enterprises from the ministries to the localities. The Ministry of Machine Building, its leaders anxious to prove their commitment to the reform drive, was the first to "send down" all its factories to provincial or municipal control.[51] The "letting the economy outgrow the plan" strategy also results in the progressive narrowing of the control these central bureaucracies have over localities and enterprises.

The example of the *baogan* or contract system granted to the Ministries of Coal, Petroleum, and Metallurgy illustrates both Zhao's willingness to compromise and the political utility of the strategy of letting the economy outgrow the plan.[52] These three ministries, as the suppliers of basic materials to the plan, were not able to take advantage of above-quota self-sale. Although officials from these ministries are generally conservative, under the dual system they considered the demands of the planners on them as a burden and resented their inability to take advantage of shortages by selling at a higher price in the extra-plan sector. When they demanded a ministerial contract system that would guarantee to the plan a certain amount of product, increasing gradually every year, in exchange for a certain amount of state investment and the freedom to self-sell all their above-quota output, the planning bureaucracies were enthusiastic and Zhao agreed. Even though the ministerial contract system was a step backward in that it strengthened the ministries' control over subordinate enterprises, it bought off these three potential opponents of the reform.

The strategy of letting the economy outgrow the plan is well suited to the preexisting decentralization of the Chinese economic system and builds political support for the economic reform drive. Still, by choosing gradually to expand the out-of-plan economy and delay in tackling some of the core structural issues within the planned economy, Zhao and his advisers created some serious problems that may threaten the future of reform. Because real charges for capital have not yet been introduced and prices have not yet been reformed, it is difficult to restrain the overheating of the economy. The dual system, with its supply shortages and gap between in-plan and out-of-plan prices, creates many possibilities for arbitrage—the buying and selling of goods between in-plan and out-of-plan sectors for profit. Such lucrative trading has been defined as corruption and has tainted the reform drive.

ADMINISTRATIVE AND ECONOMIC DECENTRALIZATION

One distinctive feature of Zhao Ziyang's strategy of economic reform is its appeal to party and government officials at the provincial and municipal levels. Zhao, who spent his entire career in provincial politics, has sought to stimulate the initiative of local officials. Included in the reform package in 1980 was a major fiscal and administrative decentralization, which permitted provinces, cities, and even counties to retain a major share of their financial revenues, much of which come from industrial profits (now taxes) and thereby gave localities the incentive and resources for economic expansion. A later policy in 1983 strengthened the autonomy of cities, especially seven "central cities," which were granted total freedom from provincial control.* In

---

*These seven cities, Wuhan, Shenyang, Chongqing, Dalian, Xian, Guangzhou, and Harbin, are now separate planning units (*jihua danlie*) like the three municipalities of Beijing, Shanghai, and Tianjin. Nanjing and Chengdu are central cities, but because the relevant provincial authorities refused to allow it, they do not have the status of independent planning units. There are a total of fifty-two experimental cities under the Economic Reform Commission which have greater autonomy than in the past (*Renmin Ribao*, Oct. 20, 1984).

many areas local officials responded to the new incentives in a surprisingly entrepreneurial fashion.* Their drive to expand local industry, however, also had the effect of draining revenues from the center, creating shortages of materials and wasting resources in the duplication of inefficient but profitable (because of price irrationalities) processing plants.

Perhaps the most serious negative consequence of the administrative decentralization was a balkanization of the market, which certainly was not conducive to economic reform. Provincial authorities sought administrative protection for their local markets instead of engaging in national economic competition. They erected local blockades against products from other provinces instead of trying to produce goods that were cheaper or better than those of other provinces.[53] They also hoarded their own fuel and materials, refusing to sell them to other provinces or charging exorbitantly high prices for them.† When provinces tried to penetrate the markets in other provinces they often were obstructed by local protectionism. This intensification of localism repeated the experience of the Soviet Union after the Khrushchev administrative decentralization of 1957.[54]

On the positive side, by introducing administrative decentralization before economic decentralization in industry, Zhao Ziyang was able to bring local officials into the reform coalition. These officials, especially those from the more dynamic coastal provinces and cities, have sought to prevent recentralization and to keep reform initiatives alive under the slogan of "increasing the liveliness of the economy." Local officials support reform because they are loath to return to the center control over their economic resources. Enhanced economic and financial autonomy has enabled even the leaders of backward areas to strengthen their local political machines. As they expand their local industrial economies, the "spoils" at their disposal, including funds for local construction, supplies, and, perhaps most valuable, jobs, also multiply. They set up new corporations to pursue profitable business opportunities and coordinate the activities of local enterprises. The local officials of the Communist party, the government, the banks, the

---

*The Heilongjiang government gave loans of 29 million yuan in 1980 and another 40 million yuan in 1981 to develop a wine industry in their province (Heilongjiang Provincial Service, Apr. 22, 1981, *BBC/FE*, May 6, 1981).

†Officials of Guangdong Province, which is poor in energy and raw materials, complain that with only 50 percent of their supplies covered by the plan, they are at the mercy of other provinces, which often "do not understand Guangdong's situation very well" (Guangdong Provincial Service, June 12, 1982, *FBIS*, June 16, 1982, p. p1).

foreign investment and trust corporations, and the managers of large enterprises, who together constitute the local power elite, use control over industry and its revenues to maintain their machines.*

By strengthening economic power at the local governmental level, Zhao has, however, made it more difficult to transfer power to the enterprises themselves. Administrative decentralization has weakened the vertical hierarchies (*tiaotiao*) and transferred power to localities (*kuaikuai*), but as Franz Schurmann predicted, it has interfered with economic decentralization at the enterprise level.[55] The press reports that even after a major effort in 1984 to separate administrative organs from the work of managing enterprises (*zheng qi fenkai*), the power that was supposed to go to enterprises has not yet been given to them; the main cause of this failure is the power struggle (*zheng chuan*) between local administrative corporations and bureaus on the one hand and basic level enterprises on the other.[56]

REPLACE OFFICIALS AND MANAGERS

Zhao Ziyang's strategy of building a reform coalition by making compromises on redistributive policies, gradually letting the economy outgrow the plan, and decentralizing fiscal and administrative power might have been for naught were it not for his elimination of many potential opponents by replacing approximately 60 to 70 percent of economic officials and enterprise managers.† This turnover of officials in the central ministries, provinces, cities, and enterprises has been accomplished over the period of partial reform under a variety of labels, including administrative reorganization, regularization of retirement, bringing up a new echelon of cadres who are younger, better trained, and more technically competent, enterprise rectification, party rectification, and changing the enterprise leading group. There have been no political attacks on incumbents (with the exception of some cadres who were criticized for corruption or opposition to reform as part of

---

*Even in a still centralized command economy these local machines can be very strong. The classic study of local power in Soviet-style systems is Jerry Hough, *The Soviet Prefects* (Cambridge, Mass.: Harvard University Press, 1969). Jean Woodall, *The Socialist Corporation and Technocratic Power: The Polish United Workers' Party, Industrial Organization and Work Force Control, 1958–80* (Cambridge, Eng.: Cambridge University Press, 1982), pp. 135, 164–66, describes how economic and fiscal decentralization in Poland strengthened local political machines. Dorothy Solinger's early reports on her research on Wuhan suggest that China is following a similar pattern ("Wuhan: Inland City on the Move," *Chinese Business Review*, Mar.–Apr. 1985, pp. 27–30.

†This is my own rough estimate based on partial reports from the Chinese press.

party rectification); they could retire or resign without stigma. If they retired they collected generous benefits, and their children received a job under the *dingti* or replacement policy.

The new managers were indoctrinated in the ideology of economic reform and trained in modern management techniques through training programs run jointly by the State Economic Commission and foreign governments such as the Dalian program cosponsored by the U.S. Department of Commerce. Economic reform was the political line taught to new economic officials in provincial and central party schools.

The new cohort of cadres owe their positions to the proreform leadership, and by virtue of their relative youthfulness and technical sophistication, they are less committed to the command economy and more open to structural change than were their predecessors. This quiet, gentle purge of the economic ranks weakened the opponents of reform and brought new allies into the reform coalition.

AGRICULTURAL REFORM AS A MODEL FOR INDUSTRIAL REFORM

The success of the agricultural reform has been put to good use by Zhao Ziyang in his effort to build support for the reform of urban industry. Although there is no evidence that the sequence—first agricultural reform, then industrial reform—was planned, the rural responsibility system was implemented more rapidly and easily because of the economic and political characteristics of the agricultural sector discussed earlier in this chapter. Even the industrial ministries, which were wary of urban reform, welcomed the rural reform because it stimulated demand for manufactured goods and by no means challenged industry's priority in state investment. The Ministry of Finance approved agricultural reform because it more than doubled rural tax revenues.

Once the success of the rural reform was established, the reform leaders could use it to make the case for urban reform. They claimed that the inability of factories to meet the farmers' increased demand for trucks, machinery, and consumer goods proved that industry had to be reformed as well. They silenced pessimistic economic officials who argued that in the short term, industrial reform did more harm than good, by pointing to the accomplishments of agricultural reform. And they propagandized reform among urban citizens by citing cases of peasants who had become wealthy under the agricultural reform.*

*In early 1985 the Chinese mass media criticized itself for "excessive propaganda on the '10,000-yuan households' in the rural areas [which] has given urban residents the mistaken idea that as a result of the rural reforms all the peasants have become rich. . . .

ATTRACTING INTERNATIONAL SUPPORT

The top Chinese leadership has expanded the reform coalition to include foreign actors. They cultivate their relations with multinational corporations as assiduously as they do their relations with foreign governments. And naturally, the multinational corporations are enthusiastic about the Chinese reform because it has opened the door to the huge China market. During the retrenchment periods of 1980–82 and 1985–86, when imports and joint investment projects were cut back or delayed, foreign executives grew anxious. Chinese leaders used this international reaction to good effect, arguing that they had to sustain the reform drive to maintain international business confidence in China.

Foreign government policies can also promote or subvert reform in China. When the United States government facilitated licensing of technology exports to China, it reinforced the position of the reformers; but when the Americans erected protectionist quotas against Chinese textiles, it weakened the hand of the reformers.[57]

International organizations, particularly the World Bank, have also become players in the domestic politics of economic reform. The recommendations of World Bank economists constitute powerful arguments for reform policies. The bank's influence stems as much from its international prestige as from its financial aid.

The political task of carrying out economic reform in a communist system is extraordinarily difficult, especially in the industrial arena, which is characterized by a high degree of interdependence and complexity and intense bureaucratic and regional competition. The Chinese case suggests, however, that an astute leader such as Premier Zhao Ziyang can manage the conflicts sparked by reform policies and devise strategies for building constituencies of support for reform.

It is too early to be confident in predicting success for industrial reform in China. Economic and political problems such as expansion-readjustment cycles and widespread corruption persist. In contrast to agriculture, which has already undergone a thorough structural transformation, much of the structure of the command economy in

---

They infer from this that with urban reforms now under way, it should be the turn of the urban employees and workers to become '10,000-yuan households'" (*Renmin Ribao*, Feb. 22, 1985). This propaganda has had the unfortunate effect of reinforcing the anti-rural prejudices of city dwellers and raising their expectations for becoming wealthy themselves from the reforms. These raised expectations put continual pressure on managers to raise wages and bonuses and create the risk of mass discontent if price reform lowers living standards.

industry remains intact. The leadership has not yet tackled the reform of prices and charges for capital, two core issues in the economic
structure, which are redistributive and bound to spark conflict. But if
Deng Xiaoping and Zhao Ziyang remain determined to carry through
industrial reform, and if Zhao Ziyang continues to use his personal
skills and the political tools of a centralized state to manage the implementation process, then one day China may be the largest market
socialist economy in the world.

Notes

Notes

1. Stark and Nee: State Socialism

This essay is the product of the authors' joint and equal efforts. We thank László Bruszt, Paul DiMaggio, István Gábor, Daniel Kleinman, and Martin Whyte for their careful reading and criticism of an earlier draft of this paper. Our special thanks to Monique Djokic for critical suggestions at various stages of conceptualizing the essay.

1. On Chinese perceptions of East European experiences with economic reform see Nina P. Halpern, "Learning from Abroad: Chinese Views of the East European Economic Experience, Jan. 1977–June 1981," *Modern China*, 11 (Jan. 1985): 77–109. For a Hungarian view of Chinese reforms see János Kornai and Zsuzsa Dániel, "The Chinese Economic Reform—As Seen by Hungarian Economists," *Acta Oeconomica*, 36 (1986): 289–305.

2. Classic statements in the 1950s include Carl J. Friedrich, ed., *Totalitarianism* (Cambridge, Mass.: Harvard University Press, 1954); and Carl J. Friedrich and Zbigniew K. Brzezinski, *Totalitarian Dictatorship and Autocracy* (Cambridge, Mass.: Harvard University Press, 1956); in the 1960s, Adam Ulam, *The New Face of Soviet Totalitarianism* (Cambridge, Mass.: Harvard University Press, 1963); and Leonard Schapiro, *The Government and Politics of the Soviet Union* (London: Hutchinson, 1967). For criticisms of the theory of totalitarianism by prominent Sovietologists see David Lane, *The Socialist Industrial State* (London: Allen & Unwin, 1976); and Stephen F. Cohen, *Rethinking the Soviet Experience* (New York: Oxford University Press, 1980), esp. pp. 3–37.

3. Richard Lowenthal, "Development vs. Utopia in Communist Policy," in Chalmers Johnson, ed., *Change in Communist Systems* (Stanford: Stanford University Press, 1970), p. 54.

4. Radovan Richta, *Civilization at the Crossroads: Social and Human Implications of the Scientific and Technical Revolution* (White Plains, N.Y.: International Arts and Sciences Press, 1969); and essays in Mark G. Field, ed., *Social Consequences of Modernization in Communist Societies* (Baltimore: Johns Hopkins University Press, 1976).

5. Thomas Baylis, *The Technical Intelligentsia and the East German Elite* (Berke-

ley: University of California Press, 1974); Frank Parkin, "System Contradiction and Political Transformation," in Anthony Giddens and David Held, eds., *Classes, Power, and Conflict* (Berkeley: University of California Press, 1982), pp. 574–87; Jack Bielasiak, "Modernization and Elite Cooptation in Eastern Europe, 1954–1971," *East European Quarterly*, 14 (Fall 1980): 345–69; Rudolf Bahro, *The Alternative in Eastern Europe* (London: New Left Books, 1979).

6. H. Gordon Skilling, "Interest Groups and Communist Politics: An Introduction," in H. Gordon Skilling and Franklyn Griffiths, eds., *Interest Groups in Soviet Politics* (Princeton: Princeton University Press, 1971), p. 17.

7. In the China field, the revisionist perspective had a broad influence on scholarship in the 1960s and 1970s and for a time became the dominant perspective. Notable examples of revisionist scholarship in the China field include James Townsend, *Political Participation in Communist China* (Berkeley: University of California Press, 1967); Mark Selden, *The Yenan Way in Revolutionary China* (Cambridge, Mass.: Harvard University Press, 1971); Richard Pfeffer, "Serving the People and Continuing the Revolution," *China Quarterly*, no. 52 (Oct.–Dec. 1972): 620–53; Victor Nee and James Peck, eds., *China's Uninterrupted Revolution* (New York: Pantheon Books, 1975); Philip Huang, "Analyzing the Twentieth-century Chinese Countryside: Revolutionaries versus Western Scholarship," *Modern China*, 1 (Apr. 1975); John G. Gurley, *China's Economy and the Maoist Strategy* (New York: Monthly Review Press, 1976); Steven Andors, *China's Industrial Revolution* (New York: Pantheon Books, 1977); Maurice Meisner, *Mao's China: A History of the People's Republic of China* (New York: Free Press, 1977); Vivienne Shue, *Peasant China in Transition* (Berkeley: University of California Press, 1980); and Carl Riskin, *China's Political Economy: The Quest for Development since 1949* (New York: Columbia University Press, 1987). In the Soviet and Eastern European fields revisionist studies tended to assume orthodox Marxist categories of analysis; examples include Charles Bettleheim, *Class Struggle in the U.S.S.R.* (New York: Monthly Review Press, 1976); Sheila Fitzpatrick, "Culture and Politics under Stalin: A Reappraisal," *Slavic Review*, 35 (June 1976): 211–31; and Sheila Fitzpatrick, "Cultural Revolution as Class War," in Sheila Fitzpatrick, ed., *Cultural Revolution in Russia, 1928–1931* (Bloomington: Indiana University Press, 1978).

8. See especially, György Márkus, "Eastern European Societies and the Western Left," in Ferenc Fehér, Agnes Heller, and György Márkus, *Dictatorship over Needs: An Analysis of Soviet Societies* (Oxford: Basil Blackwell, 1983), pp. 1–44.

9. Tamás Bauer, "Investment Cycles in Planned Economies," *Acta Oeconomica*, 21 (1978): 243–60.

10. Istrván Gábor, "The Second (Secondary) Economy," *Acta Oeconomica*, 22 (1979): 291–311; András Hegedus and Maria Márkus, "The Small Entrepreneur and Socialism," *Acta Oeconomica*, 22 (1979): 267–89.

11. Lajos Héthy and Csaba Makó, "Work Performance, Interests, Powers and Environment: The Case of Cyclical Slowdowns in a Hungarian Factory," in Paul Halmos, ed., *Hungarian Sociological Studies*, Sociological Review Series, no. 17 (1972), pp. 125–50; George Konrad and Ivan Szelenyi, "Social Conflicts of Underurbanization," in Michael Harloe, ed., *Captive Cities: Studies in the Political Economy of Cities and Regions* (New York: Wiley, 1977), pp. 157–74; Zsuzsa Ferge, *A Society in the Making: Hungarian Social and Societal Policy, 1945–*

1975 (White Plains, N.Y.: M. E. Sharpe, 1979); and Ivan Szelenyi, "Social Inequalities in State Socialist Redistributive Economies: Dilemmas for Social Policy in Contemporary Socialist Societies of Eastern Europe," *International Journal of Comparative Sociology*, 19, nos. 1–2 (1978): 63–87.

12. János Kornai, *Overcentralization in Economic Administration: A Critical Analysis Based on Experience in Hungarian Light Industry* (Oxford: Oxford University Press, 1959).

13. L. Szamuely, "The First Wave of the Mechanism Debate in Hungary (1954–1957)," *Acta Oeconomica*, 29 (1982): 15.

14. Istvǎn Gábor, "Reforms, Second Economy, State Socialism: Speculation on the Evolutionary and Comparative Economic Lessons of the Hungarian Eighties," paper presented at the Conference on Economic Reforms in China and Eastern Europe, Montecito, California, May 8–11, 1986, published in Hungarian in *Valóság*, 1986, no. 6, pp. 32–48.

15. On the problem of intransitivity of preference orderings in rational choice models and the need to specify appropriate institutional constraints see, for example, R. D. McKelvey, "Intransitivities in Multidimensional Voting Methods and Some Implications for Agenda Control," *British Journal of Sociology*, 30 (1979): 472–82; and Norman Schofield, "Instability and Development in the Political Economy," in Peter C. Ordeshook and Kenneth A. Shepsle, eds., *Political Equilibrium* (Boston: Kluwer-Nijhoff, 1982). James March and Johan Olsen survey broader institutionalist approaches in the field of political science in "The New Institutionalism: Organizational Factors in Political Life," *American Political Science Review*, 78 (1984): 734–49; and for an excellent example of this broader institutionalism see Peter Hall, *Governing the Economy* (London: Oxford University Press, 1986).

16. Oliver Williamson's "transaction cost economics" is only one of the competing theories making new institutionalist claims in economics. See his *The Economic Institutions of Capitalism: Firms, Markets, and Relational Contracting* (New York: Free Press, 1985). For discussions of this new institutionalism see Richard N. Langlois, "The New Institutional Economics: An Introductory Essay," in Richard N. Langlois, ed., *Economics as a Process* (Cambridge, Eng.: Cambridge University Press, 1986); and Terry Moe, "The New Economics of Organization," *American Journal of Political Science*, 28 (1984): 739–77. For a broader conception of institutions and a rejection of the narrow efficiency views of Williamson see, for example, Michael Piore and Charles Sabel, *The Second Industrial Divide* (New York: Basic Books, 1984).

17. John W. Meyer and Brian Rowan, "Institutionalized Organizations: Formal Structure as Myth and Ceremony," *American Journal of Sociology*, 83 (1977): 340–63; and Paul DiMaggio and Walter Powell, "The Iron Cage Revisited: Institutional Isomorphism and Collective Rationality in Organizational Fields," *American Sociological Review*, 48 (1983): 147–60. The new institutionalism in sociology builds on the assumption of the embeddedness of economic action in noneconomic social relationships and examines how markets are shaped by social institutions such as the family and kinship groups, by cultural conventions governing economic transactions, and by formal organizations such as the state, labor unions, and firms. See Mark Granovetter, "Economic Action and Social Structure: The Problem of Embeddedness," *American Journal of Sociology*, 91 (1985): 481–510; and Sharon Zukin and Paul DiMag-

gio, "Preface," *Structures of Capital*, special issue of *Theory and Society*, 15, nos. 1–2 (1986): 1–10.

18. In theoretical orientation, the new institutional analysis of state socialism most closely resembles work in comparative political economy such as Suzanne Berger et al., eds., *Organizing Interests in Western Europe* (Cambridge, Eng.: Cambridge University Press, 1981).

19. Laura D'Andrea Tyson, "The Debt Crisis and Adjustment Responses in Eastern Europe: A Comparative Perspective," *International Organization*, 40 (1986): 239–85.

20. Ivan Szelenyi, *Urban Inequalities under State Socialism* (London: Oxford University Press, 1983). For a modification of Szelenyi's argument that takes into account the inequalities produced by the market mechanisms of the new private sector see Robert Manchin and Ivan Szelenyi, "Social Policy under State Socialism: Market Redistribution and Social Inequalities in East European Socialist Societies," in Martin Rein, Gosta Esping-Anderson, and Lee Rainwater, eds., *Stagnation and Renewal in Social Policy* (White Plains, N.Y.: M. E. Sharpe, 1987), pp. 102–39.

21. Victor Nee, "From Redistribution to Markets in a Socialist Mixed Economy," paper presented at the Conference on the Social Consequences of Market Reform in China at the Fairbank Center for East Asian Research, Harvard University, May 13–15, 1988.

22. David Stark, "Rethinking Internal Labor Markets: New Insights from a Comparative Perspective," *American Sociological Review*, 51 (1986): 492–504.

23. See the essays in William L. Parish, ed., *Chinese Rural Development: The Great Transformation* (Armonk, N.Y.: M. E. Sharpe, 1985), for examples of studies based on field research in Chinese villages. The studies of Chinese peasant society based on interviews of refugees in Hong Kong have held up remarkably well. It is likely that interviews of emigrants in Hong Kong will continue to provide an alternative to direct fieldwork in China. See William L. Parish and Martin K. Whyte, *Village and Family in Contemporary China* (Chicago: University of Chicago Press, 1978); Anita Chan, Richard Madsen, and Jonathan Unger, *Chen Village: A Recent History of a Peasant Community in Mao's China* (Berkeley: University of California Press, 1984); Richard Madsen, *Power and Morality in a Chinese Village* (Berkeley: University of California Press, 1984); and Martin K. Whyte and William L. Parish, *Urban Life in Contemporary China* (Chicago: University of Chicago Press, 1984).

24. C. M. Hann, *Tazlar: A Village in Hungary* (Cambridge, Eng.: Cambridge University Press, 1980); C. M. Hann, *A Village without Solidarity: Polish Peasantry in Years of Crisis* (New Haven: Yale University Press, 1985); Katherine Verdery, *Transylvanian Villagers: Three Centuries of Political, Economic, and Ethnic Change* (Berkeley: University of California Press, 1983); and Victor Nee, "Between Center and Locality: State, Militia, and Village," in Victor Nee and David Mozingo, eds., *State and Society in Contemporary China* (Ithaca: Cornell University Press, 1983).

25. Ellen Comisso, *Workers' Control under Plan and Market* (New Haven: Yale University Press, 1979); Charles Sabel and David Stark, "Planning, Politics, and Shop-floor Power: Hidden Forms of Bargaining in Soviet-Imposed State-Socialist Societies," *Politics and Society*, 11, no. 4 (1982): 439–75; Andrew Walder, "Industrial Reform in China: The Human Dimension," in Ronald

Morse, ed., *The Limits of Reform in China* (Boulder, Colo.: Westview Press, 1983). For an illustration of the persistent grip of the totalitarianism legacy, however, see the use of the label "bureaucratic despotism" to characterize the socialist factory by Michael Burawoy in "The Politics of Production and the Production of Politics: A Comparative Analysis of Piecework Machine Shops in the United States and Hungary," in Maurice Zeitlin, ed., *Political Power and Social Theory* (Greenwich, Conn.: JAI Press, 1980), 1: 261–99. In a striking reversal of his position, Burawoy now argues the reverse—that the socialist firm is a site of workers' control and that it is more efficient than its capitalist counterpart. See Michael Burawoy and János Lukács, "Mythologies of Work: A Comparison of Firms in State Socialism and Advanced Capitalism," *American Sociological Review*, 50 (1985): 723–37.

26. Albert Simkus and Rudolf Andorka, "Inequalities in Educational Attainment in Hungary, 1923–1973," *American Sociological Review*, 47 (1982): 740–51.

27. Dwight Perkins and Shahid Yusuf, *Rural Development in China* (Baltimore: Johns Hopkins University Press, 1984); Christine Wong, "Material Allocation and Decentralization: Impact of the Local Sector on Industrial Reform," in Elizabeth J. Perry and Christine Wong, eds., *The Political Economy of Reform in Post-Mao China* (Cambridge, Mass.: Harvard University Press, 1985), pp. 253–77; and David Granick, *Enterprise Guidance in Eastern Europe: A Comparison of Four Socialist Economies* (Princeton: Princeton University Press, 1975).

28. Philip Huang, *The Peasant Economy and Social Change in North China* (Stanford: Stanford University Press, 1985); Sherman Cochran, "Economic Institutions in China's Interregional Trade: Tobacco Products and Cotton Textiles, 1850–1980," in Robert M. Hartwell et al., eds., *Region, State and Enterprise in Chinese Economic History, 980–1980* (Berkeley: University of California Press, forthcoming); Emily Honig, *Sisters and Strangers: Women in the Shanghai Cotton Mills, 1919–1949* (Stanford: Stanford University Press, 1986); James Lee, "Food Supply and Population Growth, 1250–1850," *Journal of Asian Studies*, 41 (Aug. 1982): 711–48; Elizabeth Perry, *Rebels and Revolutionaries in North China, 1845–1945* (Stanford: Stanford University Press, 1980); Laura Engelstein, *Moscow, 1905: Working-class Organization and Political Conflict* (Stanford: Stanford University Press, 1982); S. A. Smith, *Red Petrograd: Revolution in the Factories, 1917–1918* (Cambridge, Eng.: Cambridge University Press, 1983); and Victoria E. Bonnell, *Roots of Rebellion: Workers' Politics and Organization in St. Petersburg and Moscow, 1900–1914* (Berkeley: University of California Press, 1983).

29. Diane Koenker, *Moscow Workers and the 1917 Revolution*, (Princeton: Princeton University Press, 1981); Emily Honig and Gail Hershatter, *Personal Voices: Chinese Women in the 1980's* (Stanford: Stanford University Press, 1988); Ann S. Anagnost, "Politics and Magic in Contemporary China," *Modern China*, 13 (Jan. 1987): 41–61.

30. Martha Lampland, "Working through History: Ideologies of Work and Agricultural Production in a Hungarian Village, 1918–1983" (Ph.D. dissertation, University of Chicago, 1987); Gail Kligman, "Poetry and Politics in a Transylvanian Village," *Anthropological Quarterly*, 56 (1983): 83–89; Mayfair Yang, "The Art of Social Relationship and Exchange in China" (Ph.D.

dissertation, University of California at Berkeley, 1986); Jean DeBarnardi, "Chinese Rhetoric of Politeness and Persuasion," paper presented at the 86th Annual Meeting of the American Anthropological Association, November 18–22, 1987.

31. Nan Lin and Wen Xie, "Occupational Prestige in Urban China," *American Journal of Sociology*, 93 (1988): 793–832; Albert Simkus, "Structural Transformation and Social Mobility: Hungary, 1938–1973," *American Sociological Review*, 49 (1984): 291–307; Robert M. Jenkins, "Social Inequality in the State Socialist Division of Labor: Earnings Determination in Contemporary Hungary" (Ph.D. dissertation, University of Wisconsin, 1987); and Szonja Szelenyi, "Social Mobility and Class Structure in Hungary and the United States" (Ph.D. dissertation, University of Wisconsin, 1988). A number of survey research projects have been recently completed or are currently in process in China on diverse subjects. These include studies by Nan Lin on social resources and networks, Victor Nee on the peasant household economy, Martin Whyte on mate selection in urban China, Peter Blau and Andrew Walder on urban status attainment and wage distribution, and Glen Elder on the life course in Shanghai.

32. Andrew G. Walder, *Communist Neo-Traditionalism: Work and Authority in Chinese Industry* (Berkeley: University of California Press, 1986); Endre Sik, "Small Is Useful: The Reciprocal Exchange of Labour in Residential Construction," in Péter Galasi and György Sziráczki, eds., *Labour Market and Second Economy in Hungary* (Frankfurt: Campus, 1985), pp. 179–214; Thomas B. Gold, "After Comradeship: Personal Relations in China since the Cultural Revolution," *China Quarterly*, no. 104 (Dec. 1985): 657–75; Jean Oi, "Communism and Clientelism: Rural Politics in China," *World Politics*, 37 (Jan. 1985): 238–66; and Vladimir Shlapentokh, *Love, Marriage and Friendship in the Soviet Union: Ideals and Practices* (New York: Praeger, 1984).

33. T. H. Rigby, "Crypto-Politics," in Frederic J. Fleron, Jr., ed., *Communist Studies and the Social Sciences* (Chicago: Rand McNally, 1969), pp. 115–28.

34. See Vivienne Shue, *The Reach of the State* (Stanford: Stanford University Press, 1988), for an eloquent interpretation of state and society relationships in contemporary China that emphasizes the importance of focusing on subordinate groups; and Ivan Szelenyi, *Socialist Entrepreneurs: Embourgeoisement in Rural Hungary* (Madison: University of Wisconsin Press, 1988).

35. On the evolution of Solidarity see Henry Norr, "Self-Management and the Politics of Solidarity in Poland," in Carmen Sirianni, ed., *Worker Participation and the Politics of Reform* (Philadelphia: Temple University Press, 1986), pp. 267–97; Andrew Arato, "Civil Society against the State: Poland 1980–81," *Telos*, no. 47 (Spring 1981): 23–47; Timothy Garton Ash, *The Polish Revolution: Solidarity* (New York: Scribner's, 1984); Alex Pravda, "Poland 1980: From 'Premature Consumerism' to Labour Solidarity," *Soviet Studies*, 34 (Apr. 1982): 167–99; and M. C. Nagengast, "Poles Apart: Polish Farmers and the State" (Ph.D. dissertation, University of California, Irvine, 1985).

36. The argument for a state-centered political sociology of advanced capitalist democracies is presented in Peter Evans, Dietrich Reuschemeyer, and Theda Skocpol, eds., *Bringing the State Back In* (Cambridge, Eng.: Cambridge University Press, 1985); and Peter Hall, *Governing the Economy* (New York: Oxford University Press, 1986).

37. Oliver E. Williamson, *Markets and Hierarchies: Analysis and Antitrust Implications* (New York: Free Press, 1975).

38. See especially, János Kornai, "Degrees of Paternalism," in *Contradictions and Dilemmas: Studies on the Socialist Economy and Society* (Cambridge, Mass.: MIT Press, 1986), pp. 52–61.

39. Frederick Hayek, "The Use of Knowledge in Society," *American Economic Review*, 35 (1945): 519–30.

40. Wlodzimierz Brus, *The Market in a Socialist Economy* (London: Routledge & Kegan Paul, 1972), p. 142.

41. János Kornai, "Bureaucratic and Market Coordination," *Osteuropa Wirtschaft*, 29 (Dec. 1984): 310.

42. See, for example, the essays in Charles Maier, ed., *Changing Boundaries of the Political: Essays on the Evolving Balance between the State and Society, Public and Private in Europe* (Cambridge, Eng.: Cambridge University Press, 1987).

43. Albert Hirschman, *Exit, Voice, and Loyalty* (Cambridge, Mass.: Harvard University Press, 1970).

44. Dorothy J. Solinger, *Chinese Business under Socialism: The Politics of Domestic Commerce in Contemporary China* (Berkeley: University of California Press, 1984).

45. Comisso.

46. Erzsébet Szalai, *Beszélgetések a gazdasági reformról* (Conversations about the economic reform) (Budapest: Pénzügykutatási Intézet, 1985), p. 65.

47. Ed A. Hewitt, "Gorbachev at Two Years: Perspectives on Economic Reforms," *Soviet Economy*, 2, no. 4 (1986): 283–88.

48. Gertrude E. Schroeder, "Gorbachev: 'Radically' Implementing Brezhnev's Reforms," *Soviet Economy*, 2, no. 4 (1986): 299.

49. Ed A. Hewitt, "Reform or Rhetoric: Gorbachev and the Soviet Economy," *Brookings Review*, 5 (Fall 1986): 16.

50. Jerry Hough, "The Gorbachev Reform: A Maximal Case," *Soviet Economy*, 2, no. 4 (1986): 302–12; see also Peter Hausloner, "Gorbachev's Social Contract," *Soviet Economy*, 3, no. 1 (1987): 54–89.

2. Kornai: Hungarian Reform

A version of this paper with additional references to Hungarian sources appeared in the *Journal of Economic Literature*, 24 (Dec. 1986): 1687–1737. Reprinted by permission of the journal. I wish to thank many colleagues, especially Tamás Bauer, Abram Bergson, Zsuzsa Dániel, Katalin Farkas, Károly Fazekas, János Gács, Gregory Grossman, Edward A. Hewitt, Pál Juhász, János Köllő, Mária Lackó, Mihály Laki, Paul Marer, Agnes Matits, Tamás Nagy, Richard Portes, András Simonovits, Aladár Sipos, Márton Tardos, and Laura D'Andrea Tyson, for helpful suggestions and criticism of the first outline and drafts. I should like to express my thanks for the support of the Institute for Advanced Study (Princeton), the Institute of Economics of the Hungarian Academy of Sciences, and the Department of Economics at Harvard University. The devoted assistance of Maria Kovacs is gratefully acknowledged.

1. Oscar Lange, "On the Economic Theory of Socialism," *Review of Economic Studies*, 4 (Oct. 1936 and Feb. 1937): 53–71, 123–42; Paul R. Gregory and Robert C. Stuart, *Comparative Economic Systems* (Boston: Houghton Mifflin, 1980), p. 299.

2. A brief sample of literature on the Hungarian reform includes the following: Rezsó Nyers and Márton Tardos, "Enterprise in Hungary before and after the Economic Reform," *Acta Oeconomica*, 20 (1978): 21–44; József Bognár, "Further Development in Economic Reform," *New Hungarian Quarterly*, 25 (1984): 45–54; Richard Portes, "Hungary: Economic Performance, Policy and Prospects," in U.S. Congress, Joint Economic Committee, *East European Economics Post-Helsinki* (Washington, D.C.: U.S. Government Printing Office, 1977); Béla Balassa, "The Economic Reform in Hungary: Ten Years After," *European Economic Review*, 11 (Oct. 1978): 245–68; Balassa, "Reforming the New Economic Mechanism in Hungary," *Journal of Comparative Economics*, 7 (1983): 253–76; and Paul Hare, Hugo K. Radice, and Nigel Swain, eds., *Hungary: A Decade of Economic Reform* (London: Allen & Unwin, 1981).

3. For further elaboration, see János Kornai, "Bureaucratic and Market Coordination," *Osteuropa Wirtschaft*, 29 (Dec. 1984): 306–19.

4. More detailed description can be found in David Granick, *Management of the Industrial Firm in the USSR* (New York: Columbia University Press, 1954); János Kornai, *Overcentralization in Economic Administration* (1957; London: Oxford University Press, 1959); Joseph S. Berliner, *Factory and Manager in the USSR* (Cambridge, Mass.: Harvard University Press, 1957); Béla Balassa, *The Hungarian Experience in Economic Planning* (New Haven: Yale University Press, 1959); Wlodzimierz Brus, *The Market in a Socialist Economy* (1961; rpt. London: Routledge, 1972); Alec Nove, *The Soviet Economic System* (London: Allen & Unwin, 1983); Morris Bornstein, ed., *The Soviet Economy: Continuity and Change* (Boulder, Colo.: Westview Press, 1981); and Paul R. Gregory and Robert C. Stuart, *Soviet Economic Structure and Performance* (New York: Harper & Row, 1981).

5. Holland Hunter, "Optimal Tautness in Developmental Planning," *Economic Development and Cultural Change*, 9 (July 1961): 561–72.

6. János Gács, "Passive Purchasing Behaviour and Possibilities of Adjustment in the Hungarian Industry," *Acta Oeconomica*, 28 (1982): 337–49.

7. László Halpern and György Molnár, "Income Formation, Accumulation and Price Trends in Hungary in the 1970s," *Acta Oeconomica*, 35 (1985): 119.

8. János Kornai, "Resource-Constrained versus Demand-Constrained Systems," *Econometrica*, 47 (July 1979): 801–19; Kornai, *Economics of Shortage* (Amsterdam: North-Holland, 1980); and Kornai, "The Soft Budget Constraint," *Kyklos*, 39 (1986): 3–30.

9. David Granick, "Central Physical Planning, Incentives and Job Rights," in Andrew Zimbalist, ed., *Comparative Economic Systems: Present Views* (The Hague: Kluwer-Nijhoff, 1984).

10. Károly A. Soós, "A Propos the Explanation of Shortage Phenomena: Volume of Demand and Structural Inelasticity," *Acta Oeconomica*, 33 (1984): 305–20.

11. Judit Szabó and Imre Tarafás, "Hungary's Exchange Rate Policy in the 1980's," *Acta Oeconomica*, 29 (1982): 25–46.

12. János Kornai and Agnes Matits, "Softness of the Budget Constraint— An Analysis Relying on Data of Firms," *Acta Oeconomica*, 32 (1984): 223–49.

13. Zoltán Román, "The Conditions of Market Competition in Hungarian Industry," *Acta Oeconomica*, 22 (1979): 47–68. The 637 product aggregates cover about 75 percent of total manufacturing.

14. Tamás Bauer, "The Contradictory Position of the Enterprise under the New Hungarian Economic Mechanism," *Eastern European Economics*, 15 (Fall 1976): 3–23; Bauer, "The Unclearing Market," mimeo (Budapest: Institute of Economics, 1985).

15. Ferenc Donáth, *Reform and Revolution: Transformation of Hungary's Agriculture, 1945–1975* (Budapest: Corvina, 1980); Nigel Swain, "The Evolution of Hungary's Agricultural System since 1967," in Hare, Radice, and Swain, eds., pp. 225–51; Csaba Csáki, "Economic Management and Organization of Hungarian Agriculture," *Journal of Comparative Economics*, 7 (Sept. 1983): 317–28; Michael Marrese, "Agricultural Policy and Performance in Hungary," *Journal of Comparative Economics*, 7 (Sept. 1983): 329–45; and Aladár Sipos, "Relations between Enterprises in the Agro-Industrial Sphere in Hungary," *Acta Oeconomica*, 31 (1983): 53–69.

16. Kálmán Rupp, *Enterpreneurs in Red* (Albany, N.Y.: State University of New York Press, 1983).

17. Bauer, "Unclearing Market."

18. Ivan Szelenyi, *Urban Inequalities under State Socialism* (Oxford: Oxford University Press, 1983); Zsuzsa Dániel, "The Effect of Housing Allocation on Social Inequality in Hungary," *Journal of Comparative Economics*, 9 (Dec. 1985): 391–409.

19. For more detailed analysis see Teréz Laky, "Enterprise Business Work Partnership and Enterprise Interest," *Acta Oeconomica*, 34 (1985): 27–49; and David Stark, "The Micropolitics of the Firm and the Macropolitics of Reform: New Forms of Workplace Bargaining in Hungarian Enterprises," in Peter Evans, Dietrich Rueschemeyer, and Evelyne Huber Stephens, eds., *State versus Markets in the World-System* (Beverly Hills: Sage, 1985), pp. 247–69.

20. Brus; Gregory Grossman, "Gold and the Sword: Money in the Soviet Command Economy," in Henry Rosovsky, ed., *Industrialization in Two Systems* (New York: Wiley, 1966), pp. 204–36; Kornai, *Economics of Shortage*; Márton Tardos, "The Role of Money: Economic Relations between the State and the Enterprises in Hungary," *Acta Oeconomica*, 25 (1980): 19–35.

21. Péter Galasi and György Sziráczky, eds., *Labour Market and Second Economy in Hungary* (Frankfort: Campus, 1985); Károly Fazekas and János Köllő, "Fluctuations of Labour Shortage and State Intervention after 1968," ibid., pp. 42–69.

22. Kornai, *Overcentralization*; Franklyn D. Holzman, "Soviet Inflationary Pressures, 1928–1957: Causes and Cures," *Quarterly Journal of Economics*, 74 (May 1960): 167–88; Herbert S. Levine, "Pressure and Planning in the Soviet Economy," in Rosovsky, ed., pp. 266–85.

23. Tamás Bauer, "Investment Cycles in Planned Economics," *Acta Oeconomica*, 21 (1978): 243–60; Károly A. Soós, "Causes of Investment Fluctuations in the Hungarian Economy," *Eastern European Economics*, 14 (Winter 1975–76): 25–36; Mária Lackó, "Cumulating and Easing of Tensions," *Acta Oeconomica*, 24 (1980): 357–77; Lackó, "Behavioral Rules in the Distribution of Sectoral Investments in Hungary, 1951–1980," *Journal of Comparative Economics*, 8 (Sept. 1984): 290–300.

24. Soós, "A Propos the Explanation of Shortage Phenomena"; Stanislaw Gomulka, "Kornai's Soft Budget Constraint and the Shortage Phenomenon: A Criticism and Restatement," *Economic Planning*, 19 (1985): 1–11; János Kornai,

"On the Explanatory Theory of Shortage: Comments on Two Articles by K. A. Soós," *Acta Oeconomica*, 34 (1985): 145–64; Kornai, "Gomulka on the Soft Budget Constraint: A Reply," *Economic Planning*, 19 (1985): 49–55.

25. Dániel.

26. Zsuzsa Kapitány, János Kornai, and Judit Szabó, "Reproduction of Shortage on the Hungarian Car Market," *Soviet Studies*, 36 (1984): 236–56.

27. Gács.

28. Ervin Fábri, "Superficial Changes and Deep Tendencies in Inventory Process in Hungary," *Acta Oeconomica*, 28 (1982): 133–46; Attila Chikán, "Market Disequilibrium and the Volume of Stocks," in Chikán, ed., *The Economics and Management of Inventories* (Amsterdam: Elsevier, 1981), pp. 73–85.

29. Paul Marer, "The Mechanism and Performance of Hungary's Foreign Trade, 1968–79," in Hare, Radice, and Swain, eds., pp. 161–204; Béla Balassa and Laura Tyson, "Adjustment to External Shocks in Socialist and Private Market Economics," mimeo (Washington, D.C.: World Bank Development Research Department, 1983); András Köves and Gábor Obláth, "Hungarian Foreign Trade in the 1970's," *Acta Oeconomica*, 30 (1983): 89–109.

30. The problem is discussed in a wider context by Ferenc Fehrér, Agnes Heller, and György Markus, *Dictatorship over Needs* (Oxford: Blackwell, 1983).

31. For example, Szelenyi.

32. The most outstanding works in the great debate were Enrico Barone, "The Ministry of Production in the Collectivist State," in Friedrich A. Hayek, ed., *Collectivist Economic Planning* (London: Routledge, 1935), pp. 245–90; Ludwig von Mises, "Economic Calculation in the Socialist Commonwealth," ibid., pp. 87–130; Fred M. Taylor, "The Guidance of Production in a Socialist State," *American Economic Review*, 19 (Mar. 1929): 1–80; and, of course, Lange. The classical summary is Abram Bergson, "Socialist Economics," in Howard S. Ellis, ed., *A Survey of Contemporary Economics* (Homewood, Ill.: Irwin, 1948), pp. 1412–48. Important new points have been added by Bergson, "Market Socialism Revisited," *Journal of Political Economy*, 75 (1967): 655–73; Alec Nove, *The Economics of Feasible Socialism* (London: Allen & Unwin, 1983); and Don Lavoie, *Rivalry and Central Planning: The Socialist Calculation Debate Reconsidered* (Cambridge, Eng.: Cambridge University Press, 1985).

33. Teréz Laky, "The Hidden Mechanism of Recentralization in Hungary," *Acta Oeconomica*, 24 (1980): 95–109.

34. László Antal, "Development—with Some Digression: The Hungarian Economic Mechanism in the Seventies," *Acta Oeconomica*, 23 (1979): 257–73.

35. Kornai, "Bureaucratic and Market Coordination."

36. John Kenneth Galbraith, *The New Industrial State* (Boston: Houghton Mifflin, 1967); Galbraith, *American Capitalism* (1952; rpt. Boston: Houghton Mifflin, 1967).

37. Nyers and Tardos, "Enterprises in Hungary"; Nyers and Tardos, "What Economic Development Policy Should We Adopt?" *Acta Oeconomica*, 22 (1979): 11–31; Nyers and Tardos, "The Necessity for Consolidation of the Economy and the Possibility of Development in Hungary," *Acta Oeconomica*, 32 (1984): 1–19; Tardos, "The Conditions of Developing a Regulated Market," *Acta Oeconomica*, 36 (1986); Tamás Bauer, "The Second Economic Reform and Ownership Relations: Some Considerations for the Further Development of the New Economic Mechanism," *Eastern European Economics*, 22 (Spring–

Summer 1984): 33–87; Bauer, "Reform Policy in the Complexity of Economic Policy," *Acta Oeconomica*, 34 (1985): 263–74; László Antal, "About the Property Incentive," *Acta Oeconomica*, 34 (1985): 275–86.

38. For example, Bauer, "Second Economic Reform." A comprehensive survey is presented in Tamás Sárközy, "Problems of Social Ownership and of the Proprietary Organization," *Acta Oeconomica*, 29 (1982): 225–58.

39. Márton Tardos, "Developing Program for Economic Control and Organization in Hungary," *Acta Oeconomica*, 28 (1982): 295–315.

3. Lin: Economic Reform in China

1. János Kornai, *Economics of Shortage* (Amsterdam: North Holland, 1980).

2. See Cyril Lin, "The Reinstatement of Economics in China Today," *China Quarterly*, Mar. 1981, esp. pp. 39–44. The most comprehensive account of Chinese planning history is given in *Tangtai Zhongguo di Jingji Tizhi Gaige* (Recent Chinese economic structural reform) (Beijing: China Social Sciences Publishing House, 1984).

3. Lin; *Tangtai Zhongguo di Jingji Tizhi Gaige*.

4. Lin.

5. Dong Fureng, "Guanyu Wuoguo Shehuizhuyi Suoyouzi Xingshi Wenti" (Concerning the problem of the forms of socialist ownership in China), in *Jingji Yanjiu*, 1979, no. 1. Dong raised this question in greater detail in an unpublished report in 1978.

6. For Chinese views of the Sichuan reform prototype, see S. Shapiro, *Experiment in Sichuan: A Report on Economic Reform* (Beijing: New World Press, 1981), and Lin Wei and A. Chao, eds., *China's Economic Reform* (Philadelphia: University of Pennsylvania Press, 1983).

7. Ma Wenguei, "Shehuizhuyi Gongye Chiye Jihua di Tedian, Renwu he Fangfa" (The characteristics, tasks, and methods of planning in socialist industrial planning), in *Jingji Yanjiu*, 1964, no. 7.

8. Interviews, summer 1982.

9. State Statistical Bureau, *Statistical Yearbook of China, 1985*, English edition (Oxford, Eng.: Oxford University Press, 1985), pp. 215, 554.

10. For representative Chinese assessments, see note 6 above and Wei Liqun, "1980 Nian di Zhongguo Gongye" (Chinese industry in 1980); in *Zhongguo Nianjian, 1981* (China economic yearbook, 1981) (Beijing: Economic Journal Publishers, 1981), pp. IV-3 to IV-10, esp. statistics on pp. IV-6 to IV-8.

11. *Statistical Yearbook of China, 1985*, p. 420.

12. This section is based largely on interviews in summer 1982, summer 1984, and winter 1985, and on various unpublished Chinese articles. The views given here are the author's own and may not reflect those of the various Chinese economists with whom the author discussed these issues.

13. See the speeches of Chen Yun and Bo Yibo in *Eighth National Congress of the Communist Party of China*, Vol. 1: *Speeches* (Beijing: Foreign Language Press, 1956), pp. 157–76, 45–62.

14. See M. Dobb, *Soviet Economic Development since 1917*, 6th ed. (London: Routledge, 1966); P. J. D. Wiles, *The Political Economy of Communism* (Oxford, Eng.: Basil Blackwell, 1964); and P. Kende, "Planning and the Market," unpublished ms.

15. The majority of these "radical" reformers are at the State Council's Commission for Economic System Reform, the Economics Research Institute of the Chinese Academy of Social Sciences, and the Economic and Technology Center (under the State Council).

16. Sun Yefang, *Shehuizhuyi Jingji di Ruogan Lilun Wenti* (Some theoretical questions of a socialist economy) (Beijing: People's Publishers, 1979); see also the sequel published in 1982 under the same title. An analysis of Sun's ideas is available in Lin, "The Reinstatement of Economics."

17. Wlodzimierz Brus, *The Market in a Socialist Economy* (London: Routledge, 1972).

18. Central Committee of the Communist Party of China, *Circular No. 1* (Beijing, 1984).

19. Jiang Yiwei, "Guanyu Gongye Jingji Zerenzhi di Yixie Lilun Wenti" (On some theoretical questions of the industrial economic responsibility system), in *Renmin Ribao*, Jan. 21, 1983; also the "Decision on Reorganisation of State Enterprises" by the State Planning Commission and the CPC's Central Committee, as reported in *Renmin Ribao*, Aug. 19, 1982.

20. The best account of this is in Nicholas Lardy, *Agriculture in China's Modern Economic Development* (Cambridge, Eng.: Cambridge University Press, 1983).

21. *Renmin Ribao*, May 15, 1984.

22. Central Committee of the Communist Party of China, *Circular No. 1* (Beijing, 1985).

23. Interviews, summer 1984.

24. See the speech by Premier Zhao Ziyang at the 3d session of the 6th National People's Congress, in BBC, *Summary of World Broadcasts*, FE/7911/C1/3 (Mar. 28, 1985).

25. Interviews, Dec. 1985.

4. Stark: Hungary's Mixed Economy

Research for this paper was supported by a postdoctoral fellowship from the American Council of Learned Societies/Social Science Research Council and by a grant from the Graduate School of the University of Wisconsin. My appreciation to László Bruszt, Ellen Comisso, István Gábor, David Granick, Daniel Kleinman, János Lukács, Csaba Makó, Victor Nee, and László Neumann for their criticisms and suggestions.

1. László Antal, "Development with Some Digression: The Hungarian Economic Mechanism in the Seventies," *Acta Oeconomica*, 20 (1979): 257–73; Teréz Laky, "The Hidden Mechanisms of Recentralization in Hungary," *Acta Oeconomica*, 24 (1980): 95–109; William F. Robinson, *The Pattern of Reform in Hungary* (New York: Praeger, 1973); and Richard Portes, "Hungary: Economic Performance, Policy, and Prospects," in U.S. Congress, Joint Economic Committee, *East European Economic Assessment* (Washington, D.C.: U.S. Government Printing Office, 1977), pp. 757–815.

2. For an excellent concise summary of developments during this period, see Ellen Comisso and Paul Marer, "The Economics and Politics of Reform in Hungary," *International Organization*, 40 (1986): 421–54.

3. Béla Balassa, *Reforming the New Economic Mechanism in Hungary*, World Bank Staff Working Paper 534 (Washington, D.C.: World Bank Publications,

1982), Erzsébet Szalai, "The New Stage of the Reform Process in Hungary and the Large Enterprises," Acta Oeconomica, 29 (1982): 25–46; and Mihály Laki, "Liquidation and Merger in the Hungarian Industry," Acta Oeconomica, 28 (1982): 87–108.

4. World Bank, Hungary: Economic Developments and Reforms (Washington, D.C.: World Bank Publications, 1984), Comisso and Marer.

5. Paul Marer, "Hungary's Balance of Payments Crisis and Response, 1978–84," in U.S. Congress, Joint Economic Committee, East European Economics: Slow Growth in the 1980s (Washington, D.C.: U.S. Government Printing Office, 1986), 3: 298–321; World Bank.

6. On the restriction policy see László Antal, "Conflicts of Financial Planning and Regulation in Hungary: The 'Nature' of Restrictions," Acta Oeconomica, 30 (1983): 341–68; on the need for a more developed "background" industry see Márton Tardos, "The Increasing Role and Ambivalent Reception of Small Enterprises in Hungary," Journal of Comparative Economics, 7 (1983): 277–87.

7. For estimates of the scope and volume of the second economy in agricultural, industrial, and service activities, see István R. Gábor, "The Major Domains of the Second Economy," in Péter Galasi and György Sziráczki, eds., Labour Market and Second Economy in Hungary (Frankfurt: Campus, 1985), pp. 133–78. Using data from household time budget surveys, economist János Timár estimates that total working time in the Hungarian second economy in 1984 came to 4.6 billion hours compared to 9.1 billion hours in the socialist sector ("Idő és munkaidő" [Time and working time] Közgazdasági Szemle, 32 [1985]: 1306).

8. Károly Attila Soós, "Béralku és 'sérelmi politika': Adalékok a mechanizmusreform 1969 évi első megtorpanásának magyarozatához" (Wage bargaining and the 'policy of grievances': Contributions to the explanation of the reform of the Hungarian economic mechanism in the first half of 1969), Medvetánc, 1984, nos. 2–3, pp. 227–45; William Robinson, "Hungary's Industrial Workers: Increasing Success as a Pressure Group," Radio Free Europe, Background Report 2, 1973; Robinson; Portes.

9. The argument in the following paragraphs is drawn from David Stark, "Rethinking Internal Labor Markets: New Insights from a Comparative Perspective," American Sociological Review, 51 (1986): 492–504.

10. Lajos Héthy and Csaba Makó, Munkások, érdekek, érdekegyeztetés (Workers, interests, bargaining) (Budapest: Gondolat, 1978); István Kemény, Ouvriers hongrois (Paris: L'Harmattan, 1985), pp. 8–84; Csaba Makó, A Társadalmi viszonyok erőtere: A munkafolyamat (The labor process: An arena of social struggle) (Budapest: Közgazdasági és Jogi, 1985); and Gábor Kertesi and György Sziráczki, "Worker Behavior in the Labor Market," in Galasi and Sziráczki, eds., pp. 216–45.

11. Peter Doeringer and Michael J. Piore, Internal Labor Markets and Manpower Analysis (Lexington, Mass.: D. C. Heath, 1971); Robert Althauser and Arne Kalleberg, "Firms, Occupations, and the Structure of Labor Markets: A Conceptual Analysis," in Ivar Berg, ed., Sociological Perspectives on Labor Markets (New York: Academic, 1981); Paul Osterman, ed., Internal Labor Markets (Cambridge, Mass.: MIT Press, 1984).

12. Stark, p. 495.

13. Lajos Héthy and Csaba Makó, "Work Performance, Interests, Powers and Environment: The Case of Cyclical Slowdowns in a Hungarian Factory," in Paul Halmos, ed., *Hungarian Sociological Studies*, Sociological Review Series, 17 (Keele, Eng.: University of Keele, 1972), pp. 123–50; Károly Fazekas, "Wage and Performance Bargaining on the Internal Labor Market," in *Wage Bargaining in Hungarian Firms*, Studies of the Institute of Economics, 23 (Budapest: Hungarian Academy of Sciences, 1984), pp. 29–88; Zoltán Farkas, "Munkások, érdek-és érdekeltségi viszonyai" (Relations and levels of interest among workers) *Szociológia*, 1983, nos. 1–2, pp. 27–52; and György Kővári and György Sziráczki, "Old and New Forms of Wage Bargaining on the Shop Floor," in Galasi and Sziráczki, eds., pp. 133–78.

14. István Csillag, a reformer in the Finance Ministry, who helped prepare the legislation establishing the VGMs expressed such hopes in "As új 'vállalati' szervezet alapvonásai" (The basic features of the new 'enterprise' organization), *Valóság*, 1983, no. 3, pp. 39–59; see also István Kalász and György Szepesi, *Kisüzemi gazdálkodás új formái* (New forms of small-scale business) (Budapest: Kossuth Könyvkiadó, 1983).

15. Teréz Laky, "Small Enterprises in Hungary—Myth and Reality," *Acta Oeconomica*, 32 (1984): 39–62; and Laky, "Enterprise Business Work Partnerships and Enterprise Interest," *Acta Oeconomica*, 34 (1985): 27–49; István Kemény, "The Unregistered Economy in Hungary," *Soviet Studies*, 34 (1982): 349–66.

16. On the importance of "named places" on the cognitive maps of society see Luc Boltanski, *Les cadres: La formation d'un groupe social* (Paris: Minuit, 1982); and Pierre Bourdieu, "The Social Space and the Genesis of Groups," *Theory and Society*, 14 (1985): 723–44.

17. *Népszabadság*, Mar. 29, 1985, p. 3.

18. For a discussion of Stakhanovism in the Soviet Union see Kendall E. Bailes, *Technology and Society under Lenin and Stalin* (Princeton: Princeton University Press, 1978), pp. 317–18.

19. The concepts of various forms of "capital" are those of Pierre Bourdieu.

20. László Neumann reports similar figures on the composition of the VGMs in his study of work partnerships in a large steel mill: "Vállalati gazdasági munkaközösségek—a béralku változásai" (Enterprise business work partnerships—the changing wage bargain) (Ph.D. dissertation, Karl Marx University of Economics, 1986), pp. 82–95.

21. Erzsébet Szalai, *Beszélgetések a gazdasági reformról* (Conversations about the economic reform) (Budapest: Pénzügykutatási Intézet, 1985).

22. Ibid., pp. 29–30.

23. János Kornai, *Contradictions and Dilemmas: Studies on the Socialist Economy and Society* (Cambridge, Mass.: MIT Press, 1986), p. 136; István Gábor, "Reformok, második gazdaság, 'államszocializmus.' A 80-as évek tapasztalatainak fejlődéstani és összehasonlító gazdaságtani tanulságairól" (Reforms, second economy, "state socialism": Speculation on the evolutionary and comparative economic lessons of the Hungarian eighties) *Valóság*, 1986, no. 6, pp. 32–48.

5. *Nee: Entrepreneurship*

Ronald Breiger, Dong Fureng, Roger Friedland, Mark Granovetter, Peter Katzenstein, Nicholas Lardy, Thomas Lyons, William Parish, Vivienne Shue, David Stark, and Su Sijin provided helpful criticism of an earlier draft. I wish to express appreciation for the research assistance of Wang Pao-chu and Jill Major.

1. Sol Tax, *Penny Capitalism* (Washington, D.C.: Smithsonian Institution, Institute of Social Anthropology, 1953).

2. Theodore Schultz, *Transforming Traditional Agriculture* (New Haven, Conn.: Yale University Press, 1964), p. 5.

3. See Melville J. Herskovits, *Economic Anthropology* (New York: Knopf, 1940).

4. See Robert Bates, *Markets and States in Tropical Africa: The Political Basis of Agricultural Policies* (Berkeley: University of California Press, 1981).

5. Douglass North, *Structure and Change in Economic History* (New York: Norton, 1981), p. 201.

6. Nicholas R. Lardy, *Agriculture in China's Modern Economic Development* (Cambridge, Eng.: Cambridge University Press, 1983); William L. Parish and Martin K. Whyte, *Village and Family in Contemporary China* (Chicago: University of Chicago Press, 1978); Dwight Perkins, "Growth and Changing Structure of China's Twentieth Century Economy," in Perkins, ed., *China's Modern Economy in Historical Perspective* (Stanford: Stanford University Press, 1975), pp. 115–65.

7. Theda Skocpol, "Bringing the State Back In: Strategies in Current Research," in Peter Evans et al., eds., *Bringing the State Back In* (Cambridge, Eng.: Cambridge University Press, 1985), p. 6.

8. Mark Granovetter, "Economic Action and Social Structure: The Problem of Embeddedness," *American Journal of Sociology*, 91 (1985): 495.

9. G. William Skinner, "Marketing and Social Structure in Rural China," *Journal of Asian Studies*, 24, pt. 1 (Nov. 1964): 32.

10. Frederick Barth, *Ethnic Groups and Boundaries* (Boston: Little, Brown, 1969).

11. For analysis of patron-client relationships see Anton Blok, *The Mafia of a Sicilian Village, 1860–1960: A Study of Violent Peasant Entrepreneurs* (New York: Harper, 1974); and S. N. Eisenstadt and L. Roniger, *Patrons, Clients and Friends: Interpersonal Relations and the Structure of Trust in Society* (Cambridge, Eng.: Cambridge University Press, 1984).

12. Franz Schurmann, *Ideology and Organization in Communist China* (Berkeley: University of California Press, 1964), p. 416. See also Thomas P. Bernstein, "Leadership and Mobilization in the Collectivization Campaigns of 1929–30 and 1955–56: A Comparison," *China Quarterly*, 31 (1967): 1–47.

13. See Vivienne Shue, *Peasant China in Transition: The Dynamics of Development toward Socialism, 1949–1956* (Berkeley: University of California Press, 1979).

14. See Richard Madsen, *Power and Morality in a Chinese Village* (Berkeley: University of California Press, 1984), pp. 45–60. Village cadres' salaries were paid according to the workpoint system of collective agriculture, not by the state.

15. See Victor Nee, "Between Center and Locality: State, Militia, and Village," in Victor Nee and David Mozingo, eds., *State and Society in Contemporary China* (Ithaca, N.Y.: Cornell University Press, 1983), pp. 223–43.

16. Madsen, pp. 53, 51.

17. Karl Polanyi, *The Great Transformation: The Political and Economic Origins of Our Time* (1944; rpt. Boston: Beacon Press, 1957), p. 140.

18. Max Weber, *Economy and Society* (Berkeley: University of California Press, 1978), vol. 2, pp. 641–776, 956–1001.

19. *Jingji Yanjiou* (Journal of Economic Research), 1983, no. 11.

20. Personal communication, June 1, 1986. Dong Fureng is a leading reform economist. He is currently director of the Institute of Economics of the Chinese Academy of Social Science.

21. See Tamotsu Shibutani, *Social Processes* (Berkeley: University of California Press, 1986).

22. *Renmin Ribao*, Jan. 16, 1984, p. 2, Apr. 16, 1984.

23. *Fujian Ribao* (Fujian Daily), Feb. 14, 1984, p. 1.

24. *Renmin Ribao*, Jan. 16, 1984, p. 2.

25. *Foreign Broadcast Information Service: China* (hereafter *FBIS*), Feb. 6, 1984, p. 3.

26. *Renmin Ribao*, May 14, 1983, q2.

27. *FBIS*, Feb. 8, 24, 1984.

28. *Banyuetan* (Fortnightly Forum), Dec. 25, 1983, pp. 5–7.

29. David Zweig, "Opposition to Change in Rural China: The Household System of Responsibility and People's Commune," *Asian Survey*, 23 (1983): 879–900.

30. Elizabeth J. Perry, "Rural Collective Violence: The Fruits of Recent Reforms," in Elizabeth Perry and Christine Wong, eds., *The Political Economy of Reform in Post-Mao China* (Cambridge, Mass.: Harvard University Press, 1985), p. 189.

31. See Samuel Popkin, *The Rational Peasant: The Political Economy of Rural Society in Vietnam* (Berkeley: University of California Press, 1979); and Victor Nee, "Peasant Household Individualism," in William Parish, ed., *Chinese Rural Development* (New York: M. E. Sharpe, 1985), pp. 164–90.

32. *Renmin Ribao*, July 17, 1984, p. 5; *FBIS*, Jan. 27, 1984, 03.

33. *Banyuetan*, Dec. 25, 1983, pp. 5–7.

34. *Hubei Ribao* (Hubei Daily), July 2, 1985, p. 1, in *Joint Publication and Research Service*, CPS-85-105, Oct. 15, 1985 (hereafter *JPRS*-CPS).

35. *Renmin Ribao*, Apr. 21, 1983, p. 2.

36. *FBIS*, Mar. 12, 1984, s1.

37. *Renmin Ribao*, May 14, 1983, p. 2; *Xinhua* (New China News Service), June 19, 22, 1985; *Banyuetan*, June 25, 1985.

38. *Renmin Ribao*, Oct. 16, 1983, p. 2, May 14, 1983, p. 2, Feb. 3, 1983, p. 4, May 14, 1983, p. 2.

39. *Fujian Ribao*, Apr. 15, 1984, p. 2; *Renmin Ribao*, July 17, 1984, p. 5.

40. *FBIS*, Mar. 1, 1984, t3, Aug. 8, 1985, k13, Mar. 12, 1984, si, *Renmin Ribao*, May 28, 1985, p. 2.

41. Ibid., Sept. 6, 1984.

42. Ibid., Apr. 15, 1984, p. 2; *FBIS*, Apr. 18, 1984, s2.

43. *Renmin Ribao*, Apr. 6, 1984, p. 1, Apr. 21, 1984, p. 1, Apr. 15, 1984, p. 2; *FBIS*, Apr. 18, 1984 s2.

44. *Renmin Ribao*, Apr. 24, 1984, p. 2.

45. Ibid., Sept. 22, 1983, p. 5, Apr. 24, 1984, p. 2, Mar. 20, 1984, p. 2, June 9, 1984, p. 2.

46. Ibid., Feb. 21, 1984, p. 1.

47. *Shaanxi Ribao*, Sept. 23, 1983, p. 1, in *FBIS*, Oct. 14, 1983, t1.

48. *Renmin Ribao*, July 17, 1984, p. 5.

49. *FBIS*, Jan. 27, 1984, 03.

50. *Renmin Ribao*, Nov. 3, 1983, p. 2.

51. Vivienne Shue, "The Fate of the Commune," *Modern China*, 10 (1984): 278.

52. *Jingji Dili* (Economic Geography), May 1985, no. 2, pp. 146–50.

53. *China Daily*, Dec. 5, 1985, p. 4.

54. *Jingji Guanli*, Dec. 5, 1985, pp. 7–8.

55. *Xinhua*, Dec. 12, 1985, in *JPRS*-CAG-86-001.

56. *Nanfang Ribao*, Sept. 15, 1985, in *JPRS*-CAG-85-034.

57. *JPRS*-CAG-85-030, Oct. 17, pp. 19, 46.

58. *Dazhong Ribao*, Aug. 29, 1985, p. 1, in *JPRS*-CPS-85-105, Oct. 15, 1985.

59. *JPRS*-CEA-86-003, Jan. 7, 1986.

60. Polanyi, p. 140.

61. *JPRS*-CAG-85-034, Dec. 13, 1985, p. 39.

62. Beijing, *State Council Bulletin*, no. 6, Mar. 10, 1985, pp. 124–26.

63. János Kornai, *Contradictions and Dilemmas: Studies on the Socialist Economy and Society* (Cambridge, Mass.: MIT Press, 1986), pp. 6–32.

64. *China Daily*, Dec. 5, 1985, p. 1.

65. *JPRS*-CEA-86-001, Jan. 7, 1986.

66. Beijing, *State Council Bulletin*, no. 7, Mar. 20, 1985, pp. 133–36.

67. Ibid., no. 12, May 10, 1985, pp. 353–56.

68. Dwight Perkins, *Asia's Next Economic Giant* (Seattle: University of Washington Press, 1986).

69. The analysis of the determinants of state autonomy would benefit from a closer examination of the issue of boundaries. There is a growing consensus among analysts of state structures that states vary in their autonomy over time and space; yet little progress has been made in specifying the conditions for greater or lesser state autonomy. A research strategy aimed at understanding state autonomy therefore should seek to examine the determinants of "openness" and "closure" in the state's organizational boundaries, measured by the embeddedness of specific state structures in concrete social networks. Analysis of concrete networks linking states with social structures might use blockmodeling methods (see Harrison White, Scott Boorman, and Ronald Breiger, "Social Structure from Multiple Networks: I. Blockmodels of Roles and Positions," *American Journal of Sociology*, 81 [1976]: 730–80), or approaches that link exchange theory with network analysis (see George Homans, *Social Behavior: Its Elementary Forms* [New York: Harcourt Brace Jovanovich, 1974]; Karen Cook, "Network Structures from an Exchange Perspective," in Peter Marsden and Nan Lin, eds., *Social Structure and Network Analysis* [Beverly Hills: Sage, 1982], pp. 177–99; and Mark Granovetter, *Getting a Job: A Study of Contacts*

and Careers [Cambridge, Mass.: Harvard University Press, 1974] or field research methods developed by anthropologists (see P. H. Gulliver, *Neighbors and Networks: The Idiom of Kinship in Social Action among the Ndendauli in Tanzania* [Berkeley: University of California Press, 1971]; and Elizabeth Bott, *Family and Social Networks* [New York: Harper, 1957]).

6. Szelenyi: Eastern Europe

1. Michal Kalecki, "Introduction to the Theory of Growth in a Socialist Economy," in Kalecki, *Selected Essays on the Economic Growth of a Socialist and Mixed Economy* (Cambridge, Eng.: Cambridge University Press, 1972), pp. 1–118; András Bródy, "Gazdasági Növekedésünk Üteme 1924-töl 1965-ig" (Rates of our economic growth, 1924–1965), *Közgazdasági Szemle*, 14 (1967); Tamás Bauer, "A második gazdasági reform és a tulajdonviszonyok" (The second economic reform and ownership relations), *Mozgó Világ*, 1982, no. 11.

2. David Stark, "Rethinking Internal Labor Markets: New Insights from a Comparative Perspective," *American Sociological Review*, 4 (1986): 492–504; János Kornai, *The Economics of Shortage* (Amsterdam: North Holland, 1980).

3. László Antal, Lajos Bokros, István Csillag, László Lengyel, and György Matolcsy, "Fordulat és reform" (Turnaround and reform), *Közgazdasági Szemle*, 34 (1987): 642–63.

4. Alvin Gouldner, "The Dark Side of the Dialectic: Toward a New Objectivity," *Sociological Inquiry*, 46 (1976): 3–16.

5. Ferenc Jánossy, "Gazdaságunk ellentmondásainak eredete és Felszámolásuk utja" (Origins and solutions of the current contradictions of our economy), *Közgazdasági Szemle*, 1971, nos. 7–8.

6. Moshe Lewin, *Political Undercurrents in Soviet Economic Debates* (London: Pluto Press, 1974).

7. New York: International Arts and Sciences Press, 1968.

8. Oxford, Eng.: Oxford University Press, 1959.

9. *Rush versus Harmonic Growth* (Amsterdam: North Holland, 1972); *Anti-Equilibrium* (Amsterdam: North Holland, 1971).

10. Amsterdam: North Holland, 1980.

11. For the concept of the redistributively integrated economy see Karl Polanyi, "The Economy as Instituted Process," in Polanyi, *Trade and Market in Early Empires* (Glencoe, Ill.: Free Press, 1957); János Kornai, "Bürokratikus és piaci koordináció" (Bureaucratic and market coordination), *Közgazdasági Szemle*, 1983, no. 9, pp. 1025–38; George Konrad and Ivan Szelenyi, *The Intellectuals on the Road to Class Power* (New York: Harcourt Brace, 1979); Ivan Szelenyi, "Social Inequalities in State Socialist Redistributive Economies," *International Journal of Comparative Sociology*, 19 (1978): 63–87; and Ivan Szelenyi and Robert Manchin, "Social Policy under State Socialism," in Gosta Esping-Anderson, Lee Rainwater, and Martin Rein, eds., *Stagnation and Renewal in Social Policy* (White Plains, N.Y.: M. E. Sharpe, 1987). See also Tamás Bauer, *Tervgazdaság, Beruházás, Ciklusok* (Planned economy, investments, cycles) (Budapest: Közgazdasági és Jogi Kiadó, 1981).

12. Ivan Szelenyi, Robert Manchin, Pál Juhász, Bálint Magyar, and Bill Martin, *Socialist Entrepreneurs: Embourgeoisement in Rural Hungary* (Cambridge, Eng.: Polity Press, 1988).

13. Ivan Szelenyi, "The Prospects and Limits of the East European New Class Project," *Politics and Society*, 15 (1986–87): 103–44.

14. Alvin Gouldner, *The Future of the Intellectuals and the Rise of the New Class Project* (New York: Oxford University Press, 1979), pp. 49–53.

15. Szelenyi et al.

16. Konrad and Szelenyi; Szelenyi and Manchin.

17. Andrea Szegö called them the "cadre intelligentsia"; see Szegö, "Gazdaság és politika. Érdek és struktura) (Economy and politics. Interests and structure) *Medvetánc*, 1983, nos. 2–3, pp. 49–92.

18. István Huszár, "A társadalom szerkezetének átalakulásáról" (Changes in Hungarian social structure), 1985, no. 2, pp. 1–7.

19. Elemér Hankiss, "Kinek az érdeke?" (In whose interest?) *Heti Világgazdaság*, Nov. 27, 1982.

20. László Antal, Lajos Bokros, István Csillag, László Lengyel, and György Matolcsy, "Fordulat és reform" (Turnaround and reform) *Közgazdasági Szemle*, 34 (1987): 642–63; János Kis, Ferenc Köszeg, and Ottilia Solt, "Társadalmi szerződés: A politikai kibontakozás feltételei" (Social contract: Preconditions of a political rejuvenation), *Beszélö*, no. 20 (1987), pp. 1–60.

21. Hungarian Socialist Worker's Party, "Az MSZMP KB gazdasági bizottságának állásfoglalása" (Position paper of the Economic Subcommittee of the Central Committee of the Hungarian Socialist Worker's Party), *Közgazdasági Szemle*, 34 (1987): 664–70; Hungarian Socialist Worker's Party, "Az MSZMP KB állásfoglalása a gazdasági-társadalmi kibontakozás programjáról" (Statement by the Central Committee of the Hungarian Socialist Worker's Party about the economic-social reform program), *Magyar Nemzet*, July 4, 1987, pp. 1–2.

22. Antal ct al., pp. 645, 642, 656.

23. *Ibid.*, p. 656.

24. Kis ct al., pp. 7, 10–11, 22.

25. Hungarian Socialist Worker's Party, "Az MSZMP KB gazdasági bizottságának állásfoglalása," pp. 664, 667, 668.

26. Hungarian Socialist Worker's Party, "Az MSZMP KB állásfoglalása a gazdasági-társadalmi kibontakozás programjáról," p. 1.

27. Hungarian Socialist Worker's Party, "Az MSZMP KB gazdasági bizottságának állásfoglalása," p. 669.

28. Antal et al., p. 658.

7. Whyte: Who Hates Bureaucracy?

1. Dorothy Solinger, ed., *Three Visions of Chinese Socialism* (Boulder, Col.: Westview Press, 1984).

2. Alec Nove, *The Economics of Feasible Socialism* (London: Allen & Unwin, 1983), p. 44.

3. Ibid., p. 179. See also pp. 77, 233. Of course, Nove stresses that every society contains some combination of bureaucratic and market distribution.

4. Translated in Joint Publications Research Service, *Translations on Communist China*, no. 90 (Feb. 12, 1970): 40–43.

5. *People's Daily*, Aug. 29, 1984, translated in *Foreign Broadcast Information Service*, Aug. 31, 1984, pp. K-1–4.

6. *Beijing Review*, no. 40, Oct. 3, 1983, p. 18. This speech was included in the *Selected Works of Deng Xiaoping*, published in 1983, and portions of it were republished in 1986, as part of the new campaign to introduce political reforms that began in the summer of that year. See *Beijing Review*, no. 32, Aug. 11, 1986, pp. 15–19.

7. Liu Shao-ch'i, *Collected Works of Liu Shao-ch'i, 1945–1957* (Kowloon: Union Research Institute, 1969), pp. 38–39.

8. Harry Harding, *Organizing China* (Stanford: Stanford University Press, 1981).

9. Richard Solomon, *Mao's Revolution and the Chinese Political Culture* (Berkeley: University of California Press, 1971).

10. See the listing offered in Max Weber, *Economy and Society* (Berkeley: University of California Press, 1968) 1: 220–23.

11. Robert Presthus, *The Organizational Society* (New York: Knopf, 1962); Henry Jacoby, *The Bureaucratization of the World* (Berkeley: University of California Press, 1973).

12. Weber, pp. 224–25. In this same passage Weber contrasts formal bureaucratization with substantive bureaucratization, the latter corresponding to what I have called bureaucratization in content or functioning.

13. I have analyzed Mao's differences from the Weberian ideal type in my article "Bureaucracy and Modernization in China: The Maoist Critique," *American Sociological Review*, 38 (1973): 149–63.

14. See my article "Bureaucracy and Anti-bureaucracy in the People's Republic of China," in Gerald M. Britan and Ronald Cohen, eds., *Hierarchy and Society* (Philadelphia: ISHI Press, 1980), pp. 123–41.

15. See, for example, the analysis in Ronald Montaperto, "From Revolutionary Successors to Revolutionaries: Chinese Students in the Early Stages of the Cultural Revolution," in Robert Scalapino, ed., *Elites in the People's Republic of China* (Seattle: University of Washington Press, 1972).

16. See Victor Nee, "Revolution and Bureaucracy: Shanghai in the Cultural Revolution," in Victor Nee and James Peck, eds., *China's Uninterrupted Revolution* (New York: Pantheon, 1975).

17. See Liao Gailong, "Historical Experiences and Our Road to Development," trans. in *Issues and Studies*, 17 (1981): 89–90.

18. See Arnold Tannenbaum, *Control in Organizations* (New York: McGraw-Hill, 1968); Andrew Walder, "Organized Dependency and Cultures of Authority in Chinese Industry," *Journal of Asian Studies*, 43 (1983): 51–76; and Andrew Walder, *Communist Neotraditionalism* (Berkeley: University of California Press, 1986).

19. This argument is advanced by Walder, "Organized Dependency." See also Frederick Teiwes, *Leadership, Legitimacy, and Conflict in China* (Armonk, N.Y.: M. E. Sharpe, 1984); and Zheng Yefu, "Shilun guanxixue" (An exploration into relying on connections), *Shehuixue yu Shehui Diaocha*, 1984, nos. 2–3, pp. 52–56.

20. See, for example, Elizabeth Perry, "Rural Violence in Socialist China," *China Quarterly*, no. 103 (1985): 414–40; Ann Anagnost, "The Beginning and End of an Emperor," *Modern China*, (1985): 147–76.

9. Lardy: Resource Allocation

1. Hans-Herman Höhmann, "Economic Reform in the 1970's—Policy with No Alternative," in Alec Nove, Hans-Herman Höhmann, and Gertrud Seidenstecher, eds., *The East European Economies in the 1970s* (London: Butterworth, 1982), p. 2.

2. State Statistical Bureau, *Chinese Statistical Yearbook, 1983* (Beijing: Statistical Publishing House, 1983), p. 23. These growth rates are measured according to the Chinese concept "comparable prices."

3. Wu Zhenkun, "On Several Controversial Questions in Discussions on Socialist Production Goals," *Worker's Daily*, Nov. 19, 1980, p. 3.

4. Nicholas R. Lardy, "Consumption and Living Standards in China, 1978–1982," *China Quarterly*, no. 100 (Dec. 1984): 850.

5. Xue Muqiao, "Comprehensive Balance in the National Economy," *Several Current Economic Problems in China* (Beijing: People's Publishing House, 1980), trans. by K. K. Fung, ed., in *Current Economic Problems in China* (Boulder, Colo.: Westview Press, 1982), pp. 65, 18; Wang Haibo, "The Proportionate Relationship between Accumulation and Consumption," in Ma Hong and Sun Shangqing, eds., *Research in Issues on China's Economic Structure* (Beijing: People's Publishing House, 1981), pp. 562–600, esp. pp. 599–600; Zhong Renfu, "Inquiries into the Reasonable Rate of Accumulation of Our Country from Historical Experience," *People's Daily*, May 15, 1980.

6. "The Sixth Five-Year Plan of the People's Republic of China for Economic and Social Development (excerpts)," *Beijing Review*, 1983, no. 21, p. iv.

7. Frank A. Burgin, Jr., "More on the New Model of Soviet Economic Growth," *ACES Bulletin*, 25 (Spring 1983): 39.

8. Nicholas R. Lardy, *Agriculture in China's Modern Economic Development* (Cambridge, Eng.: Cambridge University Press, 1983), p. 143.

9. Chinese Communist Party Central Committee, "Decisions on Some Problems in Accelerating Agricultural Development (draft)," *Zhonggong Yanjiu*, 13, no. 5 (1979): 154–55.

10. Nicholas R. Lardy, "Prospects and Some Policy Problems of Agricultural Development in China," *American Journal of Agricultural Economics*, 68 (1986): 455.

11. State Statistical Bureau, *Chinese Statistical Abstract, 1984* (Beijing: Statistical Publishing House, 1984), pp. 63, 76, 98.

12. State Statistical Bureau, *Chinese Statistical Yearbook, 1985* (Beijing: Statistical Publishing House, 1985), p. 423.

13. Ibid., pp. 422, 424.

14. State Statistical Bureau, *Chinese Statistical Abstract, 1986* (Beijing: Statistical Publishing House, 1986), p. 96.

15. The elimination of compulsory deliveries of produce to the state actually occurred in the beginning of the 1960s, before the introduction of the NEM. See X. Richet, "Is There an 'Hungarian' Model of Planning?" in Paul Hare, Hugo Radice, and Nigel Swain, eds., *Hungary: A Decade of Economic Reform* (London: Allen & Unwin, 1981), p. 27; see also Alec Nove, *The Economics of Feasible Socialism* (London: Allen & Unwin, 1983), p. 132.

16. Nove, p. 132.

17. Chinese Communist Party Central Committee, "Decisions on Some

Problems in Accelerating Agricultural Development, adapted September 28, 1979," *Hsinhua Yuebao*, 1979, no. 10, pp. 140–50.

18. Lardy, *Agriculture in China's Modern Economic Development*, p. 118.

19. Chang Huande, "An Examination of the Elimination of the Price Subsidy for Diesel Fuel Used in Agriculture," *Caizheng*, 1983, no. 1, p. 42; Cheng Jianhe, "A Discussion of Issues in Price Subsidies," *Hsinhua Wenzhai*, 1982, no. 8, p. 57.

20. Chang Zhiping, "Market Prices and the Living Standards of Workers and Staff," *Price Theory and Practice*, 1982, no. 4, p. 6; Zhang Bingfa, "A Worthwhile and Important Trend," *Theory Monthly*, 1985, no. 11, p. 59.

21. Paul Hare, "Industrial Prices in Hungary," *Soviet Studies*, 28 (Apr. 1976): 189–206, and (July 1976): 362–90.

22. Li Peichu, "Issues in the Fixed Prices of Heavy Industry Products," *Price Theory and Practice*, 1982, no. 5, p. 7.

23. Xue Muqiao, "Price Adjustment," pp. 63–78.

24. Lardy, *Agriculture in China's Modern Economic Development*, p. 193.

25. Nicholas R. Lardy, *Agricultural Prices in China*, World Bank Staff Working Paper 606 (Washington, D.C.: International Bank for Reconstruction and Development, 1983), p. 32.

26. Li Peichu, pp. 7, 8.

27. Xue Muqiao, "Price Adjustment," pp. 71–76.

28. Li Peichu, p. 8.

29. State Statistical Bureau, "Communiqué on Fulfillment of China's 1979 National Economic Plan," *Beijing Review*, 1980, no. 19, p. 13; "Communiqué on Fulfillment of China's 1980 National Economic Plan," *Beijing Review*, 1981, no. 19, p. 23; "Communiqué on Fulfillment of China's 1981 National Economic Plan," *Beijing Review*, 1982, no. 20, p. 20.

30. Xü Yi, Chen Baosen, and Liang Wuxia, *Socialist Price Issues* (Peking: Finance and Economics Publishing House, 1982), p. 164.

31. Lu Qikang, "An Inquiry into the Issue of the Production Cost and Ex-factory Price of Coal," *Price Theory and Practice*, 1982, no. 1, p. 31.

32. Ibid., pp. 28–31. Lu provides the most explicit discussion available of the constraint posed by low or negative profitability of the coal industry on the reform of the economic system.

33. Ibid., p. 29; Ye Ruixiang, "Studies on Issues in China's Energy Pricing," *Price Theory and Practice*, 1983, no. 5, p. 16.

34. World Bank, *China: Socialist Economic Development* (Washington, D.C.: International Bank for Reconstruction and Development, 1983), 2: 198.

35. Ye Ruixiang, p. 16; World Bank, 2: 196, 195.

36. Yin Shanwen, "My Opinion Concerning Enterprises' Absorbing the Price Factor Internally," *Economic Information*, May 23, 1986, p. 6; Shu Ping, "Price Reform Last Year and a Look Ahead at Commodity Prices This Year," *Economic Information*, Apr. 22, 1986, p. 1.

37. Bill Byrd, "The Atrophy of Central Planning in Chinese Industry: Impact of the Two-Tier Plan/Market System," ms., Oct. 1986.

38. Qin Xiaoli, "Bicycle, Other Prices Decontrolled," *China Daily*, Oct. 1, 1986.

39. Kuang Rian, "A Discussion of Price Adjustment and Price Reform from

the Perspective of Transport Price Adjustment," *Economic Research*, 1984, no. 6, pp. 16–21, 15; Shu Ping, p. 1.

40. Thomas Vajna, "Problems and Trends in the Development of the Hungarian New Economic Mechanism: A Balance Sheet of the 1970s," in Nove, Höhmann, and Seidenstecher, eds., p. 209.

41. Paul Hare and P. J. Wanless, "Polish and Hungarian Reforms—A Comparison," *Soviet Studies*, 33 (Oct. 1981): 497.

42. Hu Changnuan, *Price Studies* (Beijing: People's University Publishing House, 1982), p. 496.

43. Ibid.

44. Wu Nianlu, "The Relationship between Changes in the Converted Price and Commodity Trade," *International Trade*, 1983, no. 1, p. 39.

45. Li Gonghao, "A Preliminary Study of the Problems of Pricing Import and Export Commodities," *World Economic Forum*, 1983, no. 1, trans. in Joint Publications Research Service no. 84013, Aug. 1, 1983.

46. Thomas Rawski and Victor Falkenheim, "China's Economic Reform: The International Dimension," ms. This paper contains rich interview material, dating from 1982, that supports this hypothesis.

47. Zhou Jianping and Zhao Kaitai, "Several Opinions on Resolving Losses in Foreign Trade," *Economics of Finance and Trade*, 1983, no. 1, pp. 45–46.

48. Hu Changnuan, p. 495.

49. See the article by Sha Jicai and Yang Shengming in *Economic Research —Reference Materials*, 1982, no. 38, p. 20.

50. Zhou Jianping and Zhao Kaitai, p. 48.

51. Alexander Gerschenkron, *Economic Backwardness in Historical Perspective* (Cambridge, Mass.: Harvard University Press, 1966), pp. 203–4.

52. Liu Chiguang and Chen Zhun, "Many Forms of Prices Must Be Used to Suit the Needs of Plan and Market Regulation," *Wuhan University Bulletin* (Philosophy and Social Sciences edition), 1980, no. 4, p. 77.

53. Xue Muqiao, "On the Adjustment of Prices and Reform of the System of Management of Commodity Prices," in *Several Current Problems in China's Economy*, p. 174.

54. State Statistical Bureau, *Chinese Statistical Yearbook, 1983*, p. 455.

55. Nicholas R. Lardy, "Subsidies," *Chinese Business Review*, Nov.–Dec. 1983, pp. 21–24.

10. Connor: Imperial Dilemmas

1. On the tone and content of Soviet commentary on Chinese internal change since the late 1970s, see Gilbert Rozman, *A Mirror for Socialism: Soviet Criticisms of China* (Princeton: Princeton University Press, 1985); see also Marshall I. Goldman, "Soviet Perceptions of Chinese Economic Reforms and the Implications for Reform in the U.S.S.R.," *Journal of International Affairs*, 39 (Winter 1986): 41–55.

2. Evgenii A. Ambartsumov, "Analiz V. I. Leninym prichin krizisa 1921 i putei vykhoda iz nego" (V.I. Lenin's analysis of the causes of the 1921 crisis and ways to escape it), *Voprosy istorii*, no. 4 (1984): 15–19.

3. This was not the first time Ambartsumov had argued for mixed economy private enterprise strategies to revivify the Soviet economy. See the discussion

in Elizabeth Teague, "Reformers Keep Up the Pressure," *Radio Liberty Research (RL)*, 242/84, June 18, 1984, p. 3.

4. See Moshe Lewin, *Political Undercurrents in Soviet Economic Debates* (Princeton: Princeton University Press, 1974), chap. 12; also the essays by Moshe Lewin, Alexander Erlich, and Robert C. Tucker in Robert C. Tucker, ed., *Stalinism: Essays in Historical Interpretation* (New York: Norton, 1977).

5. Evgenii Bugaev, "Strannaia pozitsiia" (Strange position) *Kommunist*, 14 (1984): 119–26.

6. In Elizabeth Teague's words; see "Stern Rebuke for Advocate of Economic Reform," *RL*, 476/84, Dec. 12, 1984.

7. *Kommunist*, 17 (1984): 127, cited ibid.

8. *Pravda*, June 21, 1985, pp. 3, 4.

9. Karoly Nemeth, "V interesakh postroeniia razvitogo sotsialisticheskogo obshchestva" (In the interests of the construction of developed socialist society), *Kommunist*, 10 (1985): 70–81.

10. Oleg Bogomolov, "Soglasovanie ekonomicheskikh interesov pri sotsializme" (Coincidence of economic interests under socialism), ibid., pp. 82–93.

11. "Bulgarian Planning Initiatives: A Surrogate for Soviet Reform?" *RL*, 258/85, Aug. 8, 1985, p. 3.

12. Released by TASS, Oct. 26, 1985.

13. "Theories of Socialist Development in Soviet–East European Relations," in Sarah Meiklejohn Terry, ed., *Soviet Policy in Eastern Europe* (New Haven, Conn.: Yale University Press, 1984), pp. 221–53.

14. Ibid., p. 232.

15. Oleg Bogomolov, "Khoziaistvennye reformy i ekonomicheskoe sotrudnichestvo sotsialisticheskikh stran" (Economic reforms and the economic cooperation of socialist countries), *Voprosy ekonomiki*, 2 (1966): 76–86, cited ibid., p. 236.

16. See Paul R. Gregory and Robert C. Stuart, *Soviet Economic Structure and Performance*, 2d ed.(New York: Harper, 1981), p. 313.

17. See *Pravda*, May 28, 1986, pp. 1–2; also my own rather pessimistic treatment in "Social Policy under Gorbachev," *Problems of Communism*, 35 (July–Aug. 1986): 42–43.

18. See the reports in the *New York Times*, Nov. 20, 1986, p. A9; *Financial Times*, Nov. 20, 1986, p. 1.

19. See Connor, p. 46.

20. See the extraordinarily interesting treatment of this "liberal" model (as opposed to the Hungarian NEM's status as a "radical" model) in Joseph S. Berliner, "Managing the USSR Economy: Alternative Models," *Problems of Communism*, 32 (Jan.–Feb. 1983): 40–56.

21. See *Pravda*, Oct. 3, 1983, p. 7 (summary in *CDSP*, Nov. 2, 1983, p. 28).

22. See the very interesting account in Aaron Trehub, "'Social Justice' and Economic Progress," *RL*, 382/86, Oct. 7, 1986.

23. V. Z. Rogovin, "Sotsial' naia spravedlivost'i sotsialisticheskoe raspredelenie zhiznennykh blag" (Social justice and the socialist distribution of welfare), *Voprosy filosofii*, no. 9 (1986): 29, cited ibid., p. 9.

24. See the discussion by Aaron Trehub, "Unemployment in the Soviet Union," *RL*, 412/85, Dec. 10, 1985.

25. *Sovetskaia kul'tura*, Jan. 4, 1986.

26. See TASS, cited in *RL*, 35/86, Jan. 17, 1986, p. 11.

27. See Charles Gati, "Soviet Empire: Alive but Not Well," *Problems of Communism*, 34 (Mar.–Apr. 1985): 75–76, citing *Magyarorszag*, July 31, 1983.

28. See Vladimir Sobell, "Mikhail Gorbachev Takes Charge of the CMEA," *Radio Free Europe Research*, RAD BR/146 (Eastern Europe), Dec. 20, 1985.

29. For an interesting treatment of the effects of increased managerial discipline *in* the critical railroad industry, which came to hand after this essay was essentially completed, see Vladimir Kontorovich, "Discipline and Growth in the Soviet Economy," *Problems of Communism*, 34 (Nov.–Dec. 1985): 18–31.

11. Shirk: Chinese Industrial Reform

1. For example, *Renmin Ribao*, Feb. 2, 1983, *Foreign Broadcast Information Service (FBIS)*, Feb. 3, 1983, p. k1.

2. There is no reliable price deflator to convert these figures to constant prices. See Nicholas R. Lardy, "Consumption and Living Standards in China, 1978–83," *China Quarterly*, no. 100 (Dec. 1984): 851, 861.

3. "Chinese Communist Party Document Number One on Rural Economic Policies," *Xinhua*, Apr. 10, 1983, *FBIS*, Apr. 13, 1983, pp. k1–k13.

4. "Chinese Communist Party Central Committee Document Number One," *Xinhua*, June 11, 1984.

5. "1985 Document Number One on Rural Economic Reform," *Xinhua*, Mar. 24, 1985, *FBIS*, Mar. 25, 1985, pp. k1–k11.

6. Peter T. Knight, *Economic Reform in Socialist Countries: The Experiences of China, Hungary, Rumania, and Yugoslavia* (Washington, D.C.: World Bank, 1983), p. 61.

7. *Xinhua*, May 23, 1983, *FBIS*, May 25, 1983, p. k1. In 1982 the combined deficit of industrial enterprises that operated at a loss came to 4.2 billion yuan (over 10 billion yuan including losses from grain and commercial enterprises —*Xinhua*, June 23, 1983, *FBIS*, June 23, 1984, p. k11). The percentages for the later years come from *China Daily*, Sept. 15, 1986, p. 3.

8. On "creeping recentralization" see Gregory Grossman, "Notes for a Theory of the Command Economy," *Soviet Studies*, 15 (Oct. 1963): 114. On the "cycle of reform" see Gertrude E. Schroeder, "The Soviet Economy on a Treadmill of 'Reforms,'" U.S. Congress, Joint Economic Committee, *Soviet Economy in a Time of Change* (Washington, D.C.: U.S. Government Printing Office, 1979), 1: 312–40; and Ronald Amann, "Industrial Innovation in the Soviet Union: Methodological Perspectives and Conclusions," in Ronald Amann and Julian Cooper, eds., *Industrial Innovation in the Soviet Union* (New Haven, Conn.: Yale University Press, 1982), pp. 30–37.

9. *Caiwu Yu Kuaiji*, Jan. 20, 1982, *Joint Publications Research Service (JPRS)*, 80591, Apr. 16, 1982, p. 22.

10. Grossman, p. 121.

11. X. Richet, "Is There an 'Hungarian' Model of Planning?" in Paul Hare, Hugo Radice, and Nigel Swain, eds., *Hungary, A Decade of Economic Reform* (London: Allen & Unwin, 1981), p. 27.

12. Frank Gibney, "A Talk with Zhao Ziyang," *Los Angeles Times*, May 6, 1984.

13. Samuel Popkin, personal communication.

14. This point was suggested to me by Nicholas R. Lardy.

15. David Zweig, "Opposition to Change in Rural China: The System of Responsibility and People's Communes," *Asian Survey*, 23 (July 1983): 885.

16. Thomas P. Bernstein made this point to me. Also see Alec Nove, "Soviet Agriculture: Problems and Prospects," in Curtis Keeble, ed., *The Soviet State: Domestic Roots of Soviet Foreign Policy* (Boulder, Colo.: Westview Press, 1985), pp. 98–99.

17. Christine P. W. Wong, "Between Plan and Market: The Role of the Local Sector in Post-Mao China," unpublished ms., Sept. 1986, p. 5.

18. *Chinese Statistical Yearbook, 1985* (Beijing: China Statistical Publishers, 1986), p. 321.

19. Wong, p. 5.

20. János Kornai, "The Dilemmas of a Socialist Economy: The Hungarian Experience," *Cambridge Journal of Economics*, 4 (June 1980): 151; also see Kornai, *Economics of Shortage* (New York: North Holland, 1980).

21. For many examples of this continuing dependency on government bureaucracy see Dorothy J. Solinger, "'Economic Readjustment' and Informal Coping Mechanisms, 1979–1982," unpublished ms., 1986.

22. *China Daily*, June 9, 1982, p. 3.

23. Nicholas R. Lardy, "Dilemmas in the Pattern of Resource Allocation in China, 1978–1984," unpublished ms., 1985.

24. For a study of enterprise bargaining with bureaucratic superiors over taxes, see Andrew G. Walder, "The Informal Dimension of Enterprise Financial Reforms," U.S. Congress, Joint Economic Committee, *China's Economy Looks toward the Year 2000* (Washington D.C., U.S. Government Printing Office, 1986), 1: 630–45.

25. *Guangming Ribao*, Apr. 8, 1979, *JPRS*, no. 73965, Aug. 6, 1979, p. 21.

26. *Jingji Ribao*, Mar. 6, 1985, *FBIS*, Mar. 8, 1985, p. k14.

27. For a good discussion of this assumption in Marxist economics see Alec Nove, *The Economics of Feasible Socialism* (London: Allen & Unwin, 1983), p. 40.

28. Susan L. Shirk, "Recent Chinese Labour Policies and the Transformation of Industrial Organization in China," *China Quarterly*, no. 88 (Dec. 1981): 579–84.

29. Andrew G. Walder, "Wage Reform and the Web of Factory Interests," in David M. Lampton, ed., *Policy Implementation in Post-Mao China* (Berkeley: University of California Press, 1987).

30. *Xinhua*, Sept. 9, 1986, *FBIS*, Sept. 25, 1986, p. k1.

31. This point was suggested to me by John Rohmer, Department of Economics, University of California, Davis.

32. On the opposition of rural cadres to the household responsibility system see David Zweig and Steven Butler, "China's Agricultural Reform: Background and Prospects" (New York: China Council of the Asia Society, 1985).

33. Much of the information for this analysis of bureaucratic conflicts in the industrial sector comes from interviews with Chinese economic bureaucrats, which I conducted during 1984.

34. Jerry F. Hough, *The Soviet Union and Social Science Theory* (Cambridge, Mass.: Harvard University Press, 1977), p. 23; Valerie Bunce, *Do New Leaders Make a Difference? Executive Succession and Public Policy under Capitalism and Socialism* (Princeton: Princeton University Press, 1981).

35. Michel Oksenberg, "China's Economic Bureaucracy," *China Business Review*, May–June 1982, pp. 22–28; David M. Lampton, "Water Politics," *ibid.*, July–Aug. 1983, pp. 10–17.

36. For example, *Jingji Ribao*, Jan. 3, 1983; *FBIS*, Jan. 18, 1983, pp. k15–16 and k23–24; *Xinhua*, Jan. 12, 1983; *FBIS*, Jan. 18, 1983, p. k8.

37. Moshe Lewin, *Political Undercurrents in Soviet Economic Debates* (Princeton: Princeton University Press, 1974), p. 173.

38. Nove, *Economics of Feasible Socialism*, p. 79.

39. Nicholas R. Lardy, *Economic Growth and Distribution in China* (Cambridge, Eng.: Cambridge University Press, 1978); Suzanne Paine, "Spatial Aspects of Chinese Development: Issues, Outcomes, and Policies, 1949–79," *Journal of Development Studies*, 17 (1981): 133–95; Nobuo Maruyama, "Regional Development Policy," Japan External Trade Relations Organization, *China Newsletter*, no. 33 (July–Aug. 1981), pp. 16–22.

40. Xue Muqiao, "Economic Management in a Socialist Country," in George C. Wang, ed., *Economic Reform in the P.R.C.* (Boulder, Colo.: Westview Press, 1982), p. 33.

41. For a Japanese example, see T. J. Pempel and Keiichi Tsunekawa, "Corporatism without Labour? The Japanese Anomaly," in Philippe C. Schmitter and Gerhard Lehmbruch, eds., *Trends toward Corporatist Intermediation* (Beverly Hills, Calif.: Sage, 1979), p. 269.

42. See David Bachman, "Implementing Chinese Tax Policy," in Lampton, ed.

43. See Chen Yun's arguments for recentralization in *Renmin Ribao*, Dec. 30, 1980.

44. *Guangming Ribao*, May 29, 1983, *FBIS*, June 15, 1983, pp. k13–14.

45. For an explicit expression of the ministry's strategy in this bureaucratic contest see Ma Daying, "On Unified Financial Authority and Concentrated Financial Resources," *Caijing wenti janjiu* (The study of finance and economic problems) (Liaoning), Jan. 1982, pp. 6–12, *JPRS*, no. 80512, Apr. 7, 1982, pp. 72–83.

46. *Hong Qi*, no. 9 (May 1, 1985): 38.

47. Audrey Donnithorne, *China's Economic System* (New York: Praeger, 1967); Dwight Perkins, *Market Control and Planning in China* (Cambridge, Mass.: Harvard University Press, 1966).

48. See Christine Wong, "Material Allocation and Decentralization: Impact of the Local Sector on Industrial Reform," in Elizabeth J. Perry and Christine Wong, eds., *The Political Economy of Reform in Post-Mao China* (Cambridge, Mass.: Harvard University Press, 1985), pp. 253–78; and Barry Naughton, "The Decline in Central Control over Investment in Post-Mao China," in Lampton, ed.

49. *Banyuetan*, July 25, 1982, *FBIS*, July 25, 1982, p. k10; *Renmin Ribao*, July 8, 1983, *FBIS*, July 12, 1983, p. k11.

50. For example, see *Renmin Ribao*, Nov. 16, 1984.

51. *Jingji Guanli*, Sept. 1984, p. 3.

52. On coal see *Renmin Ribao*, Nov. 19, 1984. On metallurgy see *ibid.*, Oct. 11 and 13, 1984.

53. For examples see Peter Kwok, *Managing Enterprises in the People's Republic of China: Seven Case Studies* (Berkeley: University of California Institute

of Business and Economic Research, 1981) p. 26; and *Renmin Ribao*, Apr. 2, 1983, *FBIS*, Apr. 8, 1983, p. k6.

54. Alec Nove, *The Economic History of the U.S.S.R.* (Harmondsworth, Eng.: Penguin, 1976), p. 359.

55. H. Franz Schurmann, *Ideology and Organization in Communist China* (Berkeley: University of California Press, 1968), pp. 175–78. A criticism of central cities as new *kuaikuai* is in *Shijie Jingji Daobao*, Sept. 24, 1984.

56. *Jingji Ribao*, Jan. 3, 1985.

57. See Bruce Cumings, "The Political Economy of China's Turn Outward," in Samuel S. Kim, ed., *China and the World* (Boulder, Colo.: Westview Press, 1984), pp. 235–65.

Index

In this index an "f" after a number indicates a separate reference on the next page, and an "ff" indicates separate references on the next two pages. A continuous discussion over two or more pages is indicated by a span of page numbers, e.g., "pp. 57–58." *Passim* is used for a cluster of references in close but not consecutive sequence.

Library of Congress Cataloging-in-Publication Data

Remaking the economic institutions of socialism: China and Eastern
Europe / edited by Victor Nee and David Stark with Mark Selden.
     p.   cm.
   Includes index.
   ISBN 0-8047-1494-0 (alk. paper)—ISBN 0-8047-1495-9
(pbk.)
     1. China—Economic policy—1949–   . 2. Europe, Eastern—Economic
policy.   3. Socialism—China.   4. Socialism—Europe, Eastern.
I. Nee, Victor, 1945–   .   II. Stark, David, 1950–   .   III. Selden,
Mark.
HC427.9.R39 1989
338.947—dc19   88-38223
                                                                              CIP